Lecture Notes in Computer Science   8595

Commenced Publication in 1973
Founding and Former Series Editors:
Gerhard Goos, Juris Hartmanis, and Jan van Leeuwen

Simon K.S. Cheung   Joseph Fong
Jiping Zhang   Reggie Kwan
Lam For Kwok (Eds.)

Hybrid Learning

Theory and Practice

7th International Conference, ICHL 2014
Shanghai, China, August 8-10, 2014
Proceedings

 Springer

Volume Editors

Simon K.S. Cheung
Open University of Hong Kong, Hong Kong
E-mail: kscheung@ouhk.edu.hk

Joseph Fong
Lam For Kwok
City University of Hong Kong, Hong Kong
E-mail:{csjfong, cslfkwok}@cityu.edu.hk

Jiping Zhang
East China Normal University, Shanghai, China
E-mail: jpz@ecnu.edu.cn

Reggie Kwan
Caritas Institute of Higher Education, Hong Kong, Hong Kong
E-mail: rkwan@cihe.edu.hk

ISSN 0302-9743   e-ISSN 1611-3349
ISBN 978-3-319-08960-7   e-ISBN 978-3-319-08961-4
DOI 10.1007/978-3-319-08961-4
Springer Cham Heidelberg New York Dordrecht London

Library of Congress Control Number: 2014942561

LNCS Sublibrary: SL 1 – Theoretical Computer Science and General Issues

Typesetting: Camera-ready by author, data conversion by Scientific Publishing Services, Chennai, India

Printed on acid-free paper

Springer is part of Springer Science+Business Media (www.springer.com)

Preface

Welcome to the 7th International Conference on Hybrid Learning (ICHL 2014). This year, ICHL 2014 was held in Shanghai, China with our new host, East China Normal University during 10–12 August 2014.

In the past decade, hybrid learning has evolved as one of the promising approaches to teaching and learning. Not only emphasizing an effective combination of face-to-face and technology-mediated instruction, hybrid learning also encompasses the strategies for teaching and learning. It provides a way forward for creating learning experience to compensate for the shortcomings of, or at least to complement, the conventional face-to-face learning. ICHL 2014 provided a platform for knowledge exchange in these areas among researchers and practitioners.

The focus of ICHL 2014 was placed on the practice of hybrid learning, especially on how hybrid learning is adopted to enhance teaching and learning effectiveness. The conference included keynote addresses and paper presentations as well as panel discussion, tutorial and tool demonstration sessions. A total of 31 papers were selected from about 90 submissions, for inclusion in this volume. The selected papers cover various aspects on hybrid learning, including computer supported collaborative learning, experiences in hybrid learning, improved flexibility on learning processes, and the pedagogical and psychological issues of hybrid learning.

We would like to take this opportunity to thank the following parties who made the conference a success: (a) the Organizing Committee; (b) the Program Committee; (c) the Conference Organizers; (d) the Conference Sponsors; (e) all the Conference Participants; and (f) all the Supporters.

We trust you will enjoy reading these papers.

August 2014

Simon K.S. Cheung
Joseph Fong
Jiping Zhang
Reggie Kwan
Lam For Kwok

Organization

Organizing Committee

Honorary Chairs

Youqun Ren   East China Normal University, China
Reggie Kwan   Caritas Institute of Higher Education, Hong Kong

Conference Chairs

Guorui Fan   East China Normal University, China
Joseph Fong   City University of Hong Kong, Hong Kong

Program Chairs

Simon K.S. Cheung   Open University of Hong Kong, Hong Kong
Fu Lee Wang   Caritas Institute of Higher Education, Hong Kong

Organization Chairs

Jiping Zhang   East China Normal University, China
Lam For Kwok   City University of Hong Kong, Hong Kong

Financial Chair

Titus Lo   Caritas Institute of Higher Education, Hong Kong

Local Arrangement Chair

Xiangdong Chen   East China Normal University, China
Oliver Au   Open University of Hong Kong, Hong Kong

Registration Chair

Kenneth Wong   Caritas Institute of Higher Education, Hong Kong

Publicity Chairs

Wilfred Fong   University of Toronto, Canada
Kanishka Bedi   U21 Global Graduate School, Singapore
Donny Lai   City University of Hong Kong, Hong Kong
Harrison Yang   Central China Normal University, China

Owen Hall Jr.   Pepperdien University, USA
Shudong Wang   Shimane University, Japan
Fowie Ng   Chinese University of Hong Kong, Hong Kong
Ivan K.W. Lai   Macau University of Science and
                              Technology, Macau

Workshop Chairs

Jeanne Lam   HKU School of Professional and Continuing
                              Education, Hong Kong
Melani Au   HKU School of Professional and Continuing
                              Education, Hong Kong
Will Ma   Hong Kong Shue Yan University, Hong Kong

Activity Chair

Xiangdong Yan   East China Normal University, China

Web Master

Donny Lai   City University of Hong Kong, Hong Kong

Steering Committee

Joseph Fong   City University of Hong Kong, Hong Kong
Victor Lee   Hong Kong Management Association,
                              Hong Kong
Reggie Kwan   Caritas Institute of Higher Education,
                              Hong Kong
Ronghuai Huang   Beijing Normal University, China
Liming Zhang   University of Macau, Mcau
Jeanne Lam   HKU School of Professional and Continuing
                              Education, Hong Kong
Kedong Li   South China Normal University, Hong Kong

International Program Committee

Oliver Au   Open University of Hong Kong, Hong Kong
Jinnong Cao   Hong Kong Polytechnic University, Hong Kong
F.T. Chan   HKU School of Professional and Continuing
                              Education, Hong Kong
Keith Chan   Hong Kong Polytechnic University, Hong Kong
Peter Chan   Brigham Young University at Hawaii, USA
Simon K.S. Cheung   Open University of Hong Kong, Hong Kong
Giuliana Dettori   Istituto di Tecnologie Didattiche del CNR, Italy
Joseph Fong   City University of Hong Kong, Hong Kong
Wilfred Fong   University of Toronto, Canada
Wolfgang Halang   Fernuniversität Hagen, Germany

Owen Hall Jr.	Pepperdine University, USA
Le Jun	Guangdong Radio and TV University, China
S.C. Kong	Hong Kong Institute of Education, Hong Kong
Reggie Kwan	Caritas Institute of Higher Education, Hong Kong
Lam For Kwok	City University of Hong Kong, Hong Kong
Donny Lai	City University of Hong Kong, Hong Kong
Jeanne Lam	HKU School of Professional and Continuing Education, Hong Kong
Yi Li	Nanjing University, China
Will Ma	Hong Kong Shue Yan University, Hong Kong
Fowie Ng	School of Continuing and Professional Studies, Chinese University of Hong Kong, Hong Kong
Liana Stanescu	University of Craiova, Romania
Stefanie Trausan-Matu	University of Bucharest, Romania
Fu Lee Wang	Caritas Institute of Higher Education, Hong Kong
Kenneth Wong	Caritas Institute of Higher Education, Hong Kong
Di Wu	Central China Normal University, China
Youru Xie	South China Normal University, China
Harrison Yang	State University of New York, USA
W.L. Yeung	Lingnan University, Hong Kong
Liming Zhang	University of Macau, Macau
Jianhua Zhao	South China Normal University, China

Organizers

International Hybrid Learning Society

East China Normal University

The Open University of Hong Kong

Sponsors

HKU School of Professional and Continuing Education

School of Continuing and Professional Studies, Chinese University of Hong Kong

City University of Hong Kong

Caritas Institute of Higher Education

Hong Kong Pei Hua Education Foundation

Table of Contents

Keynotes

The Present and the Prospect: How Far Away Are They from Blended
Learning? 1
    Huan Liu, Haijun Guo, Minyu Wu, Beirong Lu,
    Jianqiang Quan, and Youqun Ren

Is "MOOC-Mania" over? 11
    Bebo White

A Kinet-Affective Learning Model for Experiential Learning in Smart
Ambience 16
    Horace H.S. Ip and Julia Byrne

Experiences in Hybrid Learning

The Effect of Hybrid Learning in Vocational Education Based on
Cloud Space: Taking the Vocational Education Cyber-Platform
as an Example 24
    Di Wu, Xiaorong Yu, Yinghui Shi, Harrison Hao Yang, and Chun Lu

Study on the Interactions in Classroom of the Future 36
    Feng Qiu

Reconstructing New Space for Teaching and Learning: The Future
Classroom 49
    Jiping Zhang

An Empirical Study of Leveraging Information Technology in Business
through Flexible Learning, Project and Problem-Based Learning, and
Cross-Disciplinary Learning 56
    Kwan Keung Ng, Fu Lee Wang, and Louise Luk

A Practical Research of Hybrid Learning Mode in Teaching and
Research Activities 68
    Sen Wang

The Context of Blended Learning: The TIPS Blended Learning
Model 80
    Jeanne Lam

Is the Flipped Classroom Model Effective in the Perspectives of
Students' Perceptions and Benefits? 93
    Kenneth Wong and David W.K. Chu

Myths to Burst about Hybrid Learning 105
    Kam Cheong Li

Computer Supported Collaborative Learning

Trends of Cloud Computing in Education 116
    Yinghui Shi, Harrison Hao Yang, Zongkai Yang, and Di Wu

Research and Application on Web2.0-Based Sharing Modes of
Curriculum Resources 129
    Youru Xie, Jing Bai, Guanjie Li, and Rui Yin

The Development of an Augmented Reality Framework for Constructing
Circuit Learning Aids 140
    Chen Qiao and Xiangdong Chen

A Mahjong-Like Game of English Vocabulary Spelling 152
    Cheng-Yu Tsai, Jenq-Muh Hsu, Hung-Hsu Tsai, Pao-Ta Yu, and
    Wen-Feng Huang

Factors Influencing Trust and Acceptance of Electronic Sand Tables for
Higher Business Education 164
    River Chu, Yan Li, Ivan K.W. Lai, and Zhiwei Zhu

Understanding Students' Continuance Intention toward Social
Networking e-Learning... 173
    Ivan K.W. Lai and Donny C.F. Lai

Improved Flexibility of Learning Processes

An Editable Multi-media Authoring eBook System for Mobile
Learning 184
    Joseph Fong, Vincent Chung, and Kenneth Wong

A Review on the Development of an Online Platform for Open
Textbooks 196
    Simon K.S. Cheung, Kelvin K.W. Lee, and Kelvin K.L. Chan

Developing Knowledge Clusters in a Supportive Learning
Environment 208
    Wai-lap Chan and Lam-for Kwok

Forms of Instruction and Students' Preferences – A Comparative
Study 220
    Blanka Frydrychova Klimova and Petra Poulova

Borderless Education: InterUniversity Study – Successful Students'
Feedback 232
    Petra Poulova and Ivana Simonova

Creating and Delivering Learning Materials for Mobile Phones - Our
Findings in Japan   243
  Shudong Wang, Jun Iwata, and Douglas Jarrell

Pedagogical and Psychological Issues

Instructional Design and Practice of Problem-Based Collaborative
Knowledge Building under Network Environment   254
  Haixia Zhao

Personalized-Adaptive Learning – A Model for CIT Curricula   266
  *Jayshiro Tashiro, Fred Hurst, Alison Brown,
  Patrick C.K. Hung, and Miguel Vargas Martin*

A Critical Analysis of the Studies on Fostering Creativity through
Game-Based Learning   278
  Huan Nie, Haiming M. Xiao, and Junjie J. Shang

Exploring Interpersonal Relationship and Growth Need Strength on
Knowledge Sharing in Social Media   288
  Sally M. Li and Will W.K. Ma

The Analysis of Classroom Teaching Behavior Based on Knowledge
Building   300
  Wu Chen, Meilin Long, and Qionghua Duan

Evaluation of Learning Website: A Social Network Perspective   312
  Nengshan Feng and Xindong Ye

Chinese Composition Teachers' Commentary Styles and Patterns in a
Tablet-Based Marking Environment   323
  K.K. Ying, Kat Leung, Roger Lee, and Daisy Chow

An Empirical Research on Teachers' Self-Efficacy in Distance
Learning   335
  Jiangsheng Zhang, Juan Li, and Fengshan Liu

Author Index   345

The Present and the Prospect:
How Far Away Are They from Blended Learning?

Huan Liu[1], Haijun Guo[2], Minyu Wu[2], Beirong Lu[1],
Jianqiang Quan[3], and Youqun Ren[2,*]

[1] Information Technology Services Center
[2] School of Educational Science
[3] School of Foreign Languages
East China Normal University
3663 North Zhongshan Road, Shanghai, 200062, PR. China
yqren@admin.ecnu.edu.cn

Abstract. For a better understanding of the status quo of blended learning, this paper conducted a survey in five high schools in Shanghai. The results of the survey indicate that high school learners are not fully aware of the value of blended learning, and that only a small proportion of them have applied blended learning to their study. Although high school learners hold positive attitudes towards blended learning, guidance from their teachers is quite limited in this respect. Teachers seldom offer online learning resources or online courses to learners. This leads to the limited application of blended learning. The paper also discovers that learner's involvement in blended learning is heavily influenced by factors such as family commitment, learning time, and learning devices. Based on these findings, the paper finally puts forwards a number of suggestions on how to improve the effectiveness of blended learning among young learners.

Keywords: blended learning, hybrid learning, online learning, elementary education.

1   Research Background

Different scholars have defined blended learning from different perspectives [1, 2]. Driscoll defines blended learning as a way to combine or mix modes of web-based technology (e.g. live virtual classroom, self-paced instruction, collaborative learning, streaming video, audio, and text) to accomplish an educational goal, combine various pedagogical approaches (e.g. constructivism, behaviorism, cognitivism) to produce an optimal learning outcome with or without instructional technology, combine any form of instructional technology (e.g. videotape, CD-ROM, Web-based training, film) with face-to-face instructor-led training to mix or combine instructional technology with actual job tasks in order to create a harmonious effect of learning and working [3]. Singh and Reed

---

* Corresponding author.

S.K.S. Cheung et al. (Eds.): ICHL 2014, LNCS 8595, pp. 1–10, 2014.

proposed that blended learning should focus on optimizing achievement of learning objectives by applying the "right" personal learning technologies to watch the "right" personal learning style to transfer the "right" skills to the "right" person at the "right" time [4]. Bonk's definition of blended learning is very simple and brief. He holds that the concept of blended learning is established with the advent and development of the Internet [5]. Therefore blended learning is a combination of face-to-face instruction with online learning [6, 7, 8, 9, 10]. Bonk's definition of blended learning has currently become a classical version in the academic circle.

Lots of Chinese scholars have developed the theory of blended learning based on Bonk's definition. Li believes that blended learning is based on the reflection on online learning, and that it integrates face-to-face instruction with online learning. It is a teaching model which aims to reduce cost and enhance learning efficiency [11]. He proposes that blended learning is the combination of traditional learning and online learning [12]. On the one hand, the teacher plays a dominant role in monitoring the teaching process, offering guidance, and arousing learners' inspiration; on the other hand, blended learning is also a learner-directed process which aims to exert learners' initiative and creativity. Such a learning model is expected to achieve the best learning results by integrating advantages from both sides.

As two key factors of blended learning, face-to-face instruction and online learning do not always share a fixed proportion. Online learning can be either teacher guided or learner directed. Although the ultimate goal of blended learning is to improve the effectiveness of learning, it does not mean that the content of online learning should be closely related to what is taught and learned in the classroom. Blended learning can be generalized as an online learning model which involves learners with elementary educational background, higher educational background, or face-to-face lifelong educational background.

It has been widely proved that blended learning is a better learning model than pure face-to-face classroom teaching or online learning [13]. We should not only offer more theoretical support to blended learning, but also help teachers, students, and the public better understand and recognize blended learning. Due to the development of the Internet and the advancement of educational technology, various online courses and new techniques and instruments for online learning have sprung up and learners have more access to computers and such network environments which are essential for online learning. In China, blended learning is acknowledged to have been widely applied in the elementary and higher educational systems. Teachers from the elementary educational system are deeply engaged in the exploration of blended learning with a view to promoting the integration between curriculum development and information technology [14]. But currently, no specific data have supported the popularization of blended learning in schools. For this reason, the authors have decided to conduct a survey in 5 high schools in Shanghai and it aims to answer the following questions:

- Has blended learning been widely applied by high school students in Shanghai?
- What are the types and characteristics of blended learning among these learners?
- What are the factors that may influence students' blended learning?

These research questions seek to discover the actual application of blended learning among students, to explore the negative factors that hinder the application of blended learning, and therefore to offer more constructive suggestions for the further development of blended leaning in the elementary educational system.

2   Research Method

2.1   Research Subjects

The research selected 400 senior two high school students from 10 classes of 5 high schools in Shanghai. These five schools are located in different districts of Shanghai. Of the five schools, the best has 90% students enrolled by the first-class universities in China; while the poorest only has less than 30%. Such percentage reflects the average educational levels in Shanghai's high schools.

2.2   Questionnaire

The questionnaire consists of 56 questions categorized into four parts: learners' general background, classroom learning, inquiry-based learning, and the habit of online leaning. A total of 400 questionnaires have been delivered and collected, and 393 are effective. There are questions concerning the proportion of blended learning in education include: Have you ever heard of blended learning? What's your attitude towards the use of online resources for classroom teaching and learning? Do your teachers offer you the chance to read or watch some online resources for classroom teaching? There are also questions concerning the types and characteristics of blended learning: What are the online resources that your teachers have recommended? What's your method of online learning? Do you ask the Internet for help when you meet with learning difficulties? And how do you finally solve such problems? Questions concerning the negative factors that hinder the application of blended learning include: What are the factors that prevent you from learning online? What are your parents and teachers' attitudes towards net surfing?

The questionnaire contains a lot of items related to online learning. Strictly speaking, online learning is not equivalent to blended learning. But to high school students, leaning is a subject-based process and they tend to understand online learning as a hybrid concept related to various subjects and courses. In this sense, online learning and blended learning are closely connected. In the design of the questionnaire, the authors inquired some of the subjects and the result indicated that the items associated with online learning directly reflected learners' understanding of blended learning.

2.3   Data Processing

The data of this research is processed and analyzed with SPSS 20.0 software.

3   Research Method

3.1   Overview

The data of the questionnaire indicate that 89.0% students have never heard of blended learning and that 83.1% students have never heard of MOOCs. Generally speaking, learners are not fully aware of blended learning or those online learning resources that support blended learning.

However, the data also indicate that most students hold a positive attitude towards blended learning. 52.8% students believe it necessary or very necessary to support classroom learning with online resources. 41.2% students don't think it matters too much whether to use online resources or not. Only 5.9% think it unnecessary to prepare online resources for classroom learning.

Although students hold such a positive attitude, they are not actively involved in blended learning. Only 14.5% students participate in online learning. Among them, those who have studied online courses of Khan Academy, Coursera, edX, and Udacity only account for 4.0%, 1.1%, 1.8%, and 1.5% respectively. When students meet with learning difficulties, about 18.5% of them will first turn to the Internet for help. When they preview or review a certain chapter of a course, only 13.2% students agree that learning online is their top priority.

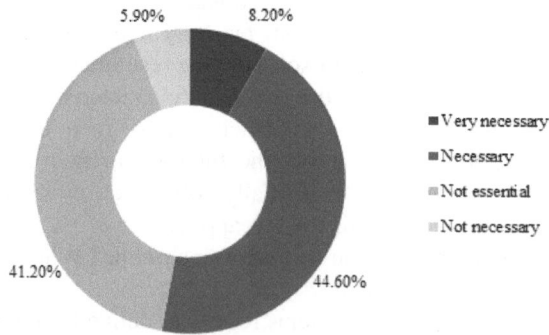

Fig. 1. Students' attitudes towards blended learning

3.2   Equipment

Good equipment is an essential guarantee of blended learning. The questionnaire inquired about the possible equipment used for blended learning, such as PC, laptop computer, pad, e-books, Mp4, and cell phones. Data indicate that cell phones are used most, Mp4 next, followed by laptop computer, pad, PC and e-books.

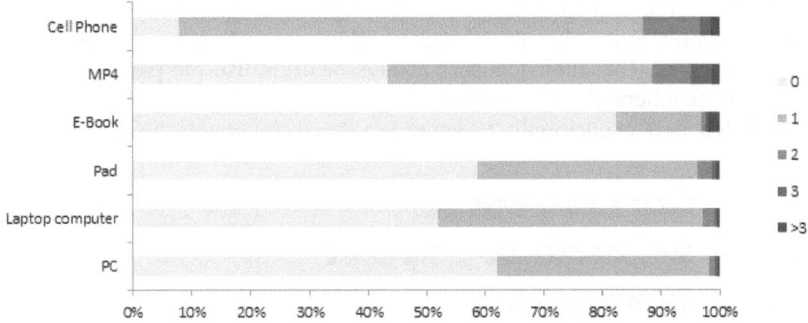

Fig. 2. Students' possession of different equipment

3.3   Teacher's Role

According to the data, 79.4% students agree that their teachers never or just occasionally arrange them to read or watch online learning resources before or after the class. As regards the forms of classroom teaching, 54.2% students do not care whether there are online resources or not, and only 6.8% welcome online resources. 86.1% students agree that their teachers never or occasionally recommend online courses or lectures to them. Only 17.4% students admit that online learning resources are mainly recommended by the teacher.

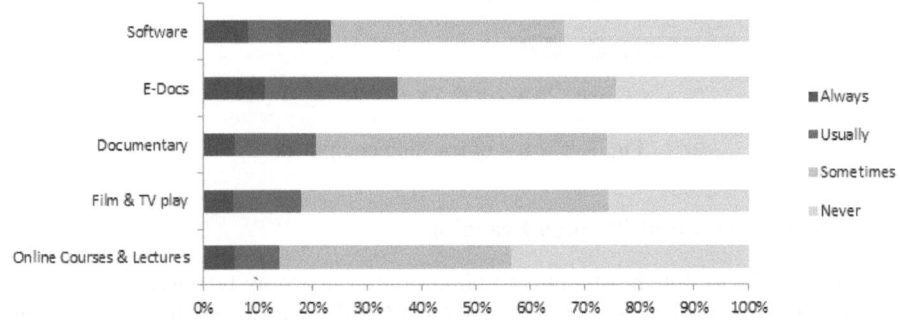

Fig. 3. Online learning resources recommended by teachers

3.4   Teacher's Information Literacy

According to the result of the questionnaire, 93.9% students agree that their teachers always or often use PPT in classroom teaching; 19.1% students agree that their teachers always or often show them movies in classroom teaching; 15.4% students agree that their teachers always or often show them documentaries; 42.8% students agree that their teachers always or often play teaching videos of the course; 66.6% students agree that their teachers always or often show them cartoons, and 50.6% students agree that their teachers always or often use teaching software. The rest of the students agree that their teachers occasionally or never use multi-media equipment.

43.8% students agree that their teachers always or often use PC in classroom teaching; 61.6% students agree that their teachers always or often use laptop computers; 19.8% students agree that their teachers always or often use the pad; 49.9% students agree that their teachers always or often use the e-board. The rest of the students admit that their teachers occasionally or never use the above-mentioned teaching aids.

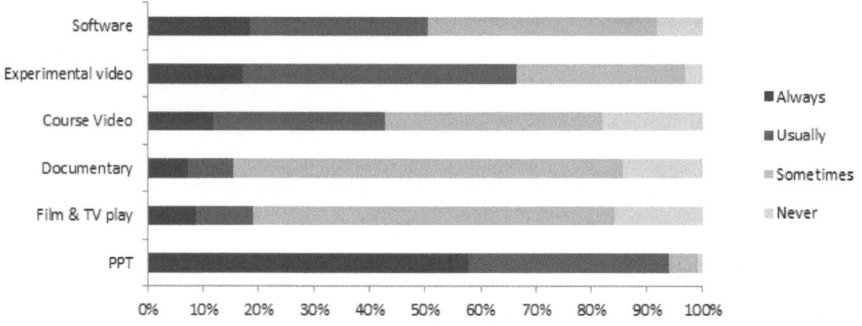

Fig. 4. The use of teaching resources

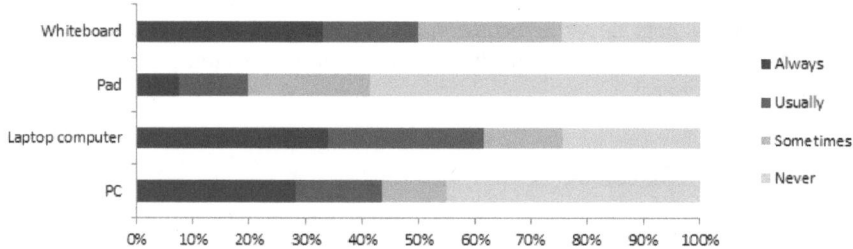

Fig. 5. The use of teaching equipment

3.5   Students' Habit of Blended Learning

The order of priority for the students to obtain online learning resources tends to follow the following pattern: scattered items (66.8%) first, followed by textbooks and reference (27.0%), academic journal (2.5%), online courses (1.9%), subscription materials (1.1%), and other materials (0.5%). When students meet with learning difficulties, 52.5% of them tend to search the Internet for the direct answer; 39.8% of them tend to search the Internet for reference materials; 5.5% of them tend to discuss these problems with other online users, and 2.1% of them tend to read or watch online courses. 85.0% students choose text materials as the major type of media of all online learning resources. 12.6% students choose visual materials while 2.4% students choose audio materials. 64.9% students search the Internet for online learning resources when they do revision after class, 6.8% students tend to search for online learning resources when they do prevision before class. As for students' motivation for online learning, it is mainly direct, problem-driven, and fragmented rather than organized, systematic, and reflective. And the online materials that students use for blended learning is mainly text based.

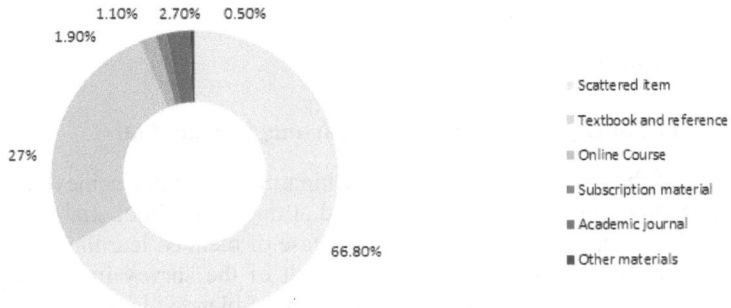

Fig. 6. Ways of obtaining online resources

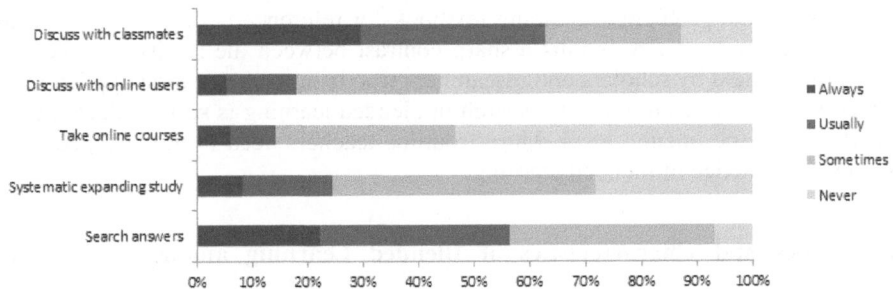

Fig. 7. Students' online learning behavior

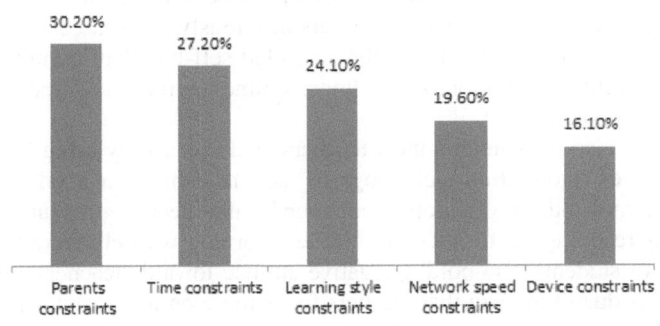

Fig. 8. Negative factors of online learning

3.6   Negative Factors

30.2% students think that they are restricted too much by their parents. 27.2% students agree that they don't have time for online learning. 24.1% students complain that online learning is not convenient at all. 19.6% students think of low Internet speed as the major negative factors. 16.1% students agree that equipment problems prevent them from learning online. Of all the students, 27.7 of them agree that they are able to learn online freely.

4   Conclusion

4.1   The Status Quo of Blended Learning in Shanghai

As one of the most developed city in China, Shanghai has achieved a fairly high level in educational informatization. Targeted at the high school students in Shanghai, this research is supposed to present the best case of blended learning in China's elementary educational system. However, the result of the survey indicates that high school students in Shanghai are still not fully aware of blended learning, their participation in blended learning is quite low, and they are unfamiliar with newly emerged online learning models such as MOOCs and seldom do they get involved in such courses. When they meet with learning difficulties, they tend to seek help from peer learners, or try to solve the problem by reading textbooks or reference books. Online learning becomes peripheral. There is thus a sharp contrast between the reality and the optimistic attitude held by scholars and researchers who believe in the wide application of blended learning. Currently most research in blended learning is still conducted at the theoretical or experimental level. More frontline teachers need to get engaged in the research and practice of blended learning.

4.2   Types and Characteristics of Blended Learning among High School Students

Despite their incomplete awareness of blended learning and low participation in it, most students hold a positive attitude towards blended learning supported with online learning resources. Some students have subconsciously integrated blended learning with their own learning style. This is the so-called self-blended learning, that is, students have the ability to autonomously choose online learning resources in the process of blended learning[15].

Research data also indicate that most teachers tend to teach by using PPT and videos. The application of information technology to their teaching is a good display of their information literacy, but they seldom recommend online learning resources to their students and they're not eager to integrate blended learning with classroom teaching. The vast majority of students also hold a negative attitude towards teacher-directed blended learning. This is due to the fact that teachers focus more on using multi-media resources in their classroom teaching but they do not offer enough guidance to encourage online learning outside the classroom. The online learning resources recommended by the teacher are also mainly text-based files and learning software. More systematic learning resources such as online courses and lectures are seldom recommended.

For lack of teachers' guidance, problems also arise in students' self-directed blended learning. Their online learning is not systematic and the effect of online learning also needs to be improved. Their online learning is mostly simple, fragmented, problem-driven, and their purpose of online learning is to solve specific problems. By searching for the answer on the Internet, they have plenty of access to text-based resources, but rarely do they choose more systematic online courses supported with various audio and visual resources. Most students tend to make use of online learning resources when they review their lessons after class. They seldom use online resources for prevision. Therefore in practice online learning becomes supplementary and superficial. This is far from the actual effect that we aim to achieve by integrating blended learning with online learning.

4.3   Factors Affecting Blended Learning

Students' insufficient participation into blended learning is not only under the influence of the general educational system, but also under the restriction of such environmental factors as the Internet devices, the Internet speed, and family control, etc. Among these factors, family control of Internet surfing accounts for the largest percentage. About 30% students agree that restrictions from parents have prevented their online learning. In the questionnaire, the data from "the habit of using the Internet" indicate that teachers and parents never completely restrict access to the Internet. On the contrary, most teachers and parents encourage students to search the Internet and practise online learning. The conflict lies in the fact that students' online learning does not follow a linear pattern. Their learning is motivated gradually in the process of net surfing. But such net surfing is usually aimless at the initial stage. Although teachers and parents support online learning, they cannot tolerate such aimless and learner-directed online behaviors. The difference in the understanding of online behaviors forces students to practice online learning with stronger purposes, such as the search for a specific answer. This in turn deprives students of more autonomous blended learning.

As regards the learning devices, most students have owned one or more of the following: personal computer, laptop, pad, e-book, MP4, and cell phone. And cell phones have the highest ownership. Considering that we are still not fully prepared to use cell phones for mobile learning, some students still think that poor equipment is one of the major negative factors against online learning. It is possible that in some underdeveloped areas outside Shanghai, the negative influence of poor equipment on online learning will remain much stronger. Besides, insufficient time of online learning, slow Internet speed, and the inconvenience of online learning are also other negative factors against blended learning.

5   Suggestions

Blended learning is still not fully understood by high school students, and only a small percentage of them have practiced blended learning. Despite students' positive attitudes towards blended learning, relevant guidance from the teacher is quite limited. Teachers seldom recommend systematic online courses and resources to students. Therefore blended learning in practice follows a simple and straightforward pattern. It is problem-directed, but not systematic or reflective. Various factors may adversely influence students' blended learning, such as family control, learning devices, and learning time, etc. To further promote the development of blended learning in the elementary educational system, we need to extend the concept of blended learning among teachers, students, and parents, help teachers offer more guidance and recommend more online learning resources, and encourage parents to create a freer online learning environment. And students' low participation in blended learning will be radically changed if we can stimulate their learning motivation and help them accept blended learning.

Acknowledgements. This research is supported by the 2012 Annual National Key Project of National Science Education of China (Grant No. ACA120005).

References

1. Oliver, M., Trigwell, K.: Can 'blended learning' be redeemed. E-learning 2(1), 17–26 (2005)
2. Osguthorpe, R.T., Graham, C.R.: Blended Learning Environments: Definitions and Directions. Quarterly Review of Distance Education 4(3), 227–233 (2003)
3. Driscoll, M.: Blended learning: Let's get beyond the hype. E-learning, 54 (March 2002)
4. Singh, H., Reed, C.: A white paper: Achieving success with blended learning. Centra software (2001)
5. Bonk, C.J., Graham, C.R.: The handbook of blended learning: Global perspectives, local designs. John Wiley & Sons (2012)
6. Young, J.R.: Hybrid teaching seeks to end the divide between traditional and online instruction. Chronicle of Higher Education 48(28), A33 (2002)
7. Reay, J.: Blended learning: A fusion for the future. Knowledge Management Review 4(3), 6 (2001)
8. Rooney, J.E.: Blending learning opportunities to enhance educational programming and meetings. Association Management 55(5), 26–32 (2003)
9. Sands, P.: Inside outside, upside downside: Strategies for connecting online and face-to-face instruction in hybrid courses. Teaching with Technology Today 8(6) (2002)
10. Ward, J., La Branche, G.A.: Blended learning: The convergence of e-learning and meetings. Franchising World 35(4), 22–23 (2003)
11. Li, K., Zhao, J.: The theory and application of blended learning. E-education Research 135, 1–6 (2004)
12. He, K.: Understanding new developments in the theory of educational technology from the perspective of blended learning. E-education Research 131, 1–6 (2004)
13. Garrison, D.R., Kanuka, H.: Blended learning: Uncovering its transformative potential in higher education. The Internet and Higher Education 7(2), 95–105 (2004)
14. Zhan, Z., Li, X.: Blended learning: Definition, strategy, present, and future tendency. E-education Research 275, 1–5 (2009)
15. Valiathan, P.: Blended learning models. Learning Circuits (2002)

Is "MOOC-Mania" over?

Bebo White

SLAC National Accelerator Laboratory, Stanford University
2575 Sand Hill Road, MailStop 88, Menlo Park CA 94117 USA
bebo@slac.stanford.edu

Abstract. The New York Times famously branded 2012 "The Year of the MOOC" given the upsurge of interest in so-called "Massive Online Open Courses." MOOCs were seen as the future of distance education and the realization of a dream to "democratize" education. Anyone with online access could become a "student" and participate freely in courses offered by the world's most knowledgeable professors at the most elite universities. Class sizes were unprecedented – it was not unusual to have tens of thousands or hundreds of thousands of participants in some very popular courses. The Times declaration followed the launch of edX, by Harvard University and MIT, and the rapid growth of MOOC platforms and providers such as Coursera and Udacity. The Sand Hill Road venture capitalists invested substantial funds in these providers even though a monetization model was not obvious. It is now almost two years since "The Year of the MOOC" and we must ask ourselves whether the enthusiasm over the MOOC model was/is still warranted. Have MOOCs been successful in changing the direction of online education? What problems, issues, and challenges have MOOC adopters encountered?

Keywords: MOOCs, "Massive Open Online Courses," Coursera, Udacity, edX, "flipped classrooms".

1   Introduction

The "Gartner Hype Cycle" is a popular and often-used tool developed by the Gartner IT research and advisory firm. [1] It seeks to track the maturity, adoption, and application of new technologies (often seen as disruptive) with respect to time. It reflects the "hype" often seen with new technologies (or applications) and what happens with that "hype" over the passage of time. In the end it hopefully indicates the important phases of a technology's life cycle. Gartner identifies five key phases in the evolution of a technology's life cycle or "period of relevance" (from Wikipedia) [2]:

Technology Trigger

A potential technology breakthrough kicks things off. Early proof-of-concept stories and media interest trigger significant publicity. Often no usable products exist and commercial viability is unproven.

S.K.S. Cheung et al. (Eds.): ICHL 2014, LNCS 8595, pp. 11–15, 2014.
© Springer International Publishing Switzerland 2014

Peak of Inflated Expectations

Early publicity produces a number of success stories—often accompanied by scores of failures. Some companies take action; many do not.

Trough of Disillusionment

Interest wanes as experiments and implementations fail to deliver. Producers of the technology shake out or fail. Investments continue only if the surviving providers improve their products to the satisfaction of early adopters.

Slope of Enlightenment

More instances of how the technology can benefit the enterprise start to crystallize and become more widely understood. Second- and third-generation products appear from technology providers. More enterprises fund pilots; conservative companies remain cautious.

Plateau of Productivity

Mainstream adoption starts to take off. Criteria for assessing provider viability are more clearly defined. The technology's broad market applicability and relevance are clearly paying off.

When graphically expressed as visibility (i.e., "hype") with respect to time, the cycle is represented as in Figure 1.

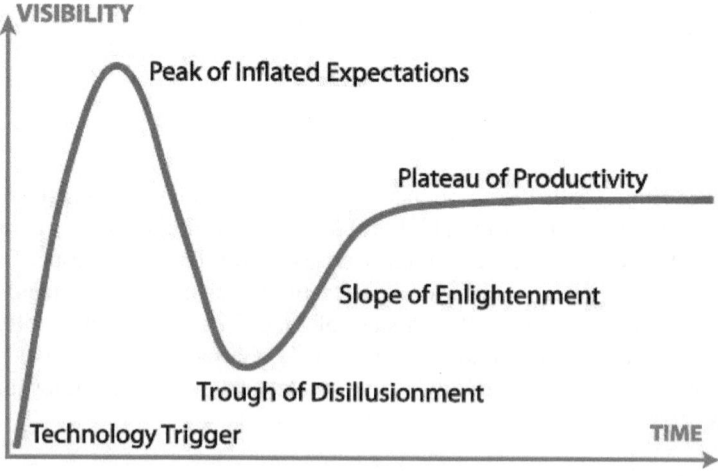

Fig. 1. The "Gartner Hype Cycle"

Assuming that it would be appropriate to apply the MOOC phenomenon to the "Gartner Hype Cycle," the relevant questions would be:

- What is the applicable time scale?
- Which phase in the cycle best describes the present influence and adoption of MOOC technology?

2   Discussion

The "Technology Trigger" in the evolution of MOOCs as a technological entity most likely came from the realization that connectivist teaching and learning could fit well on the currently defined technical and social infrastructure of the Internet/Web. It is typically acknowledged that the first MOOC was, in fact, a course and a network about the emergent practices and the theory of Connectivism taught by Stephen Downes and George Siemens through the University of Manitoba, Canada in 2008. [3] The course was not only about Connectivism but provided a demonstration of its practice through Web 2.0 concepts such as blogs and chat facilities, multimedia, and social networking.

The evolution and the growth of the MOOC concept from the Downes/Siemens course to the "Year of the MOOC" are well documented. In recent years it has been difficult to find an educational journal or conference that does not include some reference to MOOCs and the issues surrounding their adoption. Statistics abound regarding the number of MOOCs currently available, the size of enrollments, and completion rates.

There are strong indications that MOOCs may now be on the leading edge of the "Trough of Disillusionment." This proposition comes from the four groups that would be the primary stakeholders in MOOC success or failure: the institutions, the faculty, the students, and the investors.

Institutions are clearly questioning the wisdom of putting their curriculum (the intellectual capital that lies in their faculty) online for free. Some institutions have made a substantial investment into the development and support of MOOCs. For example, at Stanford University the faculty demand to create MOOCs has resulted in a backlog of three to four months in the audio-visual department. While massive participation in a Stanford MOOC could be perceived as a matter of prestige for the university (amongst the elite institutions), it is not unreasonable to ask what is their Return on Investment (ROI)? It would be hard to prove that MOOCs provide Stanford with a viable mechanism for recruiting top students. Similarly, it is unlikely that at any time in the future Stanford will allow MOOC completion to be applied towards a Stanford degree. Interestingly, Stanford is using edX as its principal MOOC platform rather than Coursera or Udacity (both of whom were developed by Stanford faculty). [4] It is possible that Stanford is finding secondary value in the collaboration with the other institutions that are members of the edX Consortium.

Faculty acceptance of MOOCs has been mixed. Motivated faculty members have found the new methods of teaching required by the development of a MOOC to be challenging. Lessons learned from teaching MOOCs and the diversity of students and student involvement can potentially result in new methods applicable to traditional, classroom, face-to-face teaching. Other faculty may be motivated by the large enrollment numbers and the opportunity to be recognized internationally as an outstanding "subject matter expert." Some faculty have also felt threatened by the concept of "flipped classrooms" and how adoption of such a course style might diminish their faculty role in the "higher education of the future." Faculty should be worried about the lack of robust student assessment mechanisms currently found in MOOCs.

As perhaps should be said for any teaching and learning environment, students stand to be the big winners with MOOCs. For motivated students, participation in MOOCs addresses the rising costs of higher education or even the need for a university degree. MOOCs can potentially satisfy one of the longtime goals of distance education and "the digital divide" by providing access to high-quality educational content to anyone anywhere in the world for little or no cost. Enrollment statistics in existing MOOCs have expanded the definition of students. MOOC "learning communities" often contain university students, lifelong learners (e.g., retirees), "learning on demand" participants, and others. Socialization between such a diversity of active students has proven to appreciably enhance the learning and teaching experience. Student disillusionment in MOOCs may be reflected in the low completion rates and the realization that many students require a more structured educational environment. To many students MOOC content has simply become another online commodity to be compared and evaluated with other options.

It is safe to say that the "hype" and "inflated expectation" surrounding MOOCs created a "new cottage industry" that some investors were eager to be a part of. The two best-known MOOC platforms, Coursera and Udacity, were both developed by faculty members who had developed successful (judging from enrollment numbers) courses. Well-known venture capitalist firms were eager to financially support their efforts in the hope that a monetization model for MOOCs could be identified. [5] Development of such a model has been "slow in coming." It is generally agreed that course content should remain free to students, but additional services and functionality may be provided at a charge. Coursera offers students completion certificates that are potentially recognized by major employers. [6] Also offered are recruitment contacts and job placement services allowing employers access to the names of high-performing MOOC students. Costs of such services may be shared between students and employers/recruiters. On Udacity non-paying students [7] have access to course videos and exercises and can view and manage their progress, but a paid subscription gives them access to in-class projects, feedback from instructors and a verified certificate. As such, MOOC platform providers are leveraging the expert content from universities and following in the footsteps of the longtime commercial online educational providers (e.g., The University of Phoenix).

In addition to providing expert content, colleges and universities are themselves exploring ways to "monetize the MOOC model." For example, in March 2014, Harvard Business School announced its HBX program. [8] HBX requires that students apply for admission and must already be pursuing at least a four-year degree at another institution. HBX is not free with tuition for its first term priced at $1,500. Instruction and assessment will be done as with other MOOCs and students successfully graduating will receive a Credential of Readiness verified by Harvard Business School. This "modified MOOC model" assumes that registration costs will offset the usual MOOC dropout rate and that students will be highly motivated by the prospect of receiving Harvard certification.

3   Conclusion

Yes – "MOOC-Mania" has likely come to an end (i.e., it has reached the "Peak of Inflated Expectations"). But rather than disillusionment (as suggested by the next phase of the "Gartner Hype Cycle"), stake-holders in the MOOC model (institutions, faculty, students, and investors) should take the opportunity to reflect on the pedagogies that can possibly be implemented via MOOCs and how they might influence future higher education both online and in the classroom. Despite the fact that to some educators MOOCs appear to be a fad or a threat, the questions that have arisen surrounding them should not be ignored. Educational researchers should continue to explore new MOOC models and paradigms (e.g., xMOOCs, cMOOCs, etc.).

A "Slope of Enlightenment" may come when it is realized that MOOCs are global events, not regional ones in the way that traditional university courses tend to be. That is, MOOCs provide the capability to transcend the specific concerns of the stakeholders. MOOCs may be one of the only ways to satisfy George Siemens' vision "learning is a social trust-based process, and limitations of language and shared context may circumscribe people's capacity to engage with others to the full potential of the [Connectivist] model."[9] Technology ownership and bandwidth certainly present barriers at this time, but they are simply technical problems that are likely to be solved in the future if there is sufficient motivation. If it is accurate to assume that the time scale on the "Gartner Hype Cycle" is approximately linear, then this "enlightenment period" should be realized within the next four to five years.

References

1. Wikipedia: Hype Cycle,
   `http://en.wikipedia.org/wiki/Gartner%27s_Hype_Cycle`
2. Wikipedia: Gartner, `http://en.wikipedia.org/wiki/Gartner`
3. Connectivism and Connective Knowledge: The Daily (September 15, 2008),
   `http://connect.downes.ca/archive/08/09_15_thedaily.htm`
4. Stanford University: Homepage of Stanford Online,
   `http://online.stanford.edu/openedx`
5. Hepler, L.: Coursera lands $20 million in new funding despite online education turmoil. Silicon Valley Business Journal (November 22, 2013),
   `http://www.bizjournals.com/sanjose/news/2013/11/22/coursera-lands-20-million-in-new.html?page=all`
6. Coursera Student Support: What is a Verified Certificate? How can I use It?,
   `http://help.coursera.org/customer/portal/articles/1167998-what-is-a-verified-certificate-how-can-i-use-it`
7. Kolowich, S.: Udacity Will No Longer Offer Free Certificates. The Chronicle of Higher Education (May 14, 2014),
   `http://chronicle.com/blogs/wiredcampus/udacity-will-no-longer-offer-free-certificates/51757`
8. Borchers, C.: Harvard Business enters online education fray. Boston Globe (March 21, 2014),
   `http://www.bostonglobe.com/business/2014/03/20/harvard-business-school-launches-online-education-program/L2x3xMuBgjR12TLlh01XYO/story.html`
9. McAuley, A., Stewart, B., Siemens, G., Cormier, D.: The MOOC model for digital practice,
   `https://www.academia.edu/2857149/The_MOOC_model_for_digital_practice`

A Kinet-Affective Learning Model
for Experiential Learning in Smart Ambience

Horace H.S. Ip[*] and Julia Byrne

AIMtech Centre and Department of Computer Science,
City University of Hong Kong
Tat Chee Avenue, Kowloon, Hong Kong
cship@cityu.edu.hk

1   Introduction

With the increasing development and implementation of 3D visualization and interactive media technologies in education under the auspices of game-based [1], experiential, virtual reality (VR) [2] or smart ambience [3] (defined here as a VR environment that is responsive to user's natural motion/gesture within it) learning, students and teachers are increasingly exposed to new and unique forms of learning experiences that go beyond those possible with traditional teaching methods.

However the corresponding development of learning / instructional models and pedagogies that serves to underpin the design of such 3D technology and sensor-driven learning scenarios are lacking behind. Such psycho-educational underpinnings are critical to our understanding and evaluation of the effectiveness and the pedagogical deployment of these new learning media and technologies, as well as gaining insight into the interplay between the three domains of learning activities [8], i.e. body movement (kinematics or psychomotor [9]), emotion (affect) and mind (cognition) within a responsive virtual reality space.

Features of game play exist in many VR-based or smart ambience learning scenarios [7], providing the learner with a multi-sensory learning experience involving body motion and gesturing, visual and audio, and in some case, olfactory stimulations. Such features of game-based learning highlight intrinsic motivation through varying aspects of control, challenge, curiosity and competition. These features also determine how the students can actively participate and control their body movements within the 3D virtual environment and experience the challenges of achieving certain learning goals. Success can lead to positive feelings resulting in greater motivation in learning.

In this paper, we will revisit a model for kinet-affective learning which we call the SAMAL Model first presented by the authors in a previous paper [4] and using it to illustrate the possible interplay between the body, mind and emotion in two distinct 3D immersive learning environments that integrate elements of game play. The two VR-based learning environments and the associated interactive learning scenarios provide the experiential learning platforms respectively for two very different groups of students with very different cognitive levels and learning objectives, namely university freshman, and severely intellectual disabled (SID) students.

---

[*] Corresponding author.

S.K.S. Cheung et al. (Eds.): ICHL 2014, LNCS 8595, pp. 16–23, 2014.

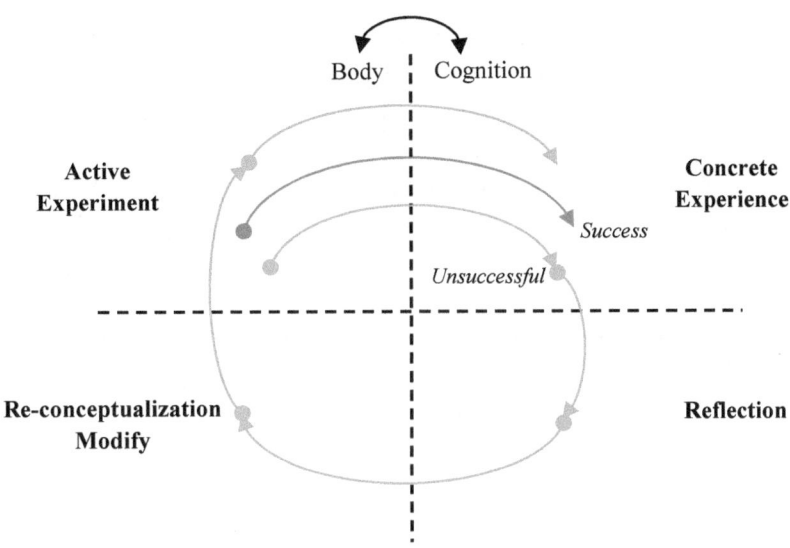

Fig. 1. Experiential Learning Cycle of the SAMAL Model

2   A Kinet-Affective Learning Model for VR-Based Learning

The SAMAL model is motivated by experiential theories in education and game-based learning, and the use of the body moving within the virtual reality space. It begins to provide a rationale that underpins the design of a 3D experiential learning platform and the associated VR-based learning scenarios. This model integrates the concepts of (a) experiential learning in VR space which is considered as an active learning process based upon trial and error through the kinesthetic interaction with the 3D virtual scene and engaging the body in the learning scenario; and (b) the concept of control and focus in relationship to learning. By drawing upon the insights from Kolb's model for experiential learning [5] and Sundstrom's model of the affective loop [6], the SAMAL Model attempts to explain how the immersive and interactive elements of the VR-based learning scenario links the aspects of kinematics (psycho-motor), affect and cognition in experiential learning.

A typical VR-based learning (game) scenario challenges a learner to navigate (move) through a series of virtual scenes or landscape, interact with virtual characters and manipulate virtual objects along the way to achieve certain learning (game play) objectives. Such multimodality activities within a trial and error process stimulate three aspects of learning domain, namely the body, mind and affect, and facilitate the practice of experiential learning, together with mental control and focus during the trial and error process. The experiential learning cycle of the SAMAL model (Figure 1) which highlights the psychomotor and cognitive aspects of learning is based upon Kolb's theory of experiential learning which suggests that learning involves an itera-tive process of concept formulation and modification, or refinement, through active experimentation which may involve physical body movement or gesturing.

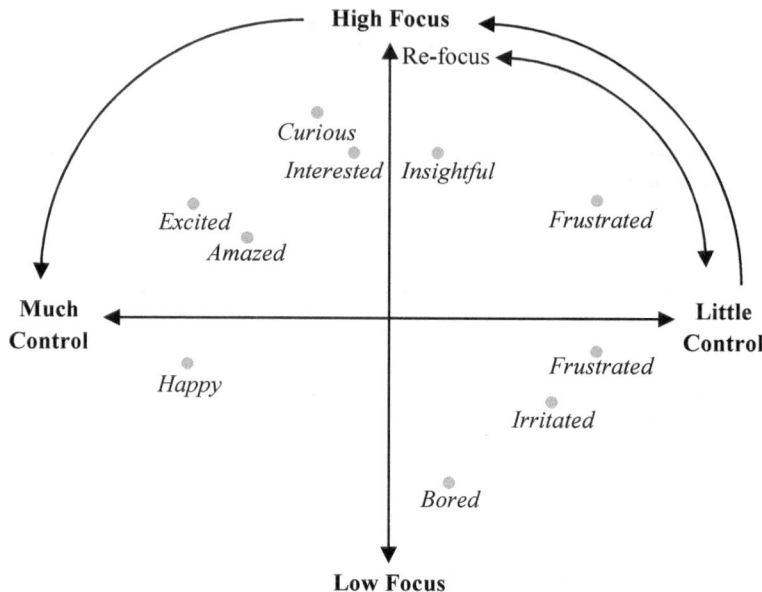

Fig. 2. Variability Component of the SAMAL Model

In an attempt to relate the affective and psychomotor aspect of learning in a responsive VR space, the SAMAL Model introduced another component called Variability, and makes use of the concept of the affective loop proposed by Sundstrom. The 'affective loop' refers to an affective interaction process 'where emotion plays an important role in interaction, involvement and evolution' [6]. Figure 2 illustrates the relationship between the possible transition of affect states with respect to changing degrees of focus and control in body gesturing during the process of technology / sensor-mediated experiential learning. This differs from the affective learning model proposed by Kort et al. [11] which directly relates phases of learning to emotions.

Merging the experiential learning cycle with the variability component gives rise to a multi-dimensional Kinet-affective model that connects the body, mind and affects in experiential learning within a smart ambience. Further detailed exposition of the SAMAL model can be found in [4]. In the following, we present two examples of a responsive VR learning environment that provide the experiential platforms for two distinct groups of students with very different degrees of physical movement and control as well as levels of cognition.

Example 1: A VR-Based Learning Scenario for University Freshman to Learning about Animal Survival

In the first Example, the learner is placed within VR environment with 3D projection of a virtual garden scene and s/he can navigate (and fly) around the virtual garden through flapping her arms while holding a motion sensing device and shifting her weigh while standing on a pressure sensing board (See Figure 3).

In the Hummingbird Flying Game Scenario, the learner will perceive herself as the hummingbird. By shifting his weight on the pressure-sensing board and, at the same time, flapping her arms, the virtual bird will fly and navigate through the garden, avoiding obstacles along the way to reach the target, ie. flowers, in order to recharge her energy level by sucking the nectar from the flowers (Figure 4). It can be a challenging task at first for the student to learn to develop appropriate strategic movements and navigation paths, while at the same time, exert the appropriate amount of energy in flapping her arms (wings) and control her body's centre of gravity to achieve controlled flight through the garden. As a result, uncontrolled flight will lead to failure and unsuccessful outcome, and hence frustration.

In game-based learning, the student is encouraged to actively develop, explore and experiment with different strategic moves which lead to concrete successful or unsuccessful experience. Through the use of the SAMAL Model, an iterative process of modification and refinement of the moves, flight paths and flight strategies followed by successive period of reflection and re-conceptualization, the students will eventually achieve successes and, in the process, learn and appreciate the challenges faced by the Hummingbird in striving to survive in the natural world, continuously trying to satisfy two conflicting goals, i.e. to *recharge* energy by sucking nectar from the flower, and to fly to get to the flower for the nectar which *consumes* energy.

The combination of motion and weight sensors, and immersive VR in the learning environment enables the simulation and sense of flying and heightens the resulting affect states of satisfaction or frustration during the trial and error process of learning.

Further detail of this VR-based learning scenario and the effectiveness of the learning scenario design can be found in [7].

Example 2: A VR-Based Learning Scenario for Severe Intellectually Disable (SID) Students to Learn Body Balancing

In the second example, the learning scenarios are designed to help SID students to acquire certain generic skills, such as balancing through controlled body weight shifting, or cognitive awareness of higher level concepts such as 'cause and effect'. SID learners typically have an IQ of 20-40 and, many of them, also have various forms of physical disability, which posed immense challenges to the design of the learning scenarios and the way the students would interact with the virtual objects within the VR environment. The VR-based learning environment consists of 3D visual projection and a Kinect (body gesture) sensor and specially developed motion analysis software that tracks and recognizes gesture and motion of SID students.

One aspect to the overall functioning of SID students is that the majority of them have mild to severe balancing difficulties, making it difficult for many of the students to maneuver their way across the room smoothly. The VR-based learning environment aims to provide a unique approach to help students develop eye-body coordination as they need to be able to use visual tracking and some level of body coordination in order to reach their target in a safe and controlled virtual space. Once acquired, this skill could be transferred into the classroom setting and home environment.

Fig. 3. A snapshot of a learner interacting with the virtual scenario using the motion and pressure sensing devices

Fig. 4. 3D virtual scene of the hummingbird flying toward its target flower

The learning scenario for training SID students to achieve greater balancing skills consists of a fantasy scenary of forests, mountains and castles (Figure 5), while the student is given the illusion that s/he is standing on a magic carpet and "flying" over the fantasy landscape, (ie) over the hill...and through the flower garden and river. The students will shift their bodies to move left or right in order to control the movement of the magic carpet and navigate to the destination which is a beautiful virtual castle. The body motion of the student is tracked by the Kinect motion sensor and analyzed by specialized software.

Fig. 5. A 3D Virtual Fantasy Scenary in the InSPAL learning scenario

Fig. 6. Actors' demonstration of navigating through a virtual fantasy scenery

The InSPAL learning scenario was designed mostly based upon the SAMAL Model, with an emphasis placed upon combining aspects of an active learning process based upon trial and error (experiential learning) and incorporating concepts of control and focus. The instuctional plan and the way that the teacher/facilitator interacted with the student lied most notably in premise that SID students can learn most effectively by 'doing'. Through kinesthetic physical interaction with the virtual characters and environment, the senses of the students are stimulated and greater learning can be achieved (kinesthetic learning). In the InSPAL programme, teachers were also involved and acted as facilitators in the learning process.

Facilitation is an enabling process with the main emphasis placed upon maximizing the student's potential at every moment. When working with students in InSPAL the teacher will train the students just long enough, so that the teacher can release the student's hand (or body in the case of the balance and coordination domain) so that the student can try to do it him/herself. If the student can do it (or partly do it) by him/herself then success can be felt, resulting in happy feelings. If success is not achieved, then the process starts over again. Repetition and training in the 'trial and error process' aides in greater success and repeated success can contribute to greater learning for the student.

3   Summary

Recent advances in sensors, natural interface and immersive 3D visualization technologies open up new ways for the design of novel learning environments. In this talk, we highlight the work being done at AIMtech Centre of City University of Hong Kong that aims to develop novel sensors and immersive VR driven learning environments that facilitate experiential learning for a diversity of student groups. At the same time, we investigate conceptual models for learning that help to provide a pedagogical underpinning of the design of technologies-mediated and sensors driven learning environments, along with a 3D immersive and responsive learning scenario that seek to invoke and synergize kinematic, affective and cognitive aspects of learning.

Acknowledgement. The authors would like to thank the support and contributions of their school partners, collaborators and research assistants to the work reported here, particularly, Dr S K Cheng, Dr Ron Kwok, Ms Kate Lau, Mr Richard Li, Ms Catherine Choi and Ms Amy Tso. The work is supported by the HKSAR Quality Education Fund, Project No. 2010/0072, and a Teaching Development Grant of City University of Hong Kong, No. 6000158.

References

1. Connolly, T.M., Boyle, E.A., et al.: A Systematic Literature Review of Empirical Evidence on Computer Games and Serious Games. Computers & Education 59, 661–686 (2012)
2. Mikropoulos, T.A., Natsis, A.: Educational Virtual Environments: A ten-year review of empirical research (1999-2009). Computers & Education 56, 769–780 (2011)
3. Kwok, R.C.W., Cheng, S.H., Ip, H.H.S., Kong, J.S.L.: Design of Affectively Evocative Smart Ambience Media for Learning. Computers & Education 56, 101–111 (2011)
4. Ip, H.H.S., Byrne, J., Cheng, S.H., Kwok, R.C.W.: The SAMAL Model for Affective Learning: A multi-dimensional model incorporating the body, mind and emotion in learning. In: Workshop on Distance Education Technology, International Conference on Distributed Multimedia Systems (2011)
5. Kolb, D.: Experiential Learning: Experience as the source of learning and development. Prentice-Hall, Englewood Cliffs (1984)
6. Sundstrom, P.: Exploring the Affective Loop. Stockholm University, Stockholm (2005)

7. Ip, H.H.S., Byrne, J., Cheng, S.H., Kwok, R.C.W., Lam, M.S.W.: Smart Ambience for Affective Learning (SAMAL): Instructional Design and Evaluation. In: Proceedings of the 18th International Conference on Computers in Education - Workshop on The Design, Implementation and Evaluation of Game and Toy Enhanced Learning (2010)
8. Bloom, B.S.: Taxonomy of Educational Objectives, Handbook I: The Cognitive Domain. David McKay Co. Inc., New York (1956)
9. Simpson, E.J.: The Classification of Educational Objectives in the Psychomotor Domain. Gryphon House, Washington, DC (1972)
10. Harrow, A.: A Taxonomy of Psychomotor Domain: A Guide for Developing Behavioral Objectives. David McKay, New York (1972)
11. Kort, B., Reilly, R., Picard, R.: An Affective Model of Interplay between emotions and Learning: Reengineering Educational Pedagogy-building a Learning Companion. In: Proceedings of the IEEE International Conference on Advanced Learning Technologies (2001)

The Effect of Hybrid Learning in Vocational Education Based on Cloud Space: Taking the Vocational Education Cyber-Platform as an Example

Di Wu[1], Xiaorong Yu[1], Yinghui Shi[1], Harrison Hao Yang[2], and Chun Lu[1,*]

[1] Collaborative & Innovative Center for Educational Technology
Central China Normal University, China
[2] Department of Curriculum and Instruction, State University of New York at Oswego, USA
{dr.wudi,yuxr402,ikkistone101}@gmail.com,
harrison.yang@oswego.edu, luchun@mail.ccnu.edu.cn

Abstract. In recent years, instructors have had an increasing interest in integrating cloud-based education platform into their classroom as part of the learning environment, especially in China's vocational education. Hunan provincial Vocational Education Cyber-Platform (VECP) is the largest vocational education cloud in China. Compared with other information systems, vocational students' attitude, effect and behavioral intention towards hybrid learning have not been assessed and thoroughly understood. This paper analyses the Technology Acceptance Model (TAM) in order to examine students' behavioral intention to use an electronic portfolio system. A Hybrid Learning Usage Questionnaire was developed using existing scales from prior TAM instruments and modified where appropriate. In our survey, 180 students completed the questionnaire measuring their responses to perceived usefulness (PU), perceived ease of use (PEOU), attitudes towards usage (ATU) and behavioral intention to use (BIU) the VECP. The results of the study indicated that students' perceived ease of use (PEOU) had a significant influence on attitude towards usage (ATU). Subsequently, perceived ease of use (PEOU) had the strongest significant influence on perceived usefulness (PU). The research further demonstrated that individual characteristics, technological factors and training experience may have a significant influence on instructors in adopting cloud-based hybrid learning into their courses in vocational education.

Keywords: education cloud, personal learning space, hybrid learning, technology acceptance model.

1   Introduction

As one of the various ways being used to deliver meaningful learning experiences, hybrid learning may significantly enhance their teaching performances and learning outcomes as well as increase student satisfaction from the learning experience. Hybrid learning has

---

* Corresponding author.

S.K.S. Cheung et al. (Eds.): ICHL 2014, LNCS 8595, pp. 24–35, 2014.
© Springer International Publishing Switzerland 2014

been an important manifestation of the trend that information technology is playing an increasingly important role in the global education development [1]. Hybrid learning, which combines traditional classroom learning and online learning has been widely used in higher education [2]. Gartner's 2008 e-learning survey for higher education revealed that the use of technology to support teaching and learning has continued to grow and hybrid learning has grown even faster [3]. Hybrid learning is also becoming an important part of the educational reform in recent years in China. Currently, a majority of universities and colleges in China have adopted network learning service platform to support teaching and learning and are able to meet the requirements of hybrid learning in both hard and software conditions.

With the emerging of cloud computing, educational service platforms or systems based on cloud computing have been effective means for schools in all levels to provide hybrid courses and programs that combine face-to-face learning with technology support for students and online learners.

In Chinese Vocational Education, a typical vocational education cyber-platform, constructed upon on a network service system and based on cloud computing, emerged at the right moment under such a situation. As the most popular vocational education cloud system in China, it provides a convenient and effective way for vocational teachers to enhance their teaching ability. It creates not only a quality learning resource sharing system, but also a personal learning space service center for teachers and students, so that students can composite face-to-face learning together with online learning.

While the vocational education cyber-platform is spreading rapidly in vocational education settings, there are some critical questions remain unanswered from this growth, including two central ones:

— How do students view the function and usage of cloud-based vocational education cyber-platform during their hybrid learning in general?
— What are the effects of cloud-based vocational education cyber-platform on students' learning attitudes, behaviors and perceptions?

Thus, the objective of this study is to examine whether the use of cloud-based vocational education cyber-platform in hybrid learning has any positive or negative impacts on both students' learning attitudes, behaviors and perceptions.

In part two of this paper, previous research on hybrid learning, cloud-based vocational education cyber-platform, and technology acceptance model will be reviewed. Also the research questions of the present study will be presented. In part three, the research method will be described. The results and discussion will be illustrated in part four. Conclusions of the investigation and suggestions for future studies will be included in the final part.

2   Literature Review

2.1   Hybrid Learning Based on Cloud Space

The concept of hybrid learning has been come out for a long time, but its terminology was not firmly established until around the beginning of the 21st century. Recently, attentions on hybrid learning are gradually booming out all over the world. Some amount of studies suggested that hybrid learning was an effective learning mode in improving the quality of teaching and learning [4]. As regarding to the core definition of hybrid learning, a bit of definitions on hybrid learning given by some researchers differ from various perspectives and in different ways, but they surely could help us to gain a better understanding of hybrid learning.

The various definitions of hybrid learning reflect the diversity and merit of hybrid learning. Generally, hybrid learning is a formal education program in which students learn at least in part through online delivery of content and instruction with some element of student control over time, place, path or pace[5]. Graham classify and induce the definition of hybrid learning by predecessors, and they found most definitions of hybrid learning can be divided into three types, one is the mix of different instructional modalities, one is the mix of different instructional methods, and the third one is the mix of online learning and face to face learning [6]. Hybrid learning reorganizes instruction resources and conducts learning activities by making full use of the advantages and potential of face-to-face learning and online learning, in order to improve the efficiency of teaching and learning [7]. In sum up, hybrid learning is composed of "brick-and-mortar" school structure with face-to-face classroom instructions and online learning that conducted with computer-mediated activities [8], which emphasizes that hybrid learning is a comprehensive reformation of ideas, models and methods of teaching. In this study, hybrid learning is used to describe student learning through traditional face to face instruction integrating with a cloud-based learning system, which is a software environment that enables the management, delivery, and share of learning content and resources.

Hybrid learning is not a simple combination of classroom and online learning, as the definition of hybrid learning implied. The advantages and potential benefits of hybrid learning to enhance teaching and learning have been reported by many researchers.

Koohang, Britz, and Seymour reported the advantages of hybrid learning in the literature, such as convenience for students' learning, increased interaction, flexibility, increased learning performance, higher retention of learning contents, reduced seat time and decreased the costs for instruction [9].

Shen summarized four advantages of hybrid learning [10]. First, students can have more choice and control over their study but under the guidance and instruction of the instructors at the same time, which will undoubtedly cultivate students' creativity and initiative; Second, under a hybrid learning context, students can make full use of the abundant resources and materials on the Internet and have a better understanding of these substantive materials with the help of teachers and other students in a traditional face-to-face classroom. Third, hybrid learning has the potential to provide students a greater opportunity to interact with each other and with their instructors and thus form a stronger sense of community. Last but not least, students in a hybrid learning context would perform better than those take mere face-to-face classes or online classes, as indicated by numerous previous studies.

Lots of researches and studies have been focused on the theoretical and practical aspects of hybrid learning in educational settings, with the purpose of exploring, utilizing and improving the effectiveness of hybrid learning in educational settings. For instance, Chen and Looi suggested that it is necessary to introduce the concept of hybrid learning to guide the discussion of instructional design (i.e., to mix the traditional discussions with online discussion), in order to improve the learning effectiveness[11]. Lopez-Perez, Perev-Lopez and Ariza studied students' perception and their relation to outcomes in hybrid learning and demonstrated that the use of hybrid learning has a positive effect in reducing dropout rates and in improving exam marks [12]. In addition, Uzun and Senturk examined the effects of blended and face to face course delivery methods on students' performance and attitudes towards computers in a computer literacy course and indicated that the blended mode course delivery method was more successful than the face to face course delivery method in terms of both students' course achievement and attitude towards computer [13].

2.2   Cloud-Based Vocational Education Cyber-Platform

The VECP referred in this study is a web-based interactive learning platform constructed in Hunan Province, China. Teachers and students can build their own online space, upload learning resource and teaching materials, launch tests and examinations. Based on VECP, students can communicate with teachers flexibly through the personal online learning space. The VECP was applied all over the whole Hunan province since it was constructed in 2009.

The homepage of VECP is a single sign on portal page, as shown in Fig. 1. From this page, students can get the latest learning resources, teaching materials and information announcements posted by administrators, teachers and other students. To ensure security and intellectual property, all users of VECP should login into the system with real name and id information.

Fig. 1. Homepage of the vocational education cyber-platform

The VECP could provide quality services, such as learning resource service, online community service, educational management service and educational management service.

The most popular service of VECP is providing resource uploading and posting platform, so that students and teachers can exchange resource and materials conveniently. Most teachers can finish the preparation of their own courses easily and students can get quality resource by themselves conveniently through this service.

The virtual online community provided by VECP is a huge scale community composed with over 2 million registered personal learning spaces. Based on these services, students can publish questions online and get answers in time. Most questions published online are questions which they are too shy to ask in class or do not have a chance to ask in face-to-face teaching.

The management of school, teaching and learning based on cloud space provides a high efficiency management model for schools and administrators. Schoolmasters and other managers can easily know the learning process of students through managers' space.

In this study, the TAM framework was used as guidance for the construction of a VECP evaluation scale. TAM mainly focuses on the adoption of technology by users who currently benefit from and/or utilize the technology by uncovering the internal decision processes at individual levels [14], in TAM was developed by Davis using several robust theories in the field of psychology, such as the theory of reasoned action (TRA), with the purpose of exploring users' acceptance towards the use of systems or platforms[15]. The advanced version of TAM (TAM-II) was based on the work of Venkatesh and Davis with the support of social pedagogical theories [16]. TAM-II basically consists of several components including perceived usefulness, perceived ease of use, behavioral intention, and actual behavior [17]. Perceived usefulness means the enhancement of work through using the technology system, perceived ease of use means the subjective perception of the usability of the technology.

To study the effectiveness of hybrid learning based on VECP, we designed a survey questionnaire for students. Because of the VECP's typical features and its distinctive usage behaviors that are not included in TAM. Therefore, specific VECP items were created after a fastidious examination of each of the TAM factors, which were primarily referring to 1) student perceptions about the VECP use; 2) student behaviors using the VECP; and 3) student attitudes toward the VECP.

3   Research Questions

In general, there is a growing number of studies on the application of vocational education cyber-platform in teaching and learning in secondary and higher vocational schools. However, little is yet known the effects of vocational education cyber-platform on students' learning attitudes, learning behaviors and learning achievements. As a consequence, to contribute to the research gaps identified in the literature review, the following research questions were proposed to help focus the present study:

— How students perceived the use of VECP for hybrid learning?
— What is the impact of VECP on students' self-report learning performance?
— What are the factors that affect the attitudes of vocational students towards VECP?
— What are the factors that affect behavioral intention of vocational students towards VECP?

4   Methodology

4.1   Sample Collection

Considering that most users of VECP are students from vocational schools and colleges inside Hunan province, over 300 students from 10 vocational schools and colleges were required to complete a student questionnaire. Furthermore, each respondent should have used VECP for at least 1 year and the answer time for them to complete the questionnaire was not limited. Finally, 180 valid samples were obtained excluding a large percentage of missing values, suggesting a 60% response rate. Statistical analysis was performed using SPSS 19 program package.

The demographic distribution among items includes school type, school level, gender, age, grade, operation proficiency and training records. 32.8% of respondents were from higher vocational colleges, followed by 67.2% from second vocational schools. The proportion of national key schools, provincial key schools and county key schools were 37.4%, 45.3% and 17.3%, respectively. The majority of respondents were female (60%), age 14-18 (77.2%). In addition, 35.6% of the respondents were in grade one, 47.2% in grade two, and 17.2% in grade three. Finally, about 61.1% of respondents did not have training experience about the operation of VECP.

4.2   Measurement Scales

Based on the literature review and the specific characteristics of the research content, the questionnaire is consisted of two sections. The first section includes 7 questions in order to investigate respondents' basic information with seven items, including school type, school level, gender, age, grade, the proficiency of platform operation and training records.

The second section of the questionnaire asked about respondents' perceived ease of use, perceived usefulness, attitude toward using and behavioral intention, including 16 questions that was measured with a five-point Likert-type scale ranging from "strongly disagree(1)" to "strongly agree(5)". Moreover, one question was designed to measure respondents' learning outcome.

The items in all constructs were adopting from prior studies having proved reliability and validity. Four items measuring ease and four items measuring usefulness of the platform were derived from O'Cass and Fenech [18]. Four items of attitude of hybrid learning were drawn from Davis, Bagozzi, and Warshaw [19]. Behavioral intention was measured with four items based on the Cheng et al. [20].

5   Results and Discussions

5.1   Descriptive Statistics

The descriptive statistics of the four factors are shown in Table 1. All means are above the midpoint of 3.30. The standard deviations range from 0.71 to 1.15 indicating a narrow spread around the mean. The factors were analyzed using Cronbach's alpha. All of the measures employed in this study demonstrated excellent internal consistency, ranging from 0.75 to 0.91. Barlett's test and Kaiser-Meyer-Olkin (KMO) tests were used to test empirically whether the data were likely to factor well. According to the test, we found values of KMO are larger than 0.6 , while Barlett's test values are all 0.00 which is less than significant level of 0.05, so we think they are suitable for the principal components analysis. The result showed that all items had factor loadings higher than 0.72.

Table 1. Descriptive statistics of the constructs and items (N=180)

Factors	Question	Mean	S.D.	Cronbach's alpha	Barlett's test	KMO
PEOU				0.91	0.83	.00
	1	3.41	1.15			
	2	3.47	0.91			
	3	3.34	1.12			
	4	3.60	1.05			
PU				0.75	0.74	.00
	5	3.42	0.99			
	6	3.54	0.71			
	7	3.61	1.03			
	8	3.56	0.96			
ATU				0.82	0.75	.00
	9	3.40	1.05			
	10	3.47	0.96			
	11	3.61	0.79			
	12	3.80	0.89			
BIU				0.89	0.77	.00
	13	3.58	1.00			
	14	3.85	0.86			
	15	3.62	1.07			
	16	3.91	0.94			

Table 2 presents the factor loadings of the e-portfolio usage questionnaire for the sample of 72 students using the individual student as the unit of analysis. The results of confirmatory factor analysis indicated that the scales were not only reliable, but also valid for the factors under study.

Table 2. Results of confirmatory factor analysis (N=180)

Item no.	Factor loading			
	PEOU	**PU**	**ATU**	**BIU**
1	0.88			
2	0.9			
3	0.88			
4	0.88			
5		0.78		
6		0.72		
7		0.69		
8		0.84		
9			0.86	
10			0.81	
11			0.82	
12			0.74	
13				0.85
14				0.85
15				0.91
16				0.87

5.2   Attitude toward Using of VECP for Hybrid Learning

We studied on the attitude of different type of schools' students and found that there are significant differences. As shown in Table 3, students from secondary vocational schools (mean=3.69) obviously tend to use VECP more than students from higher vocational colleges (mean=3.32), and students from national key schools (mean=4.01) tend to use VECP more than students from provincial key schools (mean=3.35) and students from county key schools (mean=3.16).

Table 3. Attitude differences analysis toward using of VECP for hybrid learning

School type	Mean	Mean Rank	Sig.
Higher vocational colleges	3.32	73.59	.05
Secondary vocational schools	3.69	98.74	
School level	**Mean**	**Mean Rank**	**Sig.**
National key schools	3.32	73.59	.00
Provincial key schools	3.69	98.74	
County key schools	3.16	61.48	

Table 4. Attitude toward using analysis across trained and untrained groups

	N	Mean	Median	Sig.
Not participated operation training	110	3.38	3.50	.00
Participated operation training	70	3.88	4.00	

After applying the independent samples t-test, the results show there is a significant difference between the group which attended operation training and didn't attend operation training (p=0.00). Obviously, students attended VECP operation training have better attitude than students didn't attend training (see Table 4). Therefore, necessary training is very important for enhancing the students' attitude.

5.3   Behavioral Intention of VECP for Hybrid Learning

Based on the study on the behavioral intention of VECP of students from different types of students and schools, we found that there are no significant differences between secondary vocational schools and higher vocational colleges. However, the behavioral intention of students from national key schools (mean=4.14) is better than students from provincial key schools (mean=3.48) and county key schools (mean=3.33), as shown in Table 5.

Table 5. Behavioral intention analysis of VECP for hybrid learning

School type	Mean	Mean Rank	Sig.
Higher vocational colleges	3.45	79.88	.05
Secondary vocational schools	3.83	95.68	
School level	**Mean**	**Mean Rank**	**Sig.**
National key schools	4.14	117.41	.00
Provincial key schools	3.48	73.44	
County key schools	3.34	74.03	

Based on the result of independent samples t-test, there is a significant difference between the behavioral intention of student group which attended operation training and didn't attend operation training (p=0.00), as shown in **Table 6**. Obviously, students attended operation training has more strong behavioral intention than other students.

Table 6. Adoption intention analysis

	N	Mean	Median	Sig.
Not participated operation training	110	3.47	3.25	.00
Participated operation training	70	4.08	4.25	

5.4   Influence Factor Analysis

According to the results of the correlation analysis (Table 7), the positive correlation of the following constructs was proven to be significant:

— Perceived ease of use of VECP has a positive effect on attitude toward using of VECP for hybrid learning.
— Perceived usefulness of VECP has a positive effect on attitude toward using of VECP for hybrid learning.
— Perceived usefulness of VECP has a positive effect on behavioral intention of VECP for hybrid learning.
— Attitude toward using has a positive effect on behavioral intention of VECP for hybrid learning.

Table 7. Correlation analysis for the theoretical constructs

	PEOU	PU	ATU	BIU	TE
Perceived ease of use (PEOU)	1				
Perceived usefulness (PU)	.77(**)	1.00			
Attitude toward using (ATU)	.81(**)	.81(**)	1.00		
Behavioral intention to use (BIU)	.84(**)	.70(**)	.81(**)	1.00	
Training experience (TE)	.22(**)	.24(**)	.33(**)	.36(**)	1

** Correlation is significant at the 0.01 level (2-tailed).

Fig. 2 shows Pearson correlation of each part of Technology Acceptance Model which illustrated the significant correlation for all structures that were established within this research. In addition, training experience is a factor that influence students' attitude toward using (correlation=0.33, p=0.00) and behavioral intention to use (correlation=0.36, p=0.00) of VECP for hybrid learning.

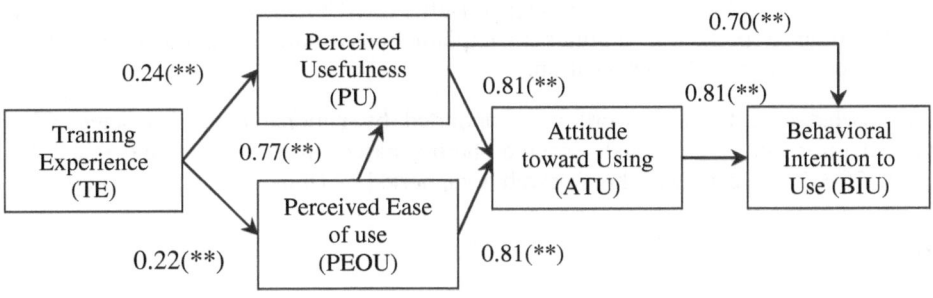

**   Correlation is significant at the 0.01 level (2-tailed).

Fig. 2. Pearson correlation model

6   Conclusions and Future Works

Given the increased application of vocational education cyber-platform in teaching and learning in vocational education, this paper aimed to study the effect of hybrid learning based on cloud-based vocational education cyber-platform, this research analyzed secondary and higher vocational school students' learning attitudes, learning behaviors and learning achievement, and investigated the factors that affect the attitudes and behavioral intention of students towards hybrid learning based on VECP. According to the analysis of the data gathered by questionnaire, the result shows that:

— Perceived ease of use of VECP has a positive effect on attitude toward using of VECP for hybrid learning.
— Perceived usefulness of VECP has a positive effect on attitude toward using of VECP for hybrid learning.
— Perceived usefulness of VECP has a positive effect on behavioral intention of VECP for hybrid learning.
— Attitude toward using has a positive effect on behavioral intention of VECP for hybrid learning.
— Training Experience has a positive effect on behavioral intention of VECP for hybrid learning.
— Training Experience has a positive effect on attitude toward using of VECP for hybrid learning.

There are numerous factors that affect users' digital archive use. In the present study, the TAM theory was adopted to elaborate on the discussion of perceived playfulness and interface design. Since the issue of digital archives has been widely discussed by researchers and others within the industry, different influential factors may be included in the discussion of digital archive users' intentions, to aid in the future development of digital archives. In addition, a follow-up study is recommended. If a favorable environment was available, a digital archives website could be used to establish a pass-back to the questionnaire design, which would facilitate an efficient questionnaire recovery rate and assist in further research in understanding digital archive usage. This study used the statistical method to test the model fit, yet, future research could include studies integrating the technology acceptance model (TAM) and computer self-efficacy (CSE), with a view to examining their combined predictive abilities to explain behavioural intention to use (BIU) among technology users in education..

Acknowledgements. This work was supported by national education science key project on quality educational resource sharing based on ICT, under the grand No. ACA120005. The survey of this research is supported by Hunan Education Department.

References

1. Information and Communication Technologies in school. UNESCO (United Nations Educational, Scientific and Cultural Organization) (2002)
2. Zuo, P., Mu, S., Han, X.: A Social Network Analysis of Students' Online Interaction in Hybrid Learning – A Case Study of "Media and Teaching" Course. In: Cheung, S.K.S., Fong, J., Kwok, L.-F., Li, K., Kwan, R. (eds.) ICHL 2012. LNCS, vol. 7411, pp. 155–164. Springer, Heidelberg (2012)

3. Zastrocky, M., Harris, M., Lowendahi, J.-M.: e-Learning for higher education: Are we reaching maturity. Industry Research. ID Number: G 1-12 (2008)
4. Cheng, J.: Blended learning in undergraduate corporate finance bilingual course at Jinan University. South China Normal University, Guangzhou (2012)
5. Staker, H., Horn, M.B.: Classifying K-12 Blended Learning, pp. 1–17. Innosight Institute (2012)
6. Graham, C.R.: Blended learning system: Definition, current trends, future directions. Pfeiffer, San Francisco (2006)
7. Lu, X., Zhao, G., Jiang, J.: Influential Factors of Blended Learning in Chinese Colleges: From the Perspective of Instructor's Acceptance and Students' Satisfaction. In: Cheung, S.K.S., Fong, J., Kwok, L.-F., Li, K., Kwan, R. (eds.) ICHL 2012. LNCS, vol. 7411, pp. 186–197. Springer, Heidelberg (2012)
8. Strauss, V.: Three fears about blended learning. The Washington Post (2012)
9. Koohang, A., Britz, J., Seymour, T.: Panel Discussion Hybrid/Blended Learning: Advantages, Challenges, Design, and Future Directions. In: Proceedings of the 2006 Informing Science and IT Education Joint Conference, June 25-28, pp. 155–158. Greater Manchester, England (2006)
10. Shen, H., Liu, W.: A Survey on the Self-regulation Efficacy in DUT's English Blended Learning Context. Journal of Language Teaching & Research 2, 1099–1110 (2011)
11. Chen, W., Looi, C.: Incorporating online discussion in face to face classroom learning: A new blended learning approach. Australasian Journal of Educational Technology 23, 307 (2007)
12. López-Pérez, M., Pérez-López, M.C., Rodríguez-Ariza, L.: Blended learning in higher education: Students' perceptions and their relation to outcomes. Computers & Education 56, 818–826 (2011)
13. Uzun, A., Senturk, A.: Blending Makes the Difference: Comparison of Blended and Traditional Instruction on Students' Performance and Attitudes in Computer Literacy. Contemporary Educational Technology 1, 196–207 (2010)
14. Usluel, Y.K., Mazman, S.G.: Adoption of Web 2.0 tools in distance education. Procedia-Social and Behavioral Sciences 1, 818–823 (2009)
15. Davis, F.D.: Perceived usefulness, perceived ease of use, and user acceptance of information technology. MIS quarterly, 319–340 (1989)
16. Venkatesh, V., Davis, F.D.: A theoretical extension of the technology acceptance model: Four longitudinal field studies. Management Science 46, 186–204 (2000)
17. Davis, F.D.: Perceived usefulness, perceived ease of use, and user acceptance of information technology. Management Information Systems Quarterly 13, 319–340 (1989)
18. Cass, A., Fenech, T.: Web retailing adoption: exploring the nature of internet users Web retailing behavior. Journal of Retailing and Consumer Services 10, 81–94 (2003)
19. Davis, F.D., Bagozzi, R.P., Warshaw, P.R.: User acceptance of computer technology: A comparison of two theoretical models. Management Science 35, 982–1003 (1989)
20. Cheng, T., Lam, D.Y., Yeung, A.C.: Adoption of internet banking: An empirical study in Hong Kong. Decision Support Systems 42, 1558–1572 (2006)

Study on the Interactions in Classroom of the Future

Feng Qiu

College of Information Technology, East China Normal University
Shanghai 200062, Shanghai, China
18602172288@163.com

Abstract. Classroom of the future is a teaching and learning space, consisting of human, technology, environment and resources. Classroom interactions can be viewed as a core in the classroom of the future. The interactions are not only between people. They also include others, namely, technology, environment, and resources. Through the studies on the classroom interactions, we can better understand how to redesign and implement the classroom of the future. This paper discusses relevance concepts, theories and various study dimensions, and reports an analysis on classroom interactions in the classroom of the future.

Keywords: interaction, classroom of the future, technology, teaching and learning environments.

1 Introduction

The 21st century is the age of knowledge economy and information. The Time Magazine in its issue on December 18, 2006 took "How to Build a Student for the 21st" as its cover. Oracle Education Foundation proposed that the 21st century talents should possess the attributes of critical thinking, creativity, team cooperation, cross-cultural understanding, interpersonal skills, technological literacy, and self-orientation [1]. Li in his letters to Chinese students mentioned that future talents should be interdisciplinary practitioners and positive optimists, with innovation, high quotients, communication and collaborative skills [2]. So, how to cultivate talents becomes an issue we are facing in the 21st century? Classroom is a key place for teaching and cultivating talents. The existing classrooms are patterned, dogma and static that are hard to meet the needs for cultivating talents. It is necessary to reform and reconstruct the existing classrooms [3].

Based on such background, the classroom of the future is put forward, where new technologies and media are provided, and new teaching strategies and pedagogies are utilized. Such classroom can be viewed as an intelligent or smart teaching space or learning environment. But the question is: What are the key elements in a classroom equipped with new technologies (intelligent or smart technologies) and new pedagogies? This is the reason why we carry out the study.

2 Relevance Concepts

Our study involves the concepts on classroom, classroom of the future, interaction, interaction in classroom, and etc.

S.K.S. Cheung et al. (Eds.): ICHL 2014, LNCS 8595, pp. 36–48, 2014.

2.1   Classroom

Classrooms "refer to the places for teaching activities" [4]. Historically, classrooms have three forms: the first form refers to a place for instruction, i.e., teaching room; the second form is the classroom teaching, which means teaching activities happened at the classroom, i.e. the place for transferring human special knowledge; the third form is the classroom syntheses, including teaching environments, teaching activities, courses, relationship between teachers and students, namely the special talent training place [5].

The classroom is the basic set-up for teaching activities at school with multiple meanings. It is a place for students to learn, communicate and socialize, where students can acquire knowledge, communicate and understand each other, and do reflection. Therefore, the ideal classroom should be interactive, intellectual and flexible space [6]. Classroom is also a main space for interpersonal interaction in school education. It is an organic "ecosystem" of continuous interactions between teachers, students, educational resources and environment [7]. A classroom should be an energetic life entity. The protagonist of the entity is the curiosity and learning desire of students and the teachers' inspiration and guidance to students on how to learn. It should be free and open [8].

2.2   Classroom of the Future (Future Classroom)

There is no clear definition on the future classroom in the literature. But, more and more exploratory researches are underway. Apple in the 1980s started the "Apple Classroom of Tomorrow" plan, where the most significant characteristic is to integrate computer technology into the classroom in order to make the students from passive learning to active learning. Dell, Intel and Microsoft started their future classroom plan, where the future classroom is regarded as a space integrated with environment, digital technologies, software, and teaching methodologies to achieve educational objectives. The classroom of the future is an integrated technology and software environment which can give students some alternative methods and rules in order to achieve learning targets [9]. The Daily Tribune defined the classroom of the future as a learning environment which employs innovative instruction activities and improves ICT uses from all aspects in the classroom [10]. Chen refers the classroom of the future as a kind of teaching environment equipped all kinds of hardware device, which changes the instruction from the one-way into an interactive two-way model for improving students' learning interests [11]. Classroom of the future is an innovative space or environment place and embodies humanism, intelligent or smart, ICT-enabled, rich resources, interactive, and new pedagogy [12].

2.3   Interaction

The word "interaction" literally means the "mutual influence and mutual effect". "Interaction" in Chinese belongs a sociological term and refers to the interaction between people. With the emergence of interactive technologies in computer science and the development of the Internet, the word "interactive" has more meanings. The emergence of computer interactive technology makes the interaction between human and human to interaction between human and computer. Intelligent machine also brings new meanings for the man-machine interaction and machine-machine interaction [13]. In summary, an interaction can be interpreted as: the interaction between bodies (also including social members and social various factors) that have mutual influence and effects, causing changes in behavior, character, attitude, values and so on [14].

2.4   Classroom Interaction

Classroom interaction refers the interaction happened within a classroom. For this interpretation, different people would give different definitions from different aspects. Classroom interaction refers to the classroom teaching scenario between teachers and students, and between students and students. It promotes or inhibits interaction, mutual influence, and thus achieves some behavioral changes of the teachers and students [15]. "Interaction" is to mobilize all the major elements involved in the classroom teaching process, around the instructional goals, and form the benign interaction between each other. Classroom interaction can be divided into dominant interaction and mind interaction [16]. Classroom interaction happens in certain situations through certain media and means, sometimes in verbal interaction, and sometime in non-verbal interaction, and dominant and recessive interaction. From the interaction-effect aspect, it has a positive impact and may also produce inhibitory effect. It reflects the diversity, but also for continuity [17].

3   Major Theories on Classroom Interaction

Currently, the study of classroom interaction is mainly from fields such as educational sociology, educational psychology, linguistics, pedagogy and educational technology. Educational sociology studies the nature and types of the classroom interaction. Linguistics focuses on the discourse interactions in the classroom and discourse analysis between teachers and students, including the classification of the verbal interaction and discourse analysis methodologies. Educational psychology focuses on the relationships between teachers and students, teacher behavior and attitude models, especially on the social psychological structures between teachers and students. Pedagogy studies the interaction types, quality and result of classroom interaction. Educational technology covers perspectives related to technologies and media on how to support the classroom interaction.

3.1   Group Dynamics

Group dynamics was created by Lewin, a famous social psychologist. He regarded the nature of a group as for leading to the "dynamic whole", having interdependence between the members (usually established by common goals). In this dynamic whole, the status change of any member can cause the status change of the other members, secondly, inherent state of tension between members can motivate a group to achieve their common expect aim [18].

3.2 Inter-Subjectivity Theory

This theory was created by Husserl, one of the most influential philosophers of the 20th century. Inter-subjectivity is also one of the main themes of transcendental phenomenology. Husserl's inter-subjectivity includes two aspects, namely, mutual understanding and consensus in inter-subject. Mutual understanding means to know and communicate each other through contacts. Consensus means to achieve the same understanding on the one thing through contact process, namely connectivity and intercommunity [19].

3.3 Interaction Determinism

This theory was created by Bandura, a famous psychologist and the originator of social learning theory. Bandura pointed out that behavior, human and environmental factors are actually interconnected and have interaction effect. Environment is the main point which is to determine the potential factors of behavior, where the interaction between people and environment decides behavior. Human factors and environmental impact are connected to each other [20]. This theory indicates that the environment is important for influencing human behavior, especially on interaction, no matter human to human or human to environment.

3.4 Mead's Interaction Theory

Mead, a sociologist and social psychologist, created the symbolic interaction theory. This theory emphasizes the "interaction" in the social practices that people act toward things based on the meaning they got, and these meanings are derived from social interaction and modified through interpretation. The basic idea is that individuals can have an ongoing dialogues and exchanges, and human communication is realized through meaningful actions. Symbolic interaction is the essential characteristic of human behavior. By means of symbolic communication, interaction between both sides can easily understand each other [21]. There are also other theories such as Bloom's symbolic interaction theory, constructivism learning theory, Fred's dialogue didactic theory and communication theory. All these provide a solid basis for us to study the interactions in the future classroom.

4   Study Dimension and Features of the Classroom Interaction

Interaction is one of the most basic and common phenomenon in human daily life. In daily life, a lot of interactions are in language and nonverbal, formal and informal, organized and unorganized, traditional and habital, modern and innovative, and so on. Traditional interaction is basically a direct and face-to-face interaction between people, but the interaction of modern society has increasingly beyond the boundaries of time and space. Modern communication media are used for interactions.

4.1 Dimensions

Andrew in his study "Campus Learning Spaces" divided classroom interaction into two categories, interpersonal interaction and interaction between people and information [22]. Classroom interactions are divided as interpersonal interaction, human-computer interaction, and ego interaction. For human-computer interaction, in 2008, Bill Gates, Microsoft founder predicted that it would have a huge revolution, where mouse and keyboard would be replaced by a more intuitive and natural technologies in which touch, vision and voice interface become more important [23]. His prediction becomes true. There is no unified definition for the classroom interaction, as each researcher is based on his or her understandings and needs for viewing interaction. We need to define a specific interaction analysis dimension involving people and technology, people and environment, people and resources, technology and technical dimensions. In short, we can identify the four dimensions of the future classroom interaction: human, technology, resources, and environments (physical and psychological). Figure 1 shows the relationship of four dimensions.

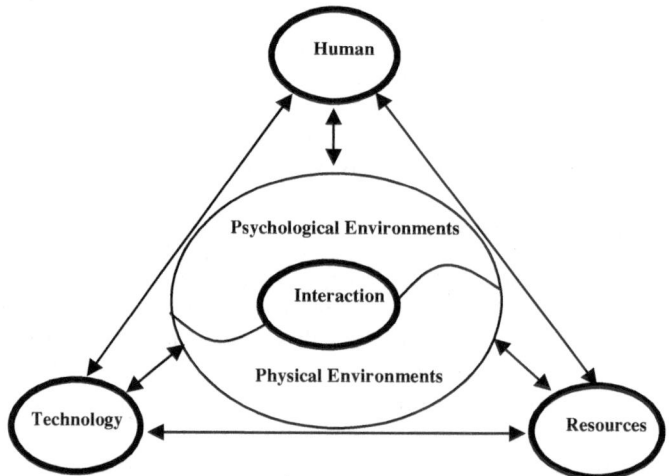

Fig. 1. Relationship of four dimensions of future classroom interaction

4.2   Forms and Characteristics

We can consider that the future classroom integrate more advanced technologies, information processing, touch and vision modes for interactions (interpersonal, people and technologies, people and resources, people and environment, technology and technology, and technology and resources).

Interpersonal Interaction

Whether in the traditional or future classroom, interpersonal interaction is one of the most common activities. This interaction is to arouse students interesting, exchange ideas, and improve understanding for the knowledge. But for the future classroom, the interpersonal interaction is more diversified, especially for interactions between teacher and student with instructional supporters, virtual person (distance or online).

Interaction between People and Environments

As Lewin pointed out, individual behavior is generated by internal factors and the interaction with environments. It can be expressed as "Behavior = f (people, environment)" which means the behavior is a function of the interaction between people and the environment [24]. In general, classroom environments can be divided into two categories: physical environment and psychological environment. Based on Bandura's interaction determinism, the classroom environment will inevitably affect classroom interaction. The physical environment refers to lighting, temperature, color, acoustic, and table and chairs, etc. The psychological environment emphasizes that there is a balance between the demands made on the students and the resources and skills he or she possesses to meet what is required. If there is imbalance, there is an increased risk of stress, conflict, dissatisfaction, more hooky, etc.

Interaction between People and Resources

Teaching process is the presentation of educational resources. Resources are presented and dynamic resources are generated. Teacher needs to present the available resources in accordance with the design scheme, and have good interaction with the resources. The resources should be easy to use and operate. Learners can also access resources for learning.

Interaction between People and Technology

Because the future classroom is equipped with advanced technologies and media, there should be adequate supports for classroom teaching or learning. In the teaching and learning process, teachers and learners have to interact with each other through technologies. Interactive media devices will have a medium to interact, generally including information input carriers, such as keyboard, mouse, light pen, track ball, infra-red sensors, audio/video input devices, and information output carriers, such as projector, whiteboard, touch screen, and audio devices [25].

5   Analysis of Classroom Interaction

Our future classroom is equipped with an intelligent audio/video recording system which can easily record whole process of teaching activities. The recorded video can be conveniently used for the analysis of interaction in the classroom. For the video analysis, two types of tools are commonly used. One is for research purpose and the other is for application. The research tool is aimed for qualitative analysis of sports or behavior, such as Nvivo and Anvil software developed by QSR Corp [26]. The application tool is for in-service and pre-service teachers, such as the VideoPaper [27]. By comparing several common video analysis tools, we choose the Interact 9.0 behavior analysis software as an analysis tool for the classroom interaction.

5.1   Analysis Indicators

Combining with the discussed features of the future classroom above and based on the mentioned four interaction dimensions, we build an evaluation indicator for the future classroom interaction shown in table 1. It is mainly around: people-people, people-technology, people-resources, and people-environments. For analysis convenience, 30 coding points and the content of each point are described.

Table 1. Categories of users and the functions available to them

Classification			Coding	Activity	Description
People-people	Teacher	Information interaction	1	Explanation	Instruction; answer questions, inspire thinking
			2	Pointing	Pointing students do something
			3	Quiz	Questioning (close issues)
		Cognitive interaction	4	Quiz	Questioning (open issues)
			5	Knowledge expanding	Deep analysis and expand of teaching contents
		Emotion interaction	6	Responding	Warmly responding student
			7	Adopt opinion	Affirm student opinion, modify or repeat student opinion
			8	Encourage and praise	Encourage & praise to student behavior
			9	Criticize and correct	Criticize & correct to student behavior
	Student	Information interaction	10	Responding	Responding teacher question or point
			11	Learning	Learning and class exercise
			12	Peer discussing	Peer discuss for teacher's question
		Cognitive interaction	13	Thinking	Deep thinking for teacher's question
			14	Active asking	Active asking queries for contents
			15	Present an idea	Give an idea for question
			16	Achievement	Explain & show group achievements
		Emotion interaction	17	Responding	Actively responding for praise and Criticize
			18	Group collaboration	Join group collaboration and actively express opinion
People-technology	Technology		19	Interaction between teacher & technology	Teacher use tech. for content presentation, process control
			20	Conferencing system	Teacher & students use conferencing system to interact with distance class
			21	Feedback technologies	Teacher use feedback tech. for testing, students using it for answering or evaluating teaching progressing

Table 1. (*Continued*)

People-resources		22	Interaction between student & technology	Student use tech. for group discuss, achievement show, learning assess
	Resources	23	Student and resources	Download, upload, or retrieve resources based on need, use resources for learning and group discussion
		24	Teacher and resources	Use resources for aided instruction and interact with resources
		25	Interaction with distance resources	Interaction with distance virtual class, with distance experts
		26	Generative resources	Use whiteboard or terminals for generating learning resources
People-environments	Environments	27	Relationship between teacher-student	Teacher go rounds for guiding group talking, joining discussion
		28	Relationship between student-student	Peer or group discussing warmly, helping each other
		29	Lighting, air condition	Adjusts lighting & air condition, making environments effect better
		30	Tables and chairs	Adjust tables & chairs for good suited to their needs, tables can combined for facilitate different group styles learning

5.2 Video Analysis

In order to analyze the interaction results, we recorded a real course process video in our future classroom and used the Interact 9.0 software tool to analyze the classroom interactions. The Interact 9.0 tool can provide good coding operation that allows automatic analysis. It is easy to obtain the analysis results. The software tool is shown in figure 2.

After coding the video, a build-in analysis function is used for analysis. We coded the video by ourselves. In addition, an expert was invited to code the video. We used the Interact9.0 build-in function of computing Kappa for comparing the two coding, the consistency reaches 98.75%.

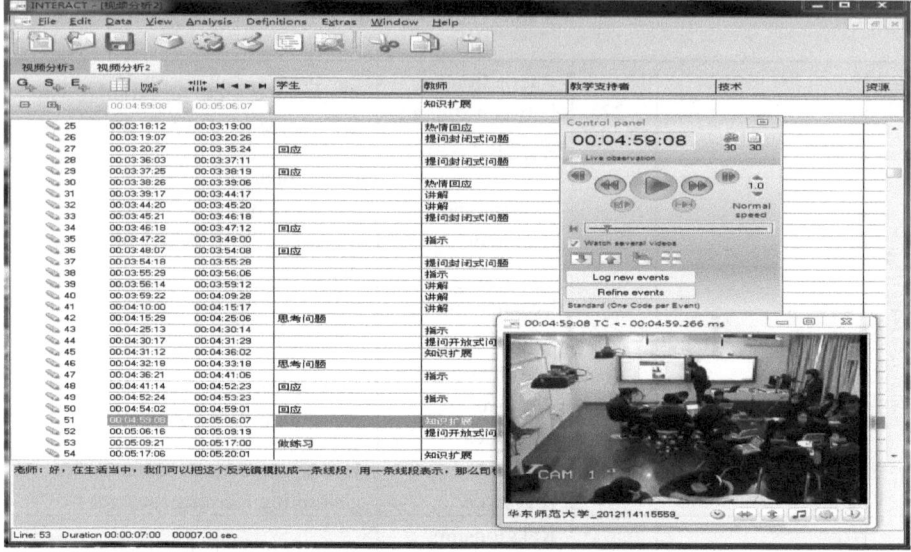

Fig. 2. Interact 9.0 Video Coding Interface

The time graph of people-centred interactive activities in classroom is shown in figure 3.

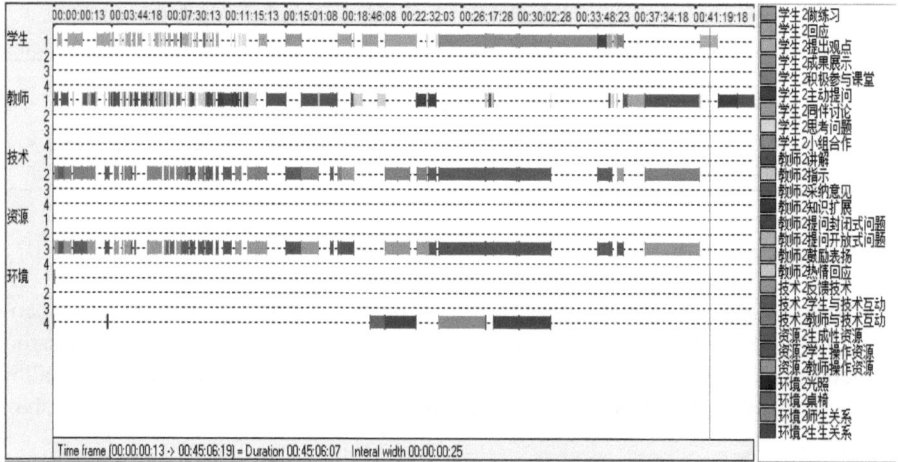

Fig. 3. Time graph of classroom interaction

5.3   Some Analysis Results

The interaction between teacher and student is an important part of classroom interaction. In the teaching and learning process, teacher would adopt different interaction forms according to different segments and stages. Also, students will have different interaction forms too in different segments and stages. Figure 4 shows the analysis of teacher interaction and figure 5 shows the student.

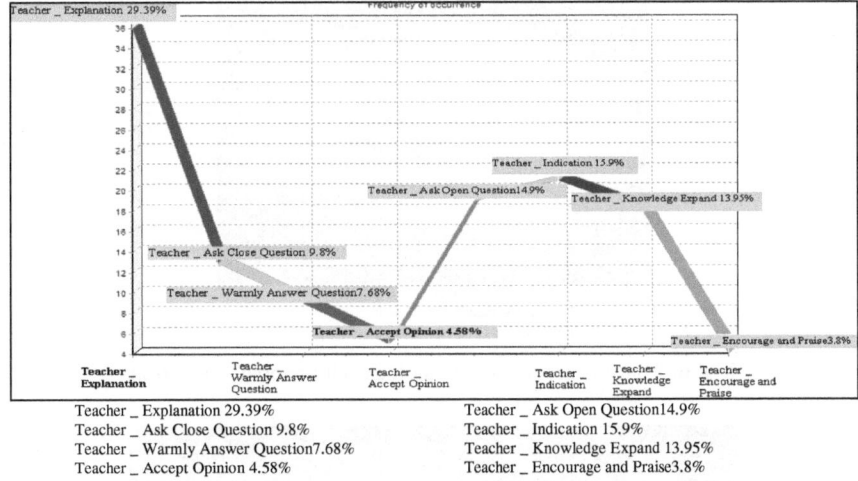

Teacher _ Explanation 29.39%   Teacher _ Ask Open Question14.9%
Teacher _ Ask Close Question 9.8%   Teacher _ Indication 15.9%
Teacher _ Warmly Answer Question7.68% Teacher _ Knowledge Expand 13.95%
Teacher _ Accept Opinion 4.58%   Teacher _ Encourage and Praise3.8%

Fig. 4. Analysis graphic of teacher interaction

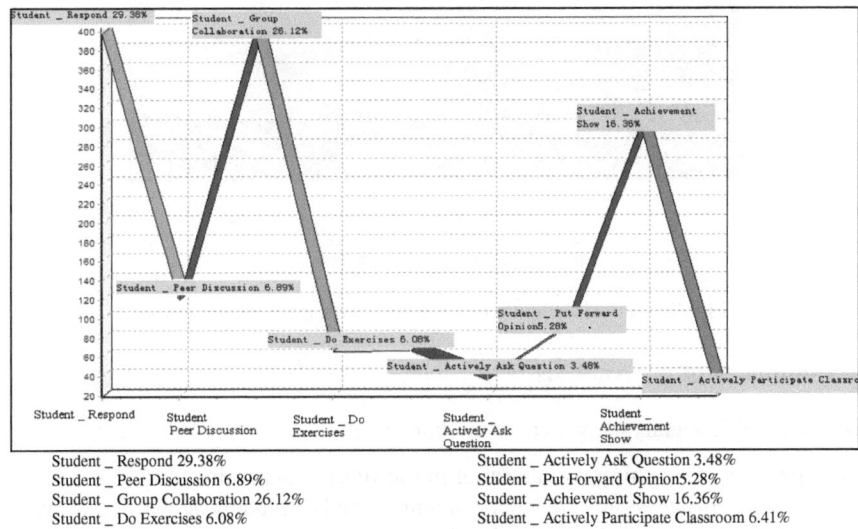

Student _ Respond 29.38%   Student _ Actively Ask Question 3.48%
Student _ Peer Discussion 6.89%   Student _ Put Forward Opinion5.28%
Student _ Group Collaboration 26.12% Student _ Achievement Show 16.36%
Student _ Do Exercises 6.08%   Student _ Actively Participate Classroom 6.41%

Fig. 5. Analysis graphic of student interaction

In the future classroom, beside the teacher and student, the technology and resources are also important. Based on the video analysis, the interaction results between technology and people show in figure 6, and between resources and people in figure 7.

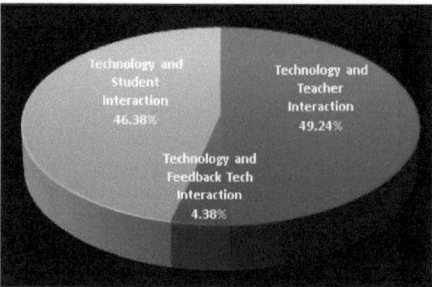

Technology and Teacher Interaction 49.24%
Technology and Student Interaction 46.38%
Technology and Feedback Tech Interaction 4.38%

Fig. 6. Analysis graphic of technology with people interaction

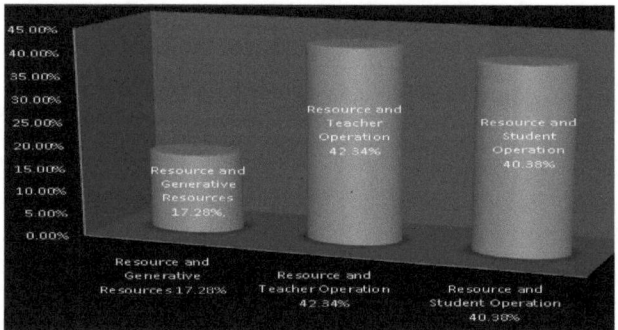

Resource and Generative Resources 17.28%
Resource and Teacher Operation 42.34%
Resource and Student Operation 40.38%

Fig. 7. Analysis graphic of resources with people interaction

5.4   Summary of the Analysis

Based on the video analysis, we can conclude that:

a.   The process of teaching and learning in the future classroom can be viewed as the interaction process on teacher-student, teacher/student-technology, teacher/ student-resources, and teacher/student- environments. In the teaching and learning process, students are the main implementers for the interaction, in which they interactive time with resources and technology for learning and group discussing reaches 52.45%.

b.   Technology plays an important role in the future classroom, where the interaction between the students and technology reaches 46.38%, between teacher and technology reaches 49.24%, and interactive feedback technology reaches 4.38%.

c.   Resources also are an important part in the teaching and learning process. From the video analysis, the time of students operating resources is 42.88%, the time of teachers operating resources is 40.14%, and the time generating resources by students and teacher is 16.98%.

   d.   Teacher is an organizer and guider of teaching activities, as well as the role of learning partners is obvious for interaction. Compared the interactions between teacher-student and student-student, the time rate is more than 15%. From actual observations, teacher's on-time guiding and participation in group discussion will significantly affect the interaction.

   e.   Students quickly adapt for the future classroom environments. They are quickly familiar with the environments, and can adjust their table and use terminals (tablet PC, ipad) for autonomous learning and cooperative learning.

   f.   For the information, cognitive, and emotional interactions, based on respective statistical results, the information interaction in the future classroom is the largest (accounting for 44.8%) which indicates that information interaction is the basis of cognitive and emotional interactions. It shows that the cognitive and emotional interactions between teachers-student will be more than information interaction in the future classroom. It also shows that the future classroom is not only for information transmission, but also a place to promote learners to improve their cognition and develop positive feelings.

6   Conclusion

Classroom of the future embodies people-oriented concepts that pay more attention to the harmonious philosophy between people, environments, and technology. Based on humanism, interaction, environmental psychology and other related theories, we explore the different elements (i.e. people, technology, resources, environment and methods, etc.) in the teaching and learning environment. Classroom interaction is regarded as the core, in order to build an active, initiative, harmonious and free development environments for teaching and learning activities. Study on the forms and characteristics of classroom interaction will help us to better understand the future classroom, and guide us how to design the classroom for meeting the demand of course characteristics and talents cultivating. We conducted an analysis on our classroom of the future, and reported the findings in this paper. There are still many challenges for us to further explore, such as new teaching methodologies, strategies, models for effective interactions in the future classroom.

References

1. Oracle Education Foundation: The 21st Century Learning Skills (January 10, 2014), http://sky-star1314.blog.163.com/blog/static/4794802420092244520259/
2. Lee, K.F.: Most need 7 kinds of talents in the 21st century. News at CSDN.NET (September 7, 2009), http://news.csdn.net/a/20090907/213569.html
3. Zheng, J.Z.: Classroom Reconstruct. Journal of East China Normal University (Education Science) 3, 53–57 (2001)
4. Chinese XinHua Dictionary, 11th edn. China People Education Press (2011)
5. Wang, J.: Classroom research overview. Educational Research 6, 20–26 (2003)
6. Hou, Y.L.: Classroom Effective Interaction Study. Master degree thesis. East China Normal University (2009)

7. Cong, L.X.: Learning to Teach (Translation from Arends, R.I.: Learning to Teach), pp. 116–117. East China Normal University Press (2007)
8. Wu, Z.Y.: Beyond the Classroom: New Vision of Teaching and Learning in the 21st Century. Shandong People's Publishing House (2009)
9. Fischler, A.S.: Disrupting Class - Highly Recommend! The Student is the Class, http://abe.thestudentistheclass.com/2009/05/disrupting-class-highly-recommend.html
10. The Daily Tribune: Classroom of the Future, Here, Now (January 18, 2014), http://telebisyon.net/balita/SCHOOL-MATTERS/artikulo/69732/
11. Chen, M.C.: You have to know - Science and Technology Teaching in the 21st century, http://epaper.hrd.gov.tw/101/EDM101-0501.htm
12. Zhang, J.P., Chen, W.D.: Study on Classroom of the Future. Journal of Educational Technology Research 8, 18–22 (2011)
13. Yin, B.: Interactive research of exhibition design. Master degree theses. Jiang Nan University, pp. 3-8 (2008)
14. Chaoyang Teachers College: Rational thinking about "interactive" teaching in primary school Chinese reading, http://www.cysz.com.cn
15. Han, Q., Zhou, Z.K., Hu, W.P.: Influence factors and teaching implications of classroom interaction. Journal of Education Theory and Practice 6, 25–29 (2008)
16. Huo, T.T.: Classroom interaction model study of feedback technical supports. Capital Normal University (2009)
17. Hou, Y.L.: Classroom Effective Interaction Study. Master degree theses. East China Normal University (2009)
18. Cheng, S.: Collaborative Learning. Fujian Education Press, pp. 26–28 (2005)
19. Mu, Z.H., Xu, T.: Chinese curriculum standard. Contemporary Education Forum (subject education research) 1, 36–41 (2008)
20. Bandura's interaction determinism overview, http://www.studyku.cn/baike/x18362
21. Tang, Y.F.: Mead's symbolic interaction theory review. Journal of Harbin Institute 7, 45–49 (2003)
22. Milne, A.J.: Entering the Interaction Age: Implementing a Future Vision for Campus Learning Spaces. EDUCAUSE Review 42, 12–31 (2007)
23. Gates, B.: Human-computer interaction will occur significant changes. China daily (March 16, 2010), http://www.chinadaily.com.cn/hqcj/bx/2010-03-16/48240.html
24. Lin, Y.L.: Environmental psychology. China Building Industry Press (2000)
25. What is an interactive projection?, http://www.souvr.com/event/200908/2322.html
26. Kipp, M.: ANVIL: Annotation of Video and Language Data 5.0. 0. Language Documentation and Conservation 5, 88–94 (2011)
27. Beardsley, L., Cogan-Drew, D., Olivero, F.: Video-paper: Bridging research and practice for pre-service and experienced teachers. In: Goldman, R., Pea, R., Barron, B., Derry, S. (eds.) Video Research in the Learning Sciences, pp. 479–493. Lawrence Erlbaum (2007)

Reconstructing New Space for Teaching and Learning: The Future Classroom

Jiping Zhang

East China Normal University
Shanghai 200062, China
jpz@ecnu.edu.cn

Abstract. Educational reform and talent cultivation require us to transform the traditional classroom. In this transformation, classrooms are reconstructed to support new styles of teaching and learning with intelligent features, blended learning, openness, and human-oriented, interactive and ecological elements. This paper reports a study on the future classroom, not only on the physical construction but also on the basic theory and application aspects. Interaction types and new styles of teaching and learning are discussed.

Keywords: future classroom, new space, teaching and learning, evaluation.

1 Introduction

Classroom innovation is essential to educational reform or development, as classroom is a place for teaching and learning [1]. General speaking, classroom should be a vibrant organism, where the teachers inspire and guide students but the students are the focus [2]. A classroom should be independent and open that helps cultivate all-round development of talents with creative and critical thinking, and a strong sense of social responsibility and team spirit.

Modern education ideas emphasize the students' capabilities on cross-discipline knowledge, independent thinking, cooperative spirit, knowledge building and problem solving, as well as the students' ability to innovate and apply the knowledge. Teaching or learning environment becomes a focus of many educators. The existing classroom is rigid, single patterned, and static in both the physical and psychological aspects [3]. Instructions in classroom are still in single or one way (teacher-centred), lacking student-oriented, independent, active and interactive features. Changes are required in order to meet the requirements of modern education. It is time to rethink how classrooms can be embodied with elements such as innovative space or environment, humanism, intelligence, ICT resources, interactive features, and new pedagogy. They cover different aspects, including people, technology, resources, environments and methodology, etc. [4]. All these motivate us to explore a new teaching and learning space, called future classroom.

2 The Future Classroom

Few years ago, the research on the future classroom was started, and it was regarded as one of new topics in the educational technology field. The research target was set out to meet different forms of the knowledge exchange and communication between people. The classroom should embody humanization, comfortable, convenient, and natural features. [5]. Definitely, these features are meaningful for effective teaching and cultivation of talented students.

There are few definitions on future classroom. A future classroom is an integrated technological and software environment that provides students a different environment to achieve the instructional goals. The students are encouraged to work together, share the experiences and lessons, and conceptualize learning [6]. The Daily Tribune in its article named "Classroom of The future, here and now" pointed out that the future classroom is a learning environment which employs innovative instruction activities and improves ICT uses in all aspects of the classroom [7]. Chen refers the future classroom as a teaching environment that equips all kinds of hardware devices which change the instruction from an one-way model to an interactive model for improving students' interest in learning [8]. In brief, the future classroom is an innovative space or environment that embodies humanism, intelligent, smart and ICT-enabled features, rich resources, interaction, and new pedagogy. It cover four key elements, namely, people, technology, resources, environments and methodology, where interaction is the main core for establishing a dynamic, free and harmonious classroom environment [9].

Currently, many studies of the future classroom are underway, especially in some famous software and hardware manufacturers, institutions and universities. Apple Co. started the "Apple Classroom of Tomorrow" plan to integrate computer technology into the classroom and change the instructional models in order to promote active learning and improve the teaching effectiveness. DELL, Intel, and Microsoft also started their plans on future classroom.

3   Characteristics of the Future Classroom

In 2010, we organized a study team and started "the future classroom" project, aiming for teaching innovation and classroom pattern-change. The project covers physical space design, new technology and media usage, instructional platform development, teaching method, and interactive features. It is expected to derive a reference model of future classrooms for all kinds of schools.

After conducting a study for more than three years, our team has a relatively clear and comprehensive description of future classrooms. A future classroom should have six characteristics: comfortable space (embodying humanity and ecology), advanced technologies (technology and media for supporting teaching and learning activities), convenient operation (intelligence and ease of use), rich resources (adequate resources for meeting the need of different subjects), real-time interaction (timely interaction), and flexible teaching modes (for diversity and effectiveness).

Characteristic 1: Comfortable Space

It means the classroom space or environment is comfortable. The environment mainly refers to the physical environment, including lighting, color, background sound, indoor temperature, air quality, furniture, per capita area, and etc. The comfortable environment directly affects students' all-round development. Traditional classroom takes the teacher as the center, which makes up of the blackboard, platform, desks, chairs, etc, as a closed space. It is a one-way transmission of teaching. In contrast, the future classroom will take students as the center, which promotes learning as the main goal, optimize the learning effective, and crate a comfortable learning environment. The environment also reflects humanization and makes teachers and students in a good state for teaching and learning.

Characteristic 2: Advanced Technology

The future classroom aims at promoting students' learning and development, and enabling happy and effective learning. Therefore, we need to consider how to provide effective technological supports for learning and interaction, including hardware and software. Our future classroom provides advanced technologies and media, including wireless equipment, mobile terminals, information gathering and processing devices, interactive electronic whiteboard, multiple screens (on synchronous, asynchronous, circulation modes). The teaching resources can be accessed through a cloud platform. With the cloud platform, the classroom can also connect to distance classrooms and virtual classrooms for distance learners.

Characteristic 3: Convenient Operation

This characteristic means the operation of all equipment should be convenience and smooth. As the classroom is for teaching and learning, all equipment or technologies should support the teaching and learning tasks. Equipment in the future classroom should be easy to use so that operation burdens can be greatly reduced. Operation can be simplified as one key or touch, such as on lighting, air conditioning, computer, projector, audio and video recording. During teaching and learning process, equipment operation is entirely spontaneous and easy so that teachers and students can focus on their teaching and learning tasks.

Characteristic 4: Rich Educational Resources

Effective teaching and learning should be supported with adequate educational resources. These resources are required in order to meet the needs of different subjects and disciplines. They include teaching and learning tools, communicating tools, audio and video tools, courseware, virtual reality experiment, and item bank. Since the future classroom also provides an environment connecting to the outside world through the cloud platform, open, online and internet resources can be effectively used in the classroom.

Characteristic 5: Timely and Smooth Interaction

Interaction is the core of teaching and learning activities. Classroom teaching should be regarded as an interaction process between students and teachers, and between students and students [10]. Teaching is originally a variety of dialogues. Through the dialogues, students not only get the knowledge but also gain development by heuristic and exploratory dialogues [11]. Therefore, the physical environment design and advanced equipment configuration should be considered on how various interaction types can be supported. They include interaction between people and technologies, between people and resources, between people and environment, between technology and technology, and between technology and resources. All interaction can be timly and smooth.

Characteristic 6: Flexible Teaching Models

In the future classroom, many flexible teaching models can be practiced, for example, interactive teaching, situation teaching, visualization teaching, collaborative inquiry, and reflective teaching and learning. Besides, diversified learning models can be used, for example, cooperative learning, inquiry learning, problem-based learning, case-based learning, flipped classroom learning, experiential learning, and e-learning. As wireless technology is applied, teaching and learning activities are no longer limited to the physical space. Teaching and learning beyond the classroom is made possible through virtual classrooms, where distance-learning students can learn, cooperate and communicate with each other, anywhere and anytime. Figure 1 shows the examples of the future classroom.

Fig. 1. Examples of the future classroom

4   Evaluation

In order to assess whether the design goals of our future classroom can be achieved, we identified the teaching and learning contents, and the teaching methodologies used for the evaluation. We invited some experts in educational technology field and some students to participate the evaluation, where the experts would focus on the prototype while the students would focus on learning experience. The results of our evaluation are reported below.

Method

Data are collected by administering a questionnaire to 26 experts and over 160 students from two secondary schools.

Instrument

Empirical data was collected by means of a questionnaire containing some questions. For the prototype evaluation, the questions were organized into the following two groups:

(1) Equipment configuration questions, related to rationality, practicability, flexibility;

(2) Environment and equipment controls, including lights, space, temperature, humidity, and automatic process recording, while for the evaluation of learning experience, the questions would focus on environment, conditions, usability, and feelings.

For both evaluations, the measuring items were on a 5-point Likert scale from "1 = strongly disagree" to "5 = strongly agree". For the prototype, the instrument was composed of 10 items on equipment configuration and 5 items on environment and equipment controls. For learning experience, there are 13 items on   environment, condition, usability, and feelings.

Analysis Results

The data collected was processed by using SPSS 19.0 (Statistical Package for Social Science). Table 1 shows a summary of the mean scores of each item surveyed in the questionnaires for prototype evaluation, in which (1) is for equipment configuration questions and (2) for environments control intellectuality. Table 2 shows a summary of student evaluation.

In both tables, the "Items" refers to the description for surveyed questions, while the "Mean" provides the representative value of the group of scores and the "Standard deviation" provides the approximate average amount that scores differ from the "Mean". As this was a small-scale research and preliminary in nature, no pilot study or pre-test were conducted.

Table 1a. Prototype evaluation data analysis (1)

Item	Mean	Standard deviation
A1: Multi-screens in front of classroom (Interactive and touch boards)	4.82	0.395
A2: One small touch screen for each student group (6-8 persons)	4.77	0.429
A3: Interactive terminal equipped for each teacher and student (tablet PC or iPad)	4.91	0.294
A4: Wireless environment and communication	5.00	0.000
A5: Arbitrary combination for student desks	4.64	0.581
A6: Personalized student seats (changeable height and rotatable)	4.91	0.294
A7: Automatically track and record whole process of teaching and learning	4.73	0.550
A8: Learning support platform based cloud computing	4.86	0.351
A9: High quality audio system	4.73	0.550
A10: Classroom lockers for students	4.55	0.510

Table 1b. Prototype evaluation data analysis (2)

Item	Mean	Standard deviation
A11: Lights, temperature, moisture control	4.41	0.590
A12: Video conferencing & auto process recording system	4.45	0.510
A13: Central control unit (CCU) for teacher table	4.45	0.596
A14: Material object display stand	4.36	0.492
A15: Commonality printer devices	4.32	0.568

For the prototype evaluation from experts, the results show that the equipment configuration gets much recognition. The average mean of 10 items is over 4.5, with a lower standard deviation. The results also indicate the expert's acceptability and satisfaction for the future classroom.

Table 2. Student evaluation data analysis

Item	Mean	Standard deviation
B1: Expecting and willing to learn in such classroom	4.56	0.509
B2: Happy and joy in such relaxed environments for learning	4.38	0.569
B3: Easy to finish my study works in such environments	4.22	0.726
B4: Wonderful to use multi-screens for showing contents of teaching	4.25	0.75
B5: Necessary using a public small touch screen for each group discussing	4.19	0.808
B6: Interactive whiteboard and touch blackboard are easy for operating	4.25	0.661
B7: Student desks can be arbitrary combination	4.45	0.561
B8: Student seats are changeable in height and rotatable	4.71	0.264
B9 : Mobile terminal is meaningful for learning and communicating	4.38	0.696
B10 : Learning resources meet real learning needs	4.31	0.583
B11: Automatically track and record whole process of teaching and learning	4.15	0.683
B12: Learning support platform based cloud computing	4.19	0.624
B13: Good quality audio system	4.31	0.652

For the students' evaluation, we want to assess the students' satisfaction and feelings for such kind of classrooms, including environment, conditions, facilities, support tools, etc. The analysis results show that the satisfaction and feelings are high, especially for the questions "Willing to learn and seats changeable" where the means are over 4.5.

5   Conclusion

Educational informatization is the premise of education modernization. In the process of educational informatization, people ignore one of the most important objects - the classroom. The classroom is a key place for teaching and learning. Informatization on classroom is essential to educational modernization. The focus of this paper is on the classroom. We consider the classroom as an important part for educational reform and development. It should embody people-oriented elements, support teaching and learning freedom and development, construct harmonious relationship among people, environment, technology and resources. Our future classroom will lead to changes in the teaching and learning enviornment. Despite the changes, the objectives of classrooms are still for meeting teaching and learning needs.

References

1. Zhang, J.P.: The future classroom: What want to change? Journal of Shanghai Education 7B, 6–8 (2013)
2. Wu, Z.Y.: Beyond the Classroom: New Vision of Teaching and Learning in the 21st Century. Shandong People's Publishing House, Shandong (2009)
3. Zheng, J.Z.: Classroom Reconstruct. Journal of East China Normal University (Education Science) 3, 53–57 (2001)
4. Zhang, J.P., Chen, W.D.: Study on Classroom of the Future. Journal of e-Education Research 8, 18–22 (2011)
5. Chen, W.D., Zhang, J.P.: Design and Application of the Future Classroom. Journal of Distance Education 4, 27–33 (2010)
6. Fischler, A.S.: Disrupting Class - Highly Recommend! Student is the Class, http://abe.thestudentistheclass.com/2009/05/disrupting-class-highly-recommend.html
7. The Daily Tribune: Classroom of the Future, Here, Now, http://telebisyon.net/balita/SCHOOL-MATTERS/artikulo/69732/
8. Chen, M.C.: You have to know - Science and Technology Teaching in the 21st century, http://epaper.hrd.gov.tw/101/EDM101-0501.htm
9. Zhang, J.P., Chen, W.D.: Study on Classroom of the Future. Journal of e-Education Research 8, 18–22 (2011)
10. Zhang, J.R.: Ideological and political classroom interaction research. East China Normal University (2007)
11. Zhong, Q.Q.: Dialogue with the text: the transformation of teaching specification. Journal of Education Research 3, 33–39 (2001)

An Empirical Study of Leveraging Information Technology in Business through Flexible Learning, Project and Problem-Based Learning, and Cross-Disciplinary Learning

Kwan Keung Ng, Fu Lee Wang, and Louise Luk

Caritas Institute of Higher Education, 18 Chui Ling Road, Hong Kong
{sng,pwang,lluk}@cihe.edu.hk

Abstract. Traditional business education studies focus on core commercial areas but graduates do not pay attention to using information technology in business environments; conversely, traditional information technology education focuses on training in compute applications and their underlying theories but graduates do not know how these applications can be utilized in the commercial environment. Application of information technology in business is an important and emerging area in modern business world. This paper summarizes how Caritas Institute of Higher Education established the Business Technology Centre to provide project and problem based flexible learning for students to customize their learning by using modern business technologies. Students formed a cross-disciplinary project teams to solve some real business problems based on group members' expertise and techniques. After having gone through this cross-disciplinary learning, students have gained practical experience in business technology and application, and enriched their learning experience as well as enhanced their employability.

Keywords: flexible learning, project-based learning, problem-based learning, cross-disciplinary learning, integrated learning, e-learning, business technology.

1 Introduction

A large volume of business data is available in the current information age, but people often have insufficient time to find and read all related material before making a decision in the dynamic and competitive business environment nowadays. Technology can support faster decision making in the modern business world; for example, performing customer relationship management by association rule mining, market segmentation by clustering, sales forecasting by regression analysis, and credit rating by classification using decision tress, among other applications.

Application of information technology in business is an important and emerging area in modern business world. However, traditional business education studies focus on core commercial areas such as accounting, marketing, management, finance, and the like. Most business programmes do not pay attention to using information technology in

S.K.S. Cheung et al. (Eds.): ICHL 2014, LNCS 8595, pp. 56–67, 2014.

business environments.   Graduates from business programmes do not know how business processes can be automated and enhanced using cutting edge technologies. Conversely, traditional information technology education focuses on training in computer applications and their underlying theories.   As a result, graduates from information technology programmes do not know how these applications can be utilized in the commercial environment. A Business Technology Centre has been established in Caritas Institute of Higher Education (CIHE).   It is the first effort in Hong Kong to introduce education of information technology in business.

Business Technology Centre started its services to the students at Caritas Institute of Higher Education and Caritas Bianchi College of Careers in 2012 with the funding supported by Education Bureau of the Government of the Hong Kong Special Administrative Region of the People's Republic of China under the Quality Enhancement Grant Scheme (QEGS)[1].

As mentioned above, a large volume of business data is available in the current information age.   Thus, technology can support faster decision making in the business world nowadays; on the other hand, conventional business education studies mostly focus on core commercial areas such as accounting, marketing, management, finance and the like.   Thus, graduates from business programmes are mostly lack of knowledge on using cutting edge technologies to automate business process and enhance efficiency; conversely, graduates from information technology programmes are also lack of knowledge on applying new technologies and applications to the practical business environment as well.

Because of this reason, Business Technology Centre provides an information exchange platform and e-learning centre for faculty members and students from the Department of Business Administration and Department of Computer Science at CIHE. The Centre provides various kinds of project for students to conduct their final year research, a graduation requirement of Bachelor of Business Administration (Hons) programme at CIHE.   For each project, a cross-disciplinary project team has been formed to solve some real business problems by using modern technologies.   Students have gained valuable experience in business knowledge, application, and technology through such project-based learning mode.   Such projects have greatly enhanced students' learning experience as well as their employability after they graduate from CIHE [7] [10] [11].

The Centre designs and provides cases collected from the real business environment for project-based learning, and provides online resources for students to conduct researches and learning through e-learning mode.   In addition, the Centre has been periodically arranging seminars and workshops in business technology education for students and faculty members to learn the state-of-art business technology in the marketplace.

The Centre provides an excellent information exchange platform and learning centre for faculty members and students.   It also provides project training to students from two departments, i.e. Department of Business Administration and Department of

[1] This project is funded by the Education Bureau of the Government of the Hong Kong Special Administrative Region under the Quality Enhancement Grant Scheme (QEGS).

Computer Science. A team of stream from different disciplines work together to solve some real business problems by using modern technologies.

Project and problem based approach provides flexibility to students to customize their learning. Given a problem from real business environment, students defined their scope of study based on the project team members' profile and also the techniques used to tackle the problem. Within the project team, members have their division of labour. Hence, students have the freedom to focus on the areas which matched their expertise.

The success of cross-disciplinary project teams has been proven by the most prestigious consulting company. Students gain valuable experience and knowledge of business technology through project-based learning. This not only greatly enhances students' learning experience, but also prepares students to work in real project teams and to develop their teamwork skills. As a consequence, students' employability has been significantly enhanced. Thus, this paper reports how the project and problem based flexible learning model do to leverage of information technology in business.

2   Flexibility Learning and Problem-Based Learning

According to Tucker & Morris's [8] review, there are many synonymous terms for "flexible learning", such as, distance learning, e-learning, open learning, self-directed learning, recourse-based / problem-based learning, etc. In recent years, flexible learning has been becoming a hot topic in the education field, and many research studies contribute different models and applications to this topic. However, Palmer [5] states that *"there is no universally agreed definition of flexible education"*. Thus, flexible learning is a response of the learners' needs in terms of flexible time, flexible content, flexible access/entry requirement, flexible instructional approach/design, and flexible delivery.

Tucker and Morris have extended 19 flexibility dimensions in response to the above five flexible categories as quoted [8]. Table 1 shows the 19 flexibility dimension of flexible learning or problem-based learning.

Table 1. Tucker and Morris's 19 Flexibility Dimensions of Flexible Learning

(A) Time		
1. time and date at which module start and finishes	2. periods of time students are able participate	
3. pace of learning	4. time when assessment occurs	5. sequence in which topics are covered
(B) Content		
6. choice of topics covered	7. amount of learning activities expected to be completed	
8. level of difficulty of module content	9. assessment standards	
(C) Access/entry requirement		
10. pre-requisites for module participation		
(D) Content		
11. social organization of learning (group or individual)	12. times available for support	
13. choice of who decides what modes of flexible learning are available	14. language for communication	
(E) Time		
15. time and place where support is available	16. methods of obtaining support	
17. types of support available	18. places for studying	19. delivery channels

According to Hill's study on flexible leaning, *"flexible learning focuses on options related to how learning occurs; that is the learning process. Flexible learning is concerned primarily with facilitating the individual student's learning process"* [2]. He further suggested that the main characteristics of flexible learning lie in providing the flexibility to the learners on <u>*what*</u> they want to learn, <u>*where*</u> they want to pursue their study, <u>*why*</u> they need to learn, and <u>*how*</u> they would like to learn. If educators intend to meet the various needs of students, institutions are expected to provide various degree of flexibility in education settings and to lead students to integrate learning with the real marketplace situation [2] [3].

In terms of flexible learning mode / problem-based learning, institutions should provide operational flexibility; its operational characteristic is to provide teaching staff and coaching staff for both face-to-face and online consultation alternatives [6].

Furthermore, Jaitip's research reported that Stanford University diagnosed the problem of blended learning as a *"mismatch"* the student's learning styles, i.e. interactive, social, mentored learning, with the delivery technology of the institution [3]. Thus, the Business Technology Centre of CIHE develops a project and problem based flexible learning model to leverage of information technology in business; and tries to apply the mentioned flexible learning / problem-based model for the final year research project in the degree programme of Bachelor of Business Administration (Hons).

3   Project-Based Learning

The idea of "learning by doing" is first introduced by John Dewey, and it was then gradually transferred to project-based education.   Project-based education is a student-centre pedagogical strategy which has been developed for more than 30 years. In recent years, project-based learning has been integrated into standard curriculum in several higher education institutes [9].

Project-based learning helps students to develop their problem-solving skills in a practical way.   Students are required to work the projects in teams.   They take social responsibility in the project teams.   Henceforth, it helps students create better work habits and attitudes towards learning. In addition, problem-based learning is a similar pedagogical approach.   Students are required to perform a number of structured activities to solve problems.   These types of pedagogical approach help students adapt to a community of practice, and help them develop their teamwork skills [9].

In the short run, such project-based learning will improve the learning experience of students across different streams in the Institute, i.e. Accounting, Finance, Corporation Management, Marketing, Human Resources, Computer Science, etc.; and in the long run, students' teamwork skills to solve technology-based business problems are also enhanced. As a result, the employability of students will be significantly improved as well.

The project-based learning emphasises integrated learning, and facilitates a flexible learning, project and problem based learning, and cross-disciplinary learning platforms for students from different programmes and disciplines. Students can base on their study field, personal interests, personality, learning styles, needs and desires to conduct research at their own pace, time and format. The following model (Figure 1) outlines how students perform the project-based / problem-based learning for their final year research project:

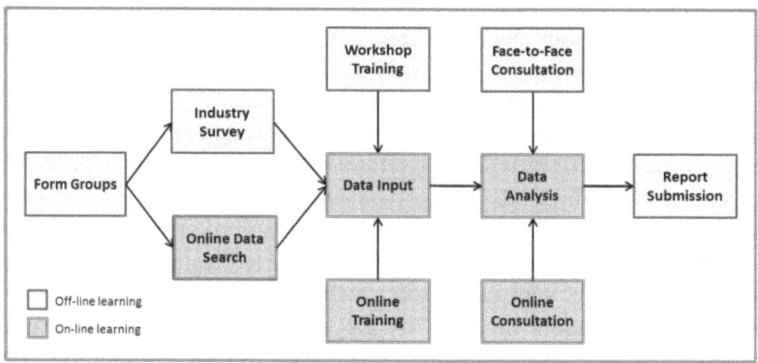

Fig. 1. Project-based or Problem-based Learning Model

4   Cases Developed for Project-Based Learning

So far, CIHE's Business Technology Centre has developed the following ten cases for the students to select in their final year projects as a tool for project-based learning:

Case #1: Market Segmentation of Real Estates in Hong Kong
- Students are required to use clustering technique to segment apartments into different clusters based on floor, facilities, selling price, rental price which aims to help customers to search the optimum selection effectively.
- Clustering technique can be applied to segment properties into different clusters based on the location, size, price range, landscape, and other factors.

Case #2: Credit Rating
- Most banks develop internal methodology to assign credit grades for their customers. Rating a customer internally is important and mandatory since such internal rating will facilitate a complementary assessment of a customer's risk profile. Students are required to use related technique to determine the credit standing of new customers.
- Decision tree can be applied to analyse customers' age, gender, income level, education level in term of debt default estimation in financial industry.

Case #3: Supply Chain Management of Chain Store
- Supply chain management comprises the cost and the flow of merchandises and services; lowering cost is vital for companies to enhance their competitive advantage. Students are required to optimize the lead-time and minimize the cost of the supply chain of a Chain Store, and meet the demand and supply requirements.

- Linear programming can be applied to analyse the supply chain management system in term of efficiency and effectiveness enhancement.

Case #4: Cross Selling for Supermarket

- In supermarket business, there is a large database of sales record; records of transactions will provide useful information to enhance transactions, promotion responses, sales, and profitability of supermarket. Students are required to analyse the captioned database, to find the association among the merchandises and the sales in the supermarket.
- Association rules can be extracted from the database of transaction so as to find the purchasing pattern of consumers in the supermarket.

Case #5: Customer Loyalty Programme

- Based on 80/20 rule, 20% customer produces 80% of the revenue, thus, it is important for companies to maintain closer relationships with customers. Students are required to identify the actual needs of customer and develop strategies maintain the relationship and enhance the profitability.
- Data mining technique can be applied to identify customer profiling, high consumption customers, and find the actual needs of customers in term of customer loyalty strategy.

Case #6: Sales Forecasting

- The use of correlation methodology to forecast sales has become popular in nowadays marketplace; students are required to identify the dependent variable and the independent variables from the sales records by using the correlation and regression analysis and methodology.
- Based on past sales records, students will use correlation and regression analysis to predict the sales of a company in coming years and suggest annual strategic plans.

Case #7: Performance Indicator for Service Industry

- Neural network is a mathematical model based on biological neural networks. The neural network is useful for data classification, and it is used to predicate the differentiation between the output value and the desired value. Students are required to evaluate the weighted contact time per sales representative, the cycle time of checking out, waiting time of customers, error rate, and customer satisfaction; and provide suggestions to enhance the above performance.
- Student will develop a method to learn from the historical records recruited from a company in service industry, and then measure & evaluate the service quality, customer satisfaction, and staff performance level of the company.

Case #8: Price Optimization

- Determine appropriate retail price is important for retailers. In order to enhance the sales, retailers simply offer discounts so as to stimulus the sales figures, however, the net profit may not be boosted up even the sales value are increased. Students are required to find the tipping point to maximize the profit by balance the sales and revenue for a designated retail shop.
- Based on past sales records, students will identify the relationship between price and sales, and identify the optimal price of the products for a company by using curve fitting methodology in their analysis.

Case #9: Online Shopping Store

- Brick-and-mortar stores are only able to serve consumers nearby locally, it is impossible for such stores to extend their sales neither to remote areas nor to overseas. The advantage of using online shopping is to expand the services with unlimited boundary with 24/7 services. Students are required to create an online shopping store which included webpages, product lists, logistics and on-line ordering for customers to place online orders.
- Student will create an online shopping website which includes webpages of stocking, product listing, order placing, order cancelling and order delivering details.

Case #10: Detection of Fraudulent Transaction

- Fraud detection is important in nowadays business since fraudulent transaction are usually associated with illegal activities and would create incalculable disasters.
- Students are required to develop a method to detect and report which transaction has probability to be suspect as a fraudulent transaction.

5   Implementation

In order to illustrate how to utilize the case study in project-based learning, Case 1 is selected as an example to explain further:

Firstly, students from different disciplines has formed a research project group of 4 ~ 6. An ideal combination of a research group should have at least one student come from the following BBA streams: namely Accountancy, Corporate Management, Marketing & Event Management, Hotel Management, Travel Management, and Information Systems.

Secondly, students are required to conduct market survey and collect property data from published materials and online as well, such as, name of the estate / property, block, location (address), saleable area, gross area, efficiency ratio, number of rooms, price/square feet in saleable area and gross area as well as the landscape (i.e. what kind of view can be observed in the property, for example, sea view, street view, factory view, mountain view, bridge view, etc. Number of property agents' websites would have the above information published online.

Thirdly, students inputted the data they have collected, developed a dataset and process the data through EXCEL's statistical tools, or Rapid Miner[2], which is an open-source software for data mining and analysis as shown in Figure 2.

After generating the segmentation reports from RapidMiner programme, students adjusted the captioned attributes in accordance with customer's preference and needs, and sorted out several segments for analysis and recommendation, as shown in Figure 3.

---

[2] RapidMiner is a Java-based program for data mining. It is an environment for machine learning, data mining, text mining, predictive analytics, and business analytics. This is an open-source software which can be downloaded by this link:
http://rapid-i.com/content/view/398/243/lang,en/

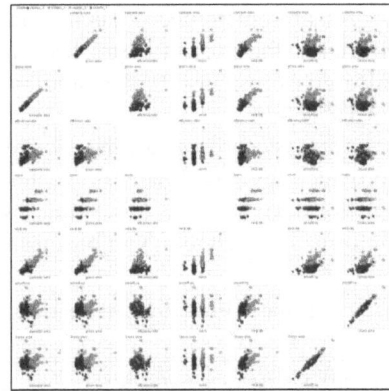

Fig. 2. Rapid Miner - Data import wizard

Fig. 3. Samples of the scatter matrix of the cluster

For example, if a customer would like to find a flat with highest efficiency ratio with sea view, the following cluster result will be generated for customer's consideration, as shown in Table 2.

Table 2. Samples of the report

Estates	Phase	Block	Floor	Saleable area	Gross area	Efficiency ratio	Room	HK$ (M)	Price/sq ft	Gross area
Metro Town	Phase 1	Tower 2	High Floor	492	658	75.00	2	6.10	$12,398	$9,271
Park Central	Phase 2	Block 1	High Floor	465	617	75.00	3	6.10	$13,120	$9,888
Ocean Shores		Block 3	Low Floor	795	1064	75.00	3	9.40	$11,824	$8,835
Residence Oasis		Block 2	High Floor	490	657	75.00	2	8.00	$16,327	$12,177
Residence Oasis		Block 2	High Floor	490	657	75.00	2	8.00	$16,327	$12,177
Park Central	Central	Block 13	Low Floor	905	1187	76.00	3	9.50	$10,497	$8,003

Furthermore, students might continue to track the price of each cluster to analyse which cluster of property is the best for investment, to survey which cluster is the best for living, or even to investigate whether bear market or bull market comes from the above data. In fact, clustering method can be applied to other business natures and industries as well. Lingras and Peters [4] suggest that clustering method can be applied on bioinformatics, engineering and marketing. Besides, clustering also plays an outstanding role for students to conduct data mining application such as scientific data exploration, information retrieval and text mining, spatial database applications, Web analysis, CRM, marketing, computational biology, etc.[1].

6   Discussion

Hill suggests the following strategies and techniques offering flexible learning environment to students; and Table 3 illustrates how the captioned project-based learning responses to the strategies and techniques [2]:

As aforementioned, Tucker and Morris's 19 flexibility dimensions of flexible learning, the project-based learning developed by the Business Technology Centre also gives response to the captioned flexible learning criteria, the checklist is shown in Table 4.

Thus, according to the above analysis, the captioned project-based learning provided by the Business Technology Centre also facilitates a flexible learning platform for students to leverage what they have learnt from their stream major with information technology in business.

Table 3. Project-based Learning vs. Hill's Strategies and Techniques for Learners

Hill's Strategies and Techniques*	CIHE's Project-Based / Problem-Based Learning
- take initiative and be self-directed	- students may decide their research method
- create a space for online work & study	- students may attend face-to-face study & seek face-to-face consultation vs. online study & online consultation
- be willing and able to commit time to the course	- students may base on their time availability to select face-to-face meeting or online discussion
- when online communication options are available and expected, logon to the course every-other day	- students will be contacted periodically to ensure their learning process is satisfied
- participate	- students will be checked regularly in order to ensure their research progress is on schedule
- sharpen abilities to communicate through writing	- students may enhance their written skill if they select the online mode to communicate with CIHE's staff
- be respectful of others, particularly in Electronic Forums	- students will be reminded to respect a productive and supportive electronic environment even though they are not meeting regularly
- let the instructor know if problems arise	- if students encounter any research problem or technical problem, they are encourage to seek guidance through face-to-face meeting with their project supervisors, and/or seek advice online.

*Source: Hill, 2006, DOI 10.1007/s10755-006-9016-6, page 191 – 192.

7   Evaluation

A preliminary project evaluation has been conducted with students and faculty members. Students responded to the survey that they enjoyed working project together in teams. The different backgrounds of project team members have enhanced their learning experience and teamwork skills. They have also appreciated the case studies collected from real business environment; particularly the way they know to make use of technology to solve problems in the cases. They believe that such project-based learning, problem-based learning, and cross-disciplinary learning have also increased their confidence to work in the real workplace in the near future.

The faculty members responded to the survey that they have also appreciated the facilities provided by the Business Technology Centre. They have commented that the training and workshops provided by the Centre to the students are very useful; and believe that students are greatly benefited from the project-based learning, problem-based learning and cross-disciplinary learning.

Table 4. Project-based Learning vs. 19 Flexibility Dimensions of Flexible Learning

19 Flexibility Dimensions of Flexible Learning*	CIHE's Project-Based / Problem-Based Learning
(A) Time	
1. time and date at which module start and finishes	- students may develop their own plan and schedule
2. periods of time students are able participate	- students may determine their own timeline to complete the project, only submission deadline is fixed
3. pace of learning	- students may decide their own pace of learning
4. time when assessment occurs	- students are required to submit their research project as schedule
5. sequence in which topics are covered	- only research procedures / steps should be in sequence
(B) Content	
6. choice of topics covered	- students may freely select their research topic
7. amount of learning activities expected to be completed	- students may determine the research objectives and methodology
8. level of difficulty of module content	- students may determine how in-depth their research will go into
9. assessment standards	- students are required to deliver a verbal presentation and written report - their project supervisor and second supervisor will responsible for the assessment, and third marker will be involved if it deemed necessary
(C) Access / entry requirements	
10. pre-requisites for module participation	- only research procedures / steps should be in sequence
(D) Instructional approach / design	
11. social organization of learning (group or individual)	- relevant industrial professions will be liaised for students to conduct interview
12. times available for support	- students may request face-to-face consultation, and online consultation at their available time
13. choice of who decides what modes of flexible learning are available	- students may consult their project supervisor to set a mode of flexible learning which is fit for them
14. language for communication	- students may use their own preferred language with their supervisor / online consultation, however, presentation and written report should be in English due to assessment criteria.
(E) Delivery	
15. time and place where support is available	- face-to-face consultation and online consultation schedule is subject to students' availability and selection.
16. methods of obtaining support	- either face-to-face consultation and online consultation are available to students
17. types of support available	- teaching staff, coaching staff, course lecturers, staff at Business Technology Centre, online resources are all available for students' selection
18. places for studying	- either at Campus, at home, or at any places which online accessibility is available
19. delivery channels	- students may submit online report to their project supervisor for comment, but final research report are required in printed form

*Source: Tucker & Morries(2012), Research in Learning Technology 2012; 20:14401 – DOI: 10.3402/rlt.v20i0/1404

In particular, faculty members commented that the teamwork skills of students have been enhanced. A summary of the survey results from both students' responses and faculty members' responses (lecturers' responses) as shown in Table 5:

Table 5. Projects Evaluation Survey Results of Students Responses and Lecturers Responses

		Students' Responses		Lecturers' Responses	
		Mean	SD (σ)	Mean	SD (σ)
1	The trainings, seminars, workshops, and project guidance provided by BTC are well-prepared and useful	3.97	0.65	4.55	0.50
2	The instructors in the BTC explain and guide the case study projects clearly and effectively to students	4.08	0.64	4.27	0.62
3	The case study projects stimulate students' interest in the cross-disciplinary learning, and enhance students' teamwork spirits & communication skills	4.00	0.58	4.18	0.72
4	The case study projects provide students a valuable cross-disciplinary learning experiences	4.08	0.64	4.64	0.48
5	The project and problem based learning provide flexibility to students to customize their learning effectively	3.92	0.76	4.45	0.50
6	Students have clear understanding of the learning objectives which help them create better work habits and attitudes towards learning	3.92	0.49	4.27	0.62
7	Knowledge of state-of-art business technology in the marketplace help students to achieve learning outcomes of the research projects	4.08	0.49	4.36	0.48
8	Skill and knowledge of using technology to solve problems have been improved and enhanced through the project-based learning	3.83	0.37	4.45	0.66
9	Recommend the project-based learning to the students who will conduct final year research projects in coming years	3.83	0.55	4.55	0.50
10	Overall speaking, the project-based learning are useful to increase students' employability and confidence to work in real workplace	3.92	0.64	4.55	0.50

Likert Scale: 1-Strongly Disagree, 2-Disagree, 3-Neutral, 4-Agree, 5-Strongly Agree

In summary, the above preliminary project evaluation has shown very positive results from both students and teaching staff. Evaluations have shown that the project-based learning helped students to develop their teamwork and communication skills; at the same time, students also have gained valuable experience and knowledge of business technology. It has significantly enhanced students' learning experience.

Furthermore, more in-depth study on quantified surveys with students and academic staff are recommended in the following years in order to quantify the satisfaction rate on the project-based learning / problem-based learning model, as well as their rating on the cross-disciplinary learning and flexible learning results.

8   Conclusion

It is undoubtedly that contemporary information technology can facilitate faster decision making in the business world nowadays; however, conventional business education mainly focus on core disciplinary areas instead of promoting cross-disciplinary project-based learning in order to broaden students' horizons and enhance their knowledge in applying up-to-date information technology in the business world.

The Business Technology Centre of Caritas Institute of Higher Education advocates the cross-disciplinary project-based / problem-based learning to the students who are pursuing the final year research project in the Bachelor of Business Administration (Hons) programme. The Centre has designed and provided cases collected from real business environment for project-based / problem-based learning, and offered online resources for students to conduct their research and learning through e-learning mode, and has arranged periodical seminars and workshops in business technology education for students to acquaint with the cutting edge information technology in the business world.

Both students and academic staff have given positive evaluation and encouragement to the Centre and this project-based / problem-based learning project. Results have showed that the project-based / problem-based learning helped students develop their teamwork and communication skills, as well as to gain practical experience and up-to-date knowledge of business technology. Participants agree that their learning experience have been enriched through this project-based learning, and they have enjoyed the process of flexible learning as well.

References

1. Berkhin, P.: Survey of clustering data mining techniques. Accrue Software, Inc., San Jose, CA65129 (2010)
2. Hill, J.R.: Flexible learning environments: Leveraging the affordances of flexible delivery and flexible learning. Innov. High Educ. 31, 187–197 (2006)
3. Jaitip, N.: Flexible learning in a workplace model: Blended a motivation to a lifelong learner in a social network environment. Global Learn Asia Pacific (2011)
4. Lingras, P., Peters, G.: Apply rough set concepts to clustering. Rough Sets: Selected Methods and applications in Management and Engineering (2012), doi: 10.1007.978-1-4471-270-4_2
5. Palmer, S.R.: The lived experience of flexible education: Theory, Policy and Practice. Journal of University Teaching & Learning Practice 8(3) (2011)
6. Schelleken, A., Pass, F., Verbraeck, A., Merrienboer, J.: Flexible programmes in higher professional education: Expert validation of a flexible educational model. Innovations in Education and Teaching International 47(3), 283–294 (2010)
7. Strobel, J., van Braneveld, A.: When is PBL more effective? A meta-synthesis of meta-analyses comparing PBL to conventional classrooms. Interdisciplinary Journal of Problem-based Learning 3(1) (2009), http://dx.doi.org/10.7771/1541-5015.1046
8. Tucker, R., Morris, G.: By design: Negotiating flexible learning in the built environment discipline. Research in Learning Technology 20 (2012)
9. Wang, F.L., Ng, K.K., Wong, K., Luk, L.: andLuk, L.: An initiative to enhance education in business and information technology. In: Ma, W.W.K., et al. (eds.) Hybrid Learning: Theory, Application and Practice, pp. 141–148. University of Toronto and City University of Hong Kong (2013)
10. Wenger, E.: Communities of practice: Learning, Meaning, and Identity. Cambridge University Press, Cambridge (2013)
11. Wenger, E., McDermott, R., Snyder, W.M.: Cultivating communities of practice. Harvard Business Press, Boston (2002)

A Practical Research of Hybrid Learning Mode in Teaching and Research Activities

Sen Wang

School of Educational Science, East China Normal University,
3663 North Zhong Shan Road, Shanghai, China, 200062
620045600@qq.com

Abstract. Along with the further improvement of education system in China and the deepening reform of new curriculum, teachers' professional quality has become critical to survive and succeed in the education industry. As the most effective means of improving teachers' professional quality, teaching and research activity has become the second biggest task for a teacher in addition to the lecture. However, the effect of traditional teaching and research activities are not ideal, owing to the limitation in time, content and resources. In this article, we revealed the disadvantages of traditional teaching and research activities, and analyzed the advantages of teaching and research activities in hybrid learning mode. Our practical research also indicates that the hybrid leaning mode can improve the effectiveness of teaching and research activities.

Keywords: hybrid learning, teaching and research activity, empirical study.

1   Introduction

In the new round of the nationwide reform of basic education curriculum, GY No. 1 Middle School conducted a top-down all-round reform in the school, starting with the innovations in teaching and research activities. This curriculum reform puts forward a lot of new education ideas. Effective application of such ideas to practical teaching is critical to the success of the reform. In this paper, we surveyed the situation of teaching and research activities in GY No. 1 Middle School, and studied its shortcomings. We proposed new methods to implement hybrid learning mode, aiming to help teachers solve common problems of operational work, to promote the level of teaching, and to improve the quality of teaching.

2   The Theoretical Concept of Hybrid Learning

In recent years, with the rapid development of computer technology and network coverage, the means of education in China have been improving gradually. Of all the newly evolved teaching methods, computer learning, also called E-Learning Model [1], is the most radical one. This kind of pure online learning mode received lots of criticism at early stage. Later, educators combined this online learning with traditional campus

S.K.S. Cheung et al. (Eds.): ICHL 2014, LNCS 8595, pp. 68–79, 2014.

learning, and formed the most remarkable way of learning - hybrid learning. Hybrid learning was developed abroad, later spread to China in 2010s. Since then, hybrid leaning has been utilized in various types of classroom teaching and quickly spread to many other activities, such as the middle school teachers' teaching and researching activities. The phenomenon fully proves that hybrid learning has unique advantages which cannot be ignored. However, successful application of hybrid learning to practice is not abundant for various reasons. Here, we studied hybrid leaning both theoretically and practically, aiming to find feasible ways to improve the effectiveness of teaching and researching activities via hybrid learning.

As a new teaching mode, hybrid learning still lacks sufficient research. Its advantages and disadvantages have been excavated in practice. As for its definition, one will get different answers from different angles. In terms of the present domestic research status, the most authoritative view comes from professor He Ke-Kang, who thinks that hybrid learning combines the advantage of the traditional learning methods and the advantages of computer learning (E-Learning) [2]. In the process of implementation, hybrid learning gives full play to the positive role of the teachers and students, and mixes different way of learning and teaching elements. With the help of two kinds of different modes of online and face-to-face, hybrid learning mode restructures teaching resources to greatly improve the quality of the teaching activities, realizing the aim of high quality teaching. Generally, hybrid learning takes the form of four operational methods: the integration of online and offline resource; the combination of learning objectives; the mixture of "learning" and "practicing" activities; and the integration of work and learning. In different teaching activities, the focuses of teaching methods are not the same. But in essence, hybrid learning is a new kind of learning style whose purpose is to make learning more convenient, and optimize the learning effect.

3   The Survey of Current Teaching and Research Activity in GY No. 1 Middle School

Research activity has been closely combined with teaching activities. Research activities can greatly improve teachers' ability to teach. Therefore, it is necessary to carry out various teaching and researching activities to achieve high quality teaching. The ongoing new round of basic education curriculum reform is a nationwide top-down comprehensive reform from teaching method to the teaching goal. In the newly promulgated curriculum reform outlined by the Ministry of Education, many innovative ideas are proposed. However, the ideas are only a kind of theory, which is different from teaching practice. Mastering the theory does not mean that one can practice the theory effectively [3]. In reality, it is not unusual for teachers who understands the theory very well, but cannot put it to actual practice. As a means of communicating and cross-training teaching skills and ideas, teaching and research activities can effectively bridge the gap between theory and practice. Such activities, when conducted effectively, can improve teachers' understanding of the teaching objectives, and promote their ability to teach.

3.1   Summary of Survey Results

Although in theory, teaching and researching activities play great effect in the improvement of teachers' teaching level, it is usually not so in reality. As the first step of our study, we carried out a survey among the teachers in GY No. 1 Middle School. The questionnaire is designed to gather information about the current situation and the teachers' understanding of teaching and research activity.

Table 1. Summary of survey results

Years of teaching				
Option	< 5	5-10	>10	Other
Number	5	30	20	0
Percentage (%)	9.1	54.5	36.4	0
Degree of teachers				
Option	Master	Bachelor	College	Other
Number	9	46	0	0
Percentage (%)	16.4	83.6	0	0
Director of teaching and researching department				
Age	< 30	30—40	41—50	> 50
Number	0	4	2	0
Percentage (%)	0	66.7	33.3	0
Yrs of Teaching	< 10	11—20	21—30	> 30
Number	0	4	2	0
Percentage (%)	0	66.7	33.3	0
Degree	Master	Bachelor	College	Other
Number	2	4	0	0
Percentage (%)	33.3	66.7	0	0
Should research staff teach?				
Option	Yes	No	Better have	No matter
Number	10	5	35	5
Percentage (%)	18.2	9.1	63.6	9.1
Level of teaching and research staffs				
Option	Teacher	Skilled	Leader	Expert
Number	0	35	20	0
Percentage (%)	0	63.6	36.4	0
Effects to campus curriculum reform				
Option	Significant	Many	Some	No
Number	10	30	15	0
Percentage (%)	18.2	54.5	27.3	0
Is there a clear topic in each teaching and research activity?				
Option	Yes	No	Sometimes Yes	Don't know
Number	15	5	30	5
Percentage (%)	27.3	9.1	54.5	9.1

Table 1. (*Continued*)

Which do you think is the most effective?				
Option	Criticism Lesson	Case study	Training	Forum
Number	15	11	27	2
Percentage (%)	27.3	20	49.1	3.6
What do you think the meaning of teaching and research is?				
Option	Research, Demonstrate, Service	Research, Guide, Administrate	Lead, Guide, Demonstrate	Research, Lead, Service
Number	9	20	12	14
Percentage (%)	16.4	36.3	21.8	25.5
What is the atmosphere of campus teaching and research?				
Option	Very good	Good	Normal	Bad
Number	9	11	19	16
Percentage (%)	16.4	20	34.5	29.1
For a closed topic with good results, what will the director of teaching and research group do?				
Option	Close and leave aside	Promulgate	Develop new topic	Investigate further
Number	27	14	6	8
Percentage (%)	49.1	25.5	10.9	14.5
Planned exchange meeting				
Option	Once a semester	Twice a semester	Once a month	Arbitrary
Number	21	9	0	25
Percentage (%)	38.2	16.4	0	45.5

What do you think the major problems are in campus teaching and research activity?					
Option	Task not research	Exam-oriented	Theory irrelevant to practice	Bad planned, no target	Mere formality
Number	49	29	26	31	11
Percentage (%)	89.1	52.7	47.3	56.4	20
What do you think the advantages are to carry out teaching and research activity?					
Option	Attention from leaders	Concept transformation	Required by curriculum reform	Supportive policy	Good research atmosphere
Number	20	20	33	29	19
Percentage (%)	36.4	36.4	60	52.7	34.5
What do you think the obstacles are to carry out teaching and research activity?					
Option	Task oriented	Lack of people	Lack of funding	Lack of leaders' support	Lack of protection, understanding
Number	35	10	46	26	8
Percentage (%)	63.6	18.2	83.6	47.3	14.5

The survey shows that all the surveyed teachers hold advanced degrees of bachelor or above. The majority of them have over 5 years of experience, and the directors of research departments have over 10 years of experience. The professional standard for researching staff is demanding, while they are not required to teach. Our survey also shows that the teaching and research activity in GY No. 1 Middle School does not fulfill its intention, due to the facts that teachers are lack of understanding of importance of teaching and research activity, and that the current teaching and research activity are not well planned. As a result, there isn't a good atmosphere of teaching and research activity. On the other hand, most teachers show great interests in training and open courses, which indicate that there are potential needs for high quality teaching and research activities. Most criticisms to current situation of teaching and research activity focus on the lack of both finance and academic support from administrative offices, and time due to too much practical work.

As for improving teaching and research activity, the majority of the surveyed people made the following suggestions. Firstly, the misunderstandings about teaching and research should be corrected. Secondly, school administrative staffs shall put teaching and research activity on high priority. Thirdly, teaching-research staff shall strive to stay in the forefront of teaching and research among teachers, and set up comprehensive and complete evaluation system. Finally, school administrative officers should let teachers take more responsibility and power, and enhance the support with more human, finance, and materials resources.

3.2 Discussion with Teachers and Directors

Through the discussions with some teachers and directors of research department, we find that the research activities in GY No. 1 Middle School are in simple traditional forms of campus-wide meeting, training and research project design. Such activities cannot get all participants involved, and have little to do with, or even irrelevant to, the actual teaching practice. For instance, teachers are not allowed to discuss and ask questions freely in campus-wide teaching meeting, thus few people can really participate in the discussion. Although qualified organizer can make the meeting more informative and interesting, one cannot change the rigid and serious nature of such meetings. As a result, teaching and researching activities becomes a mere formality without actual connotation. One the other hand, the teachers' understanding of teaching and researching activities is not enough. They didn't fully understand the meaning of teaching and researching activities existence [4]. The research activity form is inflexible, which can't arouse people's enthusiasm. Many teachers have a boring feel on teaching and researching activities, and they mostly random cope with it, not spending enough energy and enthusiasm on it [5]. As time passes, they completely overlook the non-negligible impacts of research activities on teaching practice.

As a result, most teachers don't treat such activities in a serious manner. Though they take part in the teaching and researching activities, they prepare their materials and projects without putting in much effort. Teaching and researching activities become a real perfunctory and copying collectively process, which lacks real worth. Though such phenomenon are caused by teachers' lack of good understanding of teaching and researching activities, more importantly due to the drab traditional teaching and researching activities in the long-term practice. For the moment, the most important thing is to reform the teaching and researching activities: blending it with hybrid learning mode, using a variety of forms to arouse the enthusiasm of teachers and making teachers aware of the importance of teaching and research activity through thorough analysis. Only in this way can teaching and researching activities keep going and really provide guidance for the teaching work.

4   Feasibility Analysis of Conducting Teaching and Research Activity under Hybrid Learning in GY No. 1 Middle School

Despite its advantages, hybrid learning mode requires a high standard of campus infrastructure. As mentioned in previous Section 2, there are four forms of hybrid learning [6], all of which require computer and network infrastructure. In other words, only with a high quality computer and network system can hybrid learning be applied. In this section, we will first show that GY No. 1 Middle School is capable of carrying out hybrid learning. And we will then present four practical ways to integrate hybrid learning into teaching and research activity.

4.1   Hardware and Software Infrastructure

Campus management mode of GY No. 1 Middle School is based on internet. The school implements a web-based information management system, and hosts a website on the internet, through which the campus management is achieved. The main function of the website is to publish real-times new of the school to teachers and students. Additionally, news about administration, teaching and campus events are also published through the website. This website and the school newspaper together form the campus information system to provide a transparent information center for democratic management. This web-based information management system provides an excellent and convenient hardware platform for teaching and research practice of hybrid learning mode.

The campus network provides good network environment for teachers. The campus network infrastructure was built since 2000 and continuously being developed. It uses PDS cabling system with a bandwidth of 100Mbps. There are more than 300 information terminals distributed in over 10 buildings throughout the campus. The network from one building to another is connected via optical fiber. In total, there are more than 700 PC terminals connected to the campus network. In the network center, there are PC servers and switching equipment which provides web, Email, DNS and FTP services to the campus. It is convenient for registered students and teachers owing to the campus network because it provides access to external learning resources. The campus network will connect teachers with students in the form of network, by discussing learning problems autonomously on line after classroom learning, which is more specific and targeted and can achieve better outcome.

Besides the campus wide PC network coverage, the GY No. 1 Middle School is equipped with high standard multimedia devices. It has a well-established electronic hardware system. This web-based information management system and the abundant multimedia devices provide an excellent and convenient hardware platform for teaching and research practice of hybrid learning mode. Based on the above, the GY No. 1 Middle School is fully capable to carry out the new type of teaching and researching activities - hybrid learning.

4.2   Practical Research of Teaching and Research Activities under Hybrid Learning Mode

In terms of teaching and research activities, all four forms of hybrid learning as mentioned in Section 1 can be used. In the following, we will present our practical studies in GY No. 1 Middle School of each form respectively, and finally conclude the advantages of hybrid learning in teaching and research activity.

(a) **Case Analysis.** It is a teaching and research activity based on the first form of combining online and offline resources. Teachers are required to use media devices to record a full length of lecture. Teachers are also supposed to analyze the lecture deeply and make objective comments on teaching methods. The case analysis is iterative progress where each time good thing is kept while bad is amended, thus more proper teaching method are refined.

The first step of case analysis is to plan a classroom teaching that is in line with the requirement of the reformed curriculum, that is, incorporating open-minded and active thinking elements into the lecturing, getting rid of the drawbacks of traditional teaching mode where teaching is based on textbooks and standard answers to maximize student's examination scores. The teaching strategy design shall be examined and modified to meet the requirements on middle school in the outlines of reformed curriculum. As for a qualified design, teaching is synchronized with the teaching materials, problems are in line with the key concepts, questions are hidden in the objectives, and exercises are practicability and closely related to the key concepts.

Secondly, one should also check whether the teaching idea is student-oriented, in line with the experience of students, subject to the level of the students, and is aiming to enable students to master basic classroom content. After the planned teaching is carried out, we should do analysis and reflection and give priority to reflection. The main aspects of reflection are: finding out whether the goal of curriculum design fits the students' knowledge; observing the reactions of students in the classroom; thinking about whether students are adapt to this teaching means and how they like it; and finally adjusting the plan continuously. The content of the reflection are broad, for example, a specific topic, or a thorough analysis, etc. Teachers can choose their favorite style of reflection including classroom observation records, interviews, questionnaires, homework analysis, etc. These styles can reflect issues from different angles.

Most notably, case analysis usually depends on the availability of technology and equipment, such as cameras or recorders. Sometimes questionnaire and statistical analysis are also required. These put forth higher standards for the teachers' skills besides teaching. A successful case analysis requires decently planned cooperation of a few teachers. It's obvious that this is the most time and effort consuming type of teaching and research activity. Yet this is the best way to discover problems in one's teaching which may have never found before, enabling timely adjustment to teaching means to improve the teaching quality efficiently. Due to the time-consuming characteristic, case analysis of teaching and research activities should be done in the high quality classroom to make it more productive.

(b) **Academic Salon.** It is a teaching and research activity based on the second form of combing learning objectives. In this form, teachers will be organized to form different academic groups based on type of courses they teach. Each group will hold seminars on a regular basis, and pre-determine topics to discuss before the each seminar. These seminars are of free-style where the participants can freely express their views on the academic subject, and raise questions and concerns about other's views. The leader of seminar should not rush to an agreement, instead he should encourage all participants to speak out their thoughts, and guide the direction of the seminar. This approach aims to open participants' train of thoughts, deepen the teacher's perception of an academic problem, thus design more teaching strategies, and use more flexible teaching methods [7].

This type of teaching and research activities is most suitable for primary and secondary school teachers, because they can take this opportunity to find out existing problems, and exchange teaching methods or strategies with each other. Through the in-depth discussion of an academic problem, they can seek common ground while reserving differences, to achieve optimization of the teaching means.

For instance, Mr. Li, the organizer of the Chinese language group in GY No. 1 Middle School, launched a group discussion on "How to guide students in modern poetry learning in high school". During this two-hour activity, teachers in this salon group exchanged ideas in both small groups and short question-and-answer sessions where teaching ideas are challenged and defended. Through the intense discussions on various teaching methods in a relatively short time period, teachers are forced to learn from each other, both actively and passively. This is also seen from the feedbacks from participants that the academic salon helps improve existing teaching method and stimulate new ideas. Meanwhile, although no conclusion is reached at the end of the academic salon, the majority of the teachers expressed that they now know better how to teach modern poetry, and showed great interest in the following sessions.

As mentioned above, the salon seminar is free-style and there is no pre-settled schedule as long as it focuses on the pre-determined discussion topic. For example, the seminar organizer can invite an authoritative expert to speak in the meeting, and give suggestions to participants who speaks out the teaching method. Or one can appoint a participant to write down a detailed record about the salon discussion, and distribute the meeting memo to every participant for review and re-thinking after the seminar to deepen their understanding of good teaching strategy. No matter what, the most important thing is to insist the following principle: free talking, no right and wrong, active thinking and discussion and win-win cooperation. This form aims to realize the autonomy of participants to exchange ideas and thoughts, and achieve learning and research objective in a relaxed atmosphere.

(c) **Comparative Teaching and Learning.** It is a teaching and research activity based on the third form of mixing learning and practicing activities. It closely follows the spirit of the nationwide curriculum reform, which directly incorporates new ideas, and new methods into teaching and research activity. In actual practice, the teachers need to design several different classroom-teaching methods based on theoretical research and practical experiences, then record the outcomes from each method. After thoroughly analyzing and comparing the differences of these results, one can find out the shortcomings and design the best teaching strategy. This method combines theory with practice most closely, which is more targeted and feasible. The improvement on teaching strategy is also the most obvious. There are many ways to do the comparison, and one can choose a method that best fit his style. For example, we can compare between the classroom teaching and the corresponding teaching design of pre and post curriculum reform, or we can carry out the comparison of effectiveness of teaching on heterogeneous forms for the same subject.

The applicable scope of this kind of comparative teaching research activity is to implement the new curriculum reform of the teaching area [8]. Since the aim of the new curriculum reform focus on the practice, the demand of the actual operation is higher. It can be applied to some practical subjects' teaching, such as "how to improve the students' passion for composition", "how to given priority to students and to make teachers just play guiding role in the process of teaching", "the implementation of inquiry-based reading and creative reading strategies", etc.

In order to verify the effects of such research activity, we carried out a study of "heterogeneous forms for the same subject" method in GY No. 1 Middle School. In detail, we picked up several political teachers, asked them to teach the same course in the same class using different teaching methods, and studied the influence on the students. Teacher Liu used multimedia teaching method. Because the students were curious about the multimedia, they performed actively during the class and the classroom atmosphere was good. Teacher Wu took the traditional teaching method. Since he had a very good understanding of the teaching material, the classroom atmosphere was very excellent and students are stimulated.

After the class, several teachers took part in the discussion to compare the two kinds of teaching methods, and made comments on the advantages and shortcomings of each method. Finally, Mr. Liu and Wu also reviewed their teaching effects by themselves. Mr. Liu concluded that usage of multimedia technology in classroom is a good complementary to the teaching, however, it should not be used over frequently which will then distracts the students and reduces the effectiveness of multimedia. Like a good horse should have good saddle, proficient skills are required to make multimedia teaching effective. Mr. Wu, on one hand, also shows concern on the skill required to use multimedia in classroom for average teacher. On the other hand, he agrees with Mr. Liu that involving the multimedia technology into traditional teaching is a trend in the future. This comparative teaching and research activity benefits both the speech teachers and the listener in that they learn the pros and cons of two different teaching methods directly.

The advantage of comparative teaching is straightforward, easy to understand and carry out. It presents abstract teaching concepts in the form of observable classroom teaching, which is easier for teachers to accept and to convert abstract teaching concepts into actual teaching activities.

(d) Topic Research. It is a teaching and research activity based on the fourth form of integrating work and learning simultaneously [9]. It organically combines teaching research with scientific research, taking more complex problems or contents as the research object. Its applicable scope is those difficult topics in the reformed curriculum. The first step is to determine the research topic and make a research plan, and then carefully study this topic in detail within pre-settled timelines. Combing with teaching practice, one find optimal teaching methods and gradually solve the problem. Compared with the traditional teaching and research mode, topic research is deeper and more targeted. It's also a method to tackle the difficult problems appearing in the teaching activities in general. Many teachers take part in the topic research activity to improve their level in academic research, or believe that it is powerful method to solve the difficulties in their teaching career. This indicates that academic research is no longer restricted to the higher education such as colleges and universities. And high school teachers can also get involved. Being very complicated and demanding, topic research has encountered various issues in practical application. The first most obstacles is that a large number of primary and secondary school teachers' research are superficial. Their topic research are mainly descriptions the phenomenon and lack logical in-depth theoretical analysis. These do not count actual research type of teaching and researching activities. One possible reason is that the topic itself is too vague and general, which could distract the authors. Therefore, it is important for teachers to carefully select topics that are relevant and specific to their teaching practice.

Taking the high school Chinese writing in the recent national wide curriculum reform for example, the focus on essay writing has switched from narrative and argument writing which has lasted for dozens of years to writing requirement giving priority to lyric imagination. The new guideline encourages students to imagine boldly, to stimulate students' ability to imagine. This has raised new requirements on the teacher's teaching method. For instance, how to guide the students to think, and how to teach students to write down their imaginations are two new topics that every high school Chinese teacher faces. At present, we can use the topic research teaching and researching activities to find the teaching strategies with academic research and corresponding practice. Of course, there should be a variety of teaching methods. Based on the teaching practice in teaching and research activities, teachers should choose teaching methods of their own, and continuously enhance teaching strategy to satisfy the needs of different courses.

5   Conclusion

Using GY No. 1 Middle School for example, we found that there is imminent need for effective teaching and research activity which the traditional methods are helpless. In this paper, we analyzed how to apply the four hybrid learning modes, discussed in Section 2, to improve teaching and research activity, and carried out practical studies in GY No. 1 middle school, aiming to help teachers to meet new challenges put forth by China's education reform. Our analysis shows that "case analysis" and "topic research" modes have practical application scenarios for the education reform. These two modes are ideal ways to improve one's own professional skills. Yet the shortcomings are that these consume more effort and time of individual teacher, and demand advanced skills. Under heavy lecturing tasks, these two modes are not easy to carry out for teachers in middle schools. On the other hand, our studies also show that "academic salon" and "comparative teaching and learning" yields satisfactory outcomes both from teachers and students. More importantly, these two modes can be carried out much easier in practice with high effectiveness.

In conclusion, our findings indicate that hybrid learning has a series of advantages over the traditional learning modes. When applied to teaching and research activities, hybrid learning can cause revolutionary development of such activities. First of all, hybrid learning is "free" style which enables every participant to contribute. As in the salon hosted by teacher Li, everyone shared their views and learned from each other. This free style feature of hybrid learning makes it not only suitable for classrooms, but applicable to small organization composed of teachers. Hybrid learning not only reforms the means and ways of teaching and research activity, but have positive impacts on the actual outcome of teaching and research activities, which is a great breakthrough compared to the traditional pattern. Hybrid learning makes teaching and research activities meaningful and interesting, which can improve the teacher's teaching level and scientific research ability. Therefore, applying hybrid learning mode to teaching and research activity is in imminent need for the following two advantages.

(a) Deliver More Convenient and Abundant Information

The integration of online and offline resources in hybrid learning mode is a kind of innovation of the means of teaching and researching activities. It utilizes the network media and equipment to combine the resources and information together. It uses descriptive text, graphics, images, animations, and sounds etc. to convey information. The fusion of different media makes the teaching and researching activities more interesting and more efficient, as evidenced in teacher Liu's lecture where students are motivated by the multimedia teaching. Meanwhile, hybrid learning is virtually not restricted by space and time. Teaching and research activities can be carried out anytime, anywhere, which saves time and effort of the teachers, who can choose the timing and manner of the research activity according to their own knowledge, goals, and personality characteristics. These convenient features of these types of hybrid learning enable control of the progress of teaching and research activity easier. Such activities are generally more targeted, which maximizes the effect under same cost. In addition, the teachers participating in teaching and research activities can also interact online, exchange experience and communicate synchronously or asynchronously through the network equipment.

(b) Improve Practicability of Teaching and Research Activity

After incorporating hybrid learning, the teaching and research activities can overcome the rigid shortcoming in the past, and will be able to improve the actual operability of the teaching and research activities. Hybrid learning has a variety of forms, and teachers can freely choose their favorite style based on their characteristic and actual teaching practice, making teaching and research activity more appealing to teacher and reducing the resistance participation. Since each method roots in the teachers' personal practice, it becomes high feasible, and effective in improving one's teaching ability. More importantly, each mode is not difficult to operate, and the design is reasonable, neither drab nor complex. As long as teachers follow the relevant steps in teaching and research activities, their teaching skills and lecturing quality will be improved. Only after the teachers realize that teaching and research activities are vital in promoting their abilities, will they become passionate to teaching and research activities and active in participation. As a result, teaching and research activities can play a proper role.

Under the influence of the Chinese curriculum reform tide, only through practical teaching and research activities can teachers at all levels adapt to the new teaching idea, implement the hybrid learning mode into teaching and researching activities, form a diversified forms, promote their teaching level, and improve their teaching quality.

At present, the hybrid learning mode is integrated with the research activity at a preliminary stage, playing its proper role. But this is simply an improvement to the teaching theory, there is still a long way to go to apply these theories to practice.

References

1. He, K.K.: From the Blending Learning to See the New Development of Education. Technology Theory, Electrochemical Education Research 3, 1–6 (2004)
2. Li, K., Zhao, J.H.: The Principle and Application of the Hybrid Learning Mode. Electrochemical Education Research 7(2) (2004)
3. Lv, S.L.: Blended Learning in Information Technology and Curriculum Integration of Enlightenment. Education Information Reference (2004)
4. Wu, Q.E.: A Hybrid Learning Action Research. The Academic Journal of Guangzhou Radio and TV University 3 (2008)
5. Tang, J.Y.: Look from the National Fine Course Policy in Higher Vocational Colleges Construction. China Educational Technology 21 (2006)
6. Li, K.D., Zhao, J.H.: The Principle and Application of the Hybrid Learning Mode. E-education Research 7 (2004)
7. Shen, L.Y.: The Investigation of the Network Curriculum Development Situation at Home and Abroad. Exam Week 10, 13–15 (2008)
8. Tian, S.S., Fu, G.S.: Preliminary Study of Blended Learning. E-education Research 7, 8–9 (2004)
9. Li, Y.M., Feng, W.L.: Experience of Research-oriented Teaching Mode. The Chinese University Reaching 8, 7–8 (2003)

The Context of Blended Learning:
The TIPS Blended Learning Model

Jeanne Lam

School of Professional and Continuing Education,
The Univeristy of Hong Kong
jeanne.lam@hkuspace.hku.hk

Abstract. Traditional learning in face-to-face mode has been the majority learning mode until the end of last Century. With the advent of using Internet technology, e-learning has been intensively used in higher education to enhance teaching and learning. In order to maximize the benefits and offset the constraints of both learning in pure face-to-face mode and e-learning mode, blended learning was advocated by the researchers as a solution. Throughout the years of blended learning development, the understanding on the context of blended learning was varied. This paper aims at identifying the context of blended learning in its evolution by reviewing the researches in the literature. A blended learning model, TIPS, was demonstrated as a holistic view to cover the perspectives of the context of blended learning. The TIPS blended learning model can be served as tips in designing and developing blended learning.

Keywords: Blended learning, online learning, TIPS blended learning model.

1   Introduction

Before mid-1990s, e-learning was commonly referred as computer-assisted instruction or computer-based instruction [1]. With the advent of Internet in late 1990s, the focus of e-learning has been changed to web-based learning and internet-based learning [2]. The most contemporary definition of e-learning is associated with learning in the technological environment of Web 2.0. Web 2.0, which is originally coined by O'Reilly Media in 2004, refers to the observed new forms of application, interaction and communities in the Web [3]. Downes describes e-learning in Web 2.0 as user-centred or learner centred, collaborative and interactive learning [4]. Chow and Cheung describe e-learning with the association with Web 2.0 has learner-centric, content access and content creation features [5].

E-Learning has been widely used in higher education sectors as a supplement to the traditional classroom learning environment and as in the non-traditional learning [6]. E-Learning has become one of the most popular solutions in learning to meet the changing demand for learning especially in post-secondary education [7]. The benefits of e-learning to enhance teaching and learning are recognized widely [8, 9] that e-learning allows learners to learn across context and minimize restriction of learning location. With the advent of mobile devices, e-learning has been delivered in the mode of mobile learning [10].

S.K.S. Cheung et al. (Eds.): ICHL 2014, LNCS 8595, pp. 80–92, 2014.

Zhang summarizes the development of e-learning in the last two decades in three generations based on the e-learning principles and practices. Zhang describes the characteristics of the contemporary generation of e-learning as 'adherence to a set of e-learning principles; one-stop service for e-learning; user-friendly and flexible functions and features of the e-learning platform; communication and collaboration within the learning environment; interactive and interesting learning content; sharable and co-developed learning resources; cost-effectiveness through effective management; instructional design; student support services; evaluation; and quality assurance of teaching and learning' [11].

Both e-learning and traditional face-to-face learning and have limitations. Sikora and Carroll identify that students in higher education tended to be less satisfied with fully online e-learning mode when comparing to traditional classes [12]. Cai and Yao indicate that learners' loneliness, low motivation and doubts about the effect in education were the main problem of e-learning [13]. On the other hand, a major limitation of face-to-face classroom teaching is teacher-led instruction in which learners are passive recipients of information [14].

Cheung et al suggest blended learning should be used instead of pure e-learning to maximize the benefits of both face-to-face learning and e-learning modes [15]. Cai and Yao (2010) also advocate blended learning as a solution for the limitation of e-learning [13]. Other benefits of blended learning are recognized as improve pedagogy and focus on learner-centered strategy, allow learners to participate in their studies actively, enable learners to construct knowledge socially and collaboratively and increase flexibility and cost effectiveness [16]. Ngan explains that blended learning gives significant impacts to recent teaching and learning model because it allows student to absorb a matter from different right media and different right perspectives and therefore to cater the differences of each student's need [17].

In the following sections, the context of blended learning in the literature will be reviewed. A model will be constructed for demonstrating a holistic view of blended learning.

2   Blended Learning

Blended learning is defined as combination of instruction from two educational models historically separated, the traditional face-to-face education and e-learning education [18]. Allen and Seaman quantify the definition of blended learning with the percentage of use of e-learning in a face-to-face course [19]. According to their definition, pure e-learning, blended learning, Internet-enhanced learning and tradition learning made use of e-learning delivery percentages as 80%-100%, 30-79%, 1-29% and 0% respectively. There are different terms used for the combination of technology-based learning activities with face-to-face activities, namely blended learning and hybrid learning [20].

The definition of blended learning is controversial indeed. Shroff criticizes the vague nature of blended learning, which means utilizing more than one method of providing information to the learner, has create confusion [21]. Oliver and Trigwell argue that the term 'blended learning' is ill-defined and inconsistently used as it has become a bandwagon for almost any form of teaching containing two or more different kinds of things that can then be mixed [22]. Heinze and Procter believes the understanding of blended learning should be in a more general perspective in which blended learning was the effective combination of different modes of delivery, models of teaching and styles of learning [23].

Despite of the critique of the definition, blended learning is the most common term which usually refers to the substantial blend of e-learning into traditional face-to-face learning that improves the students' learning experience. Researchers relate blended learning not only to the teaching modes but also learning instruction and learning outcomes [24, 25].

Face-to-face classroom teaching and e-learning are two important components in blended learning. Face-to-face classroom teaching is a traditional way for students to learn. It is the typical and basic way of knowledge delivery [26]. The characteristics of traditional classroom teaching included instructor-centered, sequential learning, simultaneous lecture, using static learning materials, and have teacher-student interactions [27].

Blended learning has its drawbacks. Many users, especially teachers, feel blended learning hard to apply because it consumes much time [28]. Moreover, there is age constraint when using blended learning because the technology changes so fast. It is uneasy and time-consuming for teachers to pick up new technologies [28].

The context of blended learning covers a wide range of perspectives. To understand blended learning in a more structural way, the literature about blended learning is reviewed in technological perspective, institutional perspective, pedagogical perspective and social perspective.

2.1   Technological Perspective

Online Learning Platform. Online learning platform, also known as learning management system, content learning management system and virtual learning environment, is software utilized in training and education that delivering course contents to learners, tracking learners' learning progress and managing their records [29]. Most of the contemporary online learning platforms are web-based system and can be assessed through the Internet. Chuah defines online learning platform as a means to deliver instructions which provided a virtual and rich learning environment to backup teachers that allowed them to create and manage learning materials by using of various information and communication technologies (ICT) in both synchronously and asynchronously ways   [30]. The most well-known and commonly used online learning platforms in the markets are Blackboard, WebCT and Moodle [31]. Among these platforms, Blackboard and WebCT are commercial products which hold 83% market share in higher education and universities in 2006 [32]. Moodle is open source software which became popular in the past five years [33]. Researchers also state the importance of using open source software to develop online learning platforms with the advantages of having cost effectiveness and up-to-date technological support of the platform maintenance [34].

Online Learning Objects. Learning objects are any entity, digital or non-digital, which can be used, re-used or referenced during technology-supported learning [35]. In blended learning environment, online learning objects refers to those multimedia content, pre-records audio-synced presentation, practice simulation and exercises [36]. These online learning objects can be shared and reused. It is found that students generally appreciated e-learning content with various multimedia elements, for example, audio, video, flashes and online quizzes, which were helpful to their learning as they could make learning interesting by accommodating different learning styles and fostering learning through a variety of activities that apply to different learning styles [37]. Multimedia can lead to increased retention and a stronger grasp on the subject because of the many elements that are combined in e-learning to reinforce the message.

Virtual Classroom. Synchronous communication in blended learning can be carried out in the classroom and in the virtual classroom. Virtual classroom is an environment that simulate physical classroom in the online environment. It allows teachers and students to meet and interact with each other by using their own computers at a remote location in real time [38]. Online lectures and tutorials can be conducted at any time and it enhances the flexibility and convenience of the relevant courses [39]. It can serve as a supplementary element to the classroom teaching to benefit students by incorporating frequent interactions between teachers and students even beyond teaching hours. Virtual classroom plays an important role in teaching and learning in terms of learning process [40]. The visual and synchronous communication tools enhance interactions and facilitate feedbacks between instructor and learner in a two-way communication [39]. Besides, videoconferencing in virtual classroom not only satisfies learners' social needs but promotes more naturalistic and interactive learning experiences which allow them to communicate with instructors with voice tone and facial expression [41]. It supports learners to participate and involve in the learning process actively and collaboratively with various communication and presentation tools [42].

2.2   Institutional Perspective

Strategies and Policies. At institution level, blended learning must be shown to be consistent with the values of the institution and be able to enhance institutional goal [43]. Due to different organizational structure and development strategies, the development of blended learning may diverse. Freitas et al state the formulation of e-learning policies might be varying by the practical needs of different organizational structures and their cultures [44]. Cheung et al identify that universities and higher education institutes used to have their own individual policies, operational procedures, approaches and practices in the planning, development and deployment of their e-learning systems, services and solutions [15]. Institutes' implementation of blended would base on the direction given by the government. Strategies and policies of the government play important roles in improving the quality of education. Governments of different countries understand the importance of technology enhanced learning and addresses plan in policy or strategic documents. Lam and Tsoi studied the strategies and policies in China, Hong Kong, Macau, Taiwan and Singapore and found the governments support technology enhanced education in providing direction, technical infrastructure, research fund and development fund [45]. Williams points out that blended learning will make significant impacts upon the national curricula and whether the impacts will be beneficial or destabilizing to a country will depend crucially upon the policy stances adopted by its educational establishment and how these are implemented at all levels [46].

Effective Management. Project management for blended learning course involves both course development and technical development. Lam et al define nine development stages of the development for effective development project management. The nine-stages in the blended learning course development model include project initiation, project planning, instructional design, content development, technical development, system setup, course delivery, review and production. It is advocated that a blended learning course which leads to a higher teaching effectiveness should be built with an appropriate project development model [47]. Student support service is important during blended learning implementation. In blended learning, students usually have difficulties and provision of effective support is a method to improve learning performance and to increase student retention [48]. In the blended learning environment, students sometimes find technical problems in using the computer or the e-learning website and sometimes find learning problems that need teaching support. Zhang suggests one-stop service was very important for learning in the e-learning environment [11]. Quality assurance is vital to an effective management of blended learning. The QAA extended the guidelines on quality assurance of distance learning to e-learning and other flexible and distance learning mode [49]. Endean et al critically evaluate the quality assurance environment and the e-learning standards in higher education. It conclude that the practice in quality assurance in e-learning context is diverse and ISO/IEC 19769 series international standard, which will cover harmonized quality model and guides to implement the standard, would be a truly global standard [50].

Evaluation. It is suggested that monitoring of student progress and teacher's active support using the learning management system is essential for the successful outcome from all students [51]. In the online learning environment, teachers can walk through individual's performances easily in the system and it allows them to identify slow learners and inactive participants earlier [52]. Teachers can then follow up with the students and help them to learn more actively. In such case, blended learning helps to align the academic students with the non-academic students and helps the non-academic students to achieve high-level engagement. Researchers show concerns for needs of evaluations for structure and quality of e-learning programmes [53] and emphasize the evaluation of the effectiveness of learning and feedback is an essential part of the blended learning process [54]. Yuen et al propose to use pre-survey, post-survey, focus group interview and qualitative journal to evaluate students' learning experience in blending learning [55].

2.3   Pedagogical Perspective

Instructional Design. Blended learning makes use of online learning environment to carry out teaching and learning activities. Researchers suggest an effective redesign of teaching and learning environment needed to be supported by pedagogical approaches [56]. Instructional design is emphasized during the process of pedagogy-driven blended learning development [51]. Instructional design plays a key role in differentiating the technological-driven and pedagogical-driven blended learning development project. Sikora and Carroll identify the major factor of dissatisfactory blended learning experience was ineffective use of instructional design [12]. Cheung et al point out that traditional learning and blended learning differed in many aspects that instructional design for traditional learning is not suitable for blended learning [15]. Learning hours in both classroom environment and online environment should be re-defined and learning activities in both environments should be re-designed [57]. Cheung et al introduced a paradigm with instructional design steps for blended learning courses [15]. The instructional designer will lead the teaching staff to redesign the course plan, lesson plan, online pre-class activities, face-to-fact in-class activities, online after-class activities and evaluation methodologies. The instructional designer will also collaborate with the e-learning developing staff to setup online learning platform, develop online course content, search for online educational resources, handle online resource copyright issues, and prepare e-learning objects repository for reusing.

Learner Centered Learning. Downes criticizes that activities in online learning environment were led by teachers and teachers only arranged teaching contents to be delivered to the students via the platform [4]. Pedagogy-driven approach is proposed to replace the technology-driven approach when using the online learning environment for enhancing teaching and learning effectiveness. Chow and Cheung claim that online learning moved the authorities and roles from teachers to students that learning should be controlled on the hands of learners [5]. An effective redesign of teaching and learning environment should be designed as learner-centered [58]. Learner-centered learning allows students direct learning by themselves. Wang stated the use of multimedia and online technologies allowed teaching without physical limitation and that students became self-directed in learning. Huang and Shi point out that blended learning, with self-led learning pace and content derived outside formal classroom under a virtual learning environment, allow students to experience and benefit from the learner-centered learning [59]. Such learner-centered teaching and assessment methods are more appropriate for adult learners. To cope with the existence of online learning technology, Qu et al propose a new adaptive learning model as a modern education theory which focused on situating students at the center of attention as well as individualization through studying the adaptive learning theory and considering the limitation of online learning model in teaching and learning [60] The role of teacher shifted from the sage on the stage (instructor) to the guide by the side (facilitator) in the blended learning environment.

Interactive Learning Content. In 2000s, researchers of e-learning advocate interactive and interesting learning contents are essential to effective online learning delivery. Kim, Bonk & Zeng stress interactivity is a key factor in the success of online instructional practice [61]. Sims suggests four types and levels of interactions in online learning platform: learner-teacher interaction; learner-learner interaction; learner-content interaction; and learner-interface interaction [62].

Assessment. Assessment is essential in measuring students' learning progresses. Nan suggests using integrated methods, which include formative assessment, summative assessment and diagnostic evaluation for learners' assessment in blended teaching mode [63]. In additional to the assessment carried out in the traditional classroom learning, assessment using the online learning environment can be included. Students' performance can be tested and recorded in the online learning system via online tests and online exercises. Besides, computer adaptive testing could help to test the students' abilities level and direct the students to the appropriate course content for study [64].

2.4   Social Perspective

Communication and Collaboration. Learner isolation and loneliness are the major problem of independent learning. Evans and Nation criticize independent learning as it separating teachers and students [65]. The online learning advocators suggested using and real-time communication tools to solve the problem. Cheung et al suggest the virtual classroom system increased the communication and interaction between students and students, and students and teachers [66]. Nicholson mention online learning had been shifted to a collaborative online learning environment with the rise of social constructivist theories in 1990s. Besides, online learning tools, like forum and chat room, allow students to communicate in the online learning environment [67]. Social networking tools were being used blended learning. Shiu et al study the use of social networking online tools, Facebook, to deliver learning and find that it motivated students to share and discuss for peer-to-peer learning. Students are encouraged to learn together in different ways in the blended learning environment [68]. Lee et al adopt social networking online tools, Second Life, into their blended learning course and they find such virtual environment encouraged collaborative learning. The students can learn from others and gain insights into their own learning curve [69]. Indeed, blended learning students can facilitate communication in the classroom environment. Hung et al indicate that blended learning helped teachers to allow more discussion and collaboration in class by freeing up the time using e-learning to deliver one-way lecture. Blended learning helps in facilitating communication and collaboration in the classroom environment [52].

Sharable and Co-Developed Learning Resources. Yau et al suggest the online learning environment is a platform which content are created, shared, remixed, repurposed, and exchanged [70]. Web 2.0 applications, like wikis, blogs, social bookmarking and podcasts, had emerged in online platform that allow users to read and write in the online learning environment. Students not only learn in the online environment but also build knowledge together. Wikipedia is a popular online encyclopedia that knowledge is collaboratively built and maintained by the users together [71]. e-Learning is applied for promoting the great autonomy for learners, focusing on the active learning that learner act as both a knowledge consumer and a knowledge creator [72]. It is unnecessary for blended learning course developers to build all the courseware by themselves. The use of open education resources is a common practice in online courseware development in these years. Open education resources are digitized study materials that educational institutions provided to access though the Internet for free [73]. Creative commons and Open Courseware Consortium are established to provide online environments for educators to search and obtain education resources for handling copyright issues [74].

3   The TIPS Model

The TIPS Blended Learning Model summarized the context of blended learning in technological, institutional, pedagogical and social perspectives as discussed in the above sections. The diagram in Fig. 1 shows the TIPS Blended Learning Model.

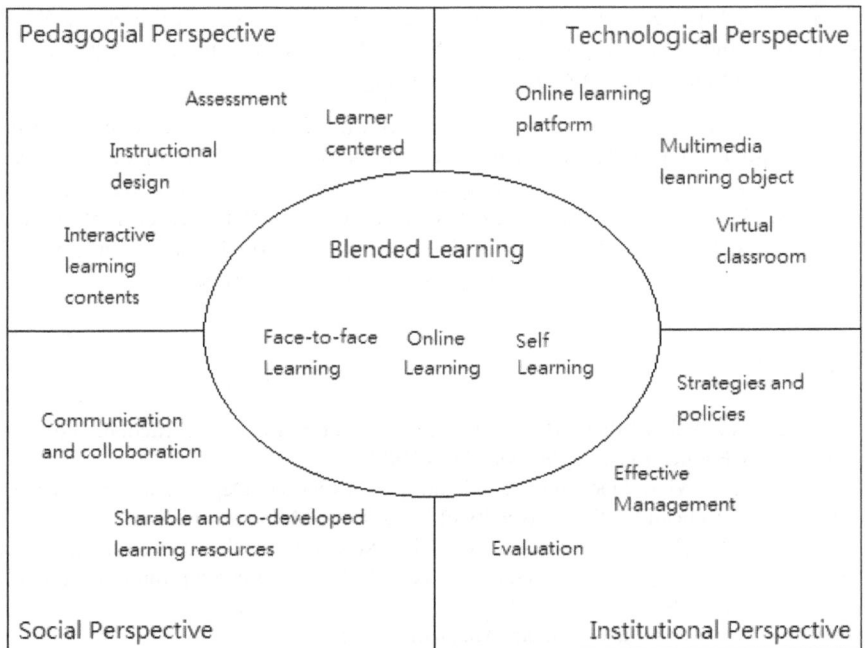

Fig. 1. The TIPS Blended Learning Model

The TIPS blended learning model proposes the areas for consideration in design and implementing blended learning in the technological, institutional, pedagogical and social perspectives. They include online learning platform, multimedia learning object, virtual classroom, strategies and policies, effective management, evaluation, instructional design, interactive learning contents, learner centered, assessment, communication and collaboration, and sharable and co-developed learning resources.

4   Conclusion

This paper identified the context of blended learning by reviewing the researches in the literature. The TIPS Blended Learning Model summarized the context of blended learning in technological, institutional, pedagogical and social perspectives.

In designing and developing blended learning, one should cover a wide range of considerations. In traditional learning, students attend lessons and have face-to-face learning. After lessons, the students learn by self-learning via reading textbooks, doing assignments and searching in the library. By combining online learning into traditional learning, students can have online learning when having face-to-face learning and self-learning. In the lesson, the students can learn from online materials and online activities with peers under the instruction of the teachers. After the lesson, the students can access the online learning platform to learn by themselves. Besides, the students can access online materials outside the learning platform by online searching. The design and development of these mix of face-to-face learning, online learning and self-learning needs the consideration from the technological, institutional, pedagogical and social perspectives.

The proposed model demonstrates the holistic view to cover all the perspectives of the context of blended learning. The TIPS blended learning model can be served as tips in designing and developing blended learning.

Acknowledgments. This paper is extracted from the literature review in the research thesis of a doctoral programme with amendment for presenting in the conference. This is to acknowledge the University of Nottingham, United Kingdom and the supervisors, Dr. Gordon Joyes and Prof. Charles Crook, of the Doctor of Education (Lifelong Education) programme to guide the research on blended learning. Their dedication in supporting and guiding the research is much appreciated.

References

1. Gibbons, A., Fairweather, P.: Designing Computer Based Instruction. Educational Technology Publications, Englewood Cliffs (1998)
2. Campbell, L.: What Does the "e" Stand for? (Report). Department of Science and Mathematics Education, The University of Melbourne, Melbourne (2004)
3. Duffy, P.: Using Youtube: Strategies for Using New Media in Teaching and Learning. In: Kwan, R., Fox, R., Chan, F.T., Tsang, P. (eds.) Enhancing Learning through Technology. World Scientific, Singapore (2008)
4. Downes, S.: E-Learning 2.0. eLearn Magazine (2005), http://elearnmag.acm.org/featured.cfm?aid=1104968
5. Chow, K.O., Cheung, K.S.: A Study on Tag Cloud Quality in e-Learning 2.0. In: Tsang, P., Kwan, R., Fox, R. (eds.) Enhancing Learning Through Technology, pp. 63–79. World Scientific, Singapore (2008)
6. Tetiwat, O., Igbaria, M.: Opportunities in Web-based Teaching: the Future of Education. In: Aggarwal, A. (ed.) Web-based Learning and Teaching Technologies: Opportunities and Challenges, pp. 17–32. Idea Group Publishing, London (2000)\

7. Shilwant, S., Haggarty, A.: Usability testing for e-Learning. Chief Learning Officer Magazine (2005),
   http://clomedia.com/articles/view/
   usability_testing_for_e_learning
8. Naidu, S. (ed.): Learning and Teaching with Technology: Principles and Practices. Kogan Page, London (2003)
9. Macdonald, J.: Blended Learning and Online Tutoring: A Good Practice Guide. Gower, Hampshire (2006)
10. Lam, J., Yau, J., Cheung, K.S.: A Review of the Use of Mobile Learning in Education. In: Proceedings of the International Conference on ICT in Teaching and Learning (2010)
11. Zhang, W.Y.: Entering the 3rd Generation of e-Learning: Characteristics and Strategies. In: Lee, V., Wang, F.L., Cheung, K.S., Hung, A. (eds.) Blended Learning: Maximization of Teaching and Learning Effectiveness, pp. 1–9. City University of Hong Kong (2011)
12. Sikora, A.C., Carroll, C.D.: Postsecondary education descriptive analysis reports (NCES 2004154), U.S. Department of Education, National Center for Education Statistics. U.S. Government Printing Office, Washington, DC (2002)
13. Cai, X.D., Yao, Y.: The Past and Present Lives of Blended Learning in the Context of Open Universities. In: Au, O., Kong, S.C., Kling, F. (eds.) Hybrid Learning 2.0, pp. 226–236. Beijing Normal University, BJ (2010)
14. Dabbagh, N., Bannan-Ritland, B.: Online learning: concepts, strategies, and application. Pearson Education, Inc., Upper Saddle River (2005)
15. Cheung, K.S., Lam, J., Lau, N., Shim, C.: A Paradigm in Instructional Design to Support Blended Learning. In: Proceedings of the International Conference on ICT in Teaching and Learning. SIMS University, Singapore (2010)
16. Ruberg, L.F., Moore, D.M., Taylor, C.D.: Student Participation, Interaction, and Regulation in a Computer-Mediated Communication Environment: A Qualitative study. Journal of Educational Computing Research 14(3), 243–268 (1996)
17. Ngan, L.: Effective Student Project Management with Peer Interaction. In: Lee, V., Wang, F.L., Cheung, S., Hung, A. (eds.) Blended Learning: Maximization of Teaching and Learning Effectiveness, pp. 178–180. City University of Hong Kong, HK (2011)
18. Graham, C.R.: Blended Learning Systems: Definition, Current Trends, and Future Directions. In: Bonk, C.J., Graham, C.R. (eds.) Handbook of Blended Learning: Global Perspectives, Local Designs, pp. 3–21. Pfeiffer Publishing, CA (2005)
19. Allen, I.E., Seaman, J.: Staying the Course: Online Education in the United States, 2008 Needham. Sloan Consortium, MA (2008)
20. McNaught, C.: The Best of Both Worlds: Effective Hybrid Learning Designs in Higher Education in Hong Kong. In: Kwan, R., Fong, J., Kwok, L.-f., Lam, J. (eds.) ICHL 2011. LNCS, vol. 6837, pp. 1–9. Springer, Heidelberg (2011)
21. Shroff, R.H.: Examining individual students' perceptions of curiosity utilizing a blend of online and face-to-face discussions: A case study. In: Ng, E.M.W. (ed.) Comparative Blended Learning Practices and Environments, pp. 125–145. Information Science Reference, Hershey (2010)
22. Oliver, M., Trigwell, K.: Can Blended Learning be Redeemed? e-Learning and Digital Media (2005),
   http://www.wwwords.co.uk/pdf/freetoview.asp?j=eleaandvol=2an
   dissue=1andyear=2005andarticle=3_Oliver_ELEA_2_1_web
23. Heinze, A., Procter, C.: Reflections on the use of blended learning. In: Education in a Changing Environment Conference Proceedings, University of Salford. Education Development Unit, Salford (2004)

24. Delialioglu, O., Yildirim, Z.: Students' Perceptions on Effective Dimensions of Interactive Learning in a Blended Learning Environment. Journal of Educational Technology and Society 10(2), 133–146 (2007)
25. Lim, D.H., Morris, M.L.: Learner and Instructional Factors Influencing Learning Outcomes within a Blended Learning Environment. Educational Technology & Society 12(4), 282–293 (2009)
26. Lam, L., Cheng, F.: Optimal Teaching Mix in Blended Team-Based Learning: A Case Study in CUUK-SCS. In: Lee, V., Wang, F.L., Cheung, K.S., Hung, A. (eds.) Blended Learning: Maximization of Teaching and Learning Effectiveness, pp. 146–156. City University of Hong Kong, HK (2011)
27. Zhang, D., Zhou, J.L., Nunamaker, J.F.: Can e-Learning Replace Classroom Learning? Communication of the ACM 47(5) (2004)
28. Chew, E., Jones, N.: Driver or Drifter? Two Case Studies of the Blended Learning Practices in Higher Education. In: Wang, F.L., Fong, J., Kwan, R. (eds.) Handbook of Research on Hybrid Learning Models: Advanced Tools, Technologies, and Applications, pp. 71–93. Information Science Publishing (2010)
29. Valuisky, V.: Platforms of Distance Learning Support: The Analysis and the Compatibility. Journal of Multimedia Aided Education Research 2(1), 103–111 (2005)
30. Chuah, C.K.P.: Experience Redesign: a Conceptual Framework for Moving Teaching and Learning into a Flexible e-Learning Environment. In: Tsang, P., Kwan, R., Fox, R. (eds.) Enhancing Learning Through Technology, pp. 37–50. World Scientific, Singapore (2007)
31. Cheung, K.S.: A Comparison of WebCT, Blackboard and Moodle for the Teaching and Learning of Continuing Education Courses. In: Tsang, P., Kwan, R., Fox, R. (eds.) Enhancing Learning Through Technology, pp. 219–228. World Scientific, Singapore (2007)
32. eSchool: eLearning Giants to Merge (2005),
    http://www.eschoolnews.com/2005/11/01/
    elearning-giants-to-merge/
33. Moodle: Moodle Website (2011), http://moodle.org/stats
34. Koong, K.S., Liu, L.C.: A Study of Web-Based Course Management Software Features. In: Tsang, P., Kwan, R., Fox, R. (eds.) Enhancing Learning Through Technology, pp. 253–266. World Scientific (2007)
35. IEEE: Draft Standard for Learning Object Metadata (2005),
    http://ltsc.ieee.org/wg12/index.html
36. Lam, J., Lau, N., Yau, J., Cheung, K.S.: A Review on the Use of Virtual Classroom in Support of Blended Learning. In: Proceedings of the 17th International Conference on Computers in Education, Hong Kong (2009)
37. Lam, J., Lau, N., Yau, J., Cheung, K.S.: A Survey on the Readiness in Adopting e-Learning among Teachers and Students. In: Fong, J., et al. (eds.) Hybrid Learning: The New Frontier, pp. 143–158. City University of Hong Kong, HK (2009)
38. Winegarden, C.R.: Visualizing Communication Structures of Nonverbal Information for Online Learning Environments. North Carolina State University, US (2005)
39. Mason, R., Rennie, F.: Elearning: the Key Concepts. Taylor and Francis Group, Routledge (2006)
40. Valenzeno, L., Alibali, M.W., Klatzky, R.: Teachers' Gestures Facilitate Students' Learning: A Lesson in Symmetry. Contemporary Educational Psychology 28(2), 187–204 (2003)
41. Hara, N., Bonk, C., Angeli, C.: Content Analysis of Online Discussion in an Applied Educational Psychology Course. Instructional Science 28(2), 115–152 (2000)

42. Wilson, B.G., Ludwig-Hardman, S., Thornam, C.L., Dunlap, J.C.: Bounded Community: Designing and Facilitating Learning Communities in Formal Courses. The International Review of Research in Open and Distance Learning (2004), http://www.irrodl.org/index.php/irrodl/article/view/204/286
43. Garrison, D.R., Vaughan, N.D.: Blended Learning in Higher Education. Jossey-Bass, US (2008)
44. Freitas, D., Sara, Oliver, M.: Does e-Learning Policy Drive Change in Higher Education: A Case Study Relating Models of Organizational Change in e-Learning Implementation. Journal of Higher Education Policy and Management 27(1), 81–95 (2003)
45. Lam, J., Tsoi, P.: Policies and Strategies of Technology Enhanced Learning in Lifelong Education in China, Hong Kong, Macau, Taiwan and Singapore. In: Kwan, R., Fong, J., Kwok, L.-F., Lam, J. (eds.) ICHL 2011. LNCS, vol. 6837, pp. 167–175. Springer, Heidelberg (2011)
46. Williams, P.: Beyond Control: Will Blended Learning Subvert National Curricula? In: Ng, E. (ed.) Comparative Blended Learning Practices and Environments, pp. 1–19. Information Science Reference (2010)
47. Lam, J., Hung, A., Chan, F.T., Zhang, W.Y., Yan, K., Woo, G.: Blended Learning Course Development Model. In: Lee, V., Wang, F.L., Cheung, K.S., Hung, A. (eds.) Blended Learning: Maximization of Teaching and Learning Effectiveness, pp. 52–64. City University of Hong Kong, HK (2011)
48. Le, J., Huang, L., Zhow, L., Li, Z.: Supporting Distance Learners for Blended Learning: A Case Study. In: Au, O., Kong, S.C., Kling, F. (eds.) Hybrid Learning 2.0, pp. 13–23. Beijing Normal University, BJ (2010)
49. QAA: Code of Practice for the Assurance of Academic Quality and Standards in Higher Education (2010), http://www.qaa.ac.uk/Publications/InformationAndGuidance/Documents/collab2010.pdf
50. Endean, M., Bai, B., Du, R.: Quality Standards in Online Distance Education. International Journal of Continuing Education and Lifelong Learning 3(1), 53–72 (2010)
51. Cheung, K.S., Lam, J., Im, T., Szeto, R.: Some Principles for Good Practices of e-Learning in Continuing Education Institutions. In: Proceedings of the International Conference on ICT in Teaching and Learning. Open University of Hong Kong, HK (2008)
52. Hung, A., Yuen, K., Lam, J., Lau, N., Kwok, I., Wong, T., Leung, H., Wong, K., Chiu, K., Pang, S.: The Experiences of Academics in Designing and Implementing the Blended Learning Project for Accounting Students at HKU SPACE Community College and HKU SPACE Po Leung Kuk Community College. In: Lee, V., Wang, F.L., Cheung, K.S., Hung, A. (eds.) Blended Learning: Maximization of Teaching and Learning Effectiveness, pp. 98–112. City University of Hong Kong, HK (2011)
53. King, K.P.: Identifying Success in Online Teacher Education and Professional Development. The Internet and Higher Education 5(3), 231–246 (2002)
54. Chen, G., Zhang, H.: Hybrid Learning in Educational Technology Training: A Perspective of Chinese University Teachers. In: Au, O., Kong, S.C., Kling, F. (eds.) Hybrid Learning 2.0, pp. 77–90. Beijing Normal University, BJ (2010)
55. Yuen, K., Hung, A., Lam, J., Lau, N., Duan, C.G.: The Learning Experiences in the Blended Learning Project at HKU SPACE Community College and HKU SPACE Po Leung Kuk Community College. In: Lee, V., Wang, F.L., Cheung, K.S., Hung, A. (eds.) Blended Learning: Maximization of Teaching and Learning Effectiveness, pp. 113–136. City University of Hong Kong, HK (2011)
56. Shim, C., Lam, J., Lau, N., Hung, A., Yuen, K., Tsang, D.: The Role of Instructional Design in Blended Accounting Courses. In: Lee, V., Wang, F.L., Cheung, K.S., Hung, A. (eds.) Blended Learning: Maximization of Teaching and Learning Effectiveness, pp. 65–74. City University of Hong Kong, HK (2011)

57. Webster, L., Murphy, D.: Enhancing Learning through Technology: Challenges and Responses. In: Kwan, R., Fox, R., Chan, F.T., Tsang, P. (eds.) Enhancing Learning through Technology, pp. 1–16. World Scientific, Singapore (2008)

58. Jolliffe, A.: The Online Learning Handbook: Developing and Using Web-based Learning. Kogan Page, London (2001)

59. Huang, J., Shi, W.: Policies and Practices of Lifelong Learning in China. International Journal of Lifelong Education 27(5), 499–508 (2008)

60. Qu, Y., Wang, C., Zhong, L.: The Research and Discussion of Web-Based Adaptive Learning Model and Strategy. In: Wang, F.L., Fong, J., Zhang, L., Lee, V.S.K. (eds.) ICHL 2009. LNCS, vol. 5685, pp. 412–420. Springer, Heidelberg (2009)

61. Kim, K., Bonk, C.J., Zeng, T.: Surveying the Future of Workplace e-Learning: The Rise of Blending, Interactivity, and Authentic Learning. eLearn Magazine, 2005(6) (2005), http://elearnmag.acm.org/archive.cfm?aid=1073202

62. Sims, R.C.: From Art to Alchemy: Achieving Success with Online Learning (2001), http://itech1.coe.uga.edu/itforum/paper55/paper55.htm

63. Nan, D.: Probing into the Ideological and Political Theory Course Hybrid Teaching Mode. In: Au, O., Kong, S.C., Kling, F. (eds.) Hybrid Learning 2.0, pp. 142–148. Beijing Normal University, BJ (2010)

64. Kandan, M.: Embedded Assessment System for Online Education, NIIT Centre for Research in Cognitive Systems (2011), http://www.kandan.org.in/articles/EmbeddedTesting.htm

65. Evans, T., Nation, D.: Critical Reflections in Distance Education. In: Evans, T., Nation, D. (eds.) Critical Reflections on Distance Education, pp. 237–263. Falmer, London (1989)

66. Cheung, K.S., Lam, J., Yau, J.: A Review of Functional Features of e-Learning Platform in the Continuing Education Context. International Journal of Continuing Education and Lifelong Learning 2(1) (2009)

67. Nicholson, P.: A History of e-Learning: Echoes of the Pioneers. In: Fernández-Manjón, B., et al. (eds.) Computers and Education: e-Learning. Springer, Netherland (2007)

68. Shiu, H., Fong, J., Lam, J.: Facebook - Education with Social Networking Websites for Teaching and Learning. In: Tsang, P., Cheung, S.K.S., Lee, V.S.K., Huang, R., et al. (eds.) ICHL 2010. LNCS, vol. 6248, pp. 59–70. Springer, Heidelberg (2010)

69. Lee, G., Fong, W., Chan, A.B.: Experiences in Hybrid Learning Utilizing Web 2.0 Social Software. In: Lee, V., Wang, F.L., Cheung, K.S., Hung, A. (eds.) Blended Learning: Maximization of Teaching and Learning Effectiveness, pp. 113–136. City University of Hong Kong, HK (2011)

70. Yau, J., Lam, J., Cheung, K.S.: A Review of e-Learning Platforms in the Age of e-Learning 2.0. In: Wang, F.L., Fong, J., Zhang, L., Lee, V.S.K. (eds.) ICHL 2009. LNCS, vol. 5685, pp. 208–217. Springer, Heidelberg (2009)

71. Wikipedia: The Wikipedia Website (2014), http://en.wikipedia.org/wiki/Main_Page

72. Grigoriadou, M., Papanikolaou, G., Magoulas, G., Kornilakis, H.: Towards New Forms of Knowledge Communication: The Adaptive Dimension of a Web-Based Learning Environment. Computers and Education 39(4), 333–360 (2001)

73. ODEC: Giving Knowledge for Free: the Emergence of Open Educational Resources (2007), http://www.oecd-ilibrary.org/education/giving-knowledge-for-free_9789264032125-en

74. Creative Commons: The Creative Commons Website (2011), http://creativecommons.org/

Is the Flipped Classroom Model Effective in the Perspectives of Students' Perceptions and Benefits?

Kenneth Wong and David W.K. Chu

Caritas Institute of Higher Education
18 Chui Ling Road, Hong Kong
{kfwong,dchu}@cihe.edu.hk

Abstract. Flipped Classroom Model is an instructional strategy that is gaining attention and adherents among instructors and educators nowadays. It is deviated from the conventional teaching method in which instructors mainly provide instructions in the classrooms. In applying the Model, students are requested by an instructor to watch a short video before the class. As a result, the instructor can instead devote more time to adopting active learning strategies in the classroom. The purpose of this study is to examine whether or not the Model is effective in students' benefits and perceptions, illustrated by a case study. Result has indicated that the Model was not only more effective than the conventional method in delivering an overview of the required materials, but also students benefitted from the inclusion of added examples about working implementations to raise their confidence level on English learning.

Keywords: Flipped Classroom, hybrid learning, e-learning, language learning, innovation, instructional strategy.

1 Introduction

In the traditional lecture-based classrooms, students take notes and are then given a minimal amount of homework at night. In other words, they do not spend the optimal amount of effort on their studies. This kind of instruction, as a consequence, allows students to take a passive role in the learning process, in which students who are motivated and engaged will perform well, but others will perhaps not meet the expectation simply because they are not required to think critically and tend therefore not to comprehend the content deeply. For a long time, educators have been endeavoring to shift from the lecture-based instructional model to student-oriented learning model. One of the models is Flipped Learning Model in which digital technologies are used to change from direct instruction to the individual learning space, mainly through videos or paper-based learning materials. This paper aims at exploring whether the Flipped Classroom Model is effective with reference to benefits and perceptions, illustrated with a case study conducted in an English course offered by a Hong Kong Post-secondary Institute.

2 Flipped Classroom Model

Flipped Classroom Model is defined as "teachers shift direct learning out of the large group learning space and move it into the individual learning space with the help of

S.K.S. Cheung et al. (Eds.): ICHL 2014, LNCS 8595, pp. 93–104, 2014.
© Springer International Publishing Switzerland 2014

one of several technologies" [1]. This Model explicitly brings active student engagement with the material (such as problem-solving exercises, discussion, case studies, etc.) into the classroom whilst moving more passive activities (such as reading notes and viewing to lectures) outside of the classroom [2]. The idea sprang from Jonathan Bergmann and Aaron Sams [3] who found that students often missed classes for some reasons. In order to measure the effectiveness, students were asked to watch YouTube videos which were video recordings on the lectures, demonstrations, and slide presentations with annotations. The educators reported, at a later stage, that students began interacting more in the class after they had flipped their classroom. In particular, stronger students continued to make progress whereas weaker students would receive more attention individually.

3   Instructional Video Platform

Video-based instruction has been recommended to be a method to enhance students' effectiveness in learning. A research from Shyu [4] indicated that it had a significant effect on student attitudes toward mathematics and improving students' problem-solving skills, regardless of their mathematics skills and scientific knowledge. Therefore, instructional videos could provide a motivating environment for students' learning. Likewise, a case study was conducted in an English course in which students had to complete a speaking assignment. In order to help students complete it, the Caritas Institute of Higher Education (thereafter Institute) developed a simple video platform for reference as shown in Figure 1.

Fig. 1. Instructional video platform login page

In this case, the platform aims at introducing practical oral skills to students who can broaden their horizons on language learning. It contains twenty one animated short films, consisting of animated short video clip and interactive exercises alike.

4   Research Methodology

In this study, the distinction between the Model and the conventional teaching method will be investigated with reference to their effectiveness particularly benefits and perceptions.

This study was conducted during the academic year 2013-14, targeting 68 students who were pursuing post-secondary programmes in the Institute, being divided into two classes. The control class was taught in the traditional method whereas the experimental class was taught with the Flipped Classroom model. In the Flipped Classroom model, students are asked by the instructor to watch a short video beforehand. Both classes were assumed to have no significant difference regarding their English language proficiency. Then, they were instructed to take a post-test on the improvement on English speaking proficiency. At last they were invited to complete a questionnaire about the perceptions on Flipped Classroom model applicable to English oral learning on voluntary basis.

4.1　Research Questions

This study attempted to answer the following research questions:

- What are students' perceptions on Flipped Classroom?
- What is students' engagement in Flipped Classroom?
- How effective is the model on students' learning?

4.2　Procedures

In early March 2014, the research team employed a random number generator to determine which class would serve as the experimental group and which class as the control group, with a particular lesson as a case study. Students in the experimental class were required to watch only one video (shown in Figure 2) a few days before the lesson. They were required to complete the interactive exercises after watching the respective video and the results would automatically be stored into the database. They were then invited to response to all problems shown in the video content on the following day. Teaching time arrangements for the Flipped Classroom were maintained as being three hours of lectures. During the class, students took part in pre-listening activity, while-listening activity and post-listening activity. Students were instructed to take a post-test to test their English speaking proficiency using a similar context provided in the video. On the other hand, students in the control group watched the video in the classroom. Similarly, they had to go through three same learning activities namely pre-listening activity, while-listening activity and post-listening activity. Then, students were invited to complete the interactive exercise after the class. At last, students were asked to take a post-test to test their English speaking proficiency.

4.3　Data Collection

Quantitative assessments were conducted to measure the effectiveness of the new Model on Likert scales. Open-ended surveys provided qualitative data to determine the attitudes of the students toward implementing the new Model.

Demographic data were limited to the number of years using internet, e-learning and internet habits. The post-test was in the format of multiple choice and fill-in-the blank in order to assess the effect of the new Model on the students' English speaking proficiency against their semester examination scores in the pre-test.

Fig. 2. Animated short video

5   Preliminary Findings

33 students and 35 students participate in the experimental group and the control group respectively. However, only 62 students attempted the post-test. According to the data analyzed by SPSS, there was a significant difference in the post-test result between the control group and the experimental group, shown in Table 1. However, there were no significant differences in the previous examination results (pre-test), shown in Table 2. There was no gender difference between both pre- and post-test results.

Table 1. ANOVA analysis on the post_test_score

ANOVA					
post_test_score					
	Sum of Squares	df	Mean Square	F	Sig.
Between Groups	60.652	1	60.652	9.795	.003
Within Groups	371.542	60	6.192		
Total	432.194	61			

Table 2. ANOVA analysis on the pre_test_score

ANOVA					
pre_test_score					
	Sum of Squares	df	Mean Square	F	Sig.
Between Groups	201.601	1	201.601	.961	.331
Within Groups	12585.367	60	209.756		
Total	12786.968	61			

A total of 10 items were designed to measure the overall effectiveness of the new Model. They were all significantly correlated, and the details were shown in Annex table 1. The results showed an average rating of 3.73 points on a five point Likert scale (as shown in Table 3) and a slightly higher than average (3 points). Furthermore, there was no gender difference on the overall effectiveness of the new Model, as shown in Annex Table 2.

Overall, 72.7% of the students agreed or strongly agreed that in contrast with the traditional instructional mode, it was able to raise their interests in learning English with the new Model. 70% of the students agreed or strongly agreed that the watching a video lecture before the class would raise their listening ability in English. Moreover, 65% of the students agreed or strongly agreed that watching a video lecture before the class helped them improve the English speaking skills. 63.6% of the students agreed or strongly agreed that watching a video lecture before the class helped them understand the lecture content, while 63.6% of the students agreed or strongly agreed that the interactive exercises helped their learning. Furthermore, 62% of the students agreed or strongly agreed that watching a video lecture before the class enhanced their understanding in English accent (stress). 58% of the students agreed or strongly agreed that they liked the new Model. Similarly, About 57% of the students agreed or strongly agreed that the new Model enriched their English language knowledge. 50% of the students agreed or strongly agreed that watching a video lecture before the class improved their understanding of English rhythm. Finally, 58% of the students agreed or strongly agreed that they liked the new Model.

Table 3. The results of measuring the overall effectiveness of the new Model

	Items	Mean	SD
1	Watching a video lecture before the class helped me understand the classroom content.	3.94	0.851
2	The interactive exercise attached to the video enhanced my English learning.	3.82	0.758
3	Watching a video lecture before the class enhanced my English listening skills.	3.85	0.702
4	Watching a video lecture before the class improved my speaking ability.	3.65	0.884
5	Watching a video lecture before the class enhanced my understanding in English accent (stress).	3.56	0.86
6	Watching a video lecture before the class improved my understanding of English rhythm.	3.44	0.786
7	In contrast with traditional instructional mode, I can raise my interests in learning English with the new Model.	3.82	0.968
8	In contrast with traditional instructional mode, I can enrich my knowledge of English with the new Model	3.74	0.828
9	In contrast with traditional instructional mode, I can enhance my motivation in English learning with the new Model	3.68	0.976
10	I like the new Model.	3.53	1.08
	Overall average	3.73	0.677

Furthermore, a total of 4 items were designed to measure the effectiveness of the students' engagement in the class. They were all significantly correlated, and the details were shown in Annex table 3. The results showed an average rating of 3.77 points on a five point Likert scale (as shown in Table 4). Furthermore, there was no gender difference on the overall effectiveness of the students' engagement in the class, as shown in Annex Table 4. However, 27% of students agreed or strongly agreed that the listening exercises were difficult to do.

Table 4. The results of measuring the effectiveness of the students' engagement in the class

	Items	Mean	SD
1	Listening activities in the classroom enhanced my understanding of English language.	3.79	0.77
2	Words and phrases activities in the classroom with providing explanatory notes enhanced my understanding of English language.	3.82	0.834
3	For the listening activities in the classroom, instructors provided more clues / comments on the exercises.	3.68	0.768
4	Learning materials for listening activities intensified my English listening learning.	3.68	0.727
	Overall	3.77	0.638

In the open-ended survey, two-third of students in the experimental group reported that it was convenient for them to watch a video lecture before the class. Over half of students in the experimental group agreed that watching a video lecture before the class could help them well prepare for the lesson. Around half of the students in the experimental group indicated that watching a video lecture before the class could enhance their interest or motivation to learn in the class. Nearly half of the students in the experimental group reported that the new Model could increase their learning motivation in the class.

However, around one-fourth of the students in the experimental group reported that the script size of the video was too small to read. Moreover, less than five students in the experimental group suggested that content of the video be further enriched. Seven students in the experimental group had not watched the video before the class and this might affect the progress of the lesson. Less than five students reported that they were bored by the fast speed of the video. Finally, about one-fourth of the students reported that they generally preferred making videos more professionally.

6   Discussion

This study has provided valuable insights for the implementation of the Flipped Classroom Model. It has been hypothesized that students in the English class would benefit with this Model from the activities conducted during the class. The result of the survey and post-test results indicated that the Model was useful for a majority of the students.

For the students' perception towards the Flipped Classroom Model, the results from the survey supported the hypothesis that the majority of students accepted this Model. Each questionnaire item that examined students' perception showed positive responses concerning the Flipped Classroom Model. No students disagreed and strongly disagreed that this Model helped them understand the classroom content. No students disagreed and strongly disagreed that this Model enhanced their English learning and improved their English listening skills. For the second research question, the results from the surveys supported the hypothesis that the majority of students engaged more in the class with this Model. Each questionnaire item that examined students' engagement showed positive responses concerning this Model. No students disagreed and strongly disagreed that words and phrases activities in the classroom with providing explanatory notes enhanced their understanding of English. Only 3% of students disagreed and strongly disagreed that listening activities in the classroom enhanced their understanding of English language, and also intensified their English listening learning. For the third research question, the overall results demonstrated overwhelmingly positive responses. Throughout the process, students were open and honest about their feedback and provided constructive suggestions on how to improve the way the Flipped Classroom model worked.

Regarding the concerns raised by the participants, more relevant exercises were proposed to articulate the difficulty by providing a bigger size of scripts with a video screen. Instructors can encourage students to watch the video before the class in various ways. Furthermore, it was also suggested to use videos which were professionally made in a series in order to ensure the quality control. In this way, Hertz [6] expressed the feasibility of using commercialized videos so that students and instructors will no longer need to create their own tailored and unique resources. The research team will further consider a balanced solution on the development of videos. Support beyond the flipped class also needs to be considered. Though some students expressed gratitude for the thoroughness of the instruction, there was still a bit of lingering hesitation as they moved into more authentic implementation. The establishment of a learning community, either online or in-person, would help students work through the initial stages and instructors provide guidance to more advanced users on the implementation.

Although findings have indicated that using the Flipped Classroom Model in English class is effective, this study still have some limitations. Firstly, the participant size was so small that only 68 students participated in this study. Secondly, the respondents were limited to students reading a diploma. As most of them intended to pursue a higher diploma or even degree programme in the near future, tracing their further learning path on English would better reflect the effectiveness of the Flipped Classroom Model. Thirdly, as all the samples were drawn from a self-financing post-secondary institute in Hong Kong, it would be doubtful whether it was a fair picture for all students reading a diploma in other institutes in Hong Kong. In this way, a comparative study with those students coming from government-funded institutes would be more fruitful. Fourthly, the result would be more comprehensive if the Model could be conducted in a whole semester instead of only a few lessons. Finally, the findings would be more convincing and reliable if the same Model could be applied to other courses than English.

7   Conclusion

This study has demonstrated that the Flipped Classroom Model is effective on enhancing students´ learning in English in terms of students´ perception and benefits, supported by a case study conducted by the Institute. The significance of the research lies in three ways. Firstly, the study has confirmed that students generally accepted this Model for it strengthens comprehension of the teaching content. Secondly, the finding has indicated that students' motivation in English learning is enhanced through the enjoyment of class activities. Thirdly, students benefited from this Model as evidenced by the post-test results which showed that the students from the experimental group earned significantly higher scores than the students from the control group did.

Future research on determining the effectiveness of the Flipped Classroom Model should be conducted continually. It may be suited for other courses. The research team will continue to pilot the Model in different courses in the coming academic years. However, the drawbacks associated with video quality, students' initiative, and activities in classroom should be also tackled. In this way, the Flipped Classroom Model would complement a future study on mobile device usage.

Acknowledgment. The research team would like to thank Education Bureau of the Hong Kong SAR Government which supported this project through Quality Enhancement Grant Scheme (QEGS).

References

1. Hamdan, N., McKnight, P., McKnight, K., Arfstrom, K.: A review of flipped learning:Flipped Learning Network,
   http://www.flippedlearning.org/cms/lib07/VA01923112/
   Centricity/Domain/41/LitReview_FlippedLearning.pdf
2. Butt, A.: Student views on the use of aflipped classroom approach: Evidence from Australia. Business Education and Accreditation 6(1), 33–43
3. Bergmann, J., Sams, A.: Flip your classroom: Reach every student in every class every day. International Society for Technology in Education, Eugene (2012)
4. Shyu, H.Y.C.: Using video-based anchored instruction to enhance learning: Taiwan's experience. British Journal of Educational Technology 31(1), 57–69 (2000)
5. Hertz, M.B.: The flipped classroom: Pro and con.,
   http://www.edutopia.org/blog/
   flipped-classroom-pro-and-con-mary-beth-hertz

Annex

Table 5. Correlations of 10 questions related to the overall effective of the new Model

Correlations

		eff_1	eff_2	eff_3	eff_4	eff_5	eff_6	eff_7	eff_8	eff_9	eff_10
eff_1	Correlation	1	0.823**	0.682**	0.521**	0.450**	0.415*	0.632**	0.478**	0.626**	0.525**
	Sig. (2-tailed)		0.000	0.000	0.002	0.009	0.016	0.000	0.005	0.000	0.002
	N	33	33	33	33	33	33	33	33	33	33
eff_2	Correlation	.823**	1	.737**	.702**	.519**	.462**	.598**	.438*	.609**	.482**
	Sig. (2-tailed)	.000		.000	.000	.002	.007	.000	.011	.000	.004
	N	33	33	33	33	33	33	33	33	33	33
eff_3	Correlation	.682**	.737**	1	.729**	.533**	.353*	.606**	.542**	.447**	.418*
	Sig. (2-tailed)	.000	.000		.000	.001	.044	.000	.001	.009	.015
	N	33	33	33	33	33	33	3 3	33	33	33
eff_4	Correlation	.521**	.702**	.729**	1	.641**	.362*	.585**	.550**	.439*	.305
	Sig. (2-tailed)	.002	.000	.000		.000	.039	.000	.001	.011	.084
	N	33	33	33	33	33	33	33	33	33	33
eff_5	Correlation	.450**	.519**	.533**	.641**	1	.754**	.556**	.677**	.577**	.549**
	Sig. (2-tailed)	.009	.002	.001	.000		.000	.001	.000	.000	.001
	N	33	33	33	33	33	33	33	33	33	33
eff_6	Correlation	.415*	.462**	.353*	.362*	.754**	1	.354*	.393*	.498**	.541**
	Sig. (2-tailed)	.016	.007	.044	.039	.000		.043	.024	.003	.001
	N	33	33	33	33	33	33	33	33	33	33
eff_7	Correlation	.632**	.598**	.606**	.585**	.556**	.354*	1	.813**	.849**	.623**
	Sig. (2-tailed)	.000	.000	.000	.000	.001	.043		.000	.000	.000
	N	33	33	33	33	33	33	33	33	33	33
eff_8	Correlation	.478**	.438*	.542**	.550**	.677**	.393*	.813**	1	.672**	.667**
	Sig. (2-tailed)	.005	.011	.001	.001	.000	.024	.000		.000	.000
	N	33	33	33	33	33	33	33	33	33	33
eff_9	Correlation	.626**	.609**	.447**	.439*	.577**	.498**	.849**	.672**	1	.769**
	Sig. (2-tailed)	.000	.000	.009	.011	.000	.003	.000	.000		.000
	N	33	33	33	33	33	33	33	33	33	33
eff_10	Correlation	.525**	.482**	.418*	.305	.549**	.541**	.623**	.667**	.769**	1
	Sig. (2-tailed)	.002	.004	.015	.084	.001	.001	.000	.000	.000	
	N	33	33	33	33	33	33	33	33	33	33

**. Correlation is significant at the 0.01 level (2-tailed).

*. Correlation is significant at the 0.05 level (2-tailed).

Table 6. The correlations between the genders and the overall effective of the Flipped Classroom Model controlled by group

Correlations

Control Variables			gender	effective
group	gender	Correlation	1.000	.167
		Significance (2-tailed)	.	.360
		df	0	30
	effective	Correlation	.167	1.000
		Significance (2-tailed)	.360	.
		df	30	0

Table 7. Correlations of 4 questions related to the overall effective of the activities during the class

Correlations

		ClassAct_1	ClassAct_2	ClassAct_3	ClassAct_4
ClassAct_1	Correlation	1	.795**	.538**	.568**
	Sig. (2-tailed)		.000	.001	.001
	N	33	33	33	33
ClassAct_2	Correlation	.795**	1	.665**	.538**
	Sig. (2-tailed)	.000		.000	.001
	N	33	33	33	33
ClassAct_3	Correlation	.538**	.665**	1	.500**
	Sig. (2-tailed)	.001	.000		.003
	N	33	33	33	33
ClassAct_4	Correlation	.568**	.538**	.500**	1
	Sig. (2-tailed)	.001	.001	.003	
	N	33	33	33	33

**. Correlation is significant at the 0.01 level (2-tailed).

Table 8. The correlations between the genders and the effective of the classroom activities controlled by group

Correlations

Control Variables			gender	eff_act
group	gender	Correlation	1.000	.080
		Significance (2-tailed)	.	.662
		df	0	30
	eff_act	Correlation	.080	1.000
		Significance (2-tailed)	.662	.
		df	30	0

Myths to Burst about Hybrid Learning

Kam Cheong Li

Unversity Research Centre, Open University of Hong Kong,
Ho Man Tin, Kowloon, Hong Kong
kcli@ouhk.edu.hk

Abstract. Given the snowballing attention to and growing popularity of hybrid learning, some take for granted that the learning mode means more effective education delivery while some who hold a skeptical view expect researchers to inform them whether hybrid learning leads to better learning effectiveness. Though diversified, both beliefs are like myths about the hybrid mode. By reporting findings concerning the use of wikis in a major project on hybrid courses piloted at a university in Hong Kong, this paper highlights the complexity concerning the effectiveness of a hybrid learning mode and the problems of a reductionistic view of its effectiveness. Means for *e*learning were blended with conventional distance learning components into four undergraduate courses. Findings show that a broad variety of factors, including subject matters, instructors' pedagogical knowledge of the teaching means, students' readiness for the new learning mode and the implementation methods, play a key role in deciding learning effectiveness, rather than just the delivery mode *per se*.

Keywords: Hybrid learning, wikis, learning effectiveness, learner readiness, teacher readiness.

1 Introduction

The popularity of hybrid learning is upsurging, and the development has been fast and the momentum strong [1, 2]. The snowballing popularity of the learning mode attracts educators to jump on the band wagon. To take a prudent stance, some have their decisions based on research support. They tend to ask academics researching hybrid learning whether blended learning should be adopted. There are two diversified views. The first group holds the belief that hybrid learning is better than their conventional mode of learning in their educational delivery. The other group believes that research can directly inform educators whether hybrid learning is a more effective education delivery mode.

This paper examines these beliefs with findings from a research study. The study investigated the effectiveness of educational delivery of four pilot blended learning courses offered in Hong Kong by an open university. The courses investigated in this study were transformed from conventional distance learning courses: i.e. courses in which students learn by studying printed materials provided by the institution and receiving tutor support through email/telephone and a small number of face-to-face tutorials. *e*Learning components were blended into these courses.

S.K.S. Cheung et al. (Eds.): ICHL 2014, LNCS 8595, pp. 105–115, 2014.
© Springer International Publishing Switzerland 2014

Within the length allowed, this paper focuses on one of the *e*learning components added to the conventional mode of course delivery — wiki. It will report the findings and discuss issues highlighted by the results. The issues linked closely to the above beliefs and precaution that educators should have in their interpretation of results from hybrid courses.

2   Hybrid Courses Investigated and the Blended Delivery Means

As noted in the analysis of the denotative and connotative senses of the term by Li and Cheung, hybrid learning may involve any two or more means to deliver a course [3]. In this study, the courses investigated were originally distance learning courses, rather than introducing *e*learning to a face-to-face curriculum setting. In an attempt to explore ways to enhance students' learning effectiveness, the institution transformed four undergraduate business administration courses originally designed and delivered in the distance-learning mode to ones presented for hybrid learning. Two of the four courses were on the general management field, one introducing students to management and the other to marketing. These two laid a strong emphasis on concepts and theories, or qualitative conceptualization. The other two were the first and second courses introducing students to accounting, stressing knowledge and skills of quantitative operations.

To re-design and transform the original distance learning courses for hybrid learning, new *e*learning means and face-to-face contacts were included in the course delivery. Each course provided a similar set of delivery means as course components to guide or facilitate learning. The conventional distance learning delivery means included tutorials for face-to-face interaction between the tutor and students, as well as detailed study material in print form was provided for students' self-study. New online self-test exercises with automatic feedback were provided to facilitate self-practice and self-checking of understanding. A set of video clips were included in the online materials as extra guidance for topics which learners' commonly found difficult to understand on their own. Recordings of the face-to-face tutorials were uploaded to the online learning platform, particularly for those who were not able to attend the tutorials and help those who would like to recall important points. Asynchronous communication platforms, discussion board and wiki, were introduced to facilitate students' interaction through texts and open-ended questions so as to stimulate student participation.

The teaching contents and course components were designed by full-time course coordinators who do not normally see or communicate with students often. Students were in contact with part-time tutors who conducted tutorials, assessed their submitted works (assignment and contributions in the wiki) and looked after individuals in his or her group. At the beginning of the course, the functions and operations of each of the delivery means were explained to the tutors.

3   Wiki

Wiki has been adopted widely as a popular education delivery means for peer interaction and collaborative learning [4, 5]. It is a web application that allows students to work with others by adding, modifying, or deleting content. It has also been commonly employed for assessment purposes (e.g. [6]). It supports knowledge creation and sharing among participants [7] and facilitates engaging students in learning within a collaborative environment [8]. Karasavvidis holds that "wikis are among the most promising elearning 2.0 tools because they require active student engagement which facilitates constructivist learning" [9] (p. 219).

As one of the course delivery means, the wiki was examined in the study and relevant findings are reported and discussed in the following sections. Students' performance in the wiki was counted 5% of their overall course results. In all four courses, students worked on the wiki in a similar way. Each student first wrote comments or ideas on the wiki platform, addressing an issue raised by their course tutor. Students could then choose a student's comments to respond to and add their feedback or comments on the platform. The student who received feedback would then respond by writing their points on the platform. Through this, students were expected to think critically and develop an in-depth understanding of the concepts discussed or commented. Tutors were not obligated to but could freely join the discussion.

4   Methodology

To assess the effectiveness of the courses, a questionnaire survey was conducted at the end of the four blended learning courses. To further explore functions and problems of each delivery means, 20 face-to-face in-depth semi-structured interviews with students individually and three focus group interviews with tutors were conducted.

An instrument was developed to gauge the students' perceived importance of the cognitive skills required for as well as perceived usefulness and satisfaction level of the wiki of each course. The revised Bloom's Taxonomy proposed by Anderson and Krathwohl categorizes cognitive process in learning into six distinctive types or levels [10]. In ascending order of cognitive demand, they are remembering, understanding, applying, analyzing, evaluating and creating. To understand the cognitive skills required for qualitative and quantitative courses, six items were developed based on the revised Bloom's Taxonomy in order to gauge students' perceived importance of different cognitive skills for learning the course.

Four measurement items were developed to gauge the corresponding perceived usefulness in students' learning. They were: "Wiki enhances my learning effectiveness in the course.", "Wiki makes it easier to learn confusing and difficult topics.", "After I had grasped the basic concept of a topic, wiki further improved myknowledge on it." and "Wiki helps me prepare for the examination". Students were requested to indicate the extent to which they agreed with each of these statements in 5-point Likert scale (with 1=strongly disagree, 2=disagree, 3=neutral, 4=agree, 5=strongly agree).

The instrument was administered to distance learners of the four blended learning courses at the end of the semester. The participants were recruited via email invitations on a voluntary basis. A total of 140 participants completed the questionnaires. Detailed demographics are presented in Table 1. As shown in the table, most participants had considerable working experience. Approximately half, 63.6%, of the participants are from the two courses emphasizing qualitative conceptualization and 36.4% of the participants are from the two stressing quantitative operations.

Table 1. Demographic Table

	Frequency	Percentage
Courses		
Introduction to accounting I (B211)	25	17.9
Introduction to accounting II (B212)	64	45.7
Principles and Practices of Management (B240)	28	20.0
Introduction to Marketing (B250)	23	16.4
Age		
<20	4	2.9
21–25	55	39.3
26–30	27	19.3
31–35	19	13.6
36–40	11	7.9
41–45	9	6.4
46–50	6	4.3
>50	9	6.4

5   Results

5.1   Whether Subject Knowledge Matters

Results suggest strongly that different subject matters call for dissimilar cognitive skills in the learning. Though the wiki was used in similar ways, students perceived that courses stressing qualitative conceptualization (qualitative courses) called for cognitive skills different from those required for emphasizing quantitative operations (quantitative courses).

Independent t-tests were conducted on samples from qualitative and quantitative courses to examine the differences in the perceived level of importance of the cognitive skills for learning the two types of courses. As shown in Table 2, the significant differences found suggest that students perceived that qualitative courses place more emphasis on "creating" and less on "applying", in comparison with quantitative courses.

To determine differences in the level of perceived usefulness and satisfaction of the wiki of the two types of courses, independent t-tests were carried out. Results shown in Table 3 suggested that perceived usefulness and satisfaction level of wiki were significantly different in the two types — the wiki in that qualitative courses had a higher level of satisfaction and perceived usefulness.

Table 2. Independent *t*-test on perceived importance of cognitive skills for two types of courses

	Qualitative courses (n=51)		Quantitative courses (n=89)		Independent *t*-test	
	$\bar{x}$	s_x	$\bar{x}$	s_x	t	p
Remember	3.80	0.775	3.82	0.732	-0.124	0.901
Understand	4.16	0.731	4.37	0.697	-1.716	0.088
Apply	3.71	0.879	4.17	0.742	-3.168	0.002**
Analyze	3.75	0.796	3.98	0.812	-1.642	0.103
Evaluate	3.57	0.831	3.76	1.012	-1.171	0.244
Create	3.71	0.729	3.39	1.040	2.080	0.039*

* Significant at the 0.05 level (2-tailed)

** Significant at the 0.01 level (2-tailed)

Table 3. Independent t-test on perceived usefulness and satisfaction levels of the wiki of two types of courses

Wiki	No. of item(s)	Cronbach Alpha	Qualitative courses (n=51)		Quantitative courses (n=89)		Independent T-test	
			$\bar{x}$	s_x	$\bar{x}$	s_x	t	p
Perceived usefulness	4	0.933	3.48	0.917	2.97	0.926	3.133	0.002**
Satisfaction level	1	-	3.47	1.007	3.03	0.872	2.695	0.008**

** Significant at the 0.01 level (2-tailed)

Table 4. One Sample t-test on perceived levels of usefulness and satisfaction of the wiki

	n	$\bar{x}$	s_x	95% Confidence Interval of Mean		Test Value = 3	
				Lower	Upper	Sig. (2-tailed)	Mean Difference
Perceived usefulness of the wiki							
Samples from qualitative courses	51	3.48	0.92	3.22	3.73	0.00**	0.48
Samples from quantitative courses	89	2.97	0.93	2.77	3.16	0.75	-0.03
Satisfaction level of the wiki							
Samples from qualitative courses	51	3.47	1.01	3.19	3.75	0.00**	0.471
Samples from quantitative courses	89	3.03	0.87	2.85	3.22	0.72	0.034

** Significant at the 0.01 level (2-tailed)

The perceived levels of usefulness of and satisfaction for the wiki were also computed by splitting samples from qualitative courses and from quantitative courses. Results of one sample *t*-tests with test values equal to 3 (neutral), as shown in Table 4, suggested that the mean scores of perceived usefulness and satisfaction level of wiki from students of qualitative courses were significantly greater than 3, but with students of quantitative courses not significantly different from 3. On average, students from qualitative courses considered the wiki useful and were satisfied with it, but not for students from quantitative courses.

5.2   Whether Individual Cognitive Domain Dominates

Results shown in Table 2 above already suggest that subject matter differences call for different learning approaches since diverse cognitive skills are required in the learning. The development of different cognitive skills may require diverse types of learning tools/tasks. The results are in line with Levine [11] that higher-order cognitive skills are "achieved through a process of interaction and dialogue".

Table 5 shows the results of individual face-to-face interviews with 20 students. It shows the frequency of students' agreement that the cognitive skill could be developed by peer interaction and the wiki. This suggests that students consider peer interaction useful for higher level cognitive skills.

Table 5. Number of students agreeing that cognitive skills could be developed by peer interaction and the wiki (n=20)

	Remember	Understand	Apply	Analyze	Evaluate	Create
Peer interaction	0	0	0	10*	12*	13*
Wiki	0	0	0	5	5	8

* Items mentioned by half or more of the respondents.

The wiki was supposed to be used for academic discussions for conceptual analysis and evaluation as well as creative use of course concepts and theories. As reported in Table 5, over 25% of the students held that wiki could enhance their higher order cognitive skills, and none of them consider that the wiki could assist them to develop lower cognitive skills. This suggests that the wiki is more suitable for courses with a heavy orientation towards higher cognitive skills.

5.3   How the Learning Medium is Used Decides

Tables 6 and 7 provide lists of students' views and comments on peer interaction and the wiki in their courses. Like what suggested by results in Table 5, Table 6 shows that students were rather positive about the function and utility of peer interactions in the course. They in general saw value in interacting with their peers.

It is worth noting that, echoing the results reported in 5.1, most students pointed out peer interaction was only needed when the topic for discussion were not restricted to a single correct answer, implying that students recognized the influence of the subject matter on the effectiveness of peer interaction.

Table 6. Student perceptions of peer interactions in their courses (n=20)

View expressed	Frequency (out of 20)
Prerequisites for peer interaction	
Topics with no single correct answer	13
Basic knowledge required for discussion	8
Engagement of counter parties	12
Creditability of information included in the discussion process	6
Tutors' feedback for facilitating the discussion process	8
Provision of interaction with peers	
Discussion with peers helps collect others' views, ideas and experience	10
Facilitation of intra action (Self checking)	
Discussion with others helps check for misunderstanding	5
Enhancement of learning interest	
Discussion enhances learning interest	4

Table 7. Students perceptions of the wiki in their courses (n=20)

View expressed	No. of students (out of 20)
Facilitating interaction with materials (Practice)	
Benefits of the wiki are similar to conventional assignments, making students practise what they have learned.	6
Provision of interaction with peers	
Reading peers' works helps gathering others' perspectives, ideas and experience	10
Problem arisen	
<u>Subject Suitability</u>	
Discussion is not necessary for topics with a single correct answer, such as calculations.	12
<u>Design of Wiki Task</u>	
There is no feedback from tutor.	7
Assessment weighting is too low. (too much workload for the small number of marks)	5
Assessment results rely on others. (Part of the marks dependent on others' participation)	5
<u>Student Readiness</u>	
Workload of wiki is heavy.	6
Peer feedback is superficial.	6
Students are not willing to criticize others' points.	5

Table 7, however, shows that students were not as positive with the learning tool requiring peer interaction. There was substantial misunderstanding and dissatisfaction or even grievances concerning the wiki.

Similar with students' view on peer interactions, they recognized the topics for discussion should have no single correct answer. Even half of them believed that wiki could help gathering others' perspectives, ideas and experience. Stduents' motivation for the wiki was low. The low motivation level reflected from some students' blamed on the workload of wiki and also complaint that the assessment weighting was too low for them to be interested in the wiki discussion. Some students were not ready for the wiki and perceived that commenting on others' point was criticizing others, and therefore avoided doing so. Some of them were not comfortable with the wiki's independent discussion context, and expected tutor's intensive guidance which however was not in the design of the course.

5.4   How Instructors Think Impinges

Tutors' views concerning the wiki were collected through three focus group interviews. The views were diverse. When asked whether the wiki could enhance students' thinking and learning, 8 out of 13 tutors indicated that the wiki did. When asked further, tutors from qualitative courses confessed that they faced difficulty in using the wiki platform at the beginning. Tutors of the quantitative courses seemed to share a general disagreement with the use of the wiki. There was much misunderstanding about the function of the wiki. For example, one said he did not even know that he could provide feedback to students on the platform. They were confused about the pedagogical functions of the wiki and what they should do with it; examples of what they said have been listed in Table 8.

Table 8. Quotations of what tutors said – Pedagogical value of the wiki

Tutor A:	I don't like the wiki. Frankly speaking, if you wish to encourage students to write more, you can set one more essay assignment task using an open-ended question. I see no points asking students to comment on each other's points.
Tutor B:	My understanding of the aim of the wiki was to give students a sense of community. In other words, it was to get individual students to feel that they are not alone and there are fellow students doing the same thing.
Tutor C:	When I saw that students wrote irrelevant comments, I have to refrain myself from saying anything. I struggled and was not sure whether I should jump in to say something and if I do, how much to say.
Tutor D:	The wiki didn't seem to be suitable for learning. It could help build a sense of belonging to a community. It is just like children's love for online games. In such games, as peers participating share a common mission, they work together. The wiki may allow students to discuss anything of their interest. It does not have to be course theories or any pre-set issues, as it is basically for interest.

6   Discussion

The results reported above show a complex picture. While students welcome the increase in provision of the course delivery means in a wider and richer variety, they have reservations about them for their learning. Tutors hardly welcomed the changes in the courses.

The likes and dislikes of key stakeholders should be interpreted in perspective and the complexity behind should be untied. Interview results show that students welcome the increased choices available to them; yet this does not mean that they enjoyed every item delivered to them. The wiki was a focus of concern.

The use of wiki was well supported by relevant studies, as the utility of wiki as a tool for collaborative learning has been well noted [12, 13]. For it to properly function and bring pedagogical benefits to students, a number of conditions need to be satisfied.

First the use of it should match with the subject matter being learned as results in 5.1 imply. The in-depth discussions of conceptual or theoretical issues through a wiki platform suit subject matters calling for qualitative discussion and creative knowledge applications. When deciding whether and how to use wiki, the nature of the subject matters should be taken into consideration.

Avoiding a reductionistic view, however, is the key. Considering that wiki is completely useless for quantitative courses will mean missing the point. It is unrealistic to expect that the other type of courses, having a heavy quantitative orientation, to go without any qualitative mastery of concepts and theories.

The learning task is linked closely to the teaching delivery means. In the wiki example, the way students learn through the wiki is linked to the way it is used. Since the means fits for the development of several cognitive domain and much less for others, as results in 5.2 show, the design of the task for the wiki plays a role on whether the means can be properly deployed for applications of designed cognitive skills.

This follows on the fact that the way the delivery means is deployed play a crucial role in its effectiveness. In the wiki case, the readiness of the learner to use it was called to question. When students did not see the reasons for using the wiki, they could hardly gain the desired pedagogic benefit of using it. They could see negative side of it, such as additional work to complete the course but only a small number of marks were allocated to the task, not being sure what comments they would receive on their points, and not having expert input from their instructors during the discussion. As a result of the low readiness and motivation, some students reported that the feedback from other students were superficial and could not facilitate learning.

Readiness of the teaching staff is another factor playing a key role. The instructor's understanding determines what they tell students about how to use the teaching delivery means and how they are involved in using the means. The confusion experienced in the reported wiki case highlight readiness could be a pre-requisite to success in implementation.

7   Conclusion

It may seem easy to say that a pedagogical approach is good or not. Evaluation in perspective, however, helps us see the complexity involved (e.g. [14, 15]) and proper evaluation warrant close look at a wide variety of factors in the learning context.

When students were asked whether they preferred continuation of the supply of the variety of learning means through the hybrid approach, the responses were virtually unanimously positive. This does not imply that blended learning fits them. A closer look reveals, as in this study, that students value the choices they have available. They could have reservations about how and whether to use the learning means given to them.

It appears reasonable to expect that research, planned and implemented properly, may provide answers to whether a learning means should be adopted. There is no simple answer.

The wiki in this study reveals the high complexity in making course design decisions. When designing the use of teaching means, a spectrum of factors should be taken into consideration. As shown in the wiki case, the design decision involves at least the subject matter, the tasks related to the wiki, cognitive skills required for the tasks, the students' readiness in terms of motivation and understanding of the tasks, the instructors' knowledge of the tasks and pedagogical underpinning behind. The complexity increases as these factors are related to each other.

The wiki is but one part of the each of courses studied. For the design of a hybrid course, consideration needs to be given to the factors operating for each of the course delivering means as well as how the various means link and interact together in students' learning process.

The study also highlights the importance of development of users' knowledge in using the learning means. As Ramanau and Geng highlight, in order to benefit from wiki, adequate training is needed to cater for the needs of both students and staff [16].

By bursting the myths about making simplistic decision about whether to blend in any new means of learning to a study course, this paper highlights the important fact that a broad range of interrelated factors need to be taken into consideration. Due attention should be given to the complexity.

This study has focused primarily on the wiki. Further studies on wiki as well as other learning means for hybrid learning may be used for triangulation and comparison.

Acknowledgment. This study was supported by research fund of the Open University of Hong Kong (2012/1.2).

References

1. Bauk, S., Scepanovic, S., Kopp, M.: Estimating students' satisfaction with e-learning system in blended learning. In: Proceedings of 8th International Technology, Education and Development Conference, pp. 263–271 (2014)
2. Bernard, R.M., Borokhovski, E., Schmid, R.F., Tamim, R.M., Abrami, P.C.: A meta-analysis of blended learning and technology use in higher education: from the general to the applied. Journal of Computing in Higher Education 26, 87–122 (2014)
3. Li, K.C., Cheung, S.K.S.: How hybrid is referred, inferred and preferred? In: Cheung, S.K.S., Fong, J., Fong, W., Wang, F.L., Kwok, L.F. (eds.) ICHL 2013. LNCS, vol. 8038, pp. 345–355. Springer, Heidelberg (2013)

4. Snodgress, S.: Wiki activities in blended learning for health professional students: Enhancing critical thinking and clinical reasoning skills. Australasian Journal of Educational Technology 27(4), 563–580 (2011)
5. Tsai, W.T., Li, W., Elston, J., Chen, Y.: Collaborative learning using wiki web sites for computer science undergraduate education: A case study. IEEE Transactions on Education 54(1), 114–124 (2011)
6. Pusey, P., Meiselwitz, G.: Assessments in large-and small-scale wiki collaborative learning environments: recommendations for educators and wiki designers. In: Ozok, A.A., Zaphiris, P. (eds.) Online Communities, HCII 2011. LNCS, vol. 6778, pp. 60–68. Springer, Heidelberg (2011)
7. Wagner, C.: Wiki: A technology for conversational Knowledge management and group collaboration. Communications of the Association for Information Systems 13, 265–289 (2004)
8. Parker, K., Chao, J.: Wiki as a teaching tool. Interdisciplinary Journal of e-learning and Learning Objects 3(1), 57–72 (2007)
9. Karasavvidis, I.: Wiki uses in higher education: exploring barriers to successful implementation. Interactive Learning Environments 18(3), 219–231 (2010)
10. Anderson, L.W., Krathwohl, D.R. (eds.): A Taxonomy for Learning, Teaching, and Assessing: A Revision of Bloom's Taxonomy of Educational Objectives. Longman, New York (2001)
11. Levine, S.J.: The online discussion board. New Directions for Adult and Continuing Education 113, 67–74 (2007)
12. Gould, D., Mi, D.S.: Use of a wiki as a collaborative learning tool to promote active learning in a neuroscience course for first-year medical students. FASEB Journal 27, 960 (2014)
13. Prokofieva, M.: Evaluating types of students' interactions in a wiki-based collaborative learning project. Australasian Journal of Educational Technology 29(4), 496–512 (2013)
14. Tselios, N., Daskalakis, S., Papadopoulou, M.: Assessing the acceptance of a blended learning university course. Educational Technology & Society 14(2), 224–235 (2011)
15. Neumann, D.L., Neumann, M.M., Hood, M.: Evaluating computer-based simulations, multimedia and animations that help integrate blended learning with lectures in first year statistics. Australasian Journal of Educational Technology 27(2), 274–289 (2011)
16. Ramanau, R., Geng, F.: Researching the use of wiki's to facilitate group work. Procedia-Social and Behavioral Sciences 1(1), 2620–2626 (2009)

Trends of Cloud Computing in Education

Yinghui Shi[1], Harrison Hao Yang[1,2,*], Zongkai Yang[1],and Di Wu[1]

[1] Central China Normal University, 430079 Wuhan, China
[2] State University of New York at Oswego, 13126 Oswego, USA
ikki.shi@hotmail.com, harrison.yang@oswego.edu,
zkyang@mail.ccnu.edu.cn, dr.wudi@gmail.com

Abstract. As an emerging technology, cloud computing has been increasingly and widely used in the field of education. Based upon 132 research studies on education of cloud computing from the Education Resources Information Center database over the recent years, this study selected 42 high-frequency descriptors to conduct co-word analysis of cloud computing in education. The results show that cloud computing in education is mainly concentrated on five areas: conceptual and pedagogical aspects, educational applications, processing of information and resources, pros and cons of cloud computing in education, and database management system integrated with cloud-based services. In addition, it provides a detailed discussion of the impact of cloud computing in these five areas.

Keywords: cloud computing, educational technology, focal themes, co-word analysis, web services.

1 Introduction

Cloud computing is one of the biggest tech buzzwords nowadays. Interestingly, a recent survey conducted by Wakefield Research for Citrix with 1,006 nationally representative American adults about cloud computing revealed, "The majority of Americans (54%) claim to never use the cloud, however 95% of those who think they're not using the cloud, actually are: 65% are banking online, 63% have shopped online, 58% report using social networking sites, 45% have played online g ames, 29% store photos online, 22% have stored music or videos online, and nearly 1 in 5 (19%) use online file-sharing services - all of these are cloud-based" [1].

Cloud computing is not a totally new concept, and it has intricate connection to other related technologies such as utility computing, cluster computing, and distributed systems [2]. The concept of cloud computing may have originally been introduced as long ago as 1961 when renowned computer scientist John McCarthy predicted that computing would become a public utility [3]. The term cloud computing was inspired by the cloud graphic that seen as a metaphor for the Internet, as cloud computing relies on the use of computing resources and applications that are delivered as a service over the Internet [4]. The National Institute of Standards and Technology (NIST) signals that

---

* Corresponding author.

S.K.S. Cheung et al. (Eds.): ICHL 2014, LNCS 8595, pp. 116–128, 2014.

cloud computing is composed of five essential characteristics from on-demand self-service, broad network access, resource pooling, rapid elasticity, and measured service; three service models such as Software as a Service - SaaS, Platform as a Service - PaaS, and Infrastructure as a Service - IaaS; and four deployment models including private cloud, community cloud, public cloud, and hybrid cloud [5].

As an emerging technology that has sparked the interest of a wide range of individuals and organizations, cloud computing has changed the way people think about computing and communication, data processing, and collaborative work [6]. Cloud computing enables individuals (e.g., teachers, students) and institutions (e.g., K-12 schools, colleges, universities) to access to these resources by offering a huge amount of compute and storage resources to the masses [7]. An important step was taken with the release of a cloud-based application named Google Apps in 2007, which is offered free to educational institutions. Inevitably and fortunately, Google is not the only cloud on the horizon, other cloud computing vendors, such as Amazon, IBM, Microsoft, are keeping in step with Google [8].

In educational contexts, cloud computing has been thought to have tremendous potential to improve efficiency and reduce costs with respect to the installation and maintenance of variety educational services [8]. Cloud computing solutions are employed by more and more schools to provide available cloud-based applications and services for teachers and students, whereas what remains to be increased is the capacity for the cloud to enhance students' engagement in real research and participation in global learning communities [9]. Cloud computing is becoming an increasingly popular and powerful approach to delivering technology to educational contexts. However, numerous factors from student and school's perspective should be paid careful attention to which helps contribute to the successful implementation of cloud computing in the educational settings [10].

While cloud computing spreads rapidly in education, there are several questions that have arisen from this growth. What is the overall impact of cloud computing in the field of education? What are the focal aspects of cloud computing that researchers and practitioners have been concerning with? In order to shed light on these questions and have a better understanding of cloud computing on teaching and learning, this study intends to provide an overall and intuitive analysis of research hotspots and development trends in the field of education of cloud computing in recent years.

The purpose of this study is two-fold. First, it provides an overview of the synthesis of key ideas, evidences, and works on cloud computing in education. Second, it provides a further discussion for researchers and practitioners to gain deep understanding and insights on cloud computing in education, and to assist them in thinking about what they are trying to do and what they hope to achieve as they integrate cloud computing services into teaching and learning.

2   Method

Co-word analysis method is used for this study. Co-word analysis method originally appeared in the late 1970s, and it has been widely applied in many fields, such as artificial intelligence, information retrieval, etc. Co-word analysis method is a comprehensive analysis method based on co-occurrence frequency of pairs of words or phrases in the literatures. According to Monarch, "co-word analysis reveals patterns and trends in technical discourse by measuring the association strengths of terms representative of relevant publications and sometimes other texts produced in a technical field" [11]. Co-word analysis is composed of co-word frequency analysis, co-word correlation analysis, co-word clustered analysis and so on [12].

2.1   Data Collection

The data of our study were from the Education Resources Information Center (ERIC) Collection. ERIC is the world's largest digital library of education literature. The ERIC Collection, begun in 1966, contains records for about 16 subject topics, and provides access to more than 1.4 million bibliographic records of journal articles and other education-related materials [13]. The ERIC Collection resources are identified with highly authoritative and comprehensive.

The following criteria was used for searching related studies from ERIC:

1) Keyword: cloud - so all other keywords which related to cloud computing were included, such as cloud-based, cloud services, cloud technologies, etc.

2) Publication Date: From 2006 up to October 2013 - the term of cloud computing was initially used by Google's CEO Eric Schmidt to represent the business model of providing services over the Internet in 2006, since then the term started to gain real popularity [14].

3) Publication Type: educational articles - including journal articles, conference article and other types of documents/materials such as computer programs, dissertations/theses, guides, etc.

As a result, 256 studies were located. After deleting the irrelevant studies (the keyword "cloud" of those studies simply related to the authors' names, institutions, weather, dark cloud, electron cloud, etc.), a total of 132 studies were finally selected.

2.2   Co-word Frequency Analysis

The Thesaurus of Descriptors produced by ERIC, is a carefully selected list of education- related words and phrases that used to tag materials by subject and thus making them easier for retrieving. Not only can the Thesaurus extract the theme of a literature, but it also can detect the linkages among these themes directly from the literatures [15]. The frequencies of thesaurus descriptors in each literature were extracted and summed up and then presented in the search results pages by ERIC automatically. The issued year and source of targeting literature were also included in the search results pages, which greatly facilitate our statistical work.

As a result, descriptors with frequency of occurrence not less than 7 times were selected as the high-frequency keywords represent for the research direction of this subject.

2.3   Construct Matrixes

Statistics treatments were applied to count the frequency of the identified 42 high-frequency descriptors pairwise appeared in the same literature. To facilitate the analysis and process of the data, while eliminating the influence of the frequency disparity on the analytical results, Ochiia coefficient was chosen for the inclusive treatment on the frequencies of word pairs, in order to transform the original co-word matrix to the similarity matrix, and finally transform to the dissimilarity matrix which represented for the dissimilarity between any two descriptors, as shown in Table 1.

Table 1. Dissimilarity matrix of descriptors

Descriptors	Internet	Computer Software	Information Technology	Educational Technology
Internet	0	0.275	0.347	0.477
Computer Software	0.275	0	0.403	0.435
Information Technology	0.347	0.403	0	0.714
Educational Technology	0.477	0.435	0.714	0

2.4   Co-word Cluster Analysis

The co-word cluster analysis was composed of the following steps:

1) Factor analysis of correlation coefficients matrix: Correlation test was conducted to the co-word matrix of high-frequency descriptors by SPSS20.0 software. The correlations among the high-frequency descriptors were significant as shown by the results, which meant that the co-word matrix was suitable for factor analysis. Factor analysis was conducted to the matrix, and as shown in Table 2, there were seven common factors, whose values of initial eigenvalues were over 1. Five components were extracted after rotated, and their cumulative contribution rate was 94.44%.

Table 2. Dissimilarity matrix of descriptors

	Initial Eigenvalues			Rotation Sums of Squared Loadings		
	Total	% of Variance	Cumulative %	Total	% of Variance	Cumulative %
1	1.33	45.62	45.62	0.87	29.79	29.79
2	0.85	29.27	74.90	0.98	33.50	63.29
3	0.37	12.81	87.71	0.64	22.00	85.29
4	0.12	4.06	91.77	0.17	5.92	91.21
5	0.08	2.68	94.44	0.09	3.23	94.44
6	0.04	1.54	95.98			
7	0.03	1.02	97.00			
8	0.02	0.85	97.85			
...						

2) Hierarchical cluster analysis of dissimilarity matrix: Hierarchical cluster analysis was applied to the dissimilarity matrix within SPSS. Five common factors were extracted after rotated and the first five factors in the scree plot could be seen clearly, as indicated by the results of factor analysis. Thus, a single solution with the number of clusters was set at five in the cluster membership in SPSS.

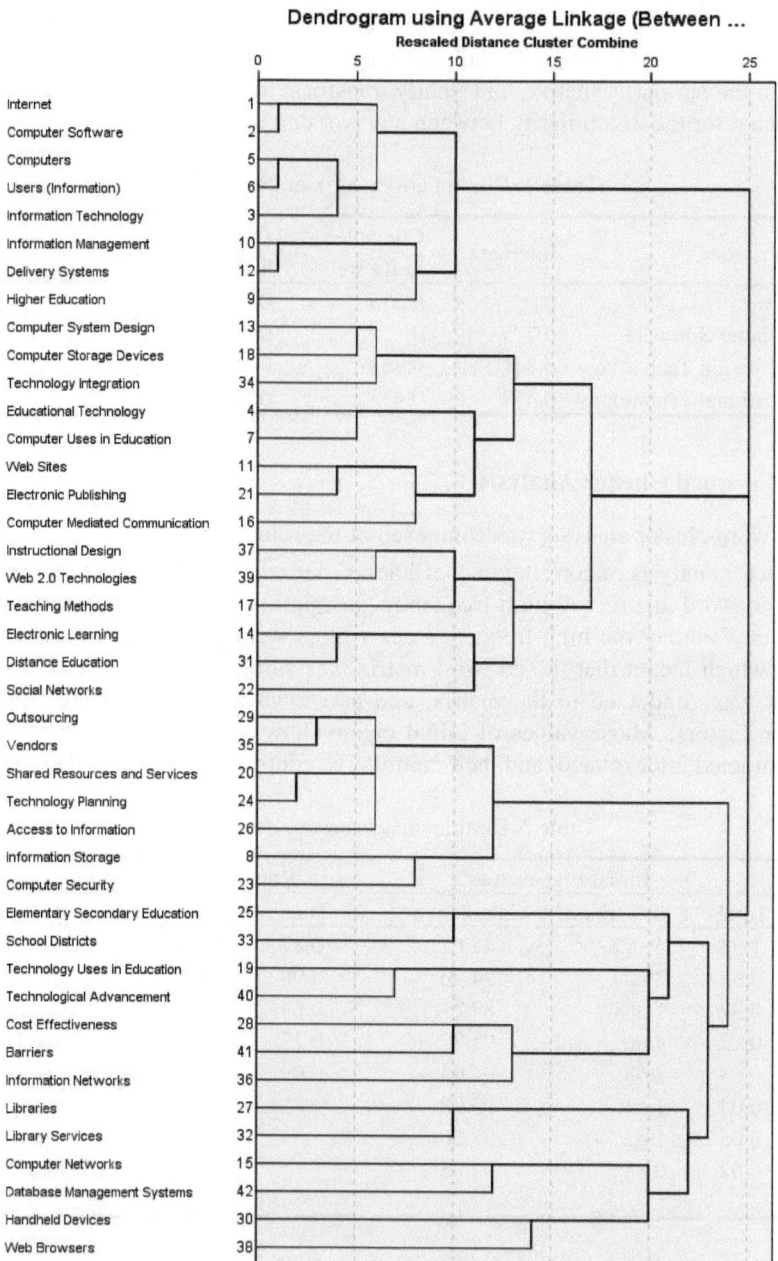

Fig. 1. Dendrogram of the hierarchical cluster analysis

Moreover, the between-groups linkage was selected as the cluster method and the squared Euclidean distance in the interval was selected as the measure method, and the Z scores method was selected to transform values after several attempts. Dendrogram of the hierarchical cluster analysis was generated as shown in Figure 1.

3   Results and Discussion

Based upon the outcomes of co-word analysis, five interrelated focal points have been formed which can basically reflect the research hotspots and priority areas of cloud computing in education from previous studies (see Table 3). They were: (1) conceptual and pedagogical aspects; (2) educational applications; (3) process of information and resources; (4) pros and cons of cloud computing; and (5) database management system integrated with cloud-based services.

Table 3. Five Focal Themes of Cloud Computing in Education

Focal Theme	Number of Studies[*]	Percent
Conceptual and Pedagogical Aspects	31	23.5%
Educational Applications	39	29.5%
Process of Information and Resources	19	14.4%
Pros and Cons of Cloud Computing	16	12.1%
Database Management System Integrated with Cloud-based Services	18	13.6%
Other	9	6.8%

Note: [*]Total number of studies was 132.

3.1   Conceptual and Pedagogical Aspects

Although many people have heard the term cloud computing and may have some ideas of what the term means, they still struggle to understand what the real meaning of cloud computing is and how it can be used to enhance teaching and learning. A bit of definitions on cloud computing given by some researchers differ from various perspectives and in different ways, but they surely could help us to gain a better understanding of cloud computing.

Generally, cloud computing is a distributed computing paradigm that pursuits on providing distributed access to scalable, virtualized hardware and software infrastructure to a broad spectrum of users over the Internet [6]. Foster et al. [2] referred cloud computing to "a large-scale distributed computing paradigm... in which a pool of abstracted, virtualized, dynamically-scalable, managed computing power, storage, platforms, and services are delivered on demand to external customers over the Internet", whereas Gartner [16] described it as "a style of computing where massively scalable IT-related capabilities are provided as a service across the Internet to multiple external customers." Furthermore, Erdogmus [17] provided a concise definition by saying that "cloud computing is an emerging computational model in which applications, data, and Information Technology (IT) resources are provided as services to users over the Web." Perhaps the most recognizable definition is the one given by the NIST, which stated cloud computing as "a model for enabling convenient, on-demand network access to a shared pool of configurable computing resources (e.g., networks, servers, storage, services) that can be rapidly provisioned and released with minimal management effort or service provider interaction" [5].

Another related issue acknowledged by educators is the cloud-enabled pedagogies. Inspecting the potential of cloud computing technologies to enhance instructional methods, Denton [18] found "cloud computing, specifically integrating with Google Docs, is a compelling approach to instruction where constructivism and cooperative learning serve as the theoretical backdrop." Exploring the destructive and innovative potential of newly emerging cloud-based pedagogies, Stevenson and Hedberg [19] addressed that cloud computing can be exploited to disseminate and scale web-based applications within and across learning contexts. In addition, based on a thorough review of the literature about cloud computing, He, Cernusca and Abdous [20] provided insights into the adoption of cloud computing for distance learning, with the purpose of helping distance learning administrators and practitioners to understand cloud computing and to make plans for successful cloud adoption.

There is a growing concern about empowering students with 21st century collaboration skills and create new learning opportunities for promoting science, technology, engineering and math (STEM) education. From this perspective, Crippen and Archambault [21] investigated the nature of scaffolded inquiry-based instruction and how it can be applied to the use of emerging technologies, such as cloud computing, so that students not only learn the content of STEM, but can also answer nowadays' critical socio-scientific questions. Furthermore, Stevenson and Hedberg [22] investigated positive individual- and group-based strategies that embody effective, genuine online collaboration when Cloud technologies were used to support real-time online collaboration between multiple learners in online spaces.

3.2   Educational Applications

The advent of cloud computing has ushered in additional options for educators and students by providing them with the means to express themselves, their research, their studies, and their creativity in distinctive ways [23]. Integrating with other instructional tools and applications, such as interactive whiteboard, cloud computing makes it possible for students to interact, simulate, and collaborate with each other, as well as to document real world problem-solving and learning experiences [24]. In addition, Denton [18] provided ten strategies for integrating cloud computing into constructivism and cooperative learning activities, such as group project, peer assessment, collaborative reflection, electronic publishing and so on.

Studies have been focused on the promotion of cloud-based services across education at all levels and how these technologies might be applied to teaching and learning integrated with curricula or existing practice [9], [25]. Discussion, planning, and usage of cloud-based applications and services are undertaking in colleges and universities throughout the world [26]. Blue and Tirotta [24] reported the advantages and challenges when incorporating cloud computing tools (e.g., social networking tools, collaborative writing tools), and interactive whiteboards into graduate teacher preparation courses, and further provided recommendations for technology integration and basic characters of cloud computing technology that enables users to make preparations for the teaching profession. In order to benefit students from learning data mining methods and using data mining tools and algorithms to analyze the data, Jafar [27] used the cloud computing as a platform to provide students with real necessary hands-on experience in data mining course. In addition, for the purpose of finding the best-available and cost-effective cloud technologies that fit well in the existing curriculum, Chen et al. [28] reported their design and experiences of integrating cloud computing into seven undergraduate-level information system, computer science, and general science courses that were related to large-scale data processing and analysis at a university in Australia.

In K-12 schools, teachers and students are trying different cloud-based solutions that allow multiple users to collaborate in innovative ways. McCrea and Weil [29] provided nine examples from K-12 educators who have found creative ways to utilize the cloud computing technologies in their classroom teaching. The sharing features of these cloud-based tools allow multiple students to develop and edit projects at the same time and thus improving their collaborative skills. Siegle [30] deliberated two cloud-based educational applications: Live- Binders and VoiceThread, and indicated, "These products harness student's creativity and build interaction into what were once static student presentations." Dorling and Johnstone [31] used the CSI (Criminal Science Investigation) Schools Project as an engaging and inspiring STEM activity for students to work on scientific hypotheses and develop higher cognitive skills, and they found cloud computing and databases have a power to develop and enhance students' learning experience.

3.3   Process of Information and Resources

The processing of information and resources, which includes the access, storage, sharing, backup and recovery of massive information and resources, is a modern fact of life [32]. As a computing technology that uses the Internet and central remote servers to maintain information, resources and applications, cloud computing technology involves much more efficient computing by centralizing storage, memory, processing, and bandwidth [23]. As Trappler [33] pointed out that cloud computing entails a paradigm shift from internal processing and storage of data to an open way that data travels over the Internet among diverse external data centers.

Information storage and sharing are important features of cloud computing. Libraries are seen as the center of data and information of colleges and universities for their powerful functionality of information storage and sharing. However, as more cloud computing services, especially the information management services are provided over the Internet, online databases and digital libraries are springing up like mushrooms. For instance, as the first web-scale, cooperative set of library management services, WorldShare Management Services (WMS) was used to move core services (e.g., circulation, acquisitions, cataloging) to the cloud. Dula et al. [34] presented how library management functions in a university were migrated to the cloud using WMS so as to share hardware, services and resources in the cloud.

Likewise, backup is also an indispensable part of processing of information and resources. Traditionally, large-scale backups have been done via local storage devices, such as hard disks, compact discs, which have limited capacities. However, these local devices are neither cheap nor fast and troublesome to move around, and the maintenance of these local devices is pretty labor-intensive compared with a backup solution that takes advantage of internet access to backup the copies of data and send them to the cloud via the Internet [35]. In order to check out whether it is possible to use the cloud to back up the data, researchers found out that there were numerous of vendors (e.g., Dropbox) able to provide one with backup solutions, and how to evaluate and choose a backup service in the cloud was further discussed [35].

Furthermore, Wheeler and Waggener [3] pointed out the growth of pervasive, high-speed digital networks and cloud services offers colleges and universities new capabilities and opportunities to rethink ways for delivering IT services. A typical case is a growing number of small libraries with limited computing resources or supporting in the cloud employs free Web applications. Since these libraries lack of certain IT-supported requirements, it would be a good choice to adopt no-cost or low-cost solutions to provide continuous library information services [36].

3.4   Pros and Cons

General speaking, cloud computing represents a crucial transformation from the old manner that IT solutions have been performed and comes with its own unique set of challenges [33]. Recent studies have focused on the pros and cons of cloud computing in educational contexts. For instance, Siegle [23] indicated that cloud computing has four main advantages for schools: time and cost, accessibility, sharing and retrieve. In addition, Romiszowski [37] discussed the potential benefits and hazards of a cloud-based approach to distance learning.

Cloud computing makes it possible for schools to use less powerful computers (e.g., netbooks) to access the cloud in order to reduce its computing costs, as the file storage services and basic applications of cloud computing are free. Moreover, many cloud-based applications have full feature sets and are compatible with standard programs, which can perform a wide array of tasks and thus pretty meet the needs of school users. Because of this, many colleges, universities and K-12 school districts in the US are already working in the cloud [4]. Cloud computing is seen not only "budget friendly," but also educationally beneficial. For example, students can learn a variety of computer production skills in a collaborative learning environment supported by cloud computing, or they can share and collaboratively edit documents and other files with others in a cloud-based application, such as Google Docs [4].

On the other hand, cloud computing in education has been facing conceptual, legal, ethical, and practical problems. There are various definitions behind the term cloud computing, the meanings of which may differ from different professionals and institutions. Moreover, cloud computing is often used for describing a variety of activities, from outsourcing a specific activity to an external provider to delivering services from the cloud. Therefore, cloud users are often confused about where their data is being stored and where it is being processed [26]. Varieties of legal issues can arise if an institution's data resides in different countries and even different states where different laws pertain to data, as Trappler [33] addressed, for those data owners, one key question with cloud computing won't go away, that is which law applies to their data, the one where they're located, or the one where their data's located.

Privacy is another significant problem, as there is a growing body of awareness on data privacy. For example, Jaeger et al. [38] discussed the policy problems of cloud computing, and argued that data privacy must be taken into account when deciding whether to move into a cloud. Also, Buckman and Gold [39] outlined the privacy and data security compliance issues facing postsecondary education institutions when they utilized cloud computing and provided with a practical list of do's and don'ts.

Furthermore, one risk associated with data is to make an appraisal of the intellectual property of the data once they are being entrusted to the cloud provider and then to build an appropriate indemnity into the contractual arrangements. A critical question has arisen: can the cloud service provider correctly value the data and make compensation to the data owner in case of a leak of privacy data [26]?

Malfunction also raises doubts about cloud computing. As clouds become a familiar thing, it is extremely common for users to upload their personal data into the cloud. The more users rely on the cloud, the more they are vulnerable to any failure or changes within the cloud [40]. The question remains: how to maintain any backup or alternate choice in case the clouds break down or not performed?

3.5   Database Management System Integration

Users now access the great mass of content and applications on the Web and they are saving more information and data in the clouds instead of on their individual devices [41]. As there is a substantial body of users and massive data, applications growing up in the clouds, more information systems and database management systems integrated with cloud-based services are needed in educational environments.

Cloud-based application features like files and resources sharing, data management, are prompting more educators to adopt these technologies [18], [42]. For instance, how to efficiently manage the data generated by numerous of students from research and/or a laboratory experiment is an important challenge. Bennett and Pence [42] found that Google Docs integrated with cloud computing provides a good solution for this data-management problem and enables researchers to coordinate their works easily.

By running applications as services on a flexible infrastructure over the Internet, cloud computing focus on providing low cost solutions to academic institutions for researchers, teachers and students. In their study, Al-Zoube, El-Seoud, and Wyne [43] presented a cloud computing based e-learning system as a solution for science education to build a virtual environment, which can be used for teaching and learning, as well as for exploring and sharing new ideas. In addition, upon a free and open-source cloud computing platform named OpenStack, Cheng, Huang and Liu [44] implemented an e-book hub system to offer content providers an easy-to-use cloud computing service with unlimited storage capacity, high usability and scalability, and high security characteristics to produce, convert, and manage their e-books, and thus enabled mobile device users to access to digital content easily.

It's noted that Geographic Information Systems (GIS) is a powerful tool for social studies on teaching and learning. However, the use of GIS has been blocked by problems such as the cost of the software and the management of large spatial data files. Recently, a free GIS application called ArcGIS Explorer takes advantage of cloud computing to deliver a virtual GIS environment, in which students and teachers can interact with maps by performing common GIS tasks, such as adding or subtracting layers and identifying features. Webster and Milson [45] described how they used ArcGIS Explorer with ninth-grade geography students to study economic development and the ways in which countries are classified. Moreover, Mumba and Zhu [46] presented a simulation-based interactive virtual classroom web system powered by the latest cloud computing technology from Google. This system allowed a quick and easy access for most users and it enabled customized course and lesson development and supported teacher and student account management.

The need, usage, benefit and potential of e-portfolio system have been analyzed and discussed in the education community. However, various challenges and limitations are in the way of the development and implementation of e-portfolios. To deal with some of these challenges and limitations, a new e-portfolio system based on Private-Public (PrPl) data index system which integrates cloud computing applications and storages with semantic web architecture has been designed and developed, which making it possible for semantic web-based visualization and advanced intelligent search [47].

4   Limitations and Conclusion

It is worthy to note that there are two limitations of this study. First, this study was relied on the frequency of occurrence of ERIC descriptors, which does not necessarily reflect the distinctive features of cloud computing in education. For future research, it is recommended to use term frequency-inverse document frequency (TF-IDF) and content analysis before the research is carried out. Second, this study was limited to the main educational database, which may not completely capture the dynamic that happen within cloud computing in education. For future research, it is recommended to include more articles from other publication databases in interdisciplinary areas.

In conclusion, periodical review is crucial to the understanding of the impact of innovative technologies on education. This study provides a glimpse into the existing research and significant work done on cloud computing in the field of education in recent years. In reviewing the previous literature, five focal points have emerged which contributing to our understanding of the overall status of priority areas and development trends in the field of education of cloud computing. It is our hope the results of this study will serve as starting point to assist researchers and practitioners in thinking about what they are trying to do and what they want to achieve as they use cloud computing to support and enhance learning and instruction in education.

Acknowledgments. This work was supported by the National Key Technology Research and Development Program under Grant NO.2013BAH18F02; Educational Informatization Strategy Research Base project of the China Ministry of Education; and Self-determined research funds of CCNU from the colleges' basic research and operation of MOE under Grant No. CCNU09A02006.

References

1. Wakefield Research.: Partly cloudy: About cloud computing, http://www.citrix.com/site/resources/dynamic/additional/ Citrix-Cloud-Survey-Guide.pdf
2. Foster, I.T., Zhao, Y., Raicu, I., Lu, S.: Cloud computing and grid computing 360-degree compared. In: Proc. IEEE Grid Computing Environments Workshop, Austin, Texas, pp. 1–10 (2008)

3. Wheeler, B., Waggener, S.: Above-campus services: Shaping the promise of cloud computing for higher education. EDUCAUSE Review 44, 52–66 (2009)
4. Johnson, D.: Computing in the clouds. Learning & Leading with Tech. 37, 16–20 (2009)
5. NIST (National Institute of Standards and Technology).: The NIST definition of cloud computing, http://csrc.nist.gov/publications/nistpubs/800-145/SP800-145.pdf
6. Strowd, H.D., Lewis, G.A.: T-check in system-of-systems technologies: Cloud computing. Software Engineering Institute, Pittsburgh (2010)
7. Voorsluys, W., Broberg, J., Buyya, R.: Introduction to cloud computing. In: Buyya, R., Broberg, J., Goscinski, A.M. (eds.) Cloud computing: Principles and Paradigms, pp. 3–41. John Wiley & Sons, Inc. Hoboken (2011)
8. Dyrli, K.O.: The start of a tech revolution. District Administration 45, 31–33 (2009)
9. Johnson, L., Levine, A., Smith, R., Haywood, K.: Key emerging technologies for elementary and secondary education. Tech Directions 70, 33–34 (2010)
10. Behrend, T.S., Wiebe, E.N., London, J.E., Johnson, E.C.: Cloud computing adoption and usage in community colleges. Behaviour & Inf. Tech. 30, 231–240 (2011)
11. Monarch, I.: Information science and information systems: converging or diverging?, http://www.cais-acsi.ca/proceedings/2000/monarch_2000.pdf
12. Zhong, W.J., Li, J.: The research of co-word analysis (1): The process and methods of co-word analysis. J. Inf. 5, 70–72 (2008)
13. ERIC (Education Resources Information Center).: About the ERIC Collection, http://eric.ed.gov/ERICWebPortal/resources/html/collection/about_collection.html
14. Zhang, Q., Cheng, L., Boutaba, R.: Cloud computing: State-of-the-art and research challenges. J. Internet Services and Applications 1, 7–18 (2010)
15. Chen, X.L., Xiao, X.D., Du, F.D.: Study on construction of a keyword-thesaurus switch table based on mutual information. Inf. Studies: Theory & Application 29, 567–569 (2006)
16. Gartner, Gartner says cloud computing will be as influential as e-business, http://www.gartner.com/newsroom/id/707508
17. Erdogmus, H.: Cloud computing: Does nirvana hide behind the nebula? IEEE Software 26, 4–6 (2009)
18. Denton, D.W.: Enhancing instruction through constructivism, cooperative learning, and cloud computing. TechTrends 56, 34–41 (2012)
19. Stevenson, M., Hedberg, J.G.: Head in the clouds: A review of current and future potential for cloud-enabled pedagogies. Educ. Media International 48, 321–333 (2011)
20. He, W., Cernusca, D., Abdous, M.: Exploring Cloud Computing for Distance Learning. Online J. Distance Learning Administration 14 (2011)
21. Crippen, K.J., Archambault, L.: Scaffolded inquiry-based instruction with technology: A signature pedagogy for STEM education. Computers in the Schools 29, 157–173 (2012)
22. Stevenson, M., Hedberg, J.G.: Learning and design with online real-time collaboration. Educational Media International 50, 120–134 (2013)
23. Siegle, D.: Cloud computing: A free technology option to promote collaborative learning. Gifted Child Today 33, 41–45 (2010)
24. Blue, E., Tirotta, R.: The benefits & drawbacks of integrating cloud computing and interactive whiteboards in teacher preparation. TechTrends 55, 3138 (2011)
25. Rabkin, A., Reiss, C., Katz, R., Patterson, D.: Using clouds for MapReduce measurement assignments. ACM Transactions on Computing Educ. 13, 2:1–2:18 (2013)
26. Bristow, R., Dodds, T., Northam, R., Plugge, L.: Cloud computing and the power to choose. Educause Review 45, 14–31 (2010)
27. Jafar, M.J.: A tools-based approach to teaching data mining methods. J. Inf. Tech. Educ. 9, IIP-2–IIP-24 (2010)

28. Chen, L., Yang, L., Gallagher, M., Pailthorpe, B., Sadip, S., Shen, H.T., Li, X.: Introducing cloud computing topics in curricula. J. Inf. Sys. Educ. 23, 315–324 (2012)
29. McCrea, B., Weil, M.: On cloud nine. The Journal, 38, 46, 48, 50–51 (2011)
30. Siegle, D.: Technology: Presentations in the cloud with a twist. Gifted Child Today 34, 54–58 (2011)
31. Dorling, M., Johnstone, E.: The CSI schools project. Educ. in Science 246, 20–21 (2012)
32. Yang, H.H., Yuen, S.C.-Y.: Handbook of research on practices and outcomes in e-learning: Issues and trends. IGI Global, Hershey (2009)
33. Trappler, T.J.: If it's in the cloud, get it on paper: Cloud computing contract issues, http://www.educause.edu/ir/library/pdf/LIVE1034b.pdf
34. Dula, M., Jacobsen, L., Ferguson, T., Ross, R.: Implementing a new cloud computing library management service: A symbiotic approach. Comput. in Libraries 32, pp. 6–11, 37–40 (2012)
35. Hastings, R.: Researching, evaluating, and choosing a backup service in the cloud. Comput. in Libraries 32, 68–71 (2012)
36. Dave, H.: Dynamic space for rent: Using commercial Web hosting to develop a Web 2.0 intranet. J. Web Librarianship 4, 115–127 (2010)
37. Romiszowski, A.J.: Distance learning and cloud computing: 'Just another buzzword or a major e-learning breakthrough?'. Educational Technology 52, 42–45 (2012)
38. Jaeger, P.T., Lin, J., Grimes, J.M.: Cloud computing and information policy: Computing in a policy cloud. J. Inf. Tech. and Politic 5, 269–283 (2008)
39. Buckman, J., Gold, S.: Privacy and data security under cloud computing arrangements: The legal framework and practical do's and don'ts. College and University 88, 10–22 (2012)
40. Ovadia, S.: Navigating the challenges of the cloud. Behavioral & Social Sciences Librarian 29, 233–236 (2010)
41. Yang, H., Yuen, S.C.-Y.: Collective intelligence and e-learning 2.0: Implications of web-based communities and networking. IGI Global, Hershey (2009)
42. Bennett, J., Pence, H.E.: Managing laboratory data using cloud computing as an organizational tool. J. Chemi. Educ. 88, 761–763 (2011)
43. Al-Zoube, M., El-Seoud, S.A., Wyne, M.F.: Cloud computing based e-learning System. Int. J. Distance Educ. Technologies 8, 58–71 (2010)
44. Cheng, J.S., Huang, E., Lin, C.L.: An e-book hub service based on a cloud platform. Int. Review of Research in Open and Distance Learning 13, 39–55 (2012)
45. Webster, M.L., Milson, A.J.: Visualizing economic development with ArcGIS Explorer. Social Educ. 75, 114–117 (2011)
46. Mumba, F., Zhu, M.X.: Development of an innovative interactive virtual classroom system for k-12 education using google app engine. J. Computers in Mathematics and Science Teaching 32, 195–217 (2013)
47. Kim, P., Ng, C.K., Lim, G.: When cloud computing meets with semantic Web: A new design for e-portfolio systems in the social media era. British Journal of Educational Technology 41, 1018–1028 (2010)

Research and Application on Web2.0-Based Sharing Modes of Curriculum Resources

Youru Xie, Jing Bai, Guanjie Li, and Rui Yin

School of Educational Information Technology, South China Normal University,
Guangzhou, China, 510631
xieyouru@aliyun.com

Abstract. Based on the analysis and research of curriculum resources sharing at home and abroad, in this paper, we constructed an overall framework of Web2.0-based sharing modes of curriculum resources. Taking one of the National Quality Courses (awarded by Chinese Ministry of Education to top quality courses offered by universities) "Principles and Methods of Instructional Design", we studied the resources applications of sharing modes based on Blog and Wiki, and verified their effectiveness.

Keywords: Web2.0, Curriculum Resources, Sharing Modes.

1   Background

"The Outline of the National Medium-and Long-Term Program for Education Reform and Development (2010-2020)" clearly states the needs to "establish an open and flexible platform for public service of educational resources, promote the universal sharing of quality education resources". In April 2003, the Chinese Ministry of Education initiated Quality Course Projects for improvement of curriculum and teaching quality in colleges and universities. In order to promote the sharing of National Quality Course, in October 2011, the Ministry of Education issued the "Opinions on the implementation of the National Quality Open Course", and upgraded the original "National Quality Course" into the "Quality Resources Sharing Course (QRSC)" to achieve universal sharing of quality instructional resources. On the other hand, Web2.0 has been infiltrated into the educational applications, its concept is consistent with the ideas of course resources sharing, and provides good technical support for the open sharing of curriculum resources. Massive Open Online Course (MOOC) use Web2.0 technologies, e.g. E-mail, Blogs, Facebook, Wiki as tools for students to discuss and construct learning content, which actively arouse their initiative, consciousness and creativity, and effectively promote openness and sharing of courses. Therefore, the research and application on Web2.0-based sharing modes of curriculum resources have positive theoretical and practical significance.

S.K.S. Cheung et al. (Eds.): ICHL 2014, LNCS 8595, pp. 129–139, 2014.
© Springer International Publishing Switzerland 2014

2   Question

The sharing of curriculum resources is an important way to promote the sustainable development to Quality Course. However, there are still issues yet to be resolved: insufficient availability and stability of resources, imperfect mechanism of updating, and lack of effective sharing platform and interaction mode. With the transformation and upgrading of Quality Course, the research of QRSC has become a hot spot, but the application research of sharing mode is still not perfect. The successful experiences of foreign open educational resources and MOOC lead our eyes to the promoting effect which Web2.0 has made to the openness and sharing of curriculum resources. Web2.0 technology, holding the ideas of people-oriented and sharing, is in consistent with the sharing ideas of curriculum resources. It has also been preliminarily applied in the sharing of curriculum resources, but is not deep enough. Based on this, the research questions are:

- How to integrate the technology and concept of Web2.0 into the sharing mode of curriculum resources ?
- How to verify the effectiveness on the sharing modes of Web2.0-based curriculum resources?

3   Current Situation

3.1   Research on Sharing of Curriculum Resources at Home and Abroad

Domestic research on "quality curriculum resources" mainly focused on four aspects: the pattern of construction, the status of application, the mode of sharing and the comparative study of open educational resources at home and abroad. Among them, the pattern of construction is most popular, and the mode of sharing has increasingly become the hot spot of researchers, but still is not deep enough. Analysis of literature shows that the sharing of quality curriculum resources have some problems: the availability and stability of curriculum resources needs to be strengthened, the updating mechanism is not perfect, there are lack of effective sharing modes and interactive communication. With the transformation and upgrading of Quality Course, related studies also sprang up. But the research content mainly focused on the construction process and method of QRSC. For example, Lailin Hu (2012) put forward to a kind of strategy for QRSC on the basis of theoretical analysis, which is "cohesion-transformation-upgrade- innovation" [1]. There are few literatures to study the sharing modes of curriculum resources.

In 2001, Open Course Ware (OCW) Project was initiated at the Massachusetts Institute of Technology (MIT) in the United States, which made the ideas of educational resources "open", "shared" and "spread" around the world [2]. In 2002, "Open Educational Resources (OER)" was proposed for the first time. OER abroad have been widely recognized, through the analysis of relevant research literatures, we could draw some successful experiences of OER. It obtains technology from standard resources, follows the standards of educational technology, and supports the sharing of content.

It provides updated information of resources via RSS, etc. It promotes the sharing of resources by the way of hosting media resources on the professional management platform of media resources. After the completion of content creation and publishing, OER project will provide tools for classification, indexing and collaborative interaction which supports users to find and use resources. These experiences bring beneficial enlightenment to the sharing of curriculum resources.

3.2   Application Research on Web2.0 in the Sharing of Curriculum Resources

In China, there was not enough application research on Web2.0 in the sharing of curriculum resources. Only several courses adopted the mode of Web2.0, such as the National Quality Courses (Online Education) in 2008 "Money and Banking" and "Discrete Mathematics". In these courses, learning resources are built by QQ space & Wiki, so independent and collaborative learning modes are also constructed by QQ group, Wiki, VOD and other tools. Some scholars focused on theoretical research related with courses construction, such as Lianbo Wen (2011) and Chenglin Huan (2008). Both of them respectively discussed promoting the sharing application of quality courses based on Blog and Moodle. As the showing and learning platform of QRSC, the website "Icourses" pays more attention to interactive function, and integrates into Microblog, BBS and Groups, etc. It adds new functions and Apps, such as Learning mates' Circle, Interactive Q & A, which make online interaction more convenient. In the research about construction strategy of QRSC, Lailin Hu (2012) mentioned that a variety of software based on Web2.0, such as Blog, Wiki, SNS, are used in the field of education. They supported the creation, storage, transmission, maintenance and management of micro-content which made it possible to enhance interaction of QRSC. But relevant application research is not enough in-depth, especially theoretical exploration and practical application is relatively less. There are still great potentials and effects on promoting the sharing of curriculum resource to be discovered and studied.

In other countries, when more and more universities and educational institutions choose to share their open quality resources, MOOC emerges [3]. MOOC would not only provide videos, text materials, and online Q & A, but also provide learners with a variety of user-interactive communities and establish the mechanism of interactive participation. MOOC uses Web2.0 technology (E-mail, Blog, Facebook, Wiki, etc.) as tools for students to discuss and constructs the learning content. The roles of students shift from consumers to developers and founders of content; meanwhile, teaching contents are generated dynamically according to participation of students. Under the support of technology tools, MOOC can positively mobilize student's initiative, consciousness and creativity [4]. It is visible that Web2.0 technologies play good roles in promoting the sharing of curriculum resource.

4   Research Process and Methods

Our research process and methods include the following tasks:

- To make a comprehensive understanding of current situation and existing problems about research on the sharing of curriculum resources by use of the *literature research method.*
- To study the construction principles and the overall framework of Web2.0-based sharing modes of curriculum resources, combining the concept and features of Web2.0.
- To use *the case-study approach* to study two typical sharing modes based on Blog and Wiki, relying on the National Quality Courses "Principles and Methods of Instructional Design"(upgraded into NQRSC in 2013) of the South China Normal University (SCNU) . Research objects are 11 undergraduate students of Grade 2010 Class 1 and 13 full-time professional postgraduate students of Grade 2012, and all of them are from School of Information Technology in Education of SCNU.
- To evaluate the effectiveness on Web2.0-based sharing modes of curriculum resources, synthetically using the *methods of evaluation research and social network analysis.*

5   The Construction on Web2.0-based Sharing Modes of Curriculum Resources

5.1   Principles of Construction

The study puts forward to the following principles to highlight Web2.0's core concept and technical characteristics according to Postmodernism Curriculum Theory, Connectionist Theory, Theory of Six Degrees of Separation [5] [6].

Dynamic Nature
On the one hand, the construction team will form new resources by applying the latest curriculum reform achievements and advanced teaching ideas into teaching. On the other hand, we need encourage users to share their own relevant curriculum resources with the public.
Integration
On the application and selection of tools, we use the Tool Concept advocated by Connectionist for reference and pay attention to the polymerized application of different Web2.0 tools.
Openness
We combine Theory of Six Degrees of Separation with the construction of sharing network of resources and knowledge, and focus on the use of software tools to establish contact with other learners or experts and form sharing network of resources.
Portability
Facing the complex situation of the course construction projects in China, the sharing modes of curriculum resources should be easy to use and be compatible with existing platform of network teaching.

5.2   The Overall Framework

According to the above principles, we got the overall framework of Web2.0-based sharing modes of curriculum resources (Fig.1). The main characteristics of this sharing mode are:

- The usage of resources and platform interaction are fully open to assure the open sharing of curriculum resources;
- The curriculum resources are updated dynamically, enriched and improved continuously;
- The supporting technology is flexible, and is easy to use with high portability.

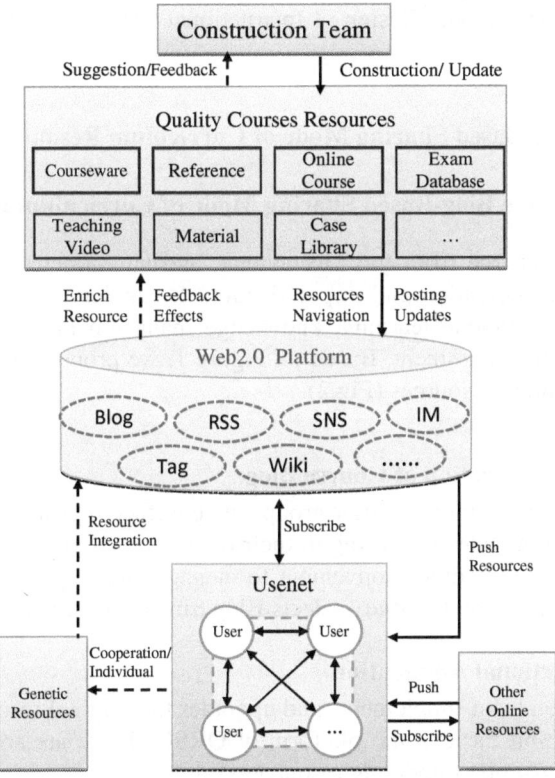

Fig. 1. The Overall Framework of Web2.0-based Sharing Modes of Curriculum Resources

6   The Application on Web2.0-based Sharing Modes of Curriculum Resource

This study focused on two typical sharing modes of curriculum resources based on Blog and Wiki.

6.1   Research Design

Use the case-study approach and choose the objects of research. They are 11 under-graduate students of Grade 2010 Class 1 and 13 full-time professional postgraduate students of Grade 2012 from School of Information Technology in Education of SCNU.

In the case-study application of Blog-based sharing modes of curriculum resources, we select three topics related to "Instructional Mode and Strategies" as contents of research. They are "Instructional Mode and Design based on the Theory of Activity", "Instructional Mode and Design based on the Construction of Knowledge", "Design of Network Teaching Evaluation ".

In the case-study application of Wiki-based sharing modes of curriculum resources, we select the topic about "Design of Instructional Process (Mode)" as contents of research.

6.2   The Blog-Based Sharing Mode of Curriculum Resources

6.3   Propose the Blog-Based Sharing Mode of Curriculum Resources

Blog is open and free from form to content, and has the characteristics of sharing, interaction and integration and popularization. It can serve as a tool of information dissemination, new-style learning, knowledge management, interactive communication and portfolio assessment. Based on Figure 1, we propose the blog-based sharing mode of curriculum resources (Fig.2).

6.2.2   The Construction of Course Blog

Blog Sina has a wide range of user groups, its interface is aesthetics, simple and users can set up custom styles according to their own interests and hobbies. It offers a rich variety of function modules convenient to manage, and supports adding self-defined components. Therefore, the study selects Blog Sina to construct Course Blog.

6.2.3   Instructional Application

The construction team supplements and upgrades the original resources of above three topics, and exhibit through the platform of QRSC. There are some pages of Course Blog and information of updating resources (Fig.3).

The Sharing of Original Curriculum Resources

Users can subscribe to or focus on Course Blog, thus forming a user network of quality curriculum resources. Users access to the website of quality curriculum resources by post link, and study or consolidate the knowledge by watching instructional videos and presentations, analysis of instructional courseware and cases. When the users have doubts, opinions or suggestions in the process of using resources, they can communicate or discuss with the team and other users through Blog Comments, Reviews and other modules. The team can give timely reply to suggestions or questions for users.

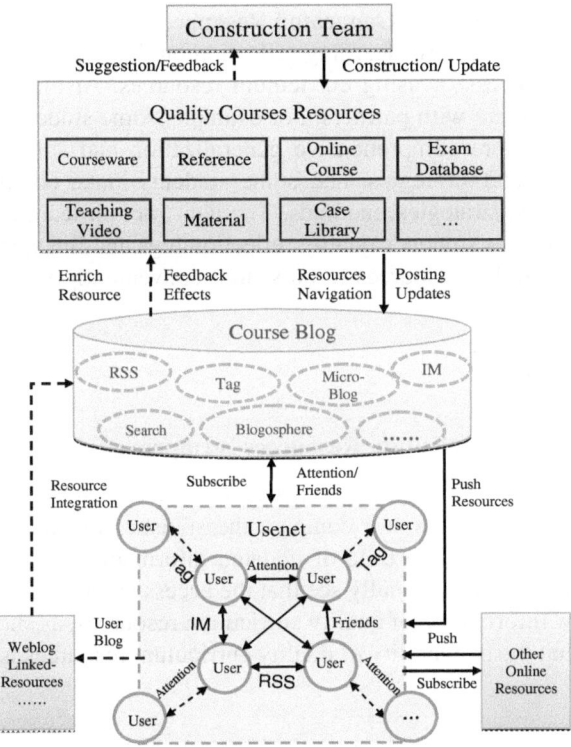

Fig. 2. The Blog-based Sharing Mode of Curriculum Resources

Fig. 3. Course Blog and Updated Resources Information of "Principles and Methods of Instructional Design"

The Sharing of Dynamically Generated Resources

Students can record their own learning reflection on the Blog with the learning narrative way in the process of using curriculum resources. At the same time, they can communicate and share with partners. For example, some students write overviews in the post to make more comprehensive generalization and summarization about instructional modes and strategies; and some students make comparative analysis to instructional modes, strategies, methods. The construction team integrates the generated resources, such as student's quality reflection logs and links, into the Course Blog and becomes renewable resources to be shared conveniently for users of other curriculum resources.

6.2.4   Effect Analysis

The Availability of Curriculum Resources is Improved.

In order to make clear the relationship between the access amount of Course Blog and quality curriculum resources, we compare the statistics about the access amount of Course Blog with the release time of updated information of quality curriculum resources. From that, we can visually see that the access amount reach a peak at the time of releasing new information of quality curriculum resources, as shown in Fig.4, which also illustrate that the availability of quality curriculum resources is improved.

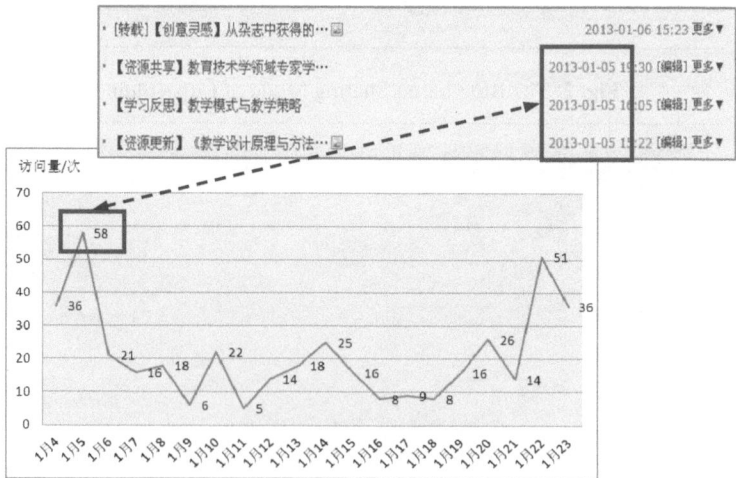

Fig. 4. the Relationship between Access Amount of Course Blog and Quality Curriculum Resources

The Updating Mechanism of Curriculum Resources is Improved.

In the case study, updated resources are from three aspects: the created and used resources by teachers of every topic during instructional process, the generated resources in the process of learning by users of quality curriculum resources and the generated resources in the process of updating the resources continually by the construction team of quality curriculum resources. The updated information of three kinds of resources can be released in time through Course Blog by the construction team of quality curriculum resources, thus forming a relatively perfect updating mechanism of quality curriculum resources.

The Sharing Scope of Curriculum Resource is Expanded.

In the case study, Course Blog, with the total access amount of 1864 times, has good effect and sharing. By using analysis method of social network to carry out specific analysis on the sharing network of quality curriculum resources (Fig.5), we can see relatively stable network of users between teams of research objects. So, the application on Blog-based sharing mode of curriculum resources improves the sharing rate of curriculum resources and expands the sharing scope of curriculum resources.

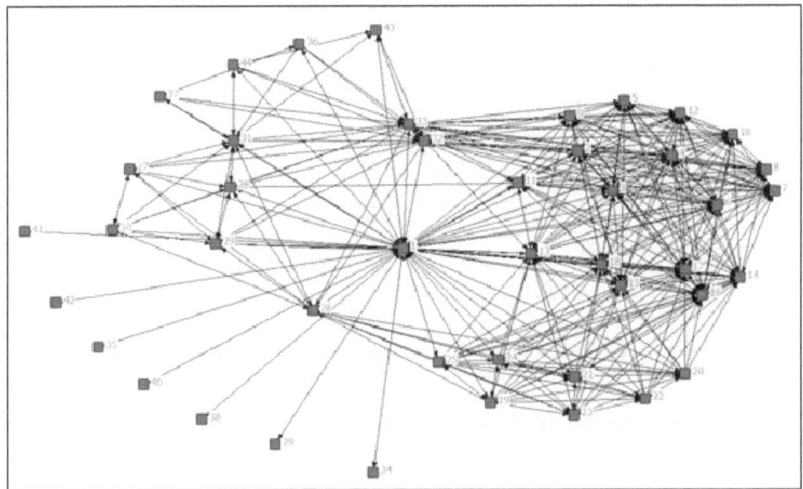

Fig. 5. the Sharing Network of Quality Curriculum Resources

6.3   The Wiki-Based Sharing Mode of Curriculum Resources

6.3.1   Propose the Wiki-Based Sharing Mode of Curriculum Resources

Wiki has the characteristics of information dissemination convenient, free and open, collaborative sharing and easy to grow. It not only emphasizes sharing, but also pays more attention to build resources on the basis of sharing, and constantly enriches the original curriculum resources. It provides the platform of collaboration for users and implements the sharing of curriculum resources based on collaborated tasks. We propose the Wiki-based sharing mode of curriculum resources (Fig.6).

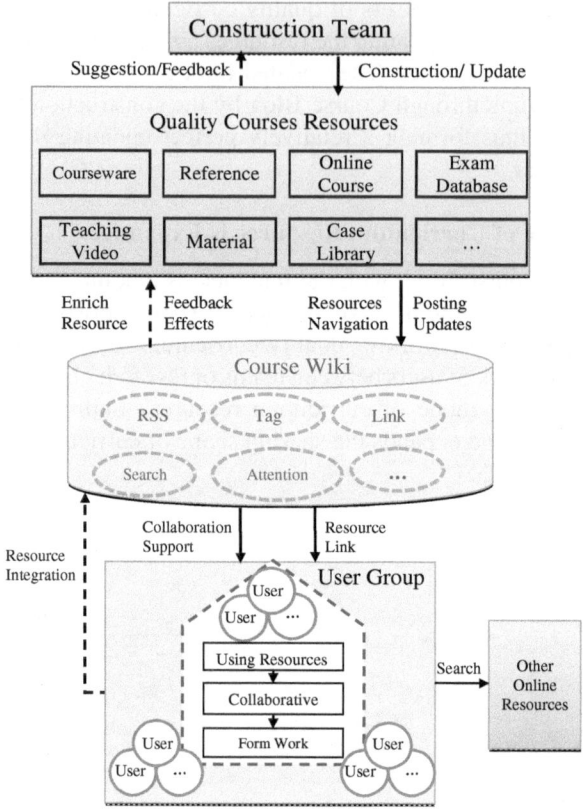

Fig. 6. the Wiki-based Sharing Mode of Curriculum Resources

6.3.2   The Construction of Course Wiki

Small Interactive Encyclopedia, which has stable function, friendly interface and many users, is a platform provided by Interactive Encyclopedia free. It supports self-defined styles of users, adding self-defined components and other functional modules, easy to manage and operate. Therefore, this study selects Small Encyclopedia site to construct Course Wiki.

6.3.3   Instructional Application

We select the topic of "Design of Instructional Process (Mode)" from "Principles and Methods of Instructional Design" as contents of research. During the study, the students are divided into five groups, and each group is 4-6 people. They complete the practical tasks of project collaboratively and make a design of instructional process (mode). Students can get access to quality curriculum resources directly through the links offered by Course Wiki platform and they can communicate on that platform, edit the works together, and exhibit their group works through Course Wiki.

6.3.4   Effect Analysis

Evaluation group was established in this case study. According to the pre-established "Evaluation Index System of Instructional Design Ability", we evaluate the original and final version of instructional design draft respectively for each group, and the results are shown in Table 1. From Table 1, we can find that team members significantly improved their abilities of instructional design through application sharing of curriculum resources and collaborative communication.

Table 1. Evaluation Scores of Group Works

Group Name	Name of Instructional Design Draft	Score of Original Draft	Score of Final Draft
"Learning and Thinking"	"The Life System of Botanic"	85	95.5
"We do"	"The Refraction of Light"	81.5	93
"First"	"Set Up the Showing Effects of PPT"	80	91.5
"The power of ID"	"The Nuclear Structure Of Atomic"	81	92
"New Moon Empire"	"The Production and Beautification of Slides"	82.5	93

7   Conclusions

Based on the analysis and research of curriculum resources sharing at home and abroad, the study constructed the overall framework of Web2.0-based sharing modes of curriculum resources. On this basis, relying on the National Quality Courses "Principles and Methods of Instructional Design", the practical applications on Blog and Wiki-based sharing modes of resources are carried out and the effectiveness is verified, including improving the availability and updating mechanism of curriculum resources, expanding the sharing scope, improving professional abilities of students.

References

1. Hu, L.L.: Research on Construction Strategies of Quality Curriculum Resources. J. Journal of Distance Education 6, 80–85 (2012)
2. MIT Open Course Ware (EB/OL) (April 10, 2012), http://ocw.mit.edu/about/site-statistics/monthly-reports/
3. Course (EB/OL) (January 23, 2014), http://en.wikipedia.org/wiki/MOOC
4. Wang, Y., Zhang, J.L., Zhang, B.H.: MOOC: Characteristics Analysis Based on Typical Projects and Its Enlightenment. J. Journal of Distance Education. 4, 67–75 (2013)
5. Wang, X.: Curriculum Studies: Modern and Postmodern. Technology and Education Press, Shanghai (2013)
6. Siemens, G.: Knowing Knowledge. Translated by Zhan, Q.L. East China Normal University Press, Shanghai (2009)

The Development of an Augmented Reality Framework for Constructing Circuit Learning Aids[*]

Chen Qiao and Xiangdong Chen

Department of Education and Information Technology,
East China Normal University
No. 3663, North Zhongshan Road, Shanghai, China
qiaochen@outlook.com, xdchen@deit.ecnu.edu.cn

Abstract. The potential of Augmented Reality (AR) as an effective approach to support learning has been discovered in numerous research studies and practical cases today. With its power to enhance the expressiveness of the real world and its multiple platform implementation choices, AR brings new visions in the organization of virtual and physical resources, thus providing a powerful hybrid learning environment. While there exits popular open source and commercial SDKs for AR application development, a way for more agile and domain specific implementation is required by non-professional developers as teachers. In this work, an AR framework was developed to support AR circuit construction. Core design issues such as object modeling, algorithms for circuit recognition and calculation were discussed, and the work flow was also illustrated by implementing a circuit demo with the framework.

Keywords: Augmented Reality, Learning Aids, Framework.

1 Introduction

Augmented Reality (AR), a concept of overlapping computer-generated objects such as video, sound or 3D modules over the live view of a real-world environment, has achieved remarkable growth and progress over the past decades. There accumulate numerous research and application outcomes of AR in virtually every field, including military, medicine, engineering, robotics, design, entertainment, advertisement as well as education [1, 2].

Like its role in many other fields, AR brings educators more imagination on instructional design and learning materials preparation. More and more education researches and projects are involving AR, among which topics and study methods vary greatly. The NMC (New Media Consortium), an international community of experts in educational technology, in its yearly published Horizon Report has twice (in year 2010 and 2011) predicted that AR will see widespread use on education in the near future.

---

[*] Periodical achievement of the project: The development and application of Augmented Reality E-books funded by Ministry of Education of the People's Republic of China (No. 12YJA880012).

S.K.S. Cheung et al. (Eds.): ICHL 2014, LNCS 8595, pp. 140–151, 2014.
© Springer International Publishing Switzerland 2014

Many research cases today have shown AR's potential of entering classrooms in the form of AR books, AR edutainment, knowledge representation tools, etc. [3].

With the prevalence of AR technology, endeavors to make easier ways of AR application development have resulted in various open source or commercial AR SDKs and IDEs. Designers now can implement their ideas conveniently, with no or little programming background. Following this trend, the main objective of this work was to develop a framework for AR circuit construction. Circuits made with the AR framework can be used as learning materials for relevant knowledge, such as basic parallel and series structures.

2   AR as Learning Aids

Over the recent years, many classroom-level AR applications have been developed and applied in practice. Despite that the forms of AR entering classrooms differentiate, they have formed several directions that yield considerable outputs. We discuss three of the many forms: AR books, AR edutainment and AR knowledge representation tools.

AR Books. AR books enhance the experience of traditional books by offering readers interactive 3D models, sounds and other information that help interpret page contents. Due to the AR features, AR books can convey information that plain texts, static graphs and illustrations cannot convey, and thus enrich ways of accessing book contents and support a kind of creative reading experience.

AR Edutainment. Unlike traditional educational games, educational AR games base their scenario on the real world environment, and extend it with virtual data and resources. AR features offer game designers unlimited resources to create connections and relationships between virtual and real objects, which are not constrained by time, shape, size, energy and other physical natures, and they also enable game players to better immerge themselves in the game scenario and interact with real or virtual resources.

AR Knowledge Representation Tools. There are always situations where a particular concept or some certain knowledge cannot be well displayed or demonstrated in the real classroom environment. AR knowledge representation tools possess the inherited AR features to enhance the expressiveness of the classroom environment, making it possible to represent phenomena that happen in vacuum, deep ocean, micro world, and many other normally unreachable conditions, or display extra information aligned with the real object being observed, e.g. the voltage value of a bulb, the inner structure of a physical texture, etc.

3   Related Work and Projects

Technically, AR is only one approach of the many to merging the virtual world with the real environment. Related technologies, or terms, such as Virtual Reality, Augmented Virtuality and Mixed Reality, all have close relationships with it, but are slightly different. Their connections can be displayed in a segment with Real and Virtual Environment as endpoints (Figure 1) and a connecting line indicating the

Mixed Reality transitional gap, in which AR stands closer to the Real end, meaning that its base is the Real Environment.

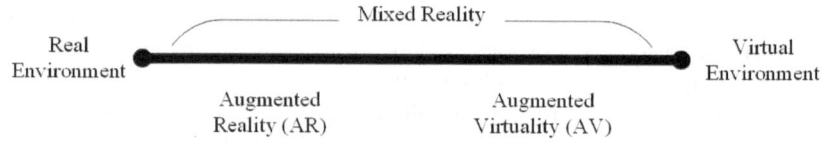

Fig. 1. Milgram's Reality-Virtuality Continuum (Adapted from [1])

The typical 4-layer architecture of an AR system can be described as what the Figure 2 shows. The lower 2 layers comprise the basics of the system, and are where SDK providers focus to relieve the work load of application developers. The application layer connects the low-layer AR building blocks with the upper client layer by organizing functioning modules to meet certain client requirements.

User
Application

Interaction Devices & Techniques	Presentation	Authoring
Tracking & Registration	Display Technology	Rendering

Fig. 2. Typical Architecture for AR System (Adapted from [4])

Several famous low-level AR SDKs or highly integrated IDEs are ARToolKit series, Metaio, Vuforia, D'fusion, Wikitude, Layer, etc. While ARToolKit is one of the most important open source AR SDKs, the others mentioned are all commercial SDKs or IDEs with powerful service support teams. In addition to the classical frame marker based AR registration and tracking techniques, modern commercial SDKs are employing many more ways to align the virtual with the real, for example, through sensory input of GPS, electronic gyro compass or natural flat textures, 3D objects, etc.

3.1   The ARToolKit Project

ARToolKit is originally a C/C++ framework for creating real-time AR applications. Because it is an open source API library and one of its license is GPLv2, it is a good choice for research or other non-commercial use. A family of products have extended from the original version, and now there are ARToolKit (C/C++), NyARToolKit (Java), FLARToolKit (Actionscript), SLARToolKit (Silverlight), versions for Android and iOS, etc.[5]

Although the ARToolKit APIs are efficient and flexible enough to be integrated into clients' projects, its tracking methods is solely through square marker patterns. The workflow of ARToolKit can be described as follows, and it is also the typical process of how a vision based AR system works.

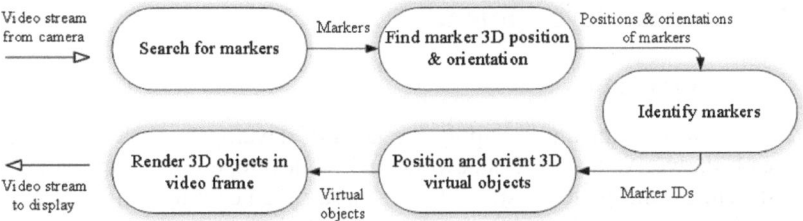

Fig. 3. Work Flow of the ARToolKit (Adapted from [5])

3.2   Commercial Solutions

The most popular commercial solutions to AR development are provided by Total Immersion, Metaio and Qualcomm, with their products D'fusion, Metaio SDK and Vuforia respectively [6-8]. They encapsulate specifics of development details by providing high level APIs and IDEs. In addition, many useful functioning modules are contained for reuse.

Here we call these commercial solutions modern AR SDKs, because they feature in that they are easy to use, have multiple approaches to aligning the virtual with the real, and support socialized use and sharing. Modern SDKs make full use of the mobile platform features, e.g. sensory data from electronic gyro compass, GPS, gravity and acceleration sensor as sources of real world perception for real-virtual mixture. Powerful as the SDKs are, they all have their own advantages and disadvantages, e.g. D'fusion allows developers to build the main part of their applications (both mobile and non-mobile platforms) in D'fusion Studio, and export the package for non-PC platform encapsulation, but the disadvantage is also obvious: it sacrifices the flexibility of development targeting non-PC platforms.

We compared the free version of the 3 commercial solutions targeting Android platform development, and found that Vuforia is best at flexibility, for it not only offers Java APIs, but also allows developers to call its C/C++ APIs for Android NDK level development; D'fusion supports most quick and convenient implementations along with a highly effective target recognition algorithm; Metaio supports the most ways of real world registration and tracking; Both three offer rich interactions between real and virtual objects.

3.3   More Specialized Solutions

While the above solutions are for general purpose development, there are also domain specific solutions that help implement a certain kind of AR application. In education, for example, ZooBurst is a helpful tool for creating AR books for interactive reading and learning. It provides teachers and students with easy ways to make their own AR books, and thus new ways in which they can tell stories, deliver presentations, write reports and express complex ideas [9].

4   Framework Development

4.1   Project Description

The AR Framework is meant to supply the need of developing such AR applications as Figure 4 shows. With the Framework, client developers can design circuits of various structures and patterns standing for circuit elements to build AR circuits as they wish. The end user of the AR circuit can fix different circuit elements (indicated by markers) in the circuit board, scan the connected circuit with a web camera and observe the changes of values of voltage, current and resistance of its components.

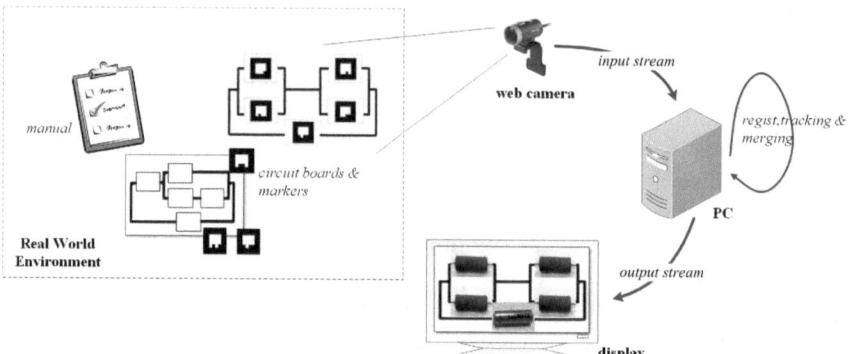

Fig. 4. Work Flow of an AR Circuit Developed by the Framework

4.2   Core Design Issues

Since we can apply third party libraries to AR registration and marker tracking, the next is to give the tracked makers electronic attributes and locate their positions in circuits. The computer can then calculate the values of electronic attributes and display them in the screen. To achieve these goals, we developed Circuit Expression Generation Algorithm (CEGA), Circuit Expression Calculation Algorithm (CECA) and used Composite design pattern in our design.

CEGA for Recognizing Circuit Structure. We use a postfix expression to describe the structure of an AR circuit, the mapping relation is shown in Figure 5, in which symbol & and # stands for series connection and parallel connection respectively.

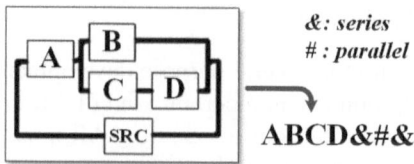

Fig. 5. A Sample Case of Mapping between Circuit and Its Expression

Because the AR Framework delays the exact structure of circuit decided by the client developers, it requires that client developers record the component connection information in the form of directed graph in profiles that can be read by the program. Thus the flow chart of CECA can be shown as Figure 6. With input of graphs indicating the structure of the circuit, CECA outputs the corresponding circuit expression. Nested sub-circuits are calculated by applying the recursion technique.

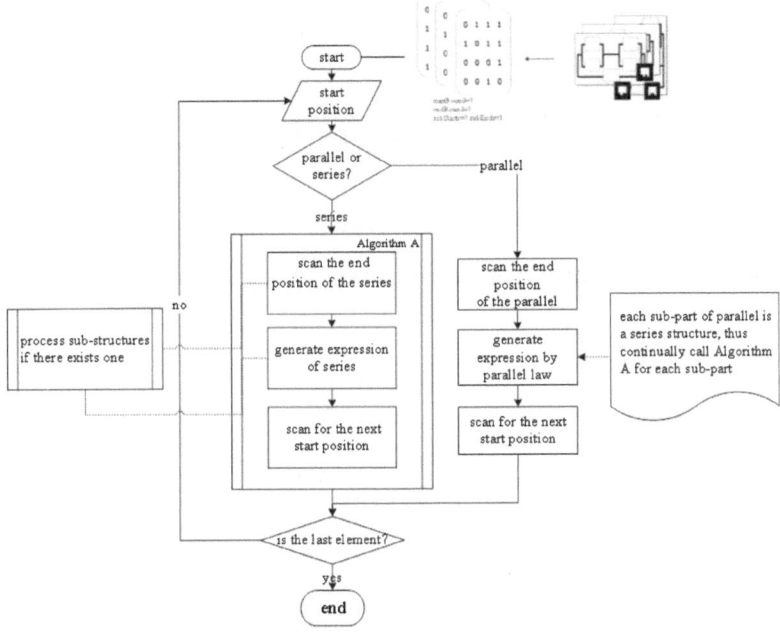

Fig. 6. Flow Chart of the Circuit Expression Generation Algorithm

CECA Implementing Composite Design Pattern for Circuit Calculation. The input of CECA is the expression generated by CEGA, and CECA calculates attribute values of all the components in the circuit. The algorithm is based on the object oriented design pattern of Composite that aimed at eliminating the differences between leaf nodes and composite nodes when they are processed together [10]. The fact that when we calculate a circuit we are continuingly merging the resistance values of electronic components according to series or parallel calculation laws until finally getting one sole merged virtual component, and that applying source values we work out the sole component's voltage and current and then backward calculate all the left circuit components provides evidence that the Composite pattern fits our situation. In our case, real components (indicated by markers) are regarded as leaf nodes, and merged virtual components can be seen as composite nodes. Hence we designed the abstract model of electronic components in the AR Framework as Figure 7 shows. Both classes, ConcreteR (leaf) and VirtualR (composite node), override the inherited abstract method "calculate (double u)". VirtualR, after calculating its own values, should further calculate the values of its merged components following the series or parallel connection law, and at last call the "calculate (double u)" methods of them. The program can thus recursively calculate all the components in the circuit.

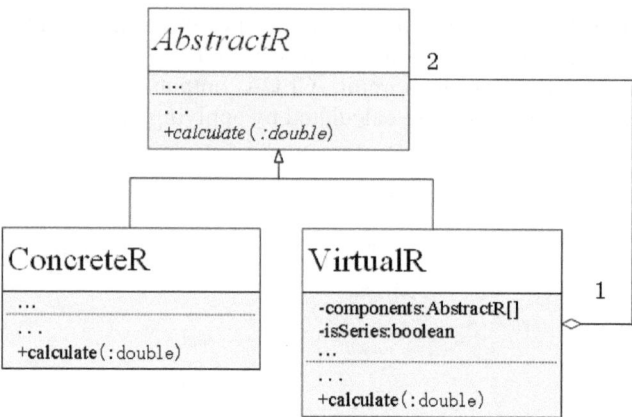

Fig. 7. The implementation of Composite Design Pattern in Framework Design

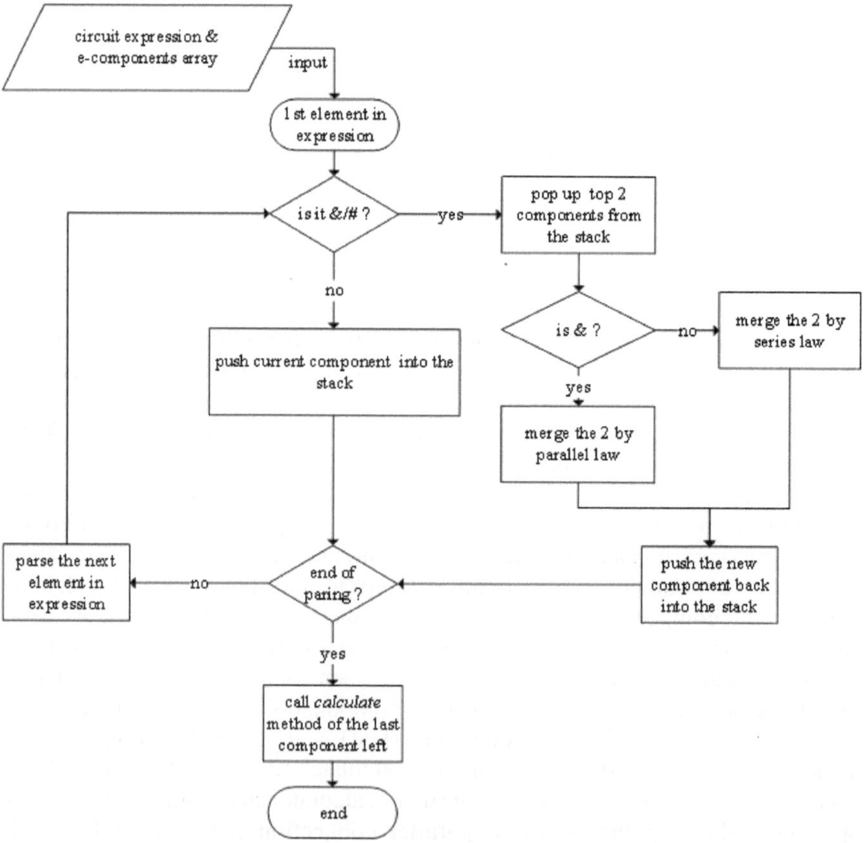

Fig. 8. Flow Chart of the Circuit Expression Calculation Algorithm

CECA uses a stack to record and do merge operations. It parses a circuit expression, and meanwhile, merges components in series or parallel ways when encountering a connection symbol. The end of parsing also leads to a final merged electronic component, leaving the last step to call its "calculate (double u)" method, and it will recursively finish the whole calculation. Figure 8 shows the process of CECA operation.

Design Implementation. There were mainly two phases in developing the AR Framework. Firstly, we developed the AR Circuit Software Development Kit (ARCSDK) that encapsulates the main algorithms and domain specific classes. Then we integrated the ARCSDK with nyar4psg SDK[1] (for AR purpose) to realize the full function of the AR Framework.

We chose Java as our programming language, and spent the first period of development in Eclipse IDE, and the latter in Processing, a powerful computational arts and visualization library and IDE.

We implemented 3 kinds of electronic components: changeable power source, bulb, and changeable resistor in our demo. The bulbs can change color depth according to their electronic energy, and the power source and resistor can both increase and decrease their values through control patterns.

After editing circuit board and selecting markers with the AR Framework, we created our demo AR circuit as the picture shows bellow.

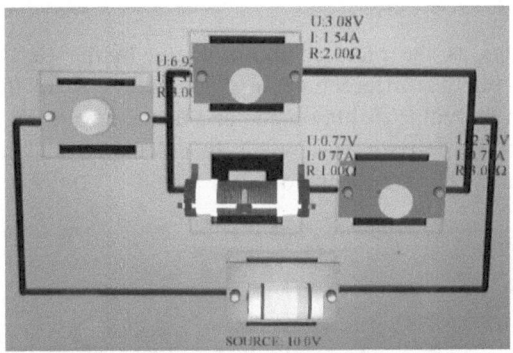

Fig. 9. Screen Shot of an AR Circuit Demo Developed by the Framework

5   Sample Implementation Case

As a sample implementation, we used the AR Framework to construct a circuit.

5.1   Constructing a Circuit

Firstly, we designed the board indicating a circuit structure, and made tracking markers standing for bulbs with 1Ω, 2Ω and 3Ω resistance values,1 changeable

---

[1] NyARToolKit for Processing, a family member of ARToolKit.

resistor(ranging from 1Ω to 20 Ω), and 1 electronic source power(10 V). In addition, we made two markers as controllers to increase or decrease the values of changeable resistor. Secondly, we created property files to record the circuit structure information and the markers with their meanings. Finally, we modified the initialization file of the Framework to load our circuit structure and marker information files. After finishing these steps, we had constructed our own AR circuit.

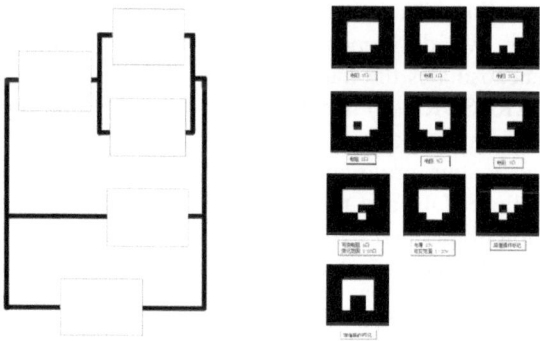

Fig. 10. Sample Design of a Circuit Board with Tracking Markers

5.2   Result Check

Our AR circuit plays as the pictures show below. In the first picture, bulbs with different electronic energy differentiate in color darkness; in the second and third pictures, we turn on the value display mode and use controller to change the value of changeable resistor. The circuit was precisely calculated and its change was also rightly displayed on its electronic components.

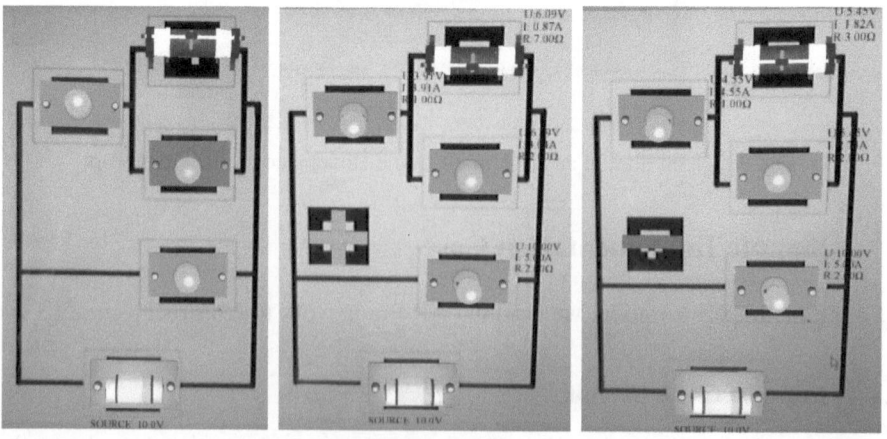

Fig. 11. Screen Shot of the Playing AR Circuit with Marker Controlled Human Computer Interactions

6   Sample Usage of the Generated Circuit Learning Aid

In this section we developed a self-learning case in which the learner was guided by a learning manual (real resource) to explore e-circuit related laws with the aid created using our framework. Usage snapshots were provided below.

Warm Up. The learner reviewed the prerequisite knowledge and did the warming up exercises (Fig. 12).

Observe and Record Phenomena by Interacting with the Learning Aid. The learner arranged circuit elements, modified changeable resistance according to tips provided by the learning manual, and recorded the observed information in the manual (Fig. 13, 14, 15, 16, 17).

Processing Raw Data. The learner drew graphs according to the recorded data, looking for possible laws (Fig. 18).

Conclude Findings and Do Independent Research. In the last stage, the learner concluded his learning work, did some independent research and recorded the results in the manual.

Fig. 12. Snapshot of Warming Up Stage

Fig. 13. Snapshot of Arranging AR Circuit

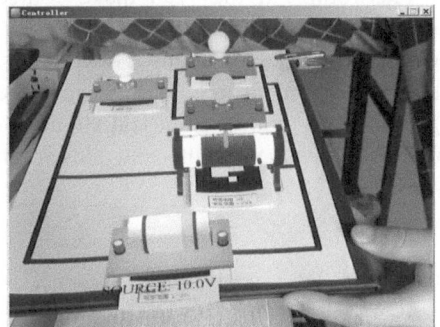

Fig. 14. AR Circuit (Normal Mode)

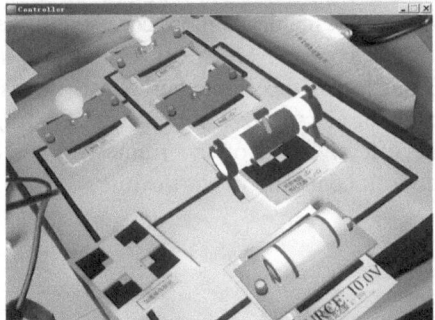

Fig. 15. Snapshot of Increasing Resistance Values

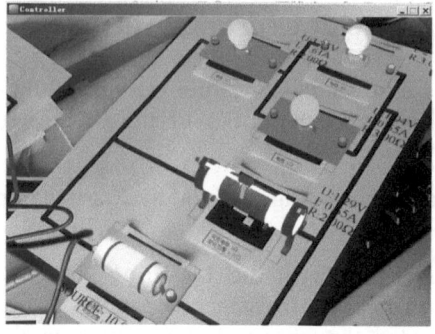

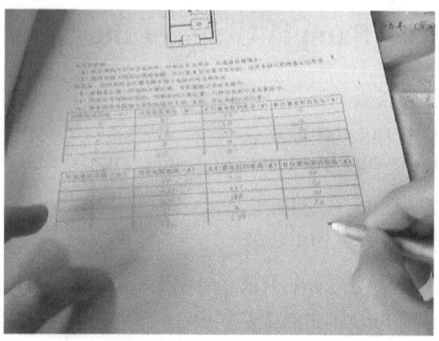

Fig. 16. AR Circuit (Numerical Mode)   **Fig. 17.** Snapshot of Data Recording

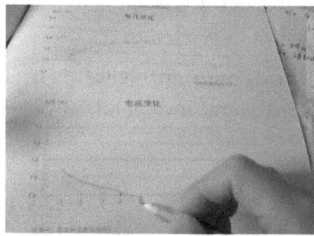

Fig. 18. Snapshot of Raw Data Processing in Learning Manual

7   Summary and Future Work

With its ability to enhance the expressiveness of the real-world environment, and the multiple choices in platform implementation, Augmented Reality is a powerful way to support hybrid learning.

To make AR more convenient to approach, it is necessary to offer easy-to-use AR SDKs to satisfy the development requirement of ordinary people. Teachers can also benefit more from the application of AR in classrooms, if they can make course related AR materials more conveniently and at will.

In this work an AR Framework was developed for constructing AR circuits. Besides that the framework itself needs further improvement, e.g. supporting more kinds of electronic components including capacitors and diodes, empirical studies of the effectiveness of the framework or its application values in the real classroom environment remain worthwhile.

References

1. Azuma, R., Baillot, Y., Behringer, R., Feiner, S., Julier, S., MacIntyre, B.: Recent Advances in Augmented Reality. J. Computer Graphics and Applications 21(6), 34–47 (2001)
2. Van Krevelen, D.W.F., Poelman, R.: A Survey of Augmented Reality Technologies, Applications and Limitations. J. The International Journal of Virtual Reality 9(2), 1–20 (2010)

3. Yuen, S.C.Y., Yaoyuneyong, G., Johnson, E.: Augmented Reality: An Overview and Five Directions for AR in Education. J. Journal of Educational Technology Development and Exchange 4(1), 119–140 (2011)
4. Bimber, O., Raskar, R.: Spatial Augmented Reality: Merging Real and Virtual Worlds: A Modern Approach to Augmented Reality. A.K. Peters Ltd., Natick (2005)
5. ARToolKit Home Page, http://www.hitl.washington.edu/artoolkit/
6. Total Immersion, Inc.,
   http://www.t-immersion.com/products/dfusion-suite
7. Metaio GmbH, http://www.metaio.com/
8. Qualcomm Connected Experiences, Inc., https://www.vuforia.com/
9. ZooBurst llc., http://www.zooburst.com/
10. Metsker, S.J., Wake, W.C.: Design Patterns in Java. Addison-Wesley Professional, Boston (2006)

A Mahjong-Like Game of English Vocabulary Spelling

Cheng-Yu Tsai[1], Jenq-Muh Hsu[2,*], Hung-Hsu Tsai[3],
Pao-Ta Yu[1], and Wen-Feng Huang[1]

[1] Dept. of Computer Science & Inf. Engineering, Nat. Chung Cheng University, Taiwan
[2] Dept. of Computer Science & Information Engineering, Nat. Chiayi University, Taiwan
[3] Dept. of Information Management, Nat. Formosa University, Taiwan
{tcy97p,csipty,hwf100m}@cs.ccu.edu.tw, hsujm@mail.ncyu.edu.tw,
thh@nfu.edu.tw

Abstract. With rapid development of the world globalization, the role of English has become an international language for people conversation. In fact, people know it but they often have no good ways to learn English efficiently. Sometimes, some people think that the procedure of learning English is boring. Therefore, it is an important issue how to engage and encourage people to effectively learn English. Many researches and experiments had indicated that the game-based learning is a joyful approach for learning. Chinese Mahjong is a traditional Chinese game for gambling and entertainment. The game rule of Mahjong is to collect the related cards combining a card sequence or the same cards in a triple pair. In the same, spelling the English vocabulary is also combined the letters to form a word. Thus, this paper tries to design and implement a Mahjong-like multi-party game spelling the English vocabulary for learners in English learning. That is, the learners play the game with other peer learners via the Internet to promote their spelling abilities of English vocabulary in multi-party networked game.

Keywords: Collaborative Learning, Game-based Learning, Vocabulary Spelling, Mahjong-like Game.

1   Introduction

In recent years, digital game-based learning has widely appreciated and received widespread attention by educators. According to the study, games are attractive and educational[1][2]. With the rise of the computer-assisted instruction and the network additionally, applications and methods of educational games expand constantly.

Applying computer games in learning is able to enhance enjoyments, and encourage students to learn topics which they originally feel bored. Students are also willing to invest much time and more efforts in gathering information, solving problems, learning during the process of interaction with classmates in the learning world and giving rise to learning intentions[3]. In this research we combine teaching contents with competitive natures of games, and their theories are based on

---

* Corresponding aurhor.

S.K.S. Cheung et al. (Eds.): ICHL 2014, LNCS 8595, pp. 152–163, 2014.

competitive and cooperative learning. We developed a Mahjong-like game to spell the English vocabularies through touchable devices. By the way, we also focus on students' cooperative learning in groups and adopt competitive game modes to attract them to learn English words. Most importantly, we can test learners with English words which they spell in the game to check their learning effects at last.

This paper is organized as follows. Section 2 briefly introduces relative technologies and learning theories, such as game-based learning, competitive learning, cooperative learning, zone of proximal development learning and language learning. Section 3 illustrates the design of Mahjong-like game-based learning for English vocabulary spelling. System implementation of our proposed game for learning English vocabulary spelling is described in section 4. Finally, Section 5 makes a conclusion and figures out further work.

2   Literature Review

Academics found that characteristics of adding games into learning activities can increase students' learning motivation, initiate their attentions on training contents, and also get them to concentrate continuously and long time[4]. Prensky had already carried out research of game learning for many years, and he proposed that 21st century is a generation of the game[5]. There are not only technological transforms, but also many changes of basic levels. In the fields of education, adding games into learning will be strong and inspiring. The design of the game gets gamers to put in the artificial conflicts, and successful game designing is able to give gamers abilities of resolution and integration.

Flow theory is proposed by Csikszentmihalyi[6]. He pointed out that during activities if people completely throw themselves into scenario because of paying attention, so that they will filter all irrelevant perceptions and then enter a flow status. Many studies supported that players about devoting into games are able to arrive at a flow status which means completely coming over. Kiili had focused on the "Flow" produced by devoting of game-integrated learning for a long time[7]. He also combined Kolb's experiential learning theory with properties of game-learning designing and devised "Experiential gaming model", and he provided references of planning and analyzing educational games to programmers.

Competition is usually considered as an effective way of promoting human to learn and progressive[8], and competitive learning environment can provoke different feelings on winners' and losers' body[9]. Therefore, we use this feature to increase users' motivation so that it becomes one of biggest significance of competitive learning environment. Students will be excited to do better performance hard in competitive game-based learning environment, so this research regards competition as an important part in activities. Students can be encouraged to complete cooperation within the group by competing between groups, and we use winners' and losers' different feelings to stimulate intention of students' learning English vocabulary actively after school. Yu also thought that competition bringing anxiety and pressure to students would make their performance not good as expected[10].

Traditional learning emphasizes copy and memory of knowledge, but cooperative learning focuses on the process of the learner constructing knowledge [11]. Cooperative learning helps much about developing acknowledge, and students can increase learning of acknowledge and memory through stimulating of interaction between group members in groups in cooperative learning [12]. However, face-to-face activity of cooperative learning may cause conflict about disagreement. So members would train ability of communication and consultation. In cooperative activities of groups, students must put their heads together. They share ideas for each other, and challenge collaborative methods of solving problems. Additionally, brainstorming and stimulating between groups can also encourage students to try hard to seek good performance.

Cooperative learning assumes that everyone is able to respect to, trust, tolerate each other, realize the target in groups and clearly know own responsibilities. By the way, the form of cooperative learning can be arbitrary. In activities, the teacher plays a role as promoting discussion between students. However, students are protagonists of really participating in cooperative learning. In classical cooperative learning, students are often divided into several small groups and they adopt cooperative learning mutually. Cooperative learning scholars claimed that learning effects always reach best conditions in students' cooperation and discussion, so the teacher has to create a kind of learning environment. Therefore in this environment, it is continuous that students help each other learning and are versed in schoolwork.

Zone of Proximal Development, ZPD is proposed by Vygotsky [13]. He thought that learning development was divided into two levels: actual and potential developmental level. Actual developmental level is just called children's developmental stage, which kind of ability children have in which stages. It means the level that children are able to solve problems independently; however, potential developmental level is that children's ability of solving problems with adults' teaching or capable peer's cooperation. Each individual basic ability "actual developmental level" is different from ZPD. Best education would take individual difference into account, and this is also the goal that school education must reach.

Learning is so important that it creates zone of proximal development. That is, internal progresses can only be operated with adults' and peers' cooperation originally. However, internal progresses can be awake by learning moreover. Once these progresses are internalized with children, they become actual developmental level. So Vygotsky said today children need other people's help so that they have ability to solve problems, and tomorrow they will finish them independently.

Vygotsky also indicated that learning is a kind of social process due to the fact produced by interacting with other people. Therefore, the game is first step of children forming abstract thinking, because the game often plays more complexly than everyday life. Children are able to learn through playing games with other people, and then improve their zone of proximal development. Some scholars also thought the game is a very important part of children's acknowledges and process of social development.

Language and thinking are correlative, and people's ability of vocabulary is considered as emphasis of ability of comprehending language. Therefore, accumulating vocabulary becomes one of the most basic ability in learning language. However, the result of emphasizing remembering words often causes that students memorize words by rote, even decreases intention and pleasure in learning. The focal point of leaning language is to do meaningful application and communication, rather than only answering the questions. However, it cannot show learning achievement [14].

As mention above, we devote to design a Mahjong-like game-based learning for English vocabulary spelling. It can improve the shortcomings of crossword puzzles which make students easily cudgel their brains, and combines advantages of game-based teaching. It even stimulates power of learning from each other and achieves fun.

3   System Design

In this section, it will briefly introduce the design of our proposed Mahjong-like game of English vocabulary spelling to enhance the ability of English vocabulary during playing the game.

Mahjong is commonly played by four players. If the player holds a constant number of Mahjong cards and combines those cards into a particular sequence as soon as earlier, he will win the game. Mahjong is also an inspired mental game which can stimulate the ability of brainstorming and encourage the mental development for the game players.

A traditional Mahjong consists of 144 cards. For following the game rule of Mahjong, our designed Mahjong-like game of vocabulary spelling has also 144 cards to try spelling the right English vocabularies based on his holding cards. The cards in the game are shown in Figure 1. These game cards are designed by Mrs. Peral Yang who is an adjunct lecturer in Takming University of Science and Technology. We thank that Mrs. Yang freely provide them for us to design the game.

The game cards are divided into three types, letter, word, and flower. The letter cards contain two categories, 26 English letters and a vowel. The player uses the English letter cards to spell the vocabularies. A vowel card can be any one of five vowels, "a", "e", "i", "o" and "u", to spell a meaningful word with other English letter cards. The word and flower cards is used to represent the winds, dragons, flowers, and seasons cards to earn the honors and bonus tiles.

For fitting the originated game rule of traditional Mahjong, game rule terms are illustrated as follows:

(a)   Applique (One more drawn card): During the game, if the player draws one "Flower" card and then drawing one more card until it is not a "Flower" card.

(b)   Chow (Only 3 "Letter" cards to spell a three-letter English word): During the game, only the previous player (always on your left) plays the card what two hand cards can spell a word.

(c)   Pong (Only 3 same "Word" cards): During the game, one of remaining three players plays the card what two hand cards are same.

(d)   Kong (Only 4 same "Word" cards or only on Chow-Pong-Kong area not in hand): During the game, one of remaining three players plays the card what three hand cards are same.

(e)   Win, that is, Hu or Self-Drawn (5 groups of "Chow", "Pong" or "Kong" which means only on Chow-Pong-Kong area not in hand and a pair which means just 2 same "Letter" or "Word" cards): During the game while you have 5 groups of "Chow", "Pong", "Kong" (only on table not in hand), one of remaining three players plays the card or you draw the card what one of your hand cards can spell a pair or two of your hand cards can spell a three-letter English word or triple.

(f)   Loss, that is, Chuck or Cheat-Hu: It condition is contrary to "Win".

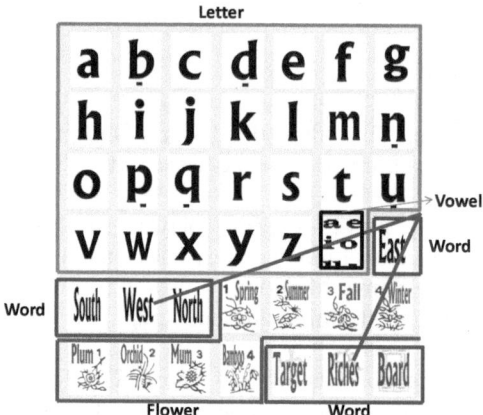

Fig. 1. Game cards of Mahjong-like game for English vocabulary spelling

For increasing the game competitiveness among players, game scoring is necessary. Table 1 is shown the scoring rule of the designed game.

Table 1. Scoring rules of the Mahjong-like game for English vocabulary spelling

Term	Result	Description	Self	Other
Hu	Win	Get Chuck player's card and win	+1	0 (without Chuck player)
Chuck	Loss	Discard to Hu player and lose	-1	0 (without Hu player)
Self-Drawn	Win	Draw and win	+3	-1
Cheat-Hu	Loss	Get Cheated-Hu player's card and lose	-1	0 (without Cheated-Hu player)
Cheated-Hu	Win	Discard to Cheat-Hu player and win	+1	0 (without Cheat-Hu player)
Self-Cheat-Hu	Loss	Draw and lose	-3	+1
Deuce	No Win or Loss	Deck is 0 and no one win or lose	0	0

Figure 2 is depicted the operational flow of our designed game based on game rule shown in Table 1. Following the game flow, the game result will be easily derived to decide which one wins the game.

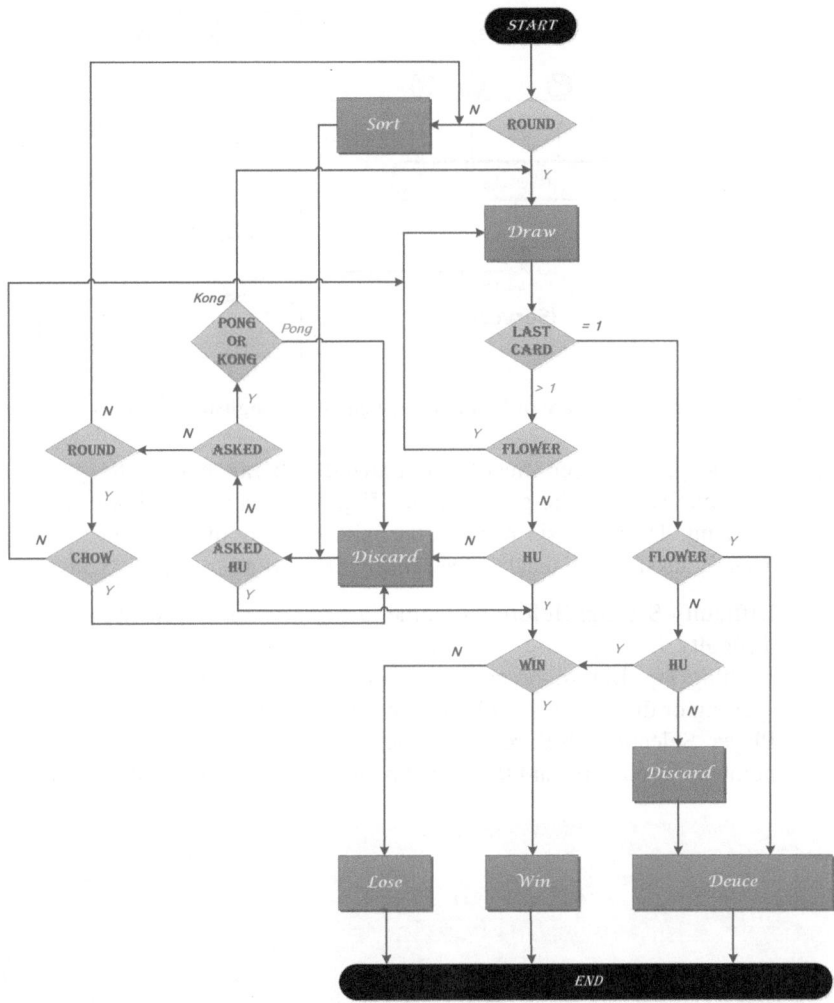

Fig. 2. Operational flow of Mahjong-like game for English vocabulary spelling

4   System Implementation

System implementation of our designed game is illustrated in this section. The detail of implementation is described in [15]. Figure 3 shows the system architecture of the designed game. It consists of one server and four clients in the same subnet. The server may be one of four clients or another fifth user, and the learners can use this system easily only with PCs, laptops or touch devices, e.g., smart phones, through a network.

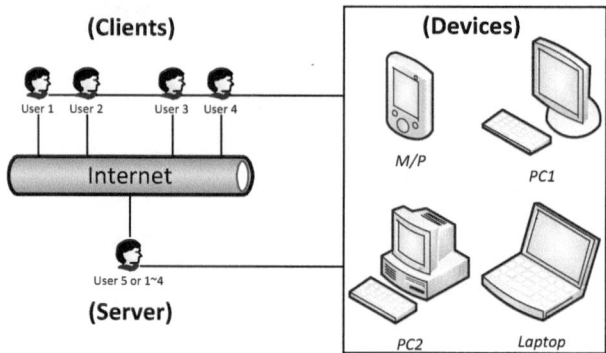

Fig. 3. System architecture of Mahjong-like game for English vocabulary spelling

At First, the game server must be initialized and ran before the game players playing the game by using the game clients. Figure 4 is a screen shot of game server while initializing. There are six parts in the initial setting of game server. The game creators (usually used by the teacher) can follow the setting to organize the game:

(a) Difficulty Setting: Before the game, the game creator can set it to decide its difficulty.

(b) Spelling Tip: Before the game, the user can set it to decide whether providing spelling or dictionary searching or not while playing.

(c) Player Selection: Before the game, the game creator can set it to decide numbers of players, and they must be multiples of four (one group) or more.

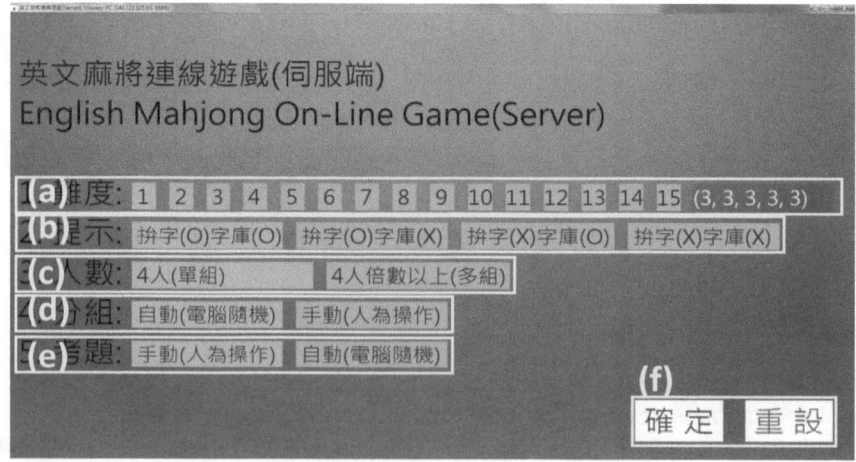

Fig. 4. The screen shot of game server for initial setting

(d) Group Selection: Before the game, the game creator can set it to decide players whose position and in which group.

(e)   Examination: Before the game, the game creator can set it to decide how to test players by choosing words which is random or artificial in exam pattern.

(f)   Setting Confirmation: Before the game, the game creator can set five options: "(a) Difficulty Setting", "(b) Spelling Tip", "(c) Player Selection", "(d) Group Selection" and "(e) Examination". Then the user can press "Confirm" to start the game or "Reset" to set them again.

After the setting of game servers and four players joining the game, the game is started. Figure 5 shows the game status on the game server. Each player draws the card and does specific action shown on the screen of game server simultaneously.

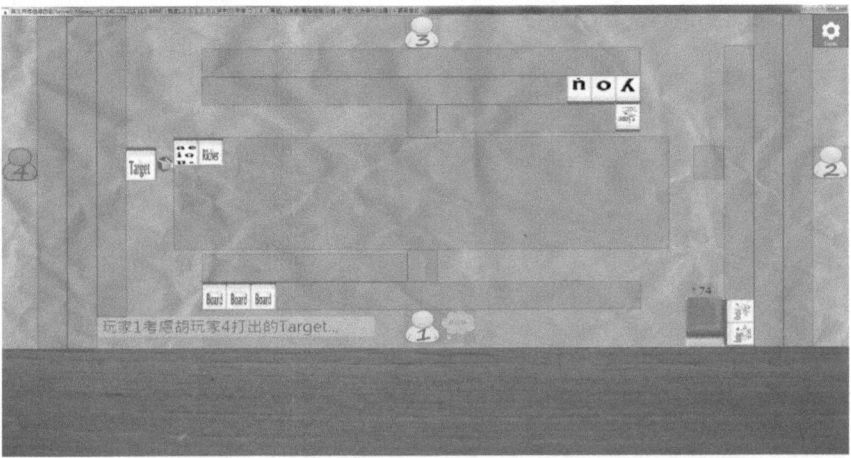

Fig. 5. The playing status of vocabulary spelling for each learner showing on the game server

A game player can use the game client to play. If there are four players joining the game server, the server will form a game learning vocabulary spelling to play for these four players. The screen of game client will be changed as shown in Figure 6. There are eight function areas controlled by the player. The corresponding description of function areas are listed below:

(a)   Hand-Card Area: During the game, the player can move them to sort in each group of three or two orange grids to spell a three-letter English word, triple, pair or empty. However, they cannot be put beyond this area except discarding, "Chow" and "Hu" the card.

(b)   Numbers of Remaindering Cards Indication Area: During the game, there is sometimes a counter to tell the user to act quickly. If time is over, the system will help the player to complete current action forcibly.

(c)   Deck Area: During the game, the player can press it and draw a card if at her/his round unless there is no card anymore.

(d)   Mahjong Button Area: During the game, the player can press it (ex. "Chow") to do something when s/he is asked.

(e)   Chow-Card Area: During the game, the player can move two of hand cards and previous user's one playing card to this area to make them a three-letter English word in his or her round.

(f)   Played Area: During the game, the player can move it when pressing "Chow" in his or her round or pressing "Hu" in other's round.

(g)   Spell Status Area: Before the game if the game creator sets "Spelling Hint" as "Spelling" on the server, and there will be total seven bars on each group of three or two lattices when playing.

(h)   Word List Area: Before the game if the game creator sets "Spelling Tip" as "Spelling" on the server, and there will be total seven lists on each group of three or two lattices when playing. When the player is moving the card, the list will immediately point all matching three-letter English words and their Chinese meanings. Figure 7 shows a screen shot of game client to prompt the spelling tips for the player.

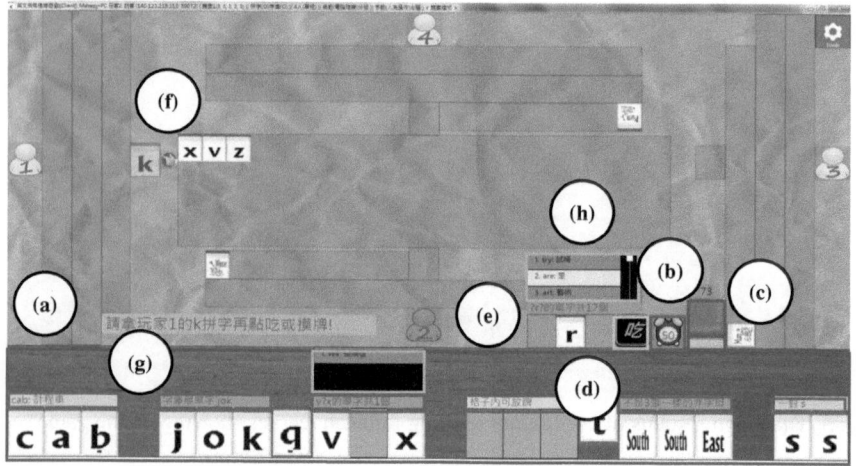

Fig. 6. The screen shot of a game client

If the player ensures that the current game status is "Hu", and then the system will automatically analyze whether s/he wins (all hand cards are in each grid and all colors of spell status are green or gray without any red) called "Self-Drawn" or lose (one color of spell status is red) called "Self-Cheat-Hu" with the message and special efficacy shown in Figure 8. If the game is over, the system will display players' scores, hand cards and remaining cards in the deck, and everyone is unable to move hand cards anymore.

Fig. 7. A Screen shot of displaying the spelling tip

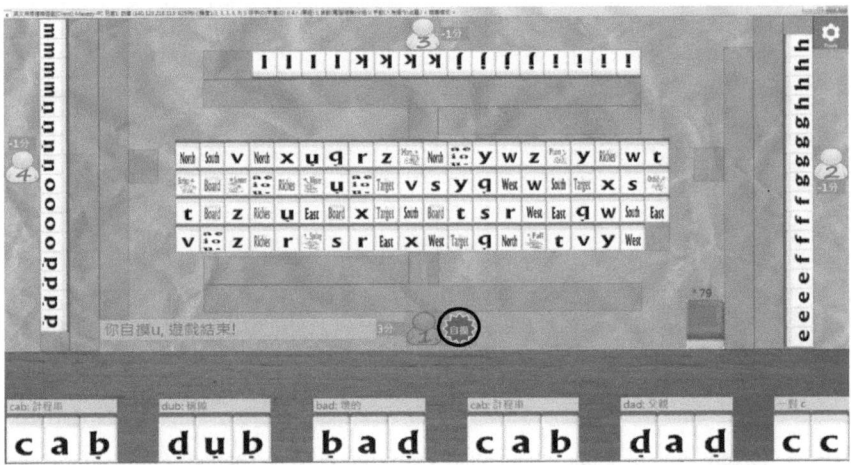

Fig. 8. A screen shot of game client while the player wining in the "Self-Drawn" condition

The game server will report the correct spelling vocabularies and show them on game client after the game finished. Each player can understand which words are spelled from different players. The result is shown in Figure 9.

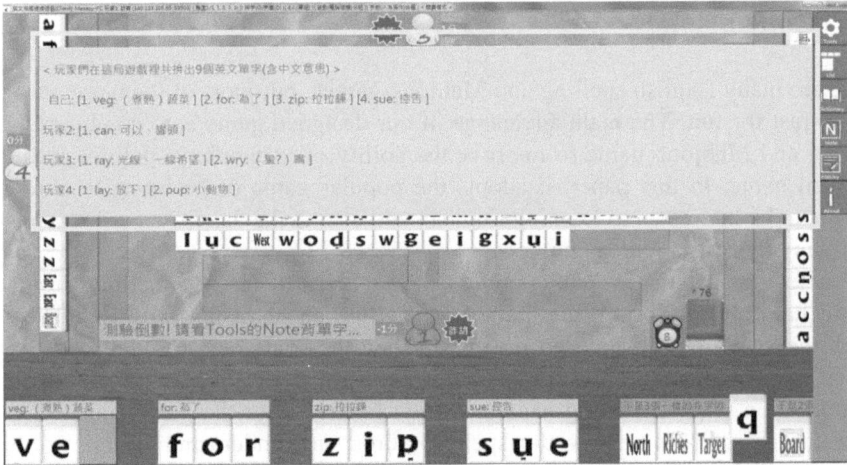

Fig. 9. A Screen shot of game client displaying the correct spelled words after the game finished

For reflecting and enhancing the ability of vocabulary spelling, the game server will form a spelling examination based on the spelled words and send it to the game clients in the game. Figure 10 shows a screen shot of a spelling examination on the game client. During the spelling examination, the player presses the white block in the screen of a game client, s/he has to use the virtual keyboard shown below inputting the English words based on the tips of the corresponding Chinese meaning.

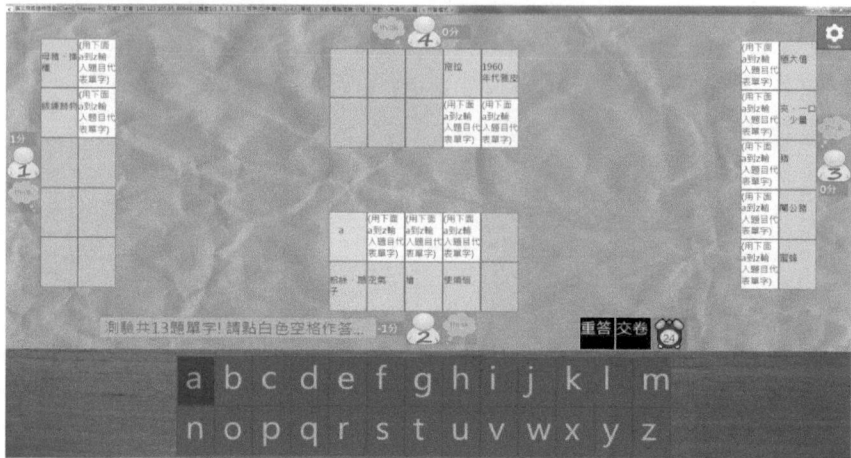

Fig. 10. A Screen shot of game client displaying the correct spelled words after the game finished

All of spelling examinations are finished. The game server will calculate the spelling scores of all game players. The teacher can investigate the ability of English vocabulary spelling and learners can compare their difference on vocabulary spelling.

5   Conclusion

There are many English spelling and Mahjong games, but most of them are only used to play just for fun. The main advantage of our designed game is to combine English spelling and Mahjong game to improve the ability of vocabulary spelling during the designed game. In this paper, it adopts the popular game of Mahjong to attract the learners to be interested in learning English, and also make the crossword much easier with many tips during the game.

Due to the fact that it really prefers the learners to learn something instead of feeling hard and giving up the game, they will even learn not only English words which they spell but also more tip words. When the learners are finding letters, they will be forced to learn more words with tips inadvertently.

In addition, a post spelling examination is formed after the game finished, it can assist the learners to review the spelled words and understand which words are remembered. It also can assist the teachers taking a remedial teaching while their learning achievement is too lower. By the way, the learners are able to learn words no matter s/he wins or loses the game or the game is deuce.

Due to the fact that it is an initiative study, we mainly focus on the implement of the system. In the future, we wish to do empirical research on students personally and to design questionnaire for proving the learning perspectives of our designed game.

Acknowledgement. This work was partially support by Nat. Science Council of Taiwan under Grants NSC 102-2511-S-194-001-MY3 and NSC 102-2511-S-194-005-MY3. We also thank Mrs. Peral Yang providing the design and rule of Mahjong game for English spelling.

References

1. Prensky, M.: Digital Game-based Learning. McGraw Hill, New York (2000)
2. Squire, K.: Video Games in Education. International Journal of Intelligent Simulations and Gaming 2(1), 49–62 (2003)
3. Kirriemuir, J., McFarlane, A.: Literature Review in Games and Learning. A report of NESTA futurelab,
   http://www.futurelab.org.uk/research/reviews/08_01.htm
4. Garris, R., Ahlers, R., Driskell, J.E.: Games, Motivation, and Learning: A Research and Practice Model. Simulation and Gaming 33(4), 441–467 (2002)
5. Prensky, M.: Digital Game-based Learning. Computer in Entertainment 1(1), 21 (2003)
6. Csikszentmihalyi, M.: Flow: The Psychology of Optimal Experience. Harper Perennial, New Yourk (1990)
7. Killi, K.: Digital Game-based Learning: Towards an Experiential Gaming Model. Internet and Higher Education 8, 13–24 (2004)
8. Julian, J., Perry, F.: Cooperation Contrasted with Intra-group and Intergroup Competition. Sociometry 30, 79–90 (1967)
9. Chang, L.J., Yang, J.C., Chan, T.W., Yu, F.Y.: Development and Evaluation of Multiple Competitive Activities in a Synchronous Quiz Game System. Innovations in Education and Teaching International 40(1), 16–26 (2003)
10. Yu, F.Y.: The Effects of Cooperation with Inter-group Competition on Performance and Attitude During a Computer-based Science Instruction. Journal of Computers in Mathematics and Science Teaching 17(4), 381–395 (1998)
11. Slavin, R.E.: Cooperative Learning: Theory, Research and Practice. Prentice Hall, NJ (1995)
12. Zurita, G., Nussbaum, M.: Computer Supported Collaborative Learning Using Wirelessly Interconnected Hand-held Computers. Computers & Education 42(3), 289–314 (2004)
13. Vygotsky, L.S.: Mind and Society: The Development of Higher Mental Processes. Harvard University Press, Cambridge (1978)
14. Chapelle, C.A.: Computer Applications in Second Language Acquisition: Foundations for Teaching, Testing and Research. Cambridge University Press, Cambridge (2001)
15. Huang, W.F.: Learning Effects of English Spelling in Mahjong-like Game Design Perspectives and Initiative Study. Master Thesis. National Chung Cheng University (2013)

Factors Influencing Trust and Acceptance of Electronic Sand Tables for Higher Business Education*

River Chu[1,2], Yan Li[3,**], Ivan K.W. Lai[4], and Zhiwei Zhu[3]

[1] Beijing Normal University, Zhuhai, Zhuhai City 519087, China
[2] Chinese Institute of Industrial Engineering, Kwun Tong, Kowloon, Hong Kong, China
[3] Guangzhou College, South China University of Technology, Guangzhou 510800, China
[4] International Graduate School of Business, University of South Australia, Adelaide, Australia
postmaster@iechina.info, 61680768@qq.com,
ivankw.lai@unisa.edu.au

Abstract. This research proposes a trust model to investigate the factors that influence students' trust and acceptance of electronic sand table (EST) learning systems. A total of 171 valid samples were collected from the students in Guangzhou College, South China University of Technology who have participated in EST-based courses. The results of this study indicate that entertanability, reliability, and auditability are key factors that determine students' trust toward EST learning systems. Furthermore, recommendations for the development and implementation of EST learning systems are provided based on the findings.

Keywords: electronic sand tables, trust, acceptance, higher business education, empirical study.

1   Introduction

Business simulations are games that illustrate management processes and principles [1]. There are different types of business simulations games designed around many different industries. "Capitalism" is the most famous business simulation game developed by Trevor Chan in 1995. The fast development of Internet technologies drives the development of online business simulation games. In China, online business simulation games are called "Electronic Sand Tables (EST) that were designed for students for hybrid learning. Literature reveals that online business simulation games which can interact with students have been observed to be an effective motivation for study [2-5], so that online business simulation games have been elevated in higher education with different business modules [4]. However, a recent study of students' experiences towards EST in the Management School of Guangzhou College, South China University of Technology (MSGC, SCUT)

---

*   This work is supported in part by Chinese Institute of Industrial Engineering under Grant No. CIIE-ABR-2014030101.
**   Corresponding author.

S.K.S. Cheung et al. (Eds.): ICHL 2014, LNCS 8595, pp. 164–172, 2014.

demonstrates that the acceptance of EST-based courses isn't as high as expected. For example, the rate in course evaluation for an EST-based "ERP Simulation Training" course is lower than a traditional teaching method "The principle of ERP" course. Literature on information technology (IT) shows that the users' acceptance of a technology or system is the premise of that the technology or system's proleptic effect can be reached [6,7]. Thus, research on factors influencing students' trust and acceptance of EST learning systems is necessary.

2   Research Background

EST is generally divided into two categories in teaching practice: one is a system developed specially for teaching, such as "Jingying Zhidao" of Kingdee and "Virtual Exchange" of China Tai'an Co., Ltd. (GTA); The other utilizes commercial software to simulate major businesses, such as "ERP Simulation Training" and "CRM Simulation Training". Either way, EST is essentially a type of information systems (IS) that is used in education.

Rational behavior theory is widely utilized in evaluating users' acceptance of a system in the field of IS and electronic business (EC). This theory contents that human behavior is determined by intention [8], and yet many studies suggested that users' trust of one system can exert a profound impact on their intension of using IS [9,10,11]. Trust is widely accepted as the expectation that a service will be provided or a commitment will be fulfilled in the field of IT [12].

Lai et al. (2011) stated that in inter-organizational context, factors and characters that may impact trust of users on IS mainly involve availability, reliability, auditability, and interoperability [13]. Chu et al. (2014) further justified this concept in compatible with the feature of cloud-based IS with a new trust factor "controllable" [10]. Furthermore, some researches indicated that entertanability exerts a positive impact on users trust of a system [11,14,15].

3   Research Hypotheses and Model

As was noted above "interoperability" and "controllability" are trust factors that are tailored for cloud-based inter-organizational systems. For the study of EST learning systems, these 2 trust factors are removed because they do not take any roles in EST learning systems. However, a new trust factor 'entertanability' is proposed because students would trust EST learning systems if they like to play with the EST learning systems. Hence, following 6 hypotheses are proposed in order to investigate students' trust toward EST learning systems.

Usability (*US*) is a set of attributes of software that affect the effort needed for use and reflects individual assessments of such use [16]. The results of Lai et al. (2011) [13] and Chu et al. (2014) [10]'s studies in the IS field demonstrated that the usability of a system shows a positive influence on users' trust of the system. Therefore, **Hypothesis 1:** Usability has a positive influence on students' trust toward EST learning systems.

Reliability *(RL)* is referred to a system that can provide continuous service without error in order to keep the enterprises running business efficiently [17]. Reliability is an important trust factor for users to trust a system [10,13]. Therefore, **Hypothesis 2:** Reliability has a positive influence on students' trust toward EST learning systems.

Auditability *(AU)* is referred to the level of easiness of auditing a system [18]. Lai et al. (2011) [13] and Chu et al. (2014) [10] found that reliability is one of the important trust factors for users to trust a system. Therefore, **Hypothesis 3**: Auditability has a positive influence on students' trust toward EST learning systems.

Entertanability *(ET)* refers to a system that is designed being able to entertains, amuses, interests users, or gives users pleasure. Studies by Koufaris & Hampton-Sosa (2002) [14], Heijden (2003) [15], Gerfen et al. (2003) [11] in IS field and Chen (2010) [19] in hybrid learning field proved the casual relations between entertanability and trust. Therefore, **Hypothesis 4**: Entertanability has a positive influence on students' trust toward EST learning systems.

Research in IS and EC fields also indicated that trust of users in a system can trigger intension of using [9,10,11,20]. Therefore, **Hypothesis 5:** Students' trust toward EST learning systems has a positive influence on their intension of using EST systems.

Chu et al. (2014) observed that in IS field, users' trust in IS plays an intermediary role between antecedent factors of trust and their intention of using the system [10]. Therefore, **Hypothesis 6**: Trust of students in participating EST learning systems plays an intermediary role between factors that responsible for causing trust and students' intension of using EST learning systems.

Figure 1 shows the research model with various measurable items of proposed trust factors. (Hypothesis 6, the intermediary effect hypothesis, does not show in the figure).

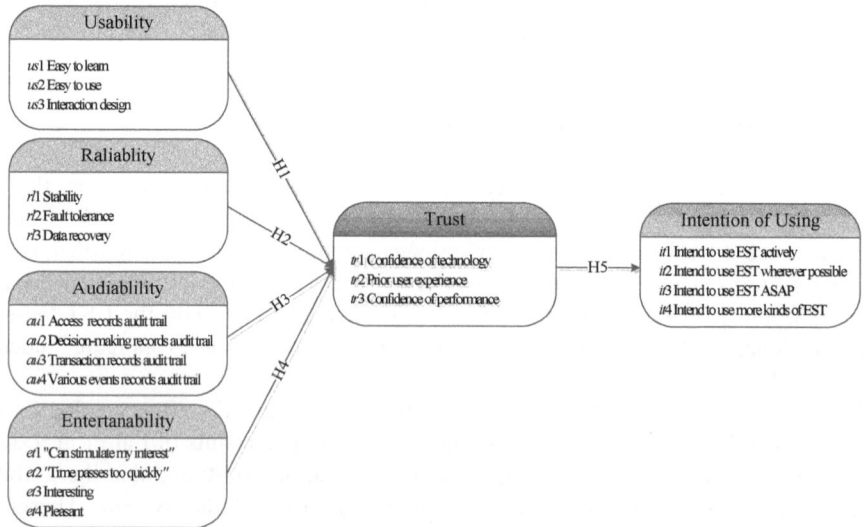

Fig. 1. Research Model

4   Results and Analysis

We used a questionnaire survey. The questionnaire consists of 2 sections: section I covers 21 questions of 6 constructs and section II is the background information of respondents. Target respondents are undergraduate students in MSGC, SCUT who are studying business and have experience in playing EST learning systems. They are required to express their opinion towards selected statements in the questionnaire in a 7-point Likert scale (7 represents "strongly agree", 1 means "strongly disagree"). Undergraduate students were invited in class or by online communication media such as QQ and Wechat to fill questionnaire online. In order to prevent duplicate entry, questionnaire was set to reject any entry from the same Mac address within 24 hours. A total of 195 answer sheets were collected in March 2014 and were carefully inspected to determine whether any problems existed in addition to being filtered by response time. 4 participants were obliviously misunderstood the questions, or even didn't get round to read it, in that answers of similar questions was disagree with each other, 20 answer sheets were also eliminated for answering "never contact with EST-based courses". A total of 171 answer sheets were finally retained for analysis.

4.1   Sample Characteristics

49.1% (84 students) of the effective respondents were females while 50.9% (87 students) were males. The percentage of students from first year to final year were 8.2% (14 students), 8.2% (14 students), 51.5% (88 students) and 32.2% (55 students) respectively. 40 students (23.4%) claimed that they were new to EST-based course, while 57 respondents (33.3%) stated that they have already completed one EST-based course, 74 students (43.3%) indicated that they attended 2 or more EST-based courses.

4.2   Reliability and Validity Assessment

Table 1 illustrates that overall Cronbach's α is 0.934 which were calculated by utilizing SPSS 19 analysis towards sample data. The highest value within all constructs is entertanability (0.866), and it can be seen that the value of audibility is the lowest (0.678). In order to ensure the acceptance of inner-reliability, Hair et al. (2010) argued that the score of Cronbach's α should be at least 0.6 [21]. This requirement was verified in the research. The result of Bartlett's Test of Sphericity (χ^2~2539.239, df~210, $Sig.$~0.000) indicates that the correlation matrix for these variables is unlikely to be an identical matrix. Further calculation on Kaiser-Meyer-Olkin test shows that $KMO = 0.880$. These results suggest that the scale is compatible for factor analysis. The graphic information presented in the far right column of Table 1 estimates each items' loading in every construct calculated by using factors rotation in principal components analysis. In factor loading, the weight of $tr2$ (confidence of system's technology) is the lowest (0.594), referring to Hair et al. (2010), minimum standards for loading of variables should reach 0.5 [21]. Thus this research is acceptable considering the structure validity of the scale.

Table 1. Reliability and Validity Analysis

Constructs	Items	Means	Std. Dev..	Cronbach's α	Factor loadings
Overall				.934	
Usability (US)	1 (us1)	5.02	1.253	.839	.775
	2 (us2)	4.98	1.166		.864
	3 (us3)	4.89	1.248		.694
Reliability (RL)	4 (rl1)	4.58	1.245	.816	.768
	5 (rl2)	4.44	1.297		.839
	6 (rl3)	4.37	1.237		.753
Auditability (AU)	7 (au1)	4.65	1.281	.678	.751
	8 (au2)	4.98	1.408		.859
	9 (au3)	5.15	1.371		.854
	10 (au4)	5.09	1.271		.626
Entertanability (ET)	11 (et1)	5.05	1.330	.866	.774
	12 (et2)	4.95	1.413		.796
	13 (et3)	5.42	1.285		.788
	14 (et4)	5.26	1.133		.697
Trust (TR)	15 (tr1)	4.77	1.133	.824	.630
	16 (tr2)	5.32	1.114		.594
	17 (tr3)	5.01	1.143		.560
Intention of Using (IT)	18 (it1)	5.36	1.147	.864	.695
	19 (it2)	5.27	1.090		.765
	20 (it3)	5.05	1.182		.844
	21 (it4)	5.16	1.396		.765

4.3   Correlation Analysis

Table 2 shows the Pearson's correlation coefficients matrix between constructs. Since the correlation coefficients are all significant at 0.01 level, but all less than 0.8, according to the criteria established by Moore (2007) [22], given that relative independence of each construct and low risks of collinearity, multiple regression analysis can be appropriated here.

Table 2. Correlation Matrix beteen Contructs

	US	RL	AU	ET	TR
RL	.490[**]				
AU	.472[**]	.501[**]			
ET	.517[**]	.370[**]	.467[**]		
TR	.482[**]	.490[**]	.512[**]	.692[**]	
IT	.426[**]	.309[**]	.361[**]	.675[**]	.740[**]

[**] P < 0.01 (two tailed test)

4.4   Regression Analysis

Utilizing stepwise regression analysis of SPSS 19, as shown in table 3, the regression equation fitted to the data is $TR = 1.193 + 0.450ET + 0.192RL + 0.132AU$, where TR is the dependent variable, US, RL, AU, ET are the independent variables and US (usability) variables are removed from the regression equation because it fail to pass significant test. Collinearity diagnostics for the above liner regression equation is done in order to justified the equation. The tolerance of each significant construct is greater than 0.2. According to the criteria Lu (2003) proposed [23], there is no obvious multicollinearity problem appears in this Model. Hence, hypotheses 2, 3, 4 and 5 are supported and hypothesis 1 is rejected.

Table 3. Regression Analysis (1)

| Model | | Non-Std. Coef. | | Std. Coef. | | | Colli. Stat. | |
		B	Std. error	β	t	Sig.	Toli.	VIF
1	Const.	2.061	.244		8.431	.000		
	ET	.575	.046	.692	12.464	.000	1.000	1.000
2	Const.	1.400	.268		5.234	.000		
	ET	.491	.047	.592	10.528	.000	.863	1.159
	RL	.245	.051	.271	4.822	.000	.863	1.159
3	Const.	1.193	.277		4.298	.000		
	ET	.450	.049	.542	9.160	.000	.757	1.321
	RL	.192	.055	.213	3.523	.001	.725	1.379
	AU	.132	.055	.153	2.411	.017	.658	1.521

Dependent variable: IT

Table 4. Regression Analysis (2)

| | Non-Std. Coef. | | Std. Coef. | | |
	B	Std. error	β	t	Sig.
Const.	1.306	.278		4.699	.000
TR	.776	.054	.740	14.314	.000

Dependent variable: IT

To examine the mediation effect of trust, first, as shown in Table 5, regression analysis is conducted where IT is dependent various and RL、AU、ET is independent various. Results from Stepwise regression analysis shows that only ET can enter into the regression equation which is $IT = 2.175 + 0.588ET$. And then, as shown in Table 6, regression analysis between dependent various IT and independent various ET and TR results in the regression equation which is $IT = 1.041 + 0.550TR + 0.271ET$, and the coefficient of ET becomes smaller while TR entered. According to the criteria posited by Baron and Kenny (1986) [24], trust of students in participating EST plays a partial intermediary role between factors that responsible for causing trust and students' intention of using EST learning systems. Hypothesis 6 is partially supported.

Table 5. Regression Analysis (3-1)

Model		Non-Std. Coef.		Std. Coef.		
		B	Std. Error	β	t	Sig.
1	Const.	2.175	.262		8.298	.000
	ET	.588	.049	.675	11.882	.000

Dependent variable: IT

Table 6. Regression Analysis (3-2)

Model		Non-Std. Coef.		Std. Coef.		
		B	Std. Error	β	t	Sig.
1	Const.	1.306	.278		4.699	.000
	TR	.776	.054	.740	14.314	.000
2	Const.	1.041	.269		3.871	.000
	TR	.550	.071	.525	7.748	.000
	ET	.271	.059	.312	4.600	.000

Dependent variable: IT

5   Discussion

Given that Hypothesis 5 is supported and Hypothesis 6 is partially supported, trust is responsible for influencing students' intention of using EST learning systems, and it is an intermediary between certain design features of EST learning systems and students' intention if using EST learning systems. Therefore, trustworthiness should regard as a significance performance indicator in the research and development of EST learning systems.

The results of this study indicate that reliability, auditability, and entertanability provide a profound impact on students' trust toward EST learning systems. The most crucial factor is entertanability (β=0.542, Sig.~0.000) which has a strong impact on students' intention of using EST learning systems in both direct and indirect means. Average score in this construct is 5.170 which is the highest of all antecedents, and has a higher recognition among students. As a result, future development of EST learning systems should continue to maintain its advantage in entertanability, however, it should be aware of that students' preference of entertanability may weaken teaching function.

Reliability is another vital factor affecting students' trust next to entertanability (β=0.213, Sig.~0.001). Average score in this construct is 4.466, which is the lowest score of all constructs, and this means a majority of students are dissatisfied with this performance of the systems. Thus, this factor needs to be improved in future development of EST learning systems.

Auditability is also an important factor affecting students' trust (β=0.153, Sig.~0.017). In 4 items of this construct, tr2 (decision-making records audit trail) has the highest factor loading (0.859), this may be due to students emphasize reviewing the process of simulation training and related courses with the audit function. The factor loading of *tr*3 (transaction records audit trail) is 0.894, very close to that of *tr*2, it shows that just as in real business environment, the incontestability of transaction behavior is appreciated in simulation training. Therefore, as an advantage of EST learning systems, auditability needs to be emphasized in future development and application of EST learning systems.

The reason for usability shows non-significant impact on EST learning systems may be due to the fact that usability is a "must" feature of EST learning systems, thus students do not pay special attention on it. Therefore, usability is a basic requirement of EST learning systems.

6   Conclusion

This research presents a trust model for EPS learning systems that is associated with system technical features and users' psychological perspectives. Questionnaires were collected and empirical data were tested for validating the proposal model. This model provides a framework for future studies of trust and acceptance of hybrid learning systems.

Single sample source and small sample size are the limitations of this study. Further consideration of more trust factors that influence trust can be added for future study. Future research can also focus on the characteristics of EST and higher education of business which can be beneficial to developing potential factors that underlying trust and acceptance for higher education.

References

1. Rollings, A., Ernest, A.: Fundamentals of Game Design. Prentice Hall, NJ (2006)
2. Adobor, H.: Management simulations: Determining their effectiveness. Journal of Management Development 25(2), 151–168 (2006)
3. Birknerová, Z.: The use of simulation business games in university education. Bulgarian Journal of Science and Education Policy 4(2), 202–215 (2010)
4. Ebner, M., Holzinger, A.: Successful Implementation of User-Centered Game Based Learning in Higher Education: An Example from Civil Engineering. Computers & Education 49(3), 873–890 (2007)
5. Tao, H.Y., Cheng, C.J., Sun, S.Y.: What Influences College Students to Continue Using Business Simulation Games? The Taiwan Experience.Computers & Education 53(3), 929–939 (2009)
6. Davis, F.D.: A Critical Assessment of Potential Measurement Biases in the Technology Acceptance Model: Three Experiments. International Journal of Human-Computer Studies 45(1), 19–45 (1996)
7. Ko, R.K.L., Jagadpramana, P., Mowbray, M., Pearson, S., Kirchberg, M., Liang, Q., Lee, B.S.: TrustCloud: A Framework for Accountability and Trust in Cloud Computing. In: The Proceedings of the 2nd IEEE Cloud Forum for Practitioners (IEEE ICFP 2011). IEEE, Washington, DC (2011)

8. Ajzen, I., Fishbein, M.: Understanding Attitudes and Predicting Social Behavior, pp. 217–242. Prentice Hall, NJ (1980)
9. Tang, T.-W., Chi, W.-H.: The Role of Trust in Customer Online Shopping Behavior: Perspective of Technology Acceptance Model. In: The Proceedings of NAACSOS Conference 2005, Notre Dame, Indiana, US (2005)
10. Chu, R., Tong, D., Lai, I.K.W.: An Empirical Study on Trust Mechanism of Cloud Based Inter-Organizational Information Systems. Application Research of Computers 31(10) (2014)
11. Gefen, D., Karahanna, E., Straub, D.: Trust and TAM in Online Shopping: An integrated Model. MIS Quarterly 27(1), 51–90 (2003)
12. Hoffman, L.J., Jenkins, L.K., Blum, J.: Trust beyond Security: An Expanded Trust Model. Communications of the ACM 49(7), 95–101 (2006)
13. Lai, I.K.W., Tong, V.W.L., Lai, D.C.F.: Trust Factors Influencing the Adoption of Internet-base Interorganizational Systems. Electronic Commerce Research and Applications 10(1), 85–93 (2011)
14. Koufaris, M., Hampton-Sosa, W.: Customer Trust Online: Examining the Role of the Experience with the Website (2002),
   http://cisnet.baruch.cuny.edu/papers/cis200205.pdf
15. Heijden, H.: Factors Influencing the usage of websites: The Care of A Generic Portal in the Netherlands. Information and Management 40(6), 541–549 (2003)
16. ISO/IEC 9126-1: Software Engineering - Product Quality - Part 1: Quality model (2001)
17. Bart, Y., Shankar, V., Sultan, F., Urban, G.L.: Are the Drivers and Role of Online Trust the Same for All Web Sites and Consumers? A Large-scale Exploratory Empirical Study. Journal of Marketing 69(4), 133–152 (2005)
18. Chu, R., Lai, I.K.W., Lai, D.C.F.: Trust Factors Influencing the Adoption of Cloud-Based Interorganizational Systems: A Conceptual Model. In: The Proceedings of ICEMSI & iCETS 2013, Macau (2013)
19. Chen, S.J.: Study on Satisfaction with Moodle in Blended Learning. Computer Education 20, 155–159 (2010)
20. Doney, P.M., Cannon, J.P.: An Examination of the Natureof Trust in Buyer-seller Relationships. Journal of Marketing 61(2), 35–51 (1997)
21. Hair, J.F., Anderson Jr., R.E., Tatham, R.L., Black, W.C.: Multivariate Data Analysis, 7th edn. Prentice Hall, NJ (2010)
22. Moore, D.S.: The Basic Practice of Statistics, 4th edn. W.H. Freeman and Company, NY (2007)
23. Lu, W.: SPSS Statistical Analysis, 4th edn., p. 323. Publishing House of Electronics Industry, Beijing (2003)
24. Baron, R.M., Kenny, D.A.: The Moderator-Mediator Variable Distinction in Social Psychological Research: Conceptual, Strategic, and Statistical Considerations. Journal of Personality and Social Psychology 51(6), 1173–1182 (1986)

Understanding Students' Continuance Intention toward Social Networking e-Learning

Ivan K.W. Lai[1,*] and Donny C.F. Lai[2]

[1] International Graduate School of Business, University of South Australia, Australia
[2] Department of Computer Science, City Unviersity of Hong Kong, Hong Kong
`ivankw.lai@unisa.edu.au`, `donnylai@cityu.edu.hk`

Abstract. With the rapid development of internet technologies, social networking e-learning has become increasingly popular that supports collaboration and sharing between students for them to solve daily learning problems. However, some students may not continually keep this practice due to some reasons. With the considering of expectation-value theory, this study tries to study students' continuance intention toward social networking e-learning by extending the UTAUT model with a critical psychological factor "perceived value". A Partial Least Squares (PLS) analysis is used to analyze the data collected from 240 students in Macau. The results of this study indicate that perceived value is an important factor followed by social influence that influence the continuance intention toward social networking e-learning. This study contributes a research model for the study of technology acceptance continuance in educational contexts and provides recommendations for educators to formulate their strategies to motive students for collaborative learning through social networking e-learning.

Keywords: social learning, technology acceptance, perceived value, UTAUT, continuance intention.

1 Introduction

According to the social constructivist approach, learning is considered to be a social and active process [1,2,3]. Social networking sites have become increasingly popular with the rise of Web 2.0 with increased collaboration and sharing between users through applications like wikis, blogs and podcasts, Facebook, etc. [4]. These social networking sites facilitate students to collaborate with others for writing assignments, doing projects, and preparing examinations. According to contemporary learning theories, student collaboration is a key element of effective learning, and many commentators have noted the synergies between the collaborative activities supported by social web technologies and the ideals of social learning theories (e.g., [5,6,7,8]). Thus, the way students learnt through social networking technologies is considered as 'social networking e-learning' in this study.

---

* Corresponding author.

S.K.S. Cheung et al. (Eds.): ICHL 2014, LNCS 8595, pp. 173–183, 2014.
© Springer International Publishing Switzerland 2014

Among all contemporary technology acceptance models, Venkatesh et al.'s [9] UTAUT model is a widely accepted one that determines users' intention to adopt different new technologies. The UTAUT model consists of two psychological factors (performance expectancy and effort expectancy), one social factor (social influence), and one technological factor (facilitating conditions). However, according to expectation-value theory, the value individuals have for succeeding is an important determinant of their motivation to perform different achievement tasks [10]. Thus, this study considers perceived value as another psychological factor that is integrated with UTAUT model to study students' continuance intention toward social networking e-learning.

Many students are trying to use social networking technologies for helping their daily learning now; however, some may give up this practice due to various reasons. Thus, identifying the factors for retaining students and encouraging their continuing use is an important task for the continued success of social network e-learning. The results of this study provide recommendations for educators to formulate strategies to motivate students for continually adapt social networking e-learning.

2   Literature Review

2.1   Social Networking e-Learning

With the rise of Web 2.0 in the last few years, social networking applications such as Facebook have become hugely popular [5,11]. These social network applications provide opportunities for communication, the forming of groups, hosting of content and small applications as well as connecting friends [12,13]. These social network applications offer students unprecedented opportunities to create and share content and to interact with others [14] and allow teachers to follow and potentially participate in the work of students [15].

Blog is one of the most properly social networking e-learning tools for educators and students. The most popular blog is Facebook which launched a high school version in early September 2005 and there are 800 million active Facebook users in 2012 [16]. In UK, 95% of undergraduate students are regularly using social networking sites [17] and 60% of them on daily [18]. Educators and students can use blogs in order to publish news and information about the course; collect learning resources and share ideas and experiences; develop interaction like in an online forum; improve researching and writing skills while preparing individual assignments; and develop collaboration and social skills in discussions over group assignments and projects [19,20,21].

Another type of common social networking e-learning tool is social web publishing such as wiki-writing. By publishing on Wikipedia, students can "showcase" their work, develop a professional profile, and invite commentary from experts outside the university [22]. Social web publishing enhances the authenticity of student writing tasks, thus students have the opportunity to produce work for a real external audience [23].

Instant messaging can be applied for social networking e-learning which is a lightweight near-synchronous communication technology that provides value as a medium for personal communication, both for peer-to-peer channels and as a conferencing platform [24]. Students who used instant messaging claimed to have a stronger sense of community and found it easier to communicate [25]. Unlike blogs and wiki, instant messaging provides synchronous e-learning environment that students feel more psychologically aroused and motivated, since this type of communication more closely resembles face-to-face communication [26]. Instant messaging gives prompt feedback that facilitates work groups collaboration and class discussions [27,28]. In this study, social network e-learning is defined as learning and teaching online through social network applications include blogs, wiki, and instant messaging.

2.2   Technology Acceptance Models for e-Learning

The Technology Acceptance Model (TAM) [29,30] has also been widely applied to many educational settings including understanding computer technology adoption by students and teachers [31] and implementation of laptop-based testing [32]. Results of TAM studies concluded that students' willingness to apply a learning technology at high levels and on an ongoing basis into the future depends upon students' perceptions of the learning technology's usefulness and ease of use.

Based on TAM model, Venkatesh et al. [9] combined other seven important user acceptance models to form a unified model named as Unified Theory of Acceptance and Use of Technology (UTAUT) model which consists of four core determinants (performance expectancy, effort expectancy, social influence, and facilitating conditions) and four control variables (gender, age, experience, and voluntariness of use). Venkatesh et al. [9] empirically validated UTAUT with six longitudinal field studies of six different departments of six large firms in six different industries. The UTAUT model accounted for 70 percent of the variance (adjusted R^2) in usage intention, better than any of the eight models alone did. In the education context,

Few researchers have applied TAM and UTAUT for studying the adoption of e-Learning. For example, Ndubisi [33] applied TAM to predict user acceptance and use of online learning systems in Malaysia. Raaij and Schepers [34] used TAM to explain the differences between individual students in the level of acceptance and use of a virtual learning environment. Chiu and Wang [35] extended the UTAUT by introducing components of subjective task value into a model for studying learners' continuance intentions in web-based learning. Their study focused on online classes offered at institutions of higher education. Sumak et al. [36] applied UTAUT to understand students' perceptions about using Moodle. These previous studies only address the e-learning platforms that allow students to access different learning resources such as program information and course content, there is no studies on social networking e-learning.

2.3   Perceived Value

Atkinson [10] originally defined expectancies as individuals' anticipations that their performance will be followed by either success or failure, and defined value as the relative attractiveness of succeeding or failing on a task. Therefore, behavior can be viewed as a function of the expectancies one holds for the behavior and the value of the behavioral outcome [37]. Eccles [38] further explained that the value is a subjective task value referred to the quality of the task that contributes to the increasing or decreasing probability that an individual will select it. Therefore, the value that people perceived to have when they try a new technology will affect their behavioral intention for continually adopting that new technology. In this study, Perceived Value (PV) is defined as the attainment value that students perceived to obtain when they are using social networking applications for collaborative learning.

3   Research Method

3.1   Research Hypothesis

Performance expectancy (PE) is the degree to which an individual believes that using the system will gain benefits or enhance job performance [9]. Students are willing to continue using social networking e-learning if they believe that social networking e-learning is useful for their study.

Effort Expectancy (EE) is the degree of ease to which an individual believes in the association with the use of the system [9]. Students will like to continue performing social networking e-learning if they believe that using social networking e-learning applications is free of effort.

Social influence (SI) is an individual perceives that important others believe the person should use the new technology [9]. Students intend to continue performing social networking e-learning if their classmates, friends, and teachers support the use of social networking e-learning.

Facilitating Conditions (FC) is defined as the degree of believing in the existence of the technical and organizational infrastructure to support the usage of a new technology [9]. Students want to continually use social networking tools for learning only if they feel that they can have sufficient supports.

Students will be more likely to engage in using social networking e-learning if they perceive it as valuable for their study. Therefore, Continuance Intention (CI) will be stimulated when students obtain attainment value from social networking e-learning for their study.

H1: Performance expectancy influences students' continuance intention toward social networking e-learning.

H2: Effort expectancy influences students' continuance intention toward social networking e-learning.

H3: Social influence influences students' continuance intention toward social networking e-learning.

H4: Facilitating conditions influence students' continuance intention toward social networking e-learning.

H5: Perceived value influence influences students' continuance intention toward social networking e-learning.

3.2   Data Collection

The aim of this study is to investigate the factors that influence students' behavior in continuous using of social network e-learning. This is a survey research and the target respondents were college students in Macau. The questionnaire is divided into two sections, including the questions for six constructs and the questions for respondent profile. In section 1, students are asked to rate the questions related to a total of 24 measurable items of the model along a 7-point Likert-type scale, with 1 set as 'strongly disagree' and 7 set as 'strongly agree'. The measurable items of the model are listed in Table 2. The measurable items of the latent variables in the model are based on previously published studies. Therefore, the items used to measure PE, EE, SI, PV, and CI are adapted from Venkatesh et al.'s [9] study and the measurable items for the PV are adapted from Chiu and Wang 's [35] study.

The questionnaire survey was conducted at campuses on four colleges in Macau from January to April 2012. Total 250 sets of questionnaire were collected. However, 10 questionnaires were eliminated (e.g., for giving the same rating for most items), leaving 240 questionnaires as valid for analysis. The summary of respondent characteristics is shown in Table 1.

Table 1. Respondent Characteristics

		Frequency	Percentage
Gender	Male	104	43.33
	Female	136	56.67
Age	Under 20	39	16.25
	20-24	171	71.25
	Over 24	30	12.50
Education	Pre-university	7	2.92
	Undergraduate	127	52.92
	Postgraduate	106	44.17
Online time	Under 4 hours	109	45.42
	4-6 hours	90	37.50
	7-9 hours	24	10.00
	Over 9 hours	17	7.08

4   Findings

4.1   Validity and Reliability

The data analysis was conducted by using SmartPLS 2.0 M3 because PLS is a variance based latent variable structural equations modeling technique, which uses an estimation approach that places minimal demands on sample size and residual distributions [39]. Table 2 shows the means, standard deviations, and PLS loadings. All factor loadings are deemed to be significant and to exceed the recommended level of 0.5, thus it assesses the construct validity of the measures.

Table 2. Means, Standard Deviations, and PLS Loadings

	Measurable Item	Mean	Std. Dev.	PLS Loading
PE1	I would find the social networking e-learning useful in my learning.	5.571	0.850	0.799
PE2	Using social networking e-learning enables me to accomplish learning tasks more quickly.	5.821	0.785	0.733
PE3	Using social networking e-learning increases my learning productivity.	5.579	0.692	0.807
PE4	If I use social networking e-learning, I will increase my chances of getting more competence.	5.600	0.857	0.701
EE1	My interaction with social network e-learning would be clear and understandable.	5.400	0.796	0.709
EE2	It would be easy for me to become skillful at using social networking e-learning.	5.704	0.808	0.812
EE3	I would find social networking e-learning easy to use.	5.554	0.811	0.804
EE4	Learning to operate social networking e-learning is easy for me.	5.492	0.697	0.731
SI1	People who influence my learning behavior think that I should use social networking e-learning.	5.579	0.698	0.810
SI2	People who are important to me think that I should use social networking e-learning.	5.563	0.746	0.659
SI3	People who are superior to me have been helpful in the use of social networking e-learning.	5.475	0.901	0.553
SI4	In general, the members of my learning community support the use of social networking e-learning.	5.725	0.950	0.771
FC1	I have the resources necessary to use social networking e-learning.	5.738	0.907	0.709
FC2	I have the knowledge necessary to use social networking e-learning.	5.758	0.882	0.752
FC3	Social networking e-learning is compatible with other systems I use.	5.571	0.850	0.829
FC4	Experts are available for assistance with social networking e-learning difficulties.	5.821	0.785	0.711
PV1	I think social networking e-learning makes me a more knowledgeable person.	5.563	0.800	0.754
PV2	I think social networking e-learning offers a forum for fulfilling achievement.	5.471	0.914	0.767
PV3	I think being successful at social networking e-learning confirms my competence.	5.658	0.892	0.830
PV4	I think being successful at social networking e-learning give me a sense of confidence	5.496	1.082	0.682
CI1	I intend to continue using social networking e-learning in the future.	5.704	0.765	0.636
CI2	I predict I will continue using social networking e-learning in the future.	5.671	0.821	0.821
CI3	I have the plan to continue using social networking e-learning in the future.	5.829	0.771	0.848
CI4	I intend to use social networking e-learning for learning as often as needed.	5.708	0.822	0.838

Table 3 shows means, standard deviations, Cronbach's alpha measures, CR values, AVE values, and all correlations among variables. It clearly shows that all correlations are statistically significant. The lowest values of AVE and CR reach the recommended standard. The square-root of the construct's AVE exceeds its correlations with other constructs in the model. These results fulfill Hair et al.'s [40] guidelines and Gefen and Straub's [41] aspect of the discriminant validity of the latent constructs.

Table 3. Reliability, Validity, and Corrections of the Constructs

	Mean	Std. Dev.	Cronbach's Alpha	CR	AVE	EE	SI	FC	PV	CI
PE	5.651	0.619	0.758	0.846	0.579	0.455	0.495	0.305	0.357	0.422
EE	5.571	0.606	0.767	0.849	0.586		0.451	0.480	0.358	0.348
SI	5.547	0.524	0.667	0.795	0.498			0.436	0.366	0.495
FC	5.674	0.685	0.744	0.838	0.565				0.390	0.495
PV	5.547	0.702	0.757	0.845	0.578					0.520
CI	5.728	0.628	0.797	0.868	0.625					

4.2   Testing of Hypotheses

Bootstrapping is performed using 240 cases and 5000 samples to assess the path coefficients' significance. The R^2 values of the endogenous constructs show the quality of PLS model [42]. The model explains 45.46% of variance in behavior intention. Fig. 1 shows a graphical representation of the outcomes of the model test. The results of model test indicate that all hypotheses are valid except H2.

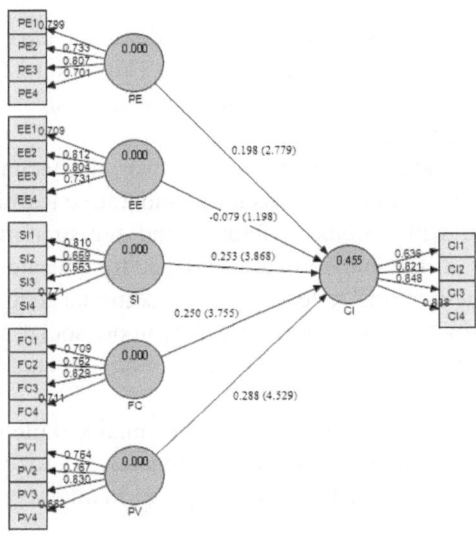

Fig. 1. Results of PLS analysis

5   Discussion and Conclusion

The results of PLS analysis indicate that PV has the highest path coefficient (β=0.288). Students consider the attainment value that they can obtain from using social networking e-learning tools. They want to successfully achieve their study objectives and to be a more knowledgeable person through continue using social networking e-learning tools. Thus, PV plays a major role in continue using social networking e-learning applications. It is not surprised that SI followed by PV is an important factor influencing continue using social networking e-learning (β=0.253), it is because existing social networking e-learning tools are highly interactive. The highly social interactive learning environment motivates students to participate group discussions that facilitate knowledge exchanges effectively. Therefore, classmates, friends and teachers' participation in social networking e-learning will affect students' continue performing social networking e-learning. FC is also an important factor as SI for continue using social networking e-learning (β=0.250). Existing social networking e-learning tools (include blogs, wiki, and instant messaging) are technically supported by application service providers. The rapid development of information and communication technologies enables the faster development of new social networking applications that gradually phase out old social networking tools, thus students are concerned about the resources and supports from the application service providers for them continually adopting social networking e-learning applications for their study. PE also has significant effect on students continue performing social networking e-learning (β=0.198) since students can ask questions through social networking e-learning applications and obtain feedbacks from classmates, friends, and teachers immediately. Thus, continue using social networking e-learning could improve students' learning productivity.

The results of PLS analysis indicate that EE does not have significant effect in continue performing social networking e-learning. This result is consistent with some previous studies [34,43] that "easy to use" may no longer important when the technologies are commonly employed.

With the continued improvement of social networking technologies, students are more likely to use social networking tools for collaborative learning. Therefore, social networking e-learning will become a future trend for supporting traditional class education. The results of this study provide guidance for educators in considering how to integrate social networking e-learning in traditional education that provides attainment value for students as well as how to promote social networking e-learning for supplementing traditional education in order motivate students for collaborative learning.

This study has a number of limitations include small sample size (n=240) and one location (Macau). The findings may not be generalized to other settings. Future research should be considered for larger sample sizes in other countries.

References

1. Vygotsky, L.S.: Mind in Society. Harvard University Press (1978)
2. Brown, J.S., Collins, A., Duguid, P.: Situated Cognition and the Culture of Learning. Educ. Res. 18(1), 32–42 (1989)
3. Jonassen, D.: Learning as Activity. Paper presented at the Meaning of Learning Project, Learning Development Institute. Presidential Session at AECT Denver, October 25-28 (2000)
4. Bosch, T.E.: Using Online Social Networking for Teaching and Learning: Facebook Use at the University of Cape Town. Communication 35(2), 185–200 (2009)
5. Alexander, B.: Web 2.0: A New Wave of Innovation for Teaching and Learning? Educause Rev. 41(2), 32–44 (2006)
6. Barnes, C., Tynan, B.: The Adventures of Miranda in the Brave New World: Learning in a Web 2.0 Millennium. Assoc. Learn. Tech. J. 15(3), 189–200 (2007)
7. Bower, M., Hedberg, J.G., Kuswara, A.: A Framework for Web 2.0 Learning Design. Educ. Media 47(3), 177–198 (2010)
8. McLoughlin, C., Lee, M.J.W.: Mapping the Digital Terrain: New Media and Social Software as Catalysts for Pedagogical Change Hello? Where Are You in the Landscape of Educational Technology? In: Proceedings of Ascilite 2008, pp. 641–652 (2008)
9. Venkatesh, V., Morris, M.G., Davis, G.B., Davis, F.D.: User Acceptance of Information Technology: Toward a Unified View. MIS Quart. 27(3), 425–478 (2003)
10. Atkinson, J.W.: Motivational Determinants of Risk Taking Behavior. Psychol. Rev. 64, 359–372 (1957)
11. Joinson, A.N.: 'Looking at', 'Looking up' or 'Keeping up with' People? Motives and Uses of Facebook. In: The Proceedings of the Twenty-Sixth Annual SIGCHI CHI 2008 Online Social Networks, Florence, Italy, April 5-10 (2008)
12. Donath, J., Boyd, D.: Public Displays of Connection. BT Tech. J. 22(4), 71–82 (2004)
13. Ellison, N., Heino, R., Gibbs, J.: Managing Impressions Online: Self-presentation Processes in the Online Dating Environment. J. Comput.-Mediat. Comm. 11(2), 415–441 (2006)
14. Sclater, N.: Web 2.0, Personal Learning Environments, and the Future of Learning Management Systems. EDUCAUSE Center for Applied Research, Res. Bull. 2008(13) (2008)
15. Richardson, W.: Morning at RSS-Blog-FurlHigh School Redux (2005), http://www.weblogg-ed.com/2005/08/21#a3906
16. Facebook Website (2014), https://www.facebook.com/facebook
17. Madge, M., Meek, J., Wellens, J., Hooley, T.: Facebook, Social Integration and Informal Learning at University: 'It is More for Socialising and Talking to Friends about Work than for Actually Doing Work'. Learn. Media Tech. 34(2), 141–155 (2009)
18. Arrington, M.: 85% of College Students Use Facebook. TechCrunch.dated (September 7, 2005)
19. Churchill, D.: Educational Applications of Web 2.0: Using Blogs to Support Teaching and Learning. Br. J. Educ. Tech. 40(1), 179–183 (2009)
20. Ellison, N.B., Wu, Y.: Blogging in the Classroom: A Preliminary Exploration of Student Attitudes and Impact on Comprehension. J. Educ. Multimed. Hypermedia 17(1), 99–122 (2008)
21. Fessakis, G., Tatsis, K.: Supporting "Learning by Design" Activities Using Group Blogs. Educ. Tech. Soc. 11(4), 199–212 (2008)

22. Schroeder, A., Minocha, S., Schneider, C.: The Strengths, Weaknesses, Opportunities, and Threats of Using Social Software in Higher and Further Education Teaching and Learning. J. Comput. Assist. Learn. 26, 159–174 (2010)
23. Rifkin, W., Longnecker, N., Leach, J., Davis, L., Orthia, L.: Motivate Students by Having Them Publish in New Media: An Invitation to Science Lecturers to Share and Test. In: Proceedings of National UniServe Science Conference 2009, Sydney, Australia, pp. 105–111 (2009)
24. Bones, E., Hasvold, P., Henriksen, E., Strandenæs, T.: Risk Analysis of Information Security in a Mobile Instant Messaging and Presence System for Healthcare. Int. J. Med. Eng. Informat. 76(9), 677–687 (2006)
25. Nicholson, S.: Socialization in the "Virtual Hallway": Instant Messaging in the Asynchronous Web-based Distance Education Classroom. Internet High. Educ. 5(4), 363–372 (2002)
26. Hrastinski, S.: Asynchronous and Synchronous e-Learning. Educause Quart. 31(4), 51–55 (2008)
27. Desai, C.M., Graves, S.J.: Instruction via Instant Messaging Reference: What's Happening? Electron. Libr. 24(2), 174–189 (2006)
28. Farmer, R.: Instant Messaging: Collaborative Tool or Educator's Nightmare! (2003), http://www.unb.ca/naweb/proceedings/2003/PaperFarmer.html
29. Davis, F.D.: A Technology Acceptance Model for Empirically Testing New End-user Information Systems: Theory and Results. Doctoral Dissertation, Sloan School of Management, Massachusetts Institute of Technology (1986)
30. Venkatesh, V., Davis, F.D.: A Theoretical Extension of the Technology Acceptance Model: Four Longitudinal Field Studies. Manag. Sci. 46(2), 186–204 (2000)
31. Ma, W.W.K., Andersson, R., Streith, K.O.: Examining User Acceptance of Computer Technology: An Empirical Study of Student Teachers. J. Comput. Assist. Learn. 21, 387–395 (2005)
32. Baker-Eveleth, L., Eveleth, D.M., O'Neill, M., Stone, R.W.: Enabling Laptop Exams Using Secure Software: Applying the Technology Acceptance Model. J. Inform. Syst. Educ. 18(1), 413–420 (2007)
33. Ndubisi, N.O.: Factors of Online Learning Adoption: A Comparative Juxtaposition of the Theory of Planned Behaviour and the Technology Acceptance Model. Int. J. e Learn. 5(4), 571–591 (2006)
34. Van Raaij, E.M., Schepers, J.J.L.: The Acceptance and Use of a Virtual learning Environment in China. Comput. Educ. 50(3), 838–852 (2008)
35. Chiu, C.M., Wang, E.T.: Understanding Web-based Learning Continuance Intention: The Role of Subjective Task Value. Inform. Manag. 45(3), 194–201 (2008)
36. Sumak, B., Polancic, G.: An Empirical Study of Virtual Learning Environment Adoption Using UTAUT. In: The Proceedings of 2010 Second International Conference on Mobile, Hybrid, and On-Line Learning, February 10-16, pp. 17–22 (2010)
37. Fishbein, M., Ajzen, I.: Belief, Attitude, Intention, and Behavior: An Introduction to Theory and Research. Addison-Wesley, Reading (1975)
38. Eccles, P.J.S., Adler, T.F., Futterman, R., Goff, S.B., Kaczala, C.M., Meece, J.L., Midgley, C.: Expectancies, Values, and Academic Behaviors. In: Spence, J.T. (ed.) Achievement and Achievement Motivation, pp. 75–146. W. H. Freeman, San Francisco (1983)
39. Chin, W.W.: The Partial Least Squares Approach to Structural Equation Modeling. In: Marcoulides, G.A. (ed.) Modern Methods for Business Research, pp. 295–336. Lawrence Erlbaum Associates, New York (1998)
40. Hair, J.F., Ringle, C.M., Sarstedt, M.: PLS-SEM: Indeed a Silver Bullet. J. Market. Theor. Pract. 19(2), 139–151 (2011)

41. Gefen, D., Straub, D.: A Practical Guide to Factorial Validity Using PLS-Graph: Tutorial and Annotated Example. Comm. Assoc. Inform. Syst. 16(5), 91–109 (2005)
42. Hulland, J.: Use of Partial Least Squares (PLS) in Strategic Management Research: A Review of Four Recent Studies. Strat. Manag. J. 2(2), 195–204 (1999)
43. Chen, J.L.: The effects of education compatibility and technological expectancy on e-learningacceptance. Comput. Educ. 57(2), 1501–1511 (2011)

An Editable Multi-media Authoring eBook System for Mobile Learning

Joseph Fong[*], Vincent Chung, and Kenneth Wong

Department of Computer Science, City University of Hong Kong, Hong Kong
csjfong@cityu.edu.hk

Abstract. Traditional eBook is to put the content of a book from hardcopy paper format into electronic mobile device format. Nevertheless, with evolution of mobile computing, information can be spread in seconds by mobile phones in multi-media format. Therefore, a student may need to put his/her learning material in an eBook which can be accessed by mobile device so that the student can study at any time and at anywhere using the mobile device. An authoring eBook allows students selects his/her own lecture slides from teacher's power point files, relevant discussion from open forum, cognitive map from course concept map, and video recording from lectures etc. This paper presents a methodology that can let students tailor make his/her own learning material from different multi-media source, and which can be edited as students' learning level improves. The stepwise development procedure includes preprocess of converting discussion panel and mind maps into images, uploading document, video, audio and images into PDF files, concatenate PDF files into an eBook PDF file, and modify the eBook PDF files if needed.

Keywords: authoring, eBook, multi-media, editable, mobile learning, PDF file.

1 Introduction

An electronic book (variously, e-book, e-book digital book, or even e-edition) is a book-length publication in digital form, consisting of text, images, or both, and produced on, published through, and readable on computers or other electronic devices.

Traditional e-books are read in e-book reader software in personal computer. The software can provide functions included: index, text, picture, login, search, reference, etc.

E-book readers have changed the way people enjoy full-length books, magazines, newspapers, and a wide range of text-based content (including PDF documents). Instead of holding a physical book or publication in your hands, an e-book reader displays text on its built-in screen. An e-book can simply be a traditionally published book that has been adapted into digital form, so it can be read on an e-book reader. When a student looks at the page of printed book versus the page of a book displayed

---

[*] Corresponding author.

S.K.S. Cheung et al. (Eds.): ICHL 2014, LNCS 8595, pp. 184–195, 2014.

on an e-book reader's screen, what the student will see can be virtually identical. Otherwise the student can customize the layout of the e-book on his/her tablet or e-book reader's screen.

There are a lot of e-book systems, but most of them only allow user to download the e-book. In other words, our system allows students select relevant learning material from multi-media resources into an e-book. The students can pick the screen layouts of the course mind maps and also individual panel discussion panel of interested subjects, teachers' power point lecture notes, video recordings, and even audios if necessary. Then the system will upload them into PDF files, which can be re-ordering accordingly by the students after preview. Then the system can concatenate these PDF files into one eBook PDF file which can be put into a mobile device for usage. Later on, the students can also revise the eBook according to his/her own requirements.

Nowadays, a smart phone has become indispensable and irreplaceable in the majority of people's daily life. Many people make use of smart phones to retrieve information on the Internet. Information can be packaged in the form of multimedia, including texts, images, audios and videos. Multimedia is often embedded into websites and mobile apps, but is rarely embedded into a single PDF file, which has been ratified as the long-term archiving solution for electronic documents in ISO standard (ISO 32000-1:2008). Until now, most applications of PDF files use merely texts and images. In fact, PDF version 1.7, which is the latest version, has been added support to contain videos and audios. The ultimate objective of the project is to develop a practical solution of producing a multimedia eBook (in the form of PDF) which can be used on smart phones for mobile learning.

2   Related Work

In these years, there is an increasing trend for University students to use mobile devices as a learning tool. Wilfred pointed out a potential reason behind the phenomenon that many educational institutions have already started using mobile devices as the primary tool to distribute course materials [1]. Still, most University students are not proficient in the way of how to manage the electronic materials well. They are often located separately, but in fact they are closely related in regarding to the content. Tortorella et al proposed an approach to provide personalized course content in mobile settings based on students' learning styles and context (cited in [1]). This allows the provision of personalized contents to individual student. To implement the approach, a personalized eBook authoring system is required in order to combine different elements intelligently for maximizing the effectiveness of students' mobile learning.

Andrew and Josie define mobile learning to be any sort of learning that happens when the learner is not at a fixed, predetermined location, or learning that happens when the learner takes advantage of the learning opportunities offered by mobile technologies [2]. The force behind which promotes and facilitates mobile learning is the advances in mobile technology such as the rapid development of mobile networks and mobile devices. Undeniably, mobile learning would be more significant among students in the future as it is expected that over one billion of the world's population will be able to access the Internet via their mobile devices within five years [3].

2.1   Multimedia eBook will be a New Breakthrough in Mobile Learning

e-Book is regarded as one of the most salient elements in mobile learning. With the existence of eBooks, students do not need to carry physical books anymore, the only thing that they need to do is to put the electronic version of the physical book into their mobile devices. In fact, the creation, modification and distribution of eBooks are not difficult to achieve by using the cutting-edge technologies nowadays. For example, Amazon Kindle Fire is one of the most popular devices for reading eBooks. And this thin and rectangular shape device enables people to access over a million eBooks from Amazon's Kindle Store. Thus, eBook is changing the way people used to read a physical book. Its digital nature enables people to share or distribute eBooks easier than ever. The ability for eBooks to be seamlessly integrated into mobile devices is a crucial advantage for mobile learning. With the rapid development of eBook, an eBook is capable to deliver not only text and images, but also audio, videos, and even programmable features which have dynamic response based on the reader's actions. Warren predicted that the future of eBooks will include more interactive formats such as hyperlinks and multimedia [5]. Therefore, the possibility for an eBook to contain innovative and interactive features will absolutely benefit students' learning experience in mobile learning.

2.2   Challenges on Mobile Learning with Multimedia eBooks

There are still a lot of challenges on mobile learning with eBooks. In fact, a compelling rationale and methodology for the adoption of eBook has not been fully utilized yet, although eBooks are increasingly popular and have a perceived value as relatively low-cost, easily accessible resources in education [6]. Up till now, a majority of eBooks do not include useful features such as cognitive map and open forum for students to apply what they have learnt after reading the eBooks [7].

Apart from the underutilization of eBooks' capabilities, it is found that many students underutilize their mobile devices to achieve mobile learning also. Indeed, there is a significant gap between students who own a mobile device and students who will actually use them for mobile learning. For instance, only 58 percent of smart phone owner and 64 percent of eBook reader owners who have the habit of using them for mobile learning. This implies that there are still a lot of students who have not yet realized mobile learning despite of the fact that their mobile devices are capable to do so. Also, we can deduce that quite large amount students still rely on using personal computers to access the course materials instead of using mobile devices.

In addition, it is found that mobile app categories related to mobile learning are much less popular than social networking among students. In fact, it is a big challenge for mobile learning to achieve the equivalent success of social networking. In order to fully utilize the processing power of mobile devices and to encourage students use it for mobile learning, it is crucial to promote mobile learning in the long run [8].

3   Methodology

Figure 1 shows the architecture of a proposed eBook system which is editable, multimedia and authoring in PDF file format.

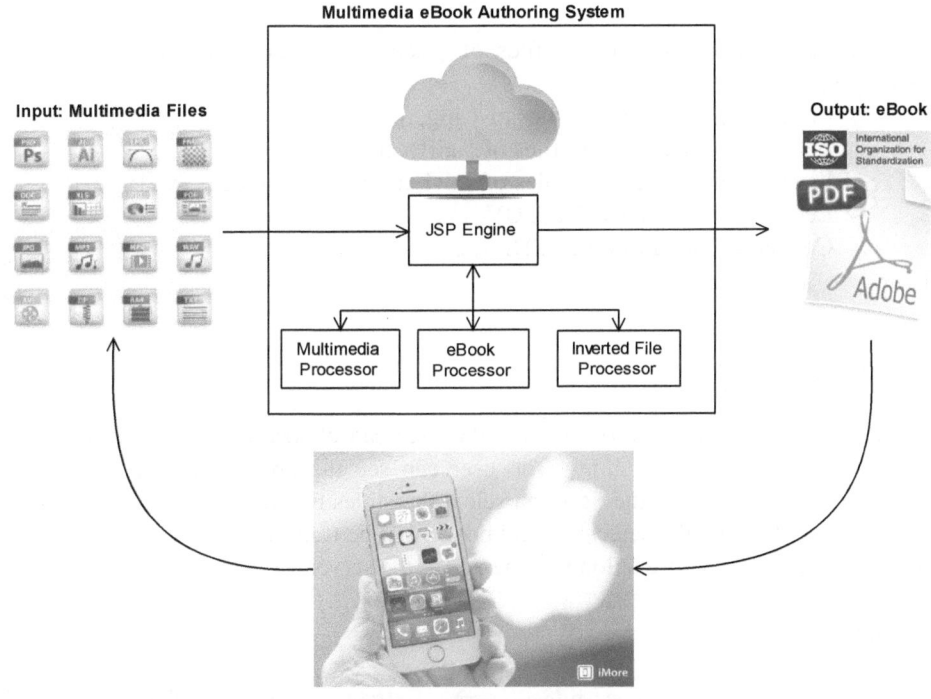

Fig. 1. Architecture of Editable Multi-media Authoring eBook System

3.1   A Stepwise Procedure of Developing an Authoring Multi-media eBook System

Step 1   Upload File

Users will be asked to upload files to the system from their computers. There are three sub-processes. (1) The first sub-process is to check whether the file format is supported by the eBook system. For example, .zip is not supported by the system. If a user tries to upload a .zip file, the eBook system will reject the upload request and return an error message. For each validated upload request, the eBook system will retrieve and store the file into a classified folder. (2) The second sub-process is that the uploaded file will be cloned and converted to a PDF automatically. (3) The third sub-process is to connect the database and execute an insertion SQL statement which inserts a new record for storing the 'file name', 'file size', 'file type', 'file format', 'file path', 'page count', 'file owner', 'upload date & time' regarding to the upload request.

Algorithm

Begin
   Let T be the set of text files of {.doc, .docx, .txt, .rtf, .html, .xml, .ppt, and .pptx};
      Let I be the set of image files of {.jpg, .png, .gif};
      Let A be the set of audio files of {.aiff, .mid, .mp3};
      Let V be the set of video files of {.avi, .mov, .mp4, .mpeg, .swf};
      Let σ be the set of T $\cup$ I $\cup$ A $\cup$ V;
      Convert σ into Ω of (.pdf) PDF file;
End;

Step 2   Extract File

If the uploaded file is PowerPoint file, the user can choose to do the extraction by selecting the only needed slides. The user can see the preview of each slide in a PowerPoint file, and then the user can select the slides by clicking the checkbox next to each slide. Finally, the selected checkboxes will be tracked by the corresponding id to do the extraction before uploading the file to the server.

Example:

test.ppt   →   *test1*.pdf   →   Extract p1, p3, p5 of *test1*.pdf   →
save as *test.pdf*

                    test-1.png   √
                    test-2.png   X
                    test-3.png   √
                    test-4.png   X
                    test-5.png   √

Step 3   Select Files

Users will be provided with a file list which consists of the files uploaded by the user previously. Each row in the file list provides the information of each file respectively. For instance, 'file name', 'file size', 'file type', 'file format', 'file path', 'page count', 'file owner' and 'upload date & time'. In addition, a checkbox will be associated with each row in the list. Users are required to select some files by clicking the checkboxes in order to proceed to the next process. If users haven't selected any files, the eBook system will be able to detect it and proceed to the next process until at least 1 checkbox is marked by users.

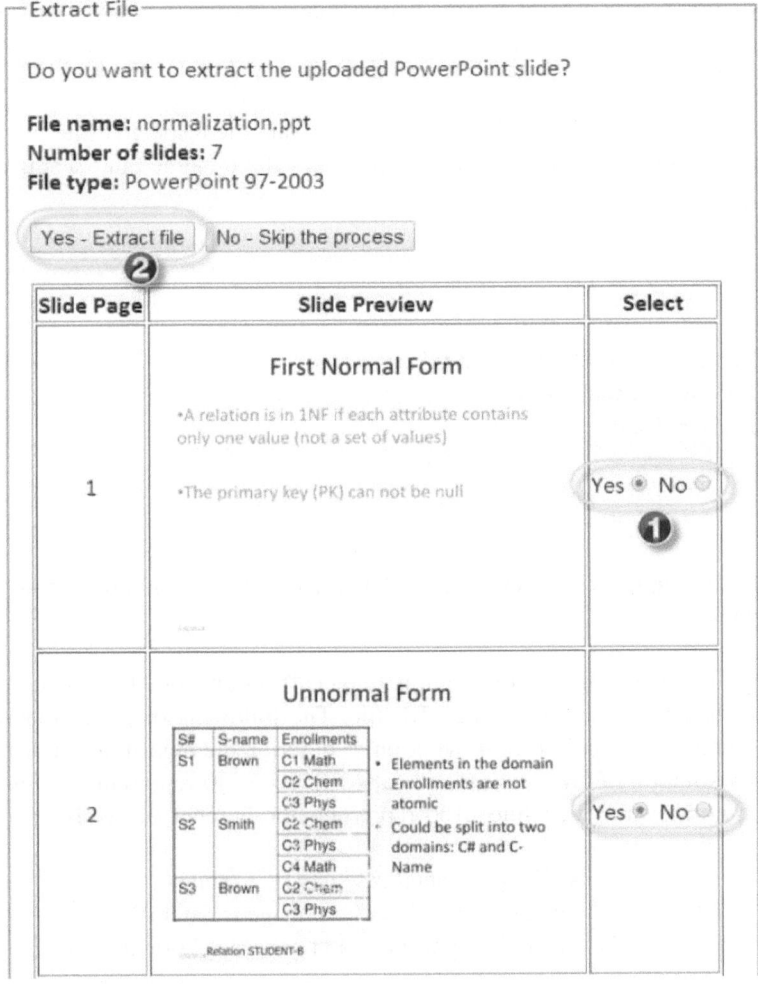

Fig. 2. Selection of the Orders of Uploaded PDF Files into eBook

Step 4   Preview & Ordering

The users will be provided with a table which consists of the selected files in the previous process. Besides, there are 'preview' column and 'ordering' column in the table. The purpose of the 'preview' column is to facilitate the ordering process because users can make an ordering decision more effectively and reduce repetitive manual effort by viewing the thumbnail of all the selected files within one single webpage. While the ordering purpose is to let users decide the file sequence in a single eBook.

For example, Figure 2 shows that user selects File 4 as first PDF file and File 2 as second PDF file in the eBook.

Step 5   Merging

The process will retrieve the ordering information and the respective file paths as the input. Based on the ordering information, the files will be merged into a single eBook as the output.

Algorithm

Begin
          Let user choose f1, f2,...,fn ∈ Ω;
          For (i==1; i<=|f|; i++)
          Do B = B ∪fi
End;

3.2   PDF Design for Detecting the Orientation of an Uploaded File (Image Type)

The design for detecting the orientation (either "Portrait" or "Landscape") of the image files before converting to the PDF file. The following diagram illustrates the image resolution concept before moving on to describe the algorithm. For instance, the image resolution of Ultra HD (4k) is 3840x2160. 3840 represents the number of pixels of a horizontal row, while 2160 represents the number of pixels of a vertical row.

If the number of pixels of a horizontal row is larger (smaller) than the number of pixels of a vertical row, then the orientation of an image is determined to be landscape (portrait). Therefore, the above diagrams have a "Landscape" orientation.

The image orientation issue is worthwhile to catch our attention because if the orientation is not determined, the image might not be fitted into the PDF page properly, or not able to fully utilize the available space of a PDF page.

Procedure:
1. For an image file which has been accepted as an authenticated upload request, the system will determine its orientation before converting to a PDF file.
2. If the image width is larger than the image height, then its orientation is landscape, and vice versa.
3. Create a blank PDF page and set the page size to A4.
4. Rotate the page by 90 degrees clockwise only if its orientation is landscape. (Skip "Step 4" for a portrait-oriented image)
5. Put the image on the blank PDF page.
6. Write the PDF file to the File Output Stream object (i.e. the destination file path).

3.3   Design of Resolving the Differentiation of the Resolution for an Uploaded File

Problem that the algorithm intended to solve: For $\forall \{n \in \Omega\}$, solve the problem of converting images with different resolution to a standardize PDF format in linear time.

The image resolution issue is worthwhile to catch our attention because if the resolution is not determined, the image might not be fitted into the PDF page properly, or will exceed the available space of a PDF page.

A4 page size is precisely 210mm x 297mm. However, computer program do not process the unit in mm directly. We need to convert the mm to dpi so that the program can do the conversion process correctly. For the conversion of mm to dpi, we need to consider how many mm for 1 inch. As 1 inch equals 2.54 cm, and 1 cm equals 10 mm, therefore, 1 inch equals 25.4 mm. After obtaining the mm per inch, we still need to consider how many pixels per inch in order to determine the actual resolution of an image.

According to ISO-32001-1, the default for the size of the unit in default user space (1/72 inch) is approximately the same as a pixel, a unit widely used in the printing industry. In short, 1 inch = 25.4mm = 72 user units (which roughly corresponds to 72 pixels).

The resolution of a PDF page (in terms of A4 page size) is to be calculated as follow:

Width = ((210mm) / (25.4mm/in)) x (72 pixels/in) = 595.2756 $\cong$ 595
Height   = ((297mm) / (25.4mm/in)) x (72 pixels/in) = 841.8898 $\cong$ 842

$\therefore$ Resolution = Width x Height = 595 x 842.

3.4   Design of an eBook System including eBook Database

An eBook database is developed to store the file id and supplemental information of each multi-media file as shown in Figure 3 in Entity Relationship Model such that the eBook and the File table are in many-to-many cardinality:

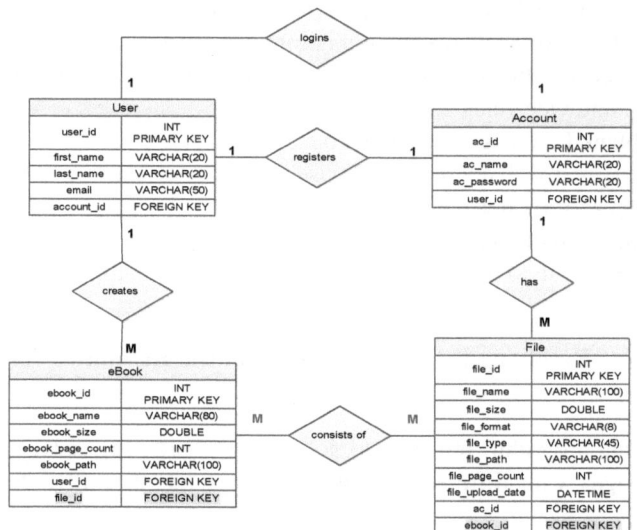

Fig. 3. The Meta Data of eBook System in Entity Relationship Model

We can show the data flow diagram of eBook system as shown in Figure 4:

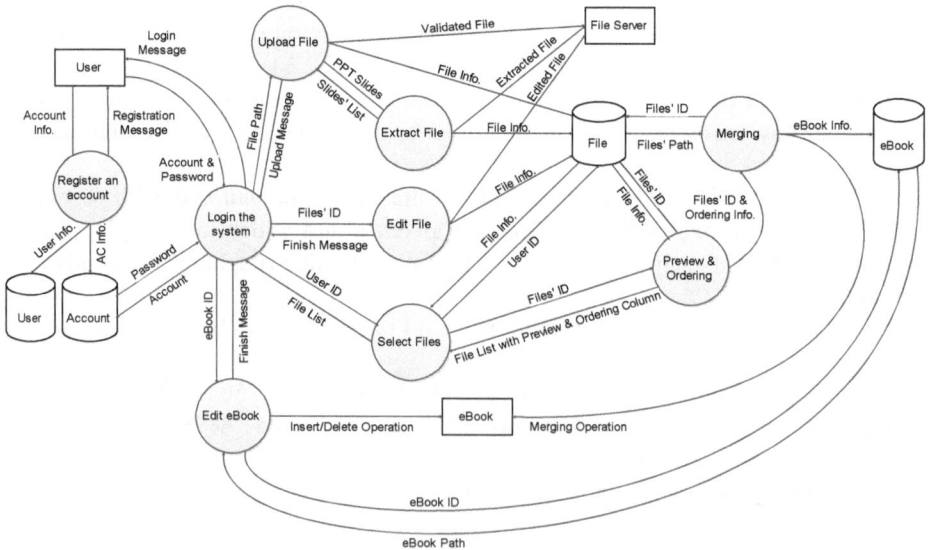

Fig. 4. Data Flow Diagram of the Editable, Multi-media, Authoring eBook System

4   Case Study

To illustrate the application of the methodology, the result of developing an eBook system on data normalization in 12 pages as shown in Figure 5:

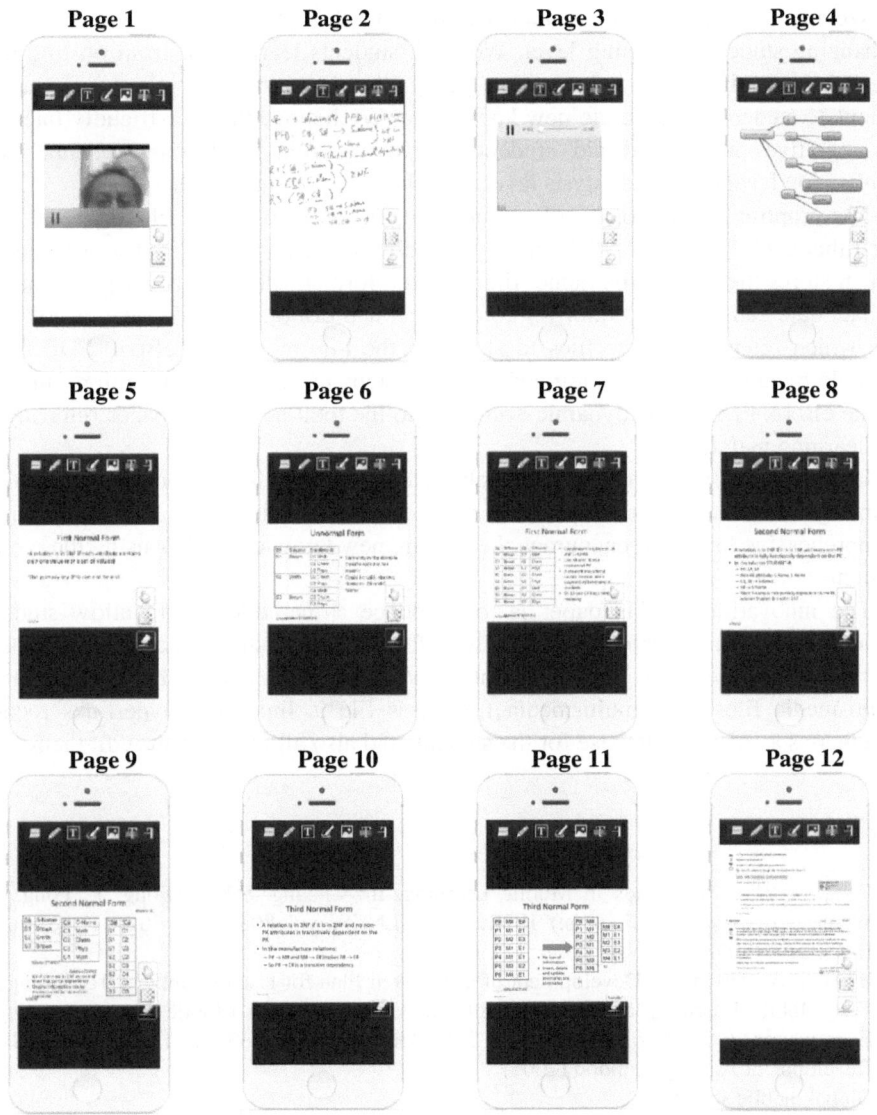

Fig. 5. A Derived Multi-media eBook in 12 Pages in PDF File Format on a Mobile Device

5   Conclusion

After teacher auto-generates a book file into e-book format, students can download and read it by their electronic device. This enables students save money to pay the cost of lecture notes or other reference book material.

We integrate the cognitive map features into the e-book system which aims at enhancing students' learning level. We wish students learn more from posting their idea through the node in cognitive map. Visualization of connecting idea can stimulate students to generate new knowledge. We believe the user-friendly interface of cognitive map could aid students' creativity. We think our students reach application level or even analysis level after they learn from the e-book.

The proposed methodology of an authoring eBook is to supply file id in PDF files such that each "resource" PDF file is uniquely identified by a file id in a File table which stores the file id, file name, file size, file format, file type, file page count, file upload date and eBook id referring to an integrated eBook PDF file. The eBook PDF file which refers to all the files id stored in the File table. The eBook PDF file is editable by doing the extraction and insertion steps in the eBook. Therefore, the size of the eBook PDF file is dynamic according to the total number of pages referring all the learning materials.

In conclusion, we develop the e-book system, not only for students to reduce their learning cost, but more important, we want our students to learn at a more comprehensive level and encourage them using new knowledge after using the e-book system.

The innovation of this paper is to introduce a methodology to allow students collect their learning materials in an eBook for study. The students can store any kind of relevant multimedia documents into his/her personal eBook by referring their multi-media files. The multi-media files uses file is link their hyperlinks records together as an eBook database for the student, and also allows students edit them.

References

1. Fong, W.W.: The Trends in Mobile Learning. In: Cheung, S.K.S., Fong, J., Fong, W., Wang, F.L., Kwok, L.F. (eds.) ICHL 2013. LNCS, vol. 8038, pp. 301–312. Springer, Heidelberg (2013)
2. Brasher, A., Taylor, J.: Development of a Research Plan for Use of Ambient Technology to Test Mobile Learning Theories. In: Jill, A., Carol, S. (eds.) Mobile Learning Anytime Everywhere: A Book of Papers from MLEARN 2004, pp. 33–37. Learning and Skills Development Agency, London (2005)
3. Global mobile statistics,
   http://mobithinking.com/mobile-marketing-tools/
   latest-mobile-stats
4. Gardiner, et al.: The Electronic Book. In: Michael, F., Woudhuysen, H. (eds.) The Oxford Companion to the Book, p. 164. Oxford University Press, Oxford (2010)

5. Warren, J.: Innovation and the Future of e-Books. The International Journal of the Book 6(1), 83–94 (2009)
6. Smith, M., Kukulska-Hulme, A.: Building Mobile Learning Capacity in Higher Education: E-books and iPads. In: Proceedings of the 11th World Conference on Mobile and Contextual Learning, pp. 298–301. CELSTEC & CICERO Learning, Helsinki (2012)
7. Fong, J., Wong, K.T.Y.: Generating E-book System Using Cloud Computing: A Cognitive Map and Open Forum Approach. In: Cheung, S.K.S., Fong, J., Fong, W., Wang, F.L., Kwok, L.F. (eds.) ICHL 2013. LNCS, vol. 8038, pp. 232–243. Springer, Heidelberg (2013)
8. Chen, B., Denoyelles, A.: Exploring Students' Mobile Learning Practices in Higher Education (2013),
   http://www.educause.edu/ero/article/
   exploring-students-mobile-learning-practices-higher-education

A Review on the Development
of an Online Platform for Open Textbooks

Simon K.S. Cheung[*], Kelvin K.W. Lee, and Kelvin K.L. Chan

The Open University of Hong Kong
Good Shepherd Street, Homantin, Kowloon, Hong Kong
kscheung@ouhk.edu.hk

Abstract. Open textbooks are typical open education resources that are freely and openly available for anyone to use and re-use, usually through an online platform which serves at least four purposes. First, it provides a repository for hosting the open textbooks. Second, it provides functions for users to access the open textbooks, both online and offline. Third, it also provides functions for users to contribute, revise, remix and redistribute the textbook contents. Forth, it allows users to rate and comment on the textbook contents. This paper shares our experience in developing an experimental platform for open textbooks, especially on the technical limitations and problems. The key functions of an open textbook platform are identified. It is learnt that user friendliness and easiness for use are the design objectives so a simple and concise user interface is required. It is however revealed that a right balance between user friendliness and functional comprehensiveness is important but difficult to achieve.

Keywords: Open textbook, open education resource, online textbook platform.

1 Introduction

With the advent of information and communication technologies and the prevalence of digital cultures together with the open licensing practices, both researchers and practitioners in education have been exploring the effective use of open education resources in teaching and learning. Open education resources are formally defined as the digitized materials offered freely and openly for educators and students to use and re-use for teaching, learning and research [1]. According to Cheung, open education resources appear in at least four forms, namely, open textbooks, open courseware, open online courses, and open-source software [2].

As a form of open education resources, open textbooks are by nature electronic books that can be accessible online and downloadable for offline usage. They consist of digital contents which can be delivered in textual and multimedia formats. They are coherent in contents and aligned to particular textbook standards. They can be readily customized to meet the individual needs and cater for the learning difference. They can be used as the traditional printed textbooks for classroom-based teaching, as well

---

[*] Corresponding author.

S.K.S. Cheung et al. (Eds.): ICHL 2014, LNCS 8595, pp. 196–207, 2014.

as for self-learning. The textbook contents are substantial enough and well organized as a single volume on a special subject or topic [3, 4].

With a short history of less than a decade, open textbooks have evolved as a major source of textbooks, not only for colleges and universities but also for primary and secondary schools. Many projects on open textbooks have been established. Some representative examples are cited below.

- College Open Textbooks aims to drive the awareness and advocacy for open textbooks, train teachers to adopt open education resources, conduct peer review, and grow online professional networks which support authors to share resources [5]. It provides hundreds of open textbooks, and a detailed guide for adopting open access textbooks and creating associated learning materials.

- The Open Access Textbooks project aims to create a sustainable model for the discovery, production and dissemination of open textbooks [6]. It builds on lessons learned in open textbook efforts and seeks to create a collaborative community to sustain the implementation of open textbooks. A repository of several hundreds of open textbooks has been deployed under this project.

- Flat World Knowledge claims itself to be one of the largest publisher of free and open textbooks [7]. Written by experts, the open textbooks are reviewed, edited, and supported by test banks, slides, and instructor manuals. These open textbooks are completely free and available online. They come with integrated audio, video, graphic, interactive features, and powerful search capabilities.

- Project Gutenberg offers over 33,000 free books, available for download on PC, Kindle, Samsung Note, Sony Reader, iPhone, iPod Touch, iPad, Android or other mobile or cell phones or tablets [8]. These books are quality assured, and previously published by bona fide publishers. The project has digitized and diligently proof-read with the keen support of thousands of volunteers.

- Connexions is a dynamic system consisting of a repository of open educational materials and textbooks [9]. Over 17,000 learning objects or study modules in mathematics, science, history, psychology and sociology are available in the repository which is currently accessed by over 2 million people per month. The books and learning materials can be downloadable to mobile devices.

- California Free Digital Textbooks was initiated in 2009, with an aim to review the existing open and free digital textbooks which can be used in schools in California [10]. It has stipulated open and free digital textbooks in high school mathematics and science, alleged to have met at least 90% of the approved academic standards. A total of 47 sets open textbooks are now available.

- CK-12 FlexBook is a non-profit-making organization with a mission to reduce the cost of textbooks for the K-12 market [11]. Using an open-content and web-based collaborative model, CK-12 FlexBook intends to create remixable textbook contents for adoption in schools. At present, remixable textbook contents for 21 subjects, mainly in science and mathematics, are available.

In any open textbook project, an online platform is provided for users to access the open textbooks as well as to revise, remix and redistribute the textbook contents. The platform also allows users to evaluate the textbook contents.

An online platform is important for the adoption of open textbooks. In 2013, we developed an experimental platform for open textbooks with an aim to investigate the usability and feasibility as well as to identify the technical limitations and problems in the development process. A group of users, including students and non-students, are also invited to evaluate the experimental platform. Very positive results are obtained. In this paper, we share our experience in developing the experimental platform. The rest of this paper is structured as follows. Section 2 states the essential functionality of an online platform for open textbooks, where our experimental platform is used for illustration. The design features of the platform as well as the technical limitations and problems are also discussed. Section 3 then reports the evaluation results. Section 4 briefly concludes this paper.

2   An Online Platform for Open Textbooks

This section begins with the functional overview of an online open textbook platform. We then describe the technical design of our experimental platform, and illustrate the key functions of the platform. This is followed by a discussion on the design features and the technical limitations and problems.

2.1   Functional Overview

In general, an online platform for open textbook should serve at least the following four functional purposes.

First, the platform should provide an online repository of the open textbooks. Users can select appropriate textbooks to meet their individual teaching and learning needs. Like traditional textbooks, from time to time, there are updates and revisions on the textbook contents. The platform should allow continuous updates and revisions on the online textbooks, and therefore, support version control of the textbook contents. The built-in architecture should anticipate and accommodate ongoing growth of contents driven by the ever expanding user community.

Second, the platform should provide functions for users to access the textbooks, both online and offline. Users can select appropriate textbooks and learning materials to meet their individual teaching and learning needs. A variety of devices, including mobile devices, tablet devices, notebook and desktop computers, should be supported. Since users can access the textbook contents through mobile or handheld devices, mobile or ubiquitous learning is made possible.

Third, the platform should provide functions for users to contribute, revise, remix and redistribute the textbook contents. Therefore, it can support a two-way interactive and iterative process for users to download, revise, remix and then upload the revised and remixed textbook contents. Also, the textbook contents can be readily customized to cater for individual learning difference.

Fourth, the platform should allow users to provide ratings and comments on the textbook contents. This essentially takes the form of peer review for reference and ongoing improvement of the open textbooks.

2.2   An Experimental Platform

With an aim to study the usability and feasibility of an online open textbook platform as well as to identify any limitations and problems in developing such a platform, in 2013, we initiated the development of an experimental platform for open textbooks as a final-year-student project [12].

In the experimental platform, users are categorized in accordance with their roles. There are three categories of users, namely, authors, teachers and students. Different categories of users would use different functions of the system. Users (authors) can contribute open textbooks by creating and revising the textbook contents and learning materials. Users (teachers) can search and select the appropriate textbook contents and learning materials. The selected contents can be customized as self-contained open textbooks to cater for specific teaching and learning needs. Users (students) can access the open textbooks online and download them for offline usage. They can also make print-on-demand requests for hard copies of the textbooks. Besides, all users can communicate with each other through an online chat room. Table 1 summarizes the functions available for users.

Table 1. Categories of users and the functions available to them

User categories	Available functions
Users (authors)	1. create the textbook contents 2. revise or delete the textbook contents 3. access the textbooks online and download the textbooks for offline usage 4. make print-on-demand requests for hard copies
Users (teachers)	1. search and select the textbook contents and the associated teaching and learning materials 2. customize the selected textbook contents as self-contained textbooks with cover pages and sections. 3. access the textbooks online and download the textbooks for offline usage 4. make print-on-demand requests for hard copies 5. rate and comment on the textbook contents 6. communicate with students through the chat room
Users (students)	1. access the textbooks online and download the textbooks for offline usage 2. make print-on-demand requests for hard copies 3. rate and comment on the textbook contents 4. communicate with teachers through the chat room

In the following, the key functions of the experimental platform are briefly described.

Create the textbook contents. There are two ways to create the textbook contents, namely, "online create" and "upload create". "Online create" allows users (authors) to create the textbook content through a HTML text editor which is available from the platform. The text editor is simple to use, and the output format is HTML files, as shown in Figure 1. "Upload create" allows users (authors) to upload external files and convert the files to HTML files, as shown in Figure 2. External files in Microsoft Word, ODT and PDF are supported. The file size is limited to 300MB.

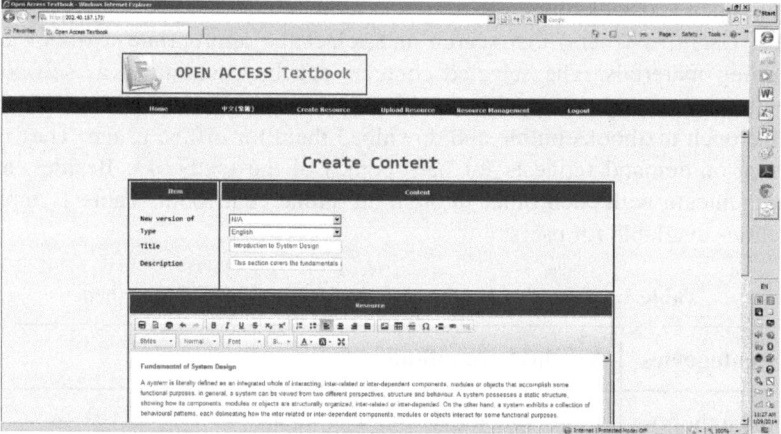

Fig. 1. The "online create" function of the experimental platform

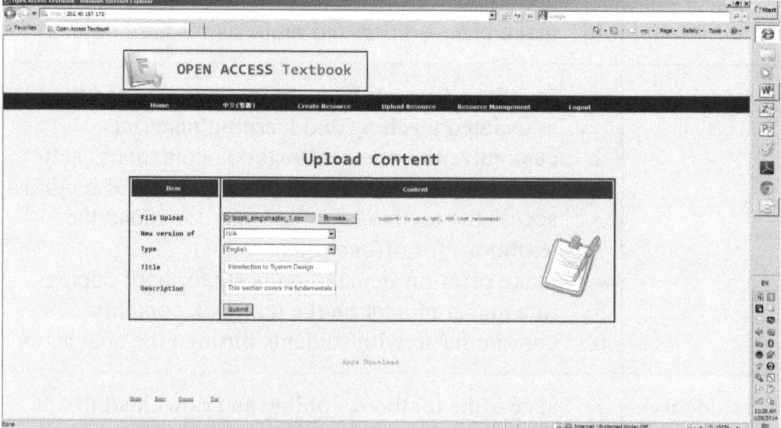

Fig. 2. The "upload create" function of the experimental platform

Revise or delete the textbook contents. Users (authors) can revise the contents through the HTML text editor to edit or delete the textbook contents.

Select the textbook contents and form a textbook. Users (teachers) can search and select the textbook contents by type, title or author, or any combination. Alternatively, users (teachers) can supply one or more keywords to search and select the textbook contents, as shown in Figure 3. After selecting the appropriate textbook contents, the users (teachers) can customize a textbook by creating a cover page and dividing the selected textbook contents as chapters. Related chapters can be grouped as sections. The table of content can be automatically generated. Figures 4 and 5 show the screens for customizing a textbook.

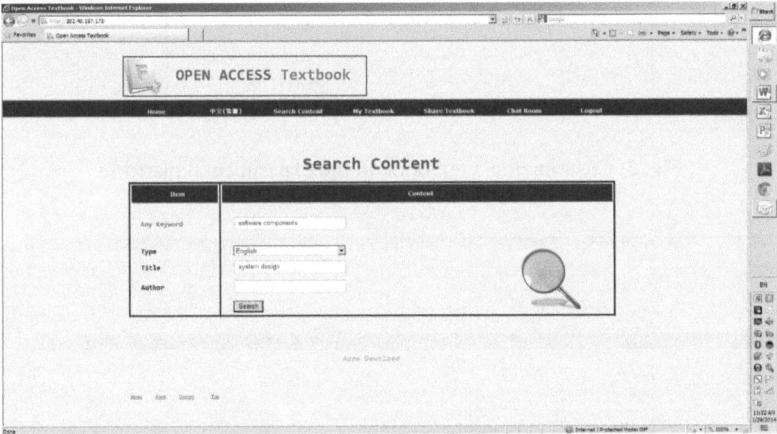

Fig. 3. Searching textbook contents in the experimental platform

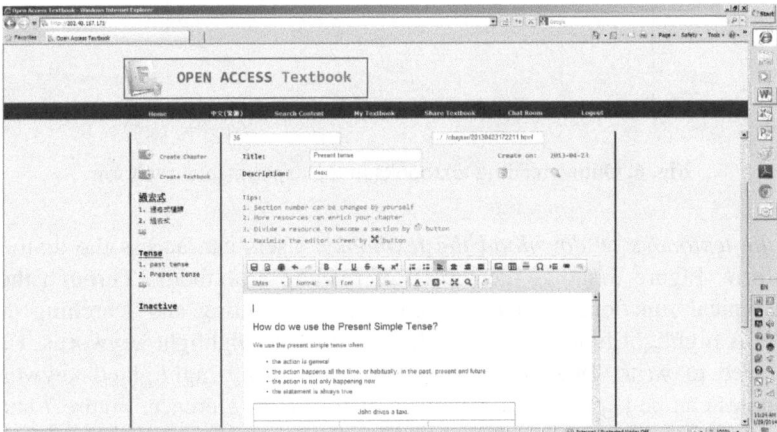

Fig. 4. Selecting textbook contents in the experimental platform

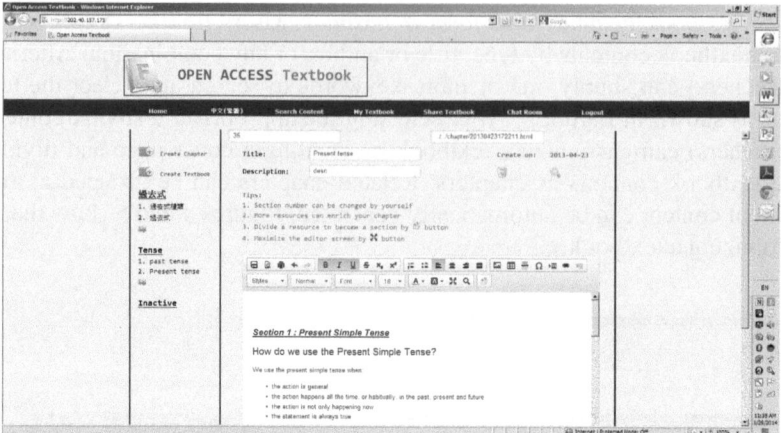

Fig. 5. Customizing a textbook in the experimental platform

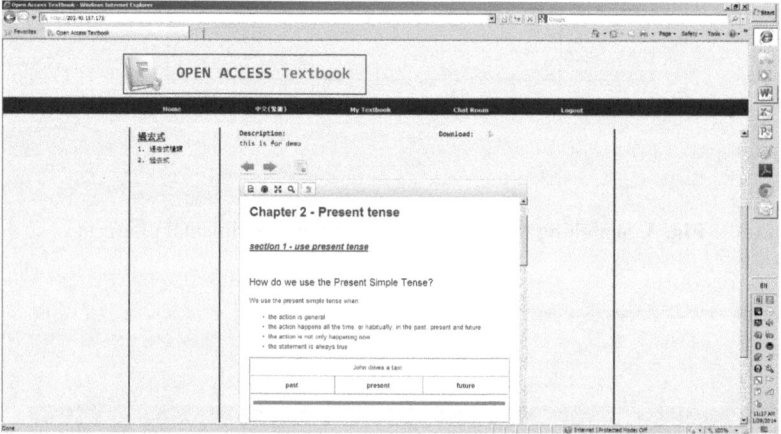

Fig. 6. Online reading textbooks in the experimental platform

Access the textbooks or download the textbooks. Users can access the textbooks on the platform. Figure 6 shows the screen of reading a textbook. Through the editor plug-in, typical functions such as screen resizing, printing and searching texts are available. A highlight function is provided for users to highlight keywords. Users are also allowed to write some notes in the textbook. Any highlighted keywords and written notes can be kept for self-reference or for other reference. Figure 7 shows the highlight function. On the other hand, textbooks can be downloaded as PDF format for offline usage, as shown in Figure 8.

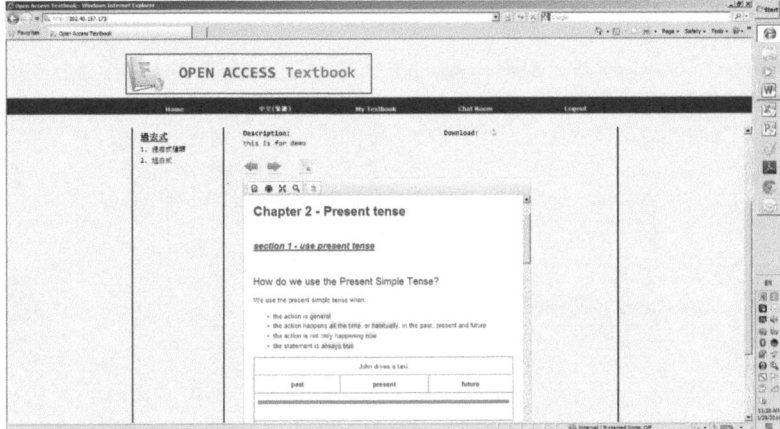

Fig. 7. Highlighting keywords in a textbook in the experimental platform

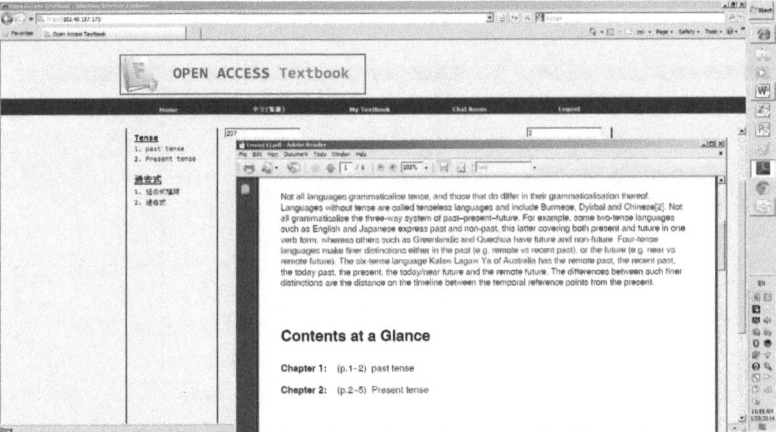

Fig. 8. Downloading a textbook as PDF format in the experimental platform

Make print-on-demand requests for hard copies. Users can make print-on-demand requests for hard copies, if necessary. These requests would be sent to designated print shops for handling the print requests.

Rate and comment on the textbooks. For any textbooks on the platform, users can freely make their own ratings and comments on the textbook through the chat room, as shown in Figure 9. These ratings and comments are visible by other users. Users can also respond to the ratings and comments provided other users. The chat room can also be used for other communications among the users.

The experimental support bilingual interfaces, that is, English and Traditional Chinese languages. A sample screen in Traditional Chinese is shown in Figure 10.

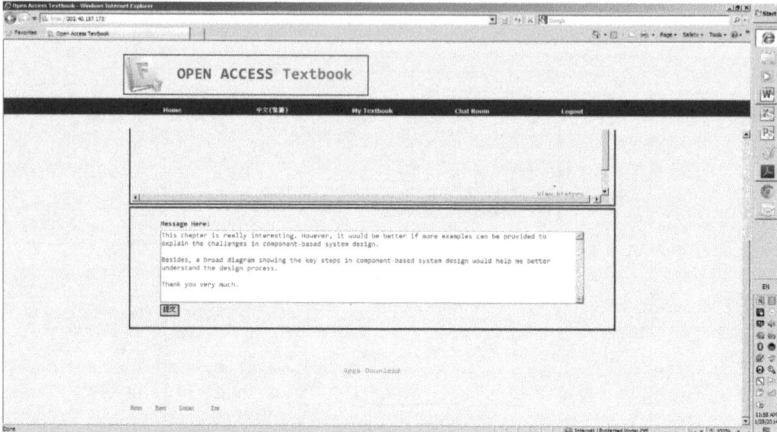

Fig. 9. Making comments through the Chat room in the experimental platform

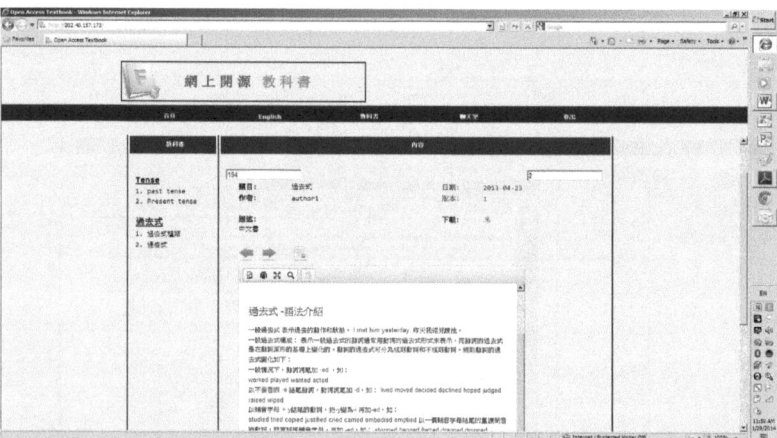

Fig. 10. A sample screen in Traditional Chinese in the experimental platform

2.3   Design Features, Limitations and Problems

In developing the experimental platform, we used the PHP programming language which is a powerful server-side scripting language. PHP can deploy on almost every operating system, so the experimental platform can be readily operated on different devices, including desktop PCs, notebook PCs, tablet devices and smart phones. Both Apple IOS-devices (iPhones, iPads and Macbooks) and Android-based devices (tablet devices and smart phones) are supported.

In the experimental platform, MySQL is used as the database management system. WampServer is used as the web servers for hosting the textbook contents and learning materials. It is a Windows-based development environment, allowing the creation of web applications using PHP and MySQL database.

The experimental platform fully supports the Android-based devices. Users can use Andriod-based tablet devices and smart phones for accessing the open textbooks via the web. This effectively supports mobile learning and ubiquitous learning. Typically in the Android operating system, Java is used as the programming language, and SDK tool is used as the compiler of the codes. For the experimental platform, Java, SDK and Eclipse are used as an integrated development environment.

Since an open textbook platform is open to the general public, the user community is diversified. The users include the authors, editors and reviewers of open textbooks as well as the teachers and students who use the textbooks for teaching and learning. The user interface should be carefully designed, and user friendliness is an important design objective. In the experimental platform, a simple and concise user interface is adopted. Menu banners are tailored for different categories of users, for example, a menu with functional items for users (authors), such as "online create" and "unload create" is shown if a user (author) is logged in.

Easiness for use is another important design objective. It is desirable that users can know how to operate without making reference to a user guide. Adopting a simple user interface, users can operate the system easily. For example, in reading a textbook online, only a few self-explanatory buttons for essential functions are shown, such as zooming in or out, moving pages forward and backward, and highlighting keywords. In editing the textbook contents, the system would load an editor with the essential buttons such as on font size and font type, boldface, italic, underline, superscript and subscript, bullet item, and left-right justification.

On the other hand, a number of technical limitations and problems are encountered. As a simple and easy-to-use user interface is adopted, complicated and sophisticated functions are not supported. For example, in editing the textbook contents, although images and graphics can be imported, the editor does not provide any online graphic editing tools for users to create or editing graphics such as lines, circles or other graphic shapes. In developing the experimental platform, we came across a technical decision on whether a graphic editing tool plug-in should be provided. If a graphic editing tool plug-in is provided, then the user interface would become too complicated for users to operate. After considering a number of factors such as user friendliness, easiness for use and functional need, it was decided not to provide the plug-in. The same issue applies to other editing tools and facilities.

Besides, there are limitations on the variety of formats of the textbook contents. The experimental platform does not support a full range of multimedia formats. Animated video and specific learning objects are not supported. In order to provide a full range of multimedia, including animated video and learning objects and other plug-ins, a lot of technical work is required. Moreover, it would also make the user interface become complicated. It also creates problems on the mobile access of the platform. This is because most of the handheld or mobile devices (Android-based and IOS-based devices) do not have sufficient memory capacity or processing power for running complicated processing tasks.

3   User Evaluation

In order to get the users' feedbacks on open textbooks and the experimental platform, an evaluation survey was conducted in 2013. Users were invited to participate, and a total of 72 replies from 30 students and 42 non-students (authors, teachers and others) were received. The survey aims to study two issues. First, would open textbooks serve the same functions as traditional printed textbooks? Second, would the experimental platform be user friendly and easy to use?

Owing to the space limitation in this paper, we cannot provide the full details of the survey results, as they are available in the student project report [12]. In summary, for the first question, it is reported that the majority (94%) strongly agree or agree that the open textbooks are similar to the traditional printed textbooks. Only 6% indicated disagreement. For the second question, it is reported that the majority (76%) strongly agree or agree that the experimental platform is user-friendly and easy to use. For the rest 24% indicating disagreement, the lack of support (due to the technical limitations and problems mentioned in the previous Section) is their key concerns. Table 2 shows the summarized results of the survey.

Table 2. Summary results of the evaluation survey

Questions	Responses	
1. Do you think the open textbooks serve the same functions as traditional printed textbooks?	Totally agree	72%
	Agree	22%
	Disagree	6%
	Totally disagree	0%
2. Do you think the experimental open textbook platform is user-friendly and easy to use?	Totally agree	5%
	Agree	71%
	Disagree	19%
	Totally disagree	5%

4   Conclusion

In the past decade, open textbooks have evolved from online resources to a major source of textbooks, serving the same purposes and functions as the traditional printed textbooks. Open textbooks have earned wide acceptance from the general public, as reflected in the rapid growth in the number of open textbooks and the establishment of more and more open textbook websites and projects. The advantages and benefits of open textbooks are well recognized.

The deployment of open textbooks needs an online platform. The online platform serves to provide a repository of the textbooks for both online access and download, as well as to allow contribution, revision, customization and redistribution of the textbook contents. We developed an experimental open textbook platform in order to investigate its usability and technical feasibility. Our experience in the development of the experimental platform is shared.

In this paper, we identify the key functions of an open textbook platform, and use the experimental platform for illustration. The design features as well as the technical limitations and problems are discussed. It is learnt that, given a diversified user community of the platform, a simple and concise user interface should be adopted. User friendliness and easiness for use are important design objectives. However, a simple and concise user interface may sacrifice the functional comprehensiveness of the platform. An evaluative survey is conducted to users. As reported by the survey results, the majority considered that open textbooks could serve the same functions as the traditional printed textbooks and that the experimental platform is user-friendly and easy to use. Based on our study, in developing an open textbook platform, a right balance between functional comprehensiveness and user friendliness is important but difficult to achieve. It is hoped that our findings would provide a reference on the development of an open textbook platform.

References

1. OECD: Giving Knowledge for Free: The Emergence of Open Education Resources, Centre for Educational Research and Innovation, Organization for Economic Cooperation and Development (2007)
2. Cheung, S.K.S., Li, K.C., Yuen, K.S.: An Overview of Open Education Resources for Higher Education. In: Lam, J., Li, K.C., Cheung, S.K.S., Wang, F.L. (eds.) ICT 2013. CCIS, vol. 407, pp. 26–34. Springer, Heidelberg (2013)
3. Cheung, S.K.S., Yuen, K.S., Li, K.C., Tsang, E.Y.M., Wong, A.: Open Access Textbooks: Opportunities and Challenges. In: Li, K.C., Wang, F.L., Yuen, K.S., Cheung, S.K.S., Kwan, R. (eds.) ICT 2012. CCIS, vol. 302, pp. 201–210. Springer, Heidelberg (2012)
4. EDUCAUSE: Open Textbook Publishing. Educause Learning Initiative, EDUCAUSE, March 2011 issue, Washington, DC (2011)
5. CCOTC: Website of College Open Textbooks, Community College Open Textbooks Collaborative (2014), http://www.collegeopentextbooks.org
6. FDLC: Open Access Textbooks: Website of Open Access Textbooks, Florida Distance Learning Consortium (2014), http://www.openaccesstextbooks.org
7. FlatWorld: Website of Flat World Knowledge (2014), http://www.flatworldknowledge.com
8. Gutenberg: Website of Project Gutenberg (2014), http://www.gutenberg.org
9. CXN: Website of Connexions (2014), http://www.cnx.org
10. CLRN: Website of California Digital Textbooks Initiative, California Learning Resource Network (2014), http://www.clrn.org/fdti
11. FlexBook: Website of CK-12 FlexBook (2014), http://flexbooks-wiki.ck12.org
12. Chan, K.K.L.: Development of an Open Access Textbook Platform, BComp (Hons) Internet Technology Final Year Project Report, School of Science and Technology, The Open University of Hong Kong (2013)

Developing Knowledge Clusters
in a Supportive Learning Environment

Wai-lap Chan and Lam-for Kwok[*]

City University of Hong Kong
83 Tat Chee Avenue, Kowloon, Hong Kong
{billchan225@gmail.com,cslfkwok@cityu.edu.hk}

Abstract. Concepts naturally have linkages with each other. Their relationships may not be so obvious to students if they are located in different learning sessions. Systematic knowledge management is desirable in learning with the use of technology in which we could control and represent knowledge with different types of connections. This paper introduces a new learning approach supported by the concept of a Knowledge Cluster. A Knowledge Cluster facilitates learning of concepts with focus on understanding the relationship of concepts across different topics, sessions and courses.

Keywords: Knowledge Management, Knowledge Cluster, Concept Maps.

1 Introduction

Learning is a process of constructing knowledge structure by interacting with a concept from the real world and the current state of knowledge in one's memory [1]. The meaning of a concept is varied. It can be a mental representation [2], ability [3] or an abstract idea lay behind objects of the physical world [4, 5]. When a new concept is identified, we are not only to understand its idea, but its relationship with concepts in our existing knowledge [6]. In a traditional learning environment, a lesson in a classroom as a learning session supports learners to build their knowledge. A teacher presents concepts to students of certain topics in a series of teaching sessions of a course. A course is a subset of a subject with topics found by a teacher based on the design of the course. A teaching session is also a learning session from the learner's point of view. Topics are a series of teaching objects and materials with concepts behind. Students participate in different lessons to understand the concepts and ideas of topics. While the efficiency and effectiveness of learning highly depends on how students construct concepts with their existing knowledge [7], it also relies on the motivation of a student, the delivery skills of a teacher [8], the design of learning activities and the supportive learning environment in a teaching session [9].

From the above described educational setting, we identify three learning targets. Basically a student starts by understanding an individual concept in a lesson. Secondly

---

[*] Corresponding author.

S.K.S. Cheung et al. (Eds.): ICHL 2014, LNCS 8595, pp. 208–219, 2014.

in a lesson there are many concepts under certain topics. While concepts naturally have linkages [10], knowing their relationships can assist a better organization of knowledge and get a whole picture of a certain subject area [11]. Finally, concepts from different courses might have linkages. Students need to understand the relationships of concepts located in different subject areas and be able to apply them.

Since motivating learners to improve their abilities and teacher training are beyond the scope of this paper, we shift the focus on designing the learning supports to achieve the above stated objectives. To support the understanding of an individual concept, more reference resources such as books and websites can be provided for further reading. To understand the relationship of different concepts in a lesson, one proposed learning activity is to draw a Concept Map (or topic Map, Mind Map) which summarizes the concepts in each lesson. A Concept Map consists of concepts in simple words and linked by lines presenting their relationships. An example of Concept Maps is given in Figure 1. It enables visual learning which engages learners to communicate concepts and knowledge visually [6, 12]. The difficulty remains on the understanding of the relationships between concepts located in different lessons. In a situation while lessons and courses are taught by different teachers, realizing their relationships largely depends on the ability of a student.

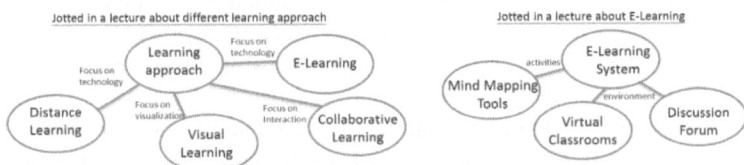

Fig. 1. An example of Concept Maps drew in two lectures

One may propose to use a Concept Mapping tool to assist the stated learning objectives. A Concept Map basically treats any kinds of information as concepts which are linked up with lines. A concept can connect to different websites, books and online materials as reference resources. It can also connect to different lessons and courses. Therefore we can use one single Concept Map which presents the connections of concepts, resources and lessons in one big picture, of which an example is shown in Figure 2.

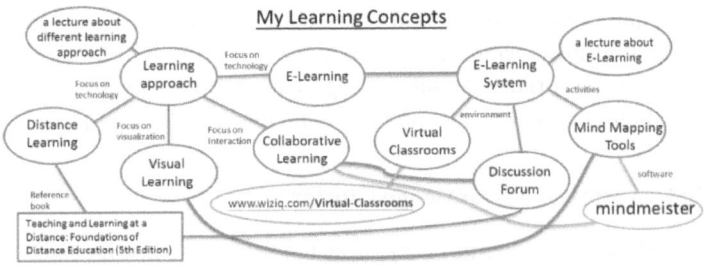

Fig. 2. An example of one Concept Map connects all information in two lectures

By using existing Concept Mapping tools, we could connect concepts, reference materials and sources together. Upon further reflection, this approach has different degree of deficiencies. Although conceptually Concept Maps are unstructured and presented in a chaotic manner, the situation might become non-comprehensible with more information attached and connected. Furthermore, this Concept Map contains not only concepts, but also different kinds of objects and information. When mixing them together and displayed in the same view with connections, the original purpose of a Concept Map, which shows the relationships between concepts, are lost in such information-rich view. Last but not least, by having only one Concept Map, the boundaries between concepts in different lessons and courses no longer exist. From another aspect, we also lost the scope of a lesson or even a course. This might become awkward if a concept simultaneously appeared in different lessons or courses. To set a boundary for a lesson and even a course is important to majority of students as it is the starting point of organizing the learning materials and thus the knowledge structure.

This study thus aims to suggest an approach on efficient knowledge management in existing educational settings based upon the existing concept of a Concept Map. In order to achieve the above stated learning objectives, an ideal tool needs to have the following features: we want to join concepts, resources and learning sessions without losing the appearance of connections between concepts; and to have boundaries between lessons but allow concepts to be connected across boundaries. With these requirements, a new learning approach is defined aiming on managing knowledge especially their relationship in existing educational learning environment. In this respect, we use the term "knowledge" to include concepts, resources and learning sessions, of which their combination provides a support to building knowledge in one's memory. Different kinds of knowledge are connected with each other with different types of linkages. Knowledge structurally clusters in different learning sessions. While knowledge inside a cluster connects to knowledge in another cluster, a Knowledge Cluster which assembles different selected pieces of knowledge is formed. In this paper, a discussion is given to the development of a Knowledge Cluster in the existing learning environment. We define its model and structure, describe its elements at a high level, and illustrate how the suggested learning activities may assist to achieve learning objectives.

2   A Conceptual Model of a Knowledge Cluster

The aim of a Knowledge Cluster is to manage knowledge in a systematic way through both individual and collaborative learning activities such that knowledge is structurally connected among all clusters. In this section we define its basic concept, extend this concept in a collaborative manner, suggest the requirements to a learning environment and explain our design in response to the three learning objectives.

2.1   Basic Concepts of a Knowledge Cluster

In a Knowledge Cluster, we define *concepts* as fundamental units. It can be presented by words, phrases or a couple of sentences. A concept has different supportive references. It can be any supportive information for further investigation. We define it as *attributes*. It may not be easy to distinguish an attribute from a concept. In general, a concept contains definitions, rules and guidelines [13]. An attribute is a reference resource. This reference resource does not limit to factual materials [13] such as books, website or files. An attribute can also be a link to a learning session where a concept is identified by a particular learner. When a concept is identified in a learning session, it can be instantiated with simple words and attached with attributes.

Concepts are clustered and connected in a learning session. They are connected by different kinds of relationships such as parent-child or sibling. It is relatively easy to identify relationships within a learning session but may be difficult for learners to sense their relationships for concepts located across different learning sessions. The attribute of reference resources is not only to provide pointers for further investigation but also provide an indirect connection of concepts across clusters. For example, while two concepts at different clusters referencing to the same chapter of a book, a learner may discover such linkage from one cluster to another. In this case, even these concepts have no explicit links but pointing to the same reference from two concepts implies a connection may exist.

2.2   Collaborative Learning with a Knowledge Cluster

Interacting with a Knowledge Cluster is a learning activity. In a learning session, a learner may be engaged in learning through discovering knowledge and identifying their relationships. As a fundamental concept of a Knowledge Cluster, individual learners perform the stated learning activities and build up an individually owned Knowledge Cluster by themselves. This simple design can be further extended into a collaborative manner with the support of a computer system. This system presents the concept of a Knowledge Cluster. Learners may directly jot down a concept into the system when participating in some learning activities. In terms of collaboration, all learners may build up their own Knowledge Cluster in a learning session or across different sessions. A Knowledge Cluster may then be further developed directly through discussion in a collaborative manner within a learning session or indirectly across different sessions. Collaborative learning achieved may increase learning effectiveness [14].

2.3   Considerations on the Learning Environment

The learning environment affects the efficiency of building a Knowledge Cluster. When learners obtain concepts, they might forget these concepts within a short period of time [15]. A Knowledge Cluster as a knowledge management system preserves such concepts for review. A good learner may put down concepts on a piece of paper or whatever means immediately in current practice. Fading memory becomes a serious problem when there is no support in recording such concepts. In the best case, a learner directly inputs concepts into the knowledge management system once identified. As a result, the learning environment and activities should be highly integrated in the form of a Knowledge Cluster. Conceptually, the learning environment contains different learning tools integrated with the Knowledge Cluster which support different learning activities. A learner may then manage concepts and their relationships learnt in a learning session.

2.4   Justification on Achieving Stated Learning Objectives

When concepts are clustered in a learning session, concepts are directly or indirectly connected. Attributes provide a direct or indirect connection between different concepts, both inside a cluster or across clusters. As such, a knowledge network is constructed across all learning sessions. When concepts are structurally connected, a learner could then enter from one point of a Knowledge Cluster, search along concepts in different clusters, through links and attributes, and reaches another point in different ends [16], as shown in Figure 3.

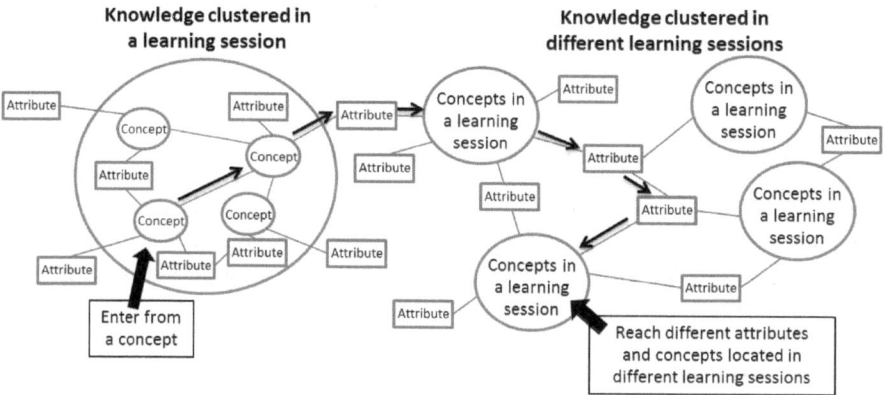

Fig. 3. A conceptual model of a Knowledge Cluster

When there are more attributes attaching to a single concept, these attributes may provide implicit or explicit links to other knowledge clusters which in turn provide a trace of connections between concepts. When concepts are clustered and connected inside a learning session, a visual image of such connections may provide learners with better understanding of the relationships between concepts. When attributes provide indirectly linkages of concepts located in different learning sessions, a learner may search along different concepts via these links and attributes and their relationships can be implicitly shown. In this respect, different clusters of knowledge in the system may be joined together with those overlapped with one's memory.

3   A Design and Implementation of a Knowledge Cluster

This section proposes the design of a Knowledge Cluster. This design composes of four major elements: the representation of a Knowledge Cluster, presenting and managing a Knowledge Cluster, initializing a cluster of knowledge and the design of a supportive learning environment.

3.1   Representation of a Knowledge Cluster

The basic data unit of a Knowledge Cluster is a concept. A Concept consists of attributes. Attributes can be generalized into three types: *fundamental*, *supportive* and *systemic*. Fundamental attributes represent the basics of a Concept. Supportive attributes are extra descriptions of a Concept. Systemic attributes are built for internal usage. A concept may be generalized by words or phrases but different learners may have their own elaborations on an instance of a concept. As such, some attributes of a concept have consensus by all learners while the others do not. To assist the collaborative learning activities, we further classified attributes into two types: *shared* and *personal*. They are summarized in Table 1.

Table 1. List of attributes of a concept

General classification	Interpretation
(Shared type)	
Basic Representation (fundamental)	Basic Representation is the basic form of a concept presented by words or phrases. This attribute presents the foundation existence of a concept inside the system.
Concept ID (systemic)	Concept ID is the standardized identifier of an instance of a concept replacing the Basic Representation.
Primary source (supportive)	A learning session usually conducted with learning materials such as presentation slides in form of PowerPoint file. A primary source of materials is that presentation slides.
Parent Concept ID (supportive/systemic)	Parent Concept is a direct linkage. A concept is a sub-concept of its parent concept. Concepts under the same parent concept are sibling concepts. This attribute represents the direct relationship.
Access count (supportive)	Access count is the number of access on a concept which shows a potential signal of its importance.
(Personal type)	
Keywords (supportive)	When a concept may present in a couple of long sentences, keywords telescope and provide a higher chance of creating indirect relationship. A keyword is also a type of category.
Reference Files (supportive)	Files are documents uploaded by teachers and stored in the system.
Reference Books (supportive)	It is used for reference resource. It also increases the chance of creating indirect linkage.
Reference Websites (supportive)	Same as above.
Detail Elaboration (supportive)	Detail Elaborations can be any other reference supports that further elaborate a concept.
Proposed Users (supportive/systemic)	While different Learners can have different elaboration on a certain concept, the name of the proposed user bounds to a concept and its personal attributes.
Last Modified Date (supportive)	It is used to identify the date of a concept's creation. Learners can use it to justify if the concept is updated or not.

In a learning session, a learner acquires concepts and identifies attributes. Those concepts and attributes can be shared by means of a Knowledge Cluster. While the other learners read a concept shared by others, they can give their own elaborations on it. A shared concept with attributes may be defined as one proposed by a learner. When such a concept is agreed by other learners, it can be used directly. In most cases, other learners might have different views or have slightly different set of attributes to such a concept, they may elaborate on ones' personal copy and propose to modify the shared one. When most of the other learners in the group agree to the proposal, such change may be included into the shared concept as shown in Figure 4.

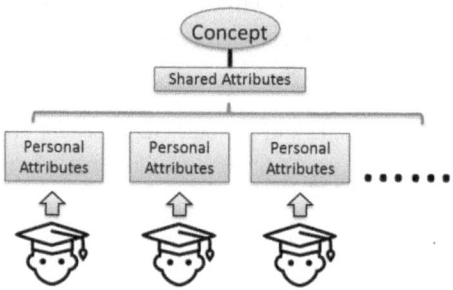

Fig. 4. Shared and personal attributes

3.2   Presenting and Managing a Knowledge Cluster

The concepts and their relationships can be organized and presented in a structural manner in the form of a tree as shown in Figure 5. Learners may take this shared visual form as a personal copy of the cluster for further development or elaboration. Such a cluster may be bounded by a learning session initially and learners may directly manage these concepts using the facilities provided simultaneously on this shared copy.

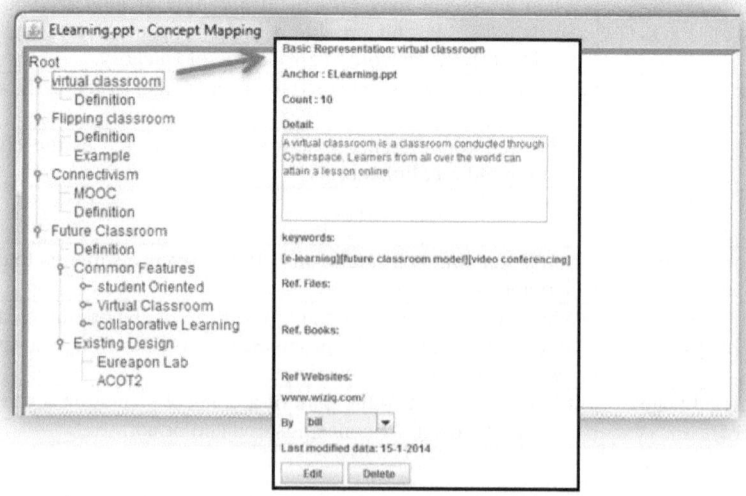

Fig. 5. A conceptual interface of a cluster of knowledge

The above conceptual interface may present a cluster of knowledge based on the learning material in a lesson. This design is constructed with boundary of a learning session as shown in Figure 6a and 6b, in which we reconstruct and redefine the boundary of a cluster by using different attributes. Figure 6c shows a more complicated design in which we define a group of clusters is contained in a larger cluster of knowledge.

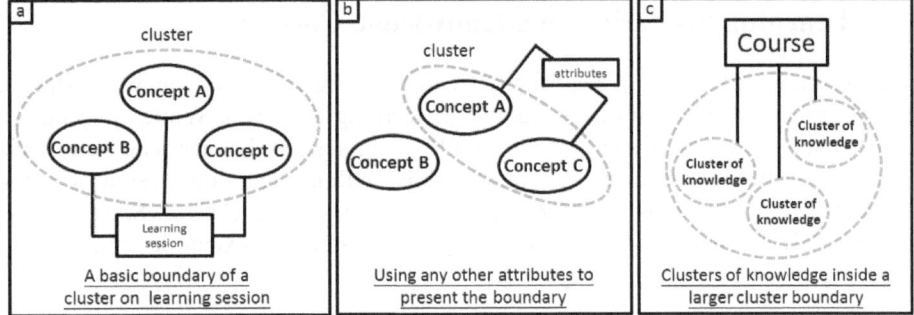

Fig. 6. Different conceptual boundaries of knowledge clusters

When concepts are located in different clusters of knowledge, their relationships can be seen through searching. There is a searching panel in the system which allows learners to input words and search for relating attributes. With more attributes included, there will be more indirect linkages connecting concepts located in different learning sessions.

3.3   Initializing a Cluster of knowledge on Top of Material

A learner may start learning with the supportive material of a learning session. For example, a lecture is often supported by presentation slides in the PowerPoint format. A cluster of knowledge may be formed initially on top of the presentation slides by extracting key items from such content.

When the course materials are uploaded, some key items such as topics, sub-titles and keywords are extracted. Further searching becomes possible with these extracted items. There are web-services which allow searching keywords relating to certain words, and thus provide a possibility for further expanding the resources and relationships of concepts. The teacher may then obtain some extracted items based on the course materials to justify and initialize a simple cluster of concepts.

3.4   Design of Supportive Learning Environment

To reduce the degree of fading memory, we need to take into considerations of the supportive learning environment. A learning environment equipping with computers provides basic supports to learning and enables further integration with the Knowledge Cluster system. For example, the system allows learners to directly read a piece of learning material without downloading. As such, learners could immediately input a concept into the system once they identify it. We further provide communication functions in such an environment to increase the degree of collaboration. An ideal supportive learning environment needs to facilitate learning engagement and collaboration. Such systems can be developed based upon the features of a virtual classroom environment [17], which facilitates collaborative learning to learners from all over the world.

4   Learning Scenarios on a Knowledge Cluster

Learners may participate in learning activities in a learning session with which a learning process usually starts in traditional learning approach. While concepts are captured and organized systematically in a learning session, learners can share these concepts and further discover their relationships within a learning session or across different learning sessions with the support of a Knowledge Cluster. Such cycle of learning activities may repeat and the knowledge cluster may extend learning beyond a learning session as shown in Figure 7.

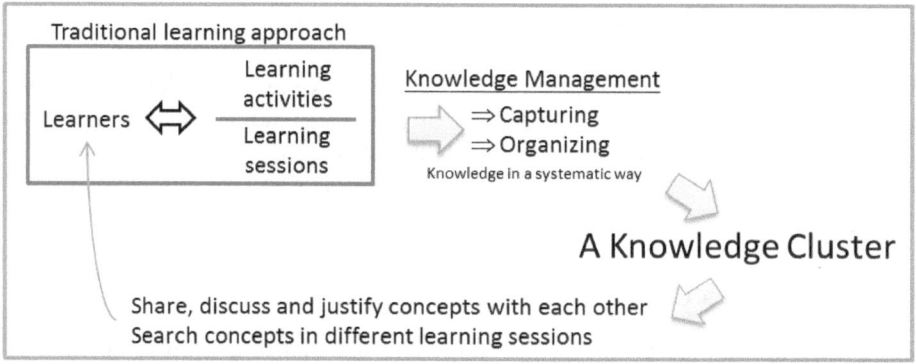

Fig. 7. The learning cycle of a knowledge cluster

At the beginning, we identify three learning objectives as the understanding on concepts and their relationships within or across different courses. With the support of a Knowledge Cluster, learning sessions are structurally managed and connected. A concept identified in a certain learning session is supported by attributes and linkages identification connecting to concepts in other learning sessions. This learning network allows learners to realize the relationship within or across different lessons and courses they participate in. We further illustrate this with several user scenarios.

4.1   Supporting Learning on a Single Concept

A student attends an algorithm course which covers the topics of Greedy algorithm. In a learning session, the teacher introduces this Greedy algorithm together with some examples such as a minimum spanning tree and their possible applications. Learners may take this further with the support of a Knowledge Cluster. When a learner finds out a website which shows the drawing of a minimum spanning tree step-by-step with animation, a learner may create a concept relating to Greedy algorithm and define the website as an attribute of the concept of minimum spanning tree as shown in Figure 8. Such a concept may be shared to others via the knowledge cluster and other learners may follow the website defined in the attribute of minimum spanning tree for further reading. This collaboration may enrich the learning of a concept and might facilitate better understanding of the concept.

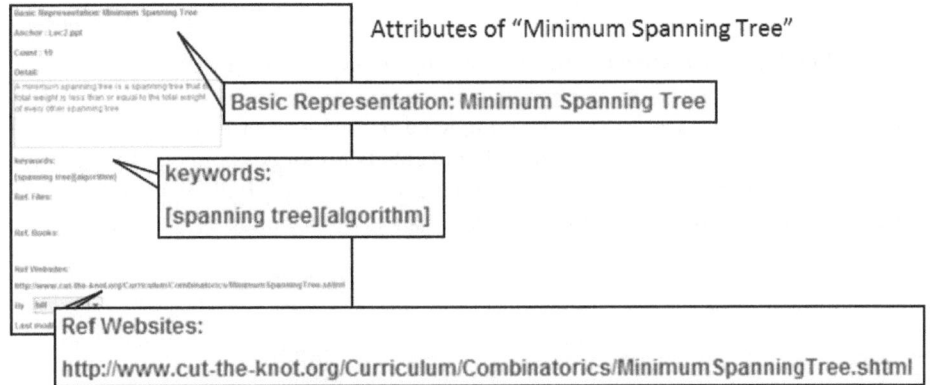

Fig. 8. The attributes of a concept

4.2   Understanding the Relationships of Concepts within a Subject

Learners share concepts and collaborate with each other to create a Knowledge Cluster bounded by a learning session initially. Take the algorithm lesson as an example, learners may discover concepts and identify their relationships present them visually as shown in Figure 9. By visualizing the concepts and their relationships, learners get better understanding on the knowledge relationships within the lesson.

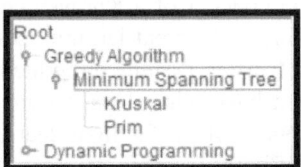

Fig. 9. A cluster of knowledge in a learning session

4.3   Connecting Concepts Located in Different Learning Sessions

Learners may come across the concepts of broadcasting and a spanning tree protocol in a network course. With the support of knowledge clusters, a learner may define "spanning tree" and "network protocol" as an attribute of keywords appending to the concept of "spanning tree protocol" and then share it via the knowledge cluster. Learners may then realize the linkage between "spanning tree" in the network course and "minimum spanning tree" in the algorithm course by searching through Knowledge Clusters as shown in Figure 10. In this sense, a connection is made between two concepts in clusters of knowledge.

spanning tree		Search	
Concept	Primary source		keywords
Minimum Spanning Tree	algorithm_Lec3.ppt		[spanning tree][algorithm]
Spanning Tree Protocol	05_ComputerNetwork.ppt		[spanning tree][network]

Fig. 10. A connection is made by searching the attribute of "spanning tree"

It is noted that this scenario can be completed by one learner or many learners collaboratively. In any cases, the learning of concepts is no longer bounded by a particular learning session. Different levels of connections can be built between different concepts located in different learning sessions as shown in Figure 11.

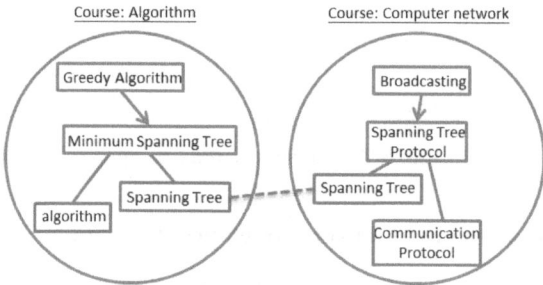

Fig. 11. Connecting concepts in different learning sessions

5   Conclusion

In this study, we introduce the concept of a Knowledge Cluster which manages and connects concepts within or across different learning sessions. We have developed a prototype of the Knowledge Cluster system integrated with a supportive learning environment with features of a basic virtual classroom. We have illustrated the assembly of concepts with attributes which facilitate learning within a learning session and extends learning across different learning sessions. While comparing with existing Concept Mapping tools, a Knowledge Cluster has a much tighter structure with different levels of linkages and boundaries. A concept is supported by reference resources in the form of attributes. Learners may get a whole picture of concepts in a learning session where concepts and attributes can be clearly classified. In other words, a Knowledge Cluster extends the capability of existing Concept Map by incorporating it with layers and structures together with enhanced descriptive power in terms of attributes to suit the current educational settings. While existing concept mapping tools allow collaborative learning for multiply users, a knowledge cluster extends this capability by allowing concurrent assess to and work on a concept in different learning sessions. If these works were shared back to a Knowledge Cluster, their implicit relationships can be discovered. Different learning sessions are implicitly connected with defined boundaries initially. The concept of attributes can be further developed by analyzing the types and characteristics of attributes and be supported by means of classification technology like ontology. When attributes are refined more precisely, we could redefine the boundary of clusters of a learning session, a course and a subject. A learner may then freely choose an attribute of a concept in a Knowledge Cluster and visualizing those relating concepts of that attribute such that different views can be formed with original physical boundaries fade. A trial of the system is expected to explore its effectiveness.

References

1. Ormrod, J.E., Davis, K.M.: Human learning. Merrill (2004)
2. Fodor, J.: Concepts: Where Cognitive Science Went Wrong. Oxford University Press, New York (1998)
3. Kenny, A.: Concepts, Brains, and Behaviour. Grazer Philosophische Studien 81(1) (2010)
4. Peacocke, C.: A study of concepts. The MIT Press (1992)
5. Concepts: Stanford Encyclopedia of Philosophy. Metaphysics Research Lab at Stanford University, http://plato.stanford.edu/entries/concepts/
6. Novak, J.D.: Learning, creating, and using knowledge: Concept maps as facilitative tools in schools and corporations. Routledge (2010)
7. Biggs, J.: What the student does: teaching for enhanced learning. Higher Education Research & Development 18(1), 57–75 (1999)
8. Valenzeno, L., Alibali, M.W., Klatzky, R.: Teachers' gestures facilitate students' learning: A lesson in symmetry. Contemporary Educational Psychology 28(2), 187–204 (2003)
9. Savery, J.R., Duffy, T.M.: Problem based learning: An instructional model and its constructivist framework. Educational Technology 35(5), 31–38 (1995)
10. Peacocke, C.: Interrelations: Concepts, knowledge, reference and structure. Mind & Language 19(1), 85–98 (2004)
11. Bransford, J.D., Brown, A.L., Cocking, R.: How People Learn: Brain, Mind, Experience, and School. National Academy Press, Washington (2000)
12. Willis, C.L., Miertschin, S.L.: Mind maps as active learning tools. Journal of Computing Sciences in Colleges 21(4), 266–272 (2006)
13. Priestley, M.: DITA XML: A reuse by reference architecture for technical documentation. In: Proceedings of the 19th Annual International Conference on Computer Documentation, pp. 152–156. ACM (2001)
14. Soller, A.: Supporting social interaction in an intelligent collaborative learning system. International Journal of Artificial Intelligence in Education (IJAIED) 12, 40–62 (2001)
15. Markovitch, S., Scott, P.D.: The Role of Forgetting in Learning. ML, 459–465 (1988)
16. Dunaway, M.K.: Connectivism: Learning theory and pedagogical practice for networked information landscapes. Reference Services Review 39(4), 675–685 (2011)
17. Hiltz, S.R., Wellman, B.: Asynchronous learning networks as a virtual classroom. Communications of the ACM 40(9), 44–49 (1997)

Forms of Instruction and Students' Preferences – A Comparative Study

Blanka Frydrychova Klimova and Petra Poulova

University of Hradec Kralove, Rokitanskeho 62, Hradec Kralove, Czech Republic
blanka.klimova@uhk.cz, petra.poulova@uhk.cz

Abstract. Online teaching and learning is increasingly common nowadays at many types of higher education institutions, ranging from hybrid/blended courses that offer a combination of face-to-face and online instruction, to fully online experiences and distance learning. The purpose of this article is to firstly outline the main benefits of online teaching and learning. Secondly, the authors survey which of the forms of instruction currently prevails and thirdly, to what extent students' learning preferences correspond to the selected form of instruction. This survey is conducted both in the Czech Republic and abroad, in this case in Kazakhstan, in order to obtain more reliable results.

Keywords: Online learning, traditional teaching, blended learning, learning preferences, survey.

1   Introduction

Online teaching and learning is increasingly common nowadays at many types of higher education institutions, ranging from hybrid/blended courses that offer a combination of in-person and online instruction, to fully online experiences and distance learning [1] The main reasons why online learning environment is widely used are as follows:

- it contributes to pedagogy because it supports more interactive strategies, not only face-to-face teaching [2], [3];
- it thus encourages collaborative learning; students or educators can work together on some projects from anywhere and at any time   [4], [5];
- it deepens intercultural awareness since it puts together re-searchers, educators, and students from anywhere in the world;
- it reduces costs of teaching and learning since students do not have to undertake so many frequent travels to complete their education [2]; and
- it might match students' learning style although there is no clear consensus on this issue [6], [7], [8], [9], [10], [11].

Also in the Czech Republic tertiary education is partly run online [12], [13]. [14]. For example, the Faculty of Informatics and Management (FIM) of the University of Hradec Kralove, Czech Republic, runs more than 230 e-courses which are exploited in different ways. They are run purely as online courses or they are led as blended courses

S.K.S. Cheung et al. (Eds.): ICHL 2014, LNCS 8595, pp. 220–231, 2014.

(see [15] for their definition) or they serve as an additional support for students after their regular, face-to-face classes so that students can read once again the information already obtained during the lecture. Several surveys and research performed at the faculty confirmed that students welcomed the possibility to exploit online courses but mainly as blended learning courses (see, for example, [16], [17]. Thanks to the cooperation with Karaganda State Technical University, the research team had an opportunity to work at the oldest Kazakh university and survey e-learning environment in this Central Asian republic in order to ensure the representativeness of the survey sample at an international level. The aim of this article is to survey which of the forms of instruction currently prevails at both institutions and to examine to what extent students' learning preferences correspond to the selected form of instruction.

2   Material and Methods

In January of 2014, 42 part-time students of Management of Tourism at FIM were given a questionnaire in order to discover whether their attitude towards online teaching has altered or not and to what extent their learning preferences correspond to the selected form of instruction. The same was performed at Karaganda State Technical University in January 2013 among 65 students from managerial fields. Both groups of the selected students were involved in the same field of study, which was management. The research tools used were as follows:

- pen and paper questionnaires;
- descriptive statistical methods of processing the results of the survey; and
- observations.

The level of students' English was in most cases B2 according to the Common European Framework of Reference for languages [18].

All Czech students submitted the questionnaires. 35 (83%) of them were females and 7 (17%) were males (Fig. 1). The biggest groups of the students were between

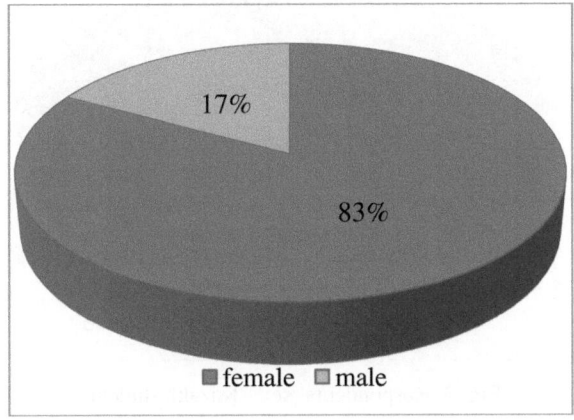

Fig. 1. Respondents' sex - Czech students

20-24 years old (31%) and between 25-29 years old (31%), while 19% of the respondents were between 30-34 years old. 12% were aged between 35-39 years. See Fig. 2 below for further description.

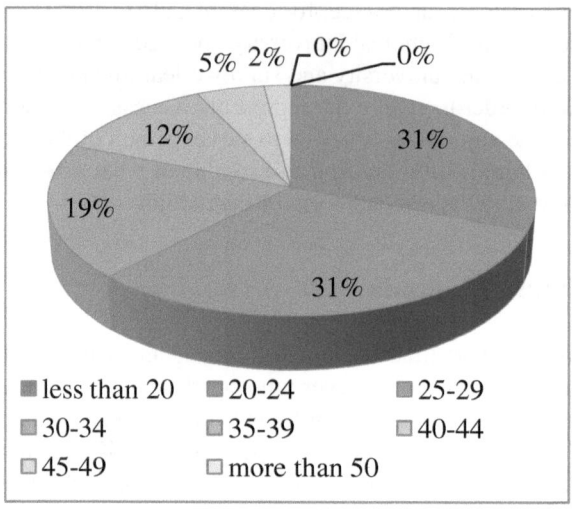

Fig. 2. Respondents' age - Czech students

As far as the Kazakh students are concerned, 65 were given a questionnaire but eight (12%) students did not respond. Out of the total number thus 33 (51%) were males and 24 (37%) were females (Fig. 3). The largest group of respondents was again between 20-24 years old (80%). See Fig. 4 below for further description.

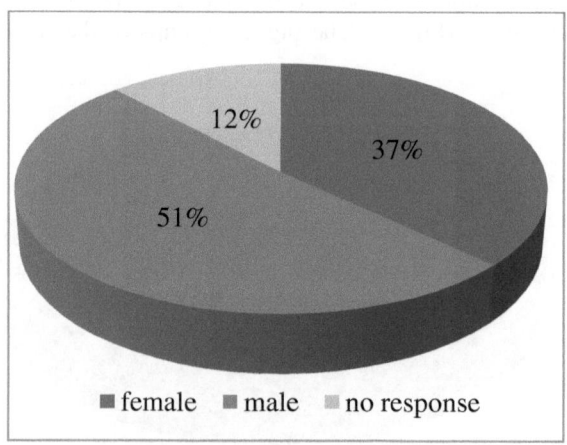

Fig. 3. Respondents' sex - Kazakh students

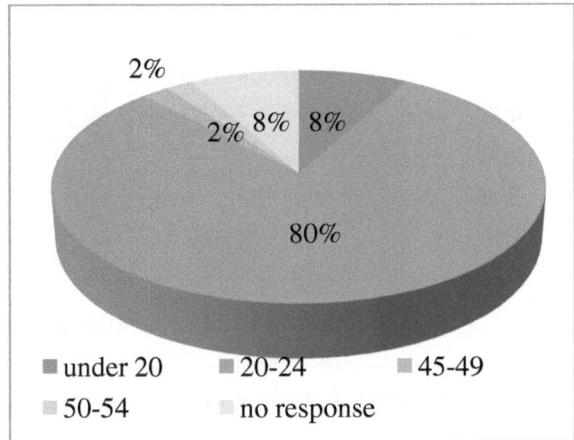

Fig. 4. Respondents' age - Kazakh students

3   Results of the Survey

Within a larger survey focused on the development of students' productive language skills, students were asked two core questions which are a subject of this article and they are as follows:

Which form of instruction would you prefer in the teaching of English? Please tick one option only.

a)   traditional, face-to-face;
b)   online/eLearning; or
c)   blended (a combination of traditional and online teaching).

What are your learning preferences while learning a foreign language? Please tick one option only.

• visual (seeing);
• auditory (hearing);
• kinaesthetic (moving); or
• tactile (touching).

Compare to [19]

Question 1 (Czech students): As for the form of instruction, 21 students (50%) prefer a combination of online and traditional teaching; 16 respondents (38%) would rather be exposed to face-to-face teaching and only five students (12%) would favour pure online teaching. See Fig. 5 below.

Question 1 (Kazakh students): As Fig. 6 shows, most of the Kazakh students still stick to the traditional form of instruction (34 students/ 52%). 24 (37%) respondents prefer a combination of traditional and online forms of instruction and only two students (3%) favour pure online teaching. Five students (8%) again did not respond to this question.

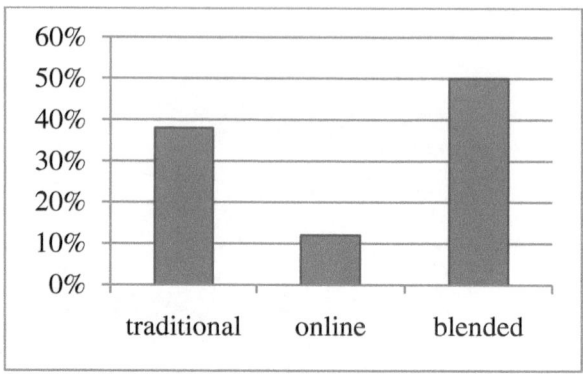

Fig. 5. Form of instruction - Czech students

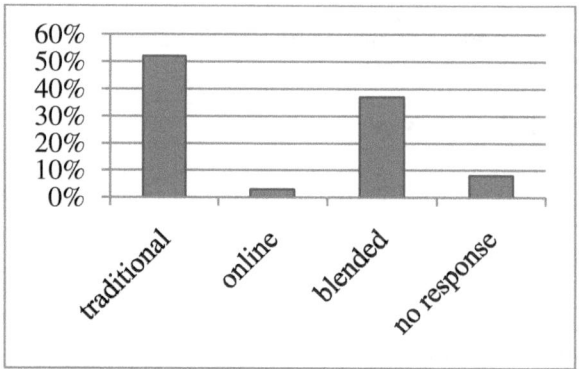

Fig. 6. Form of instruction - Kazakh students

Question 2 (Czech students): As far as the students' learning preferences are concerned, the numerical proportions of the options were quite balanced. In most cases students, however, preferred a kinaestheic learning style (13 students/ 31%); 10 students (24%) favoured an auditory learning style and the same number of respondents (10/ 24%) preferred a visual learning style, while nine students (21%) preferred a tactile learning style. See Fig. 7 below.

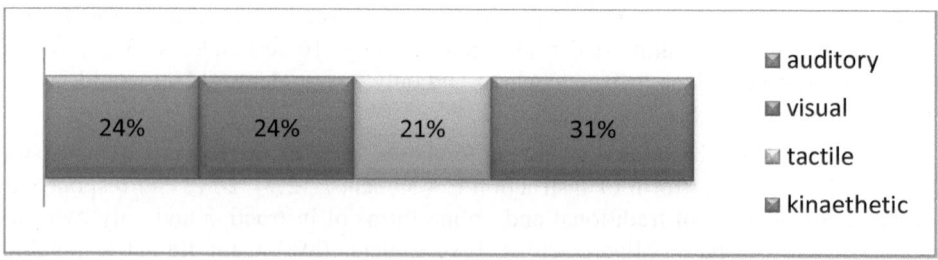

Fig. 7. Students' learning styles - Czech students

Question 2 (Kazakh students): As Fig. 8 indicates, a vast majority of the Kazakh students prefer an auditory learning style (41 students/ 63%); 14 students (22%) favour a visual learning style; six respondents (9%) prefer a tactile learning style and only two students (3%) are fond of a kinaesthetic learning style. Two students (3%) did not again respond to this question.

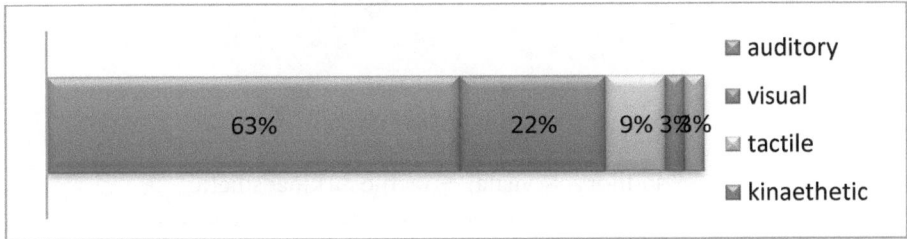

Fig. 8. Students' learning styles - Kazakh students

In addition, the authors of this article analysed the learning preferences with respect to the form of instruction since she was interested to discover whether there was any connection between the form of instruction and the relevant student's learning style which justified the selected form of instruction. The survey findings showed that the Czech students who favoured the traditional form of instruction preferred mostly the auditory learning style (eight students/ 19%); five students who liked better online learning had the kinaesthetic (two respondents/ 4%) and visual (two respondents/ 4%) learning preferences; and the students who fancied the combined form of study favoured mostly the kinaesthetic learning style (eight students/ 19%), followed by the tactile learning style (six students/ 14%) and the visual learning style (five students/ 12%). See Fig. 9, 10 and 11 below for further descriptions.

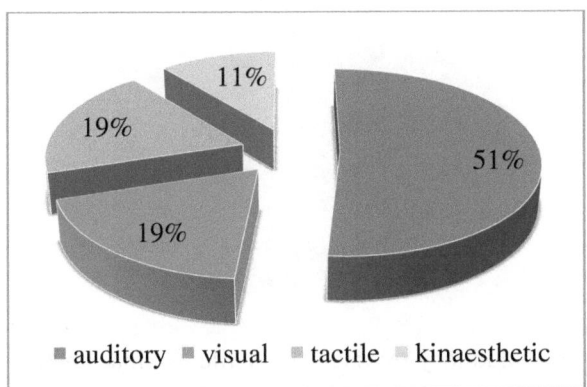

Fig. 9. Traditional form of instruction and students' learning preferences – Czech students

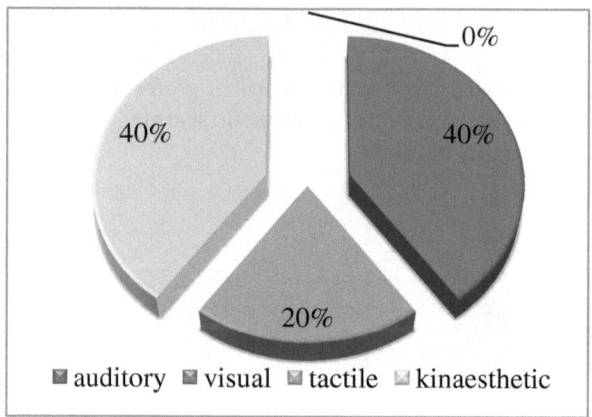

Fig. 10. Online form of instruction and students' learning preferences – Czech students

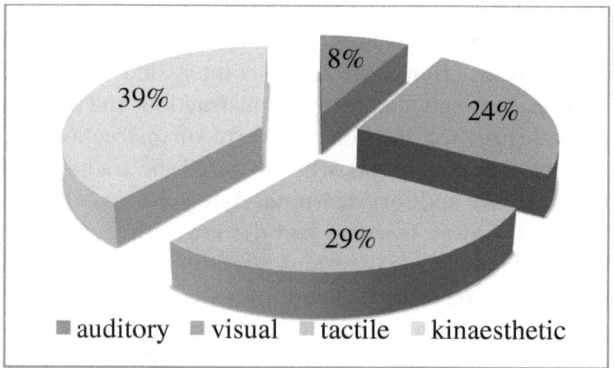

Fig. 11. Blended form of instruction and students' learning preferences – Czech students

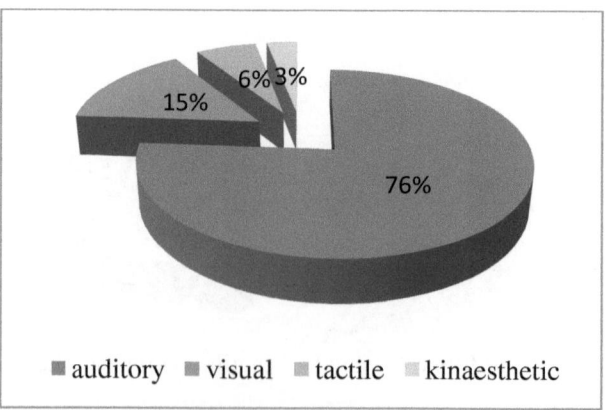

Fig.12. Traditional form of instruction and students' learning preferences – Kazakh students

As for the Kazakh students are concerned, those who prefer the traditional form of instruction favour the auditory learning style (26 students/ 76%), while five students (15%) fancy the visual learning style. Only two students stated that they would rather have the online form of instruction and they both (100%) preferred the visual learning style. As for the blended form of instruction, a majority of respondents (15 students/ 54%) prefer the auditory learning style, followed by the visual learning style (seven students/ 25%) and the tactile learning style (four students/ 14%). See Fig. 12, 13 and 14 below for further descriptions.

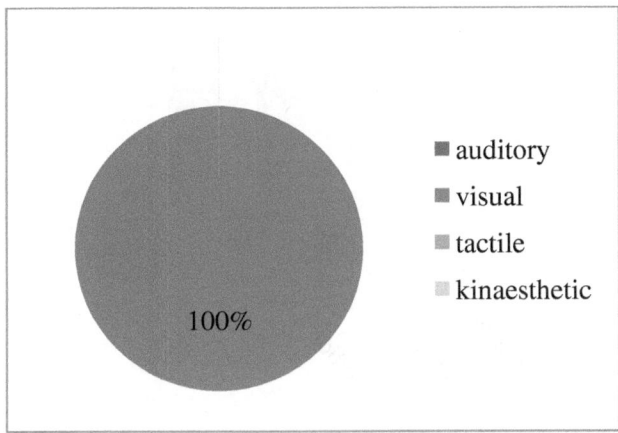

Fig. 13. Online form of instruction and students' learning preferences – Kazakh students

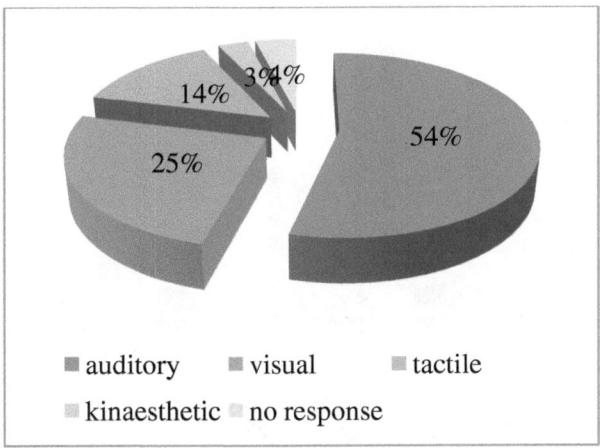

Fig. 14. Blended form of instruction and students' learning preferences – Kazakh students

Moreover, the authors were also curious to discover whether there are some differences between males and females as far as the forms of instruction and learning styles are concerned. See Fig. 15 and 16 for the results. As Fig. 15 shows, both Kazakh males and females tend to prefer the traditional form of instruction, while in the

Czech Republic only males favour the traditional teaching and females prefer the blended learning. In addition, Fig. 16 explores their learning preferences and it confirms the findings about the learning styles mentioned above that both Kazakh males and females favour the auditory learning style which best corresponds to the face-to-face teaching. However, this style is preferred by the Czech male students, while the Czech female students favour it least and they prefer the other three learning styles which are more or less balanced.

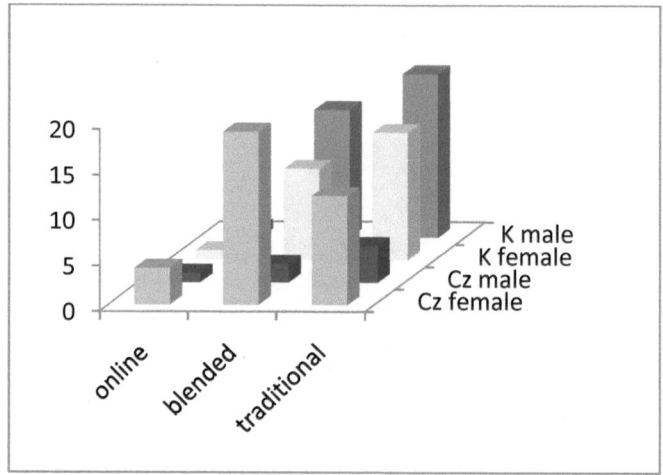

Fig. 15. Forms of instruction – a comparison of sexes in both countries

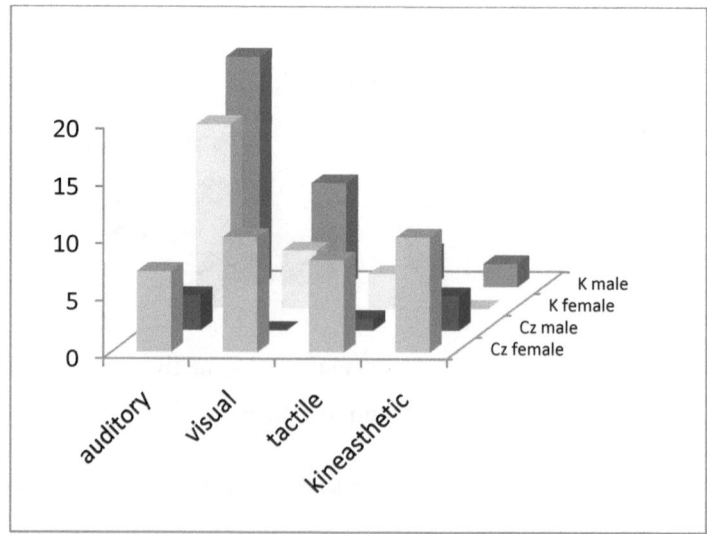

Fig. 16. Students' learning styles – a comparison of sexes in both countries

4   Discussion

Findings from Question 1 (Czech students) in fact confirm the previous research and surveys [8], [17] carried out across the disciplines taught at the Faculty of Informatics and Management in Hradec Kralove. Thus, from the above described results of the survey, it is clear that the Czech students welcome an opportunity to work online although, predominantly, in the so-called combined/blended/hybrid form of learning, which is now together with connectivism and self-regulated learning, a common method in teaching enhanced by ICT. Moreover, through blended learning students can complete their knowledge and thus finish their learning process, which they did not manage to do during the face-to-face classes. They are not forced to do it immediately at school or in the library because they can access the online course from the cosines of their homes any time they feel like that. In addition, if they did not understand anything during the lecture, they can contact their teacher online and ask him/her. Similarly, the Kazakh students also exploit the blended form of learning. However, most of them still welcome the traditional, face-to-face classes since not all of them can afford to have a computer at home and moreover, at school they do not have such frequent access to a computer. Although the university is equipped with a large number of computer laboratories, these are mostly used for the scheduled classes and students are thus not able to use them for their self-study so often.

The findings of the analysis of students' learning preferences in the Czech Republic were quite surprising and might indicate some general conclusions, which are as follows: the students who prefer the traditional, face-to-face teaching, favour mostly the auditory learning style, which might mean that they want to be exposed to spoken English as much as possible. This in fact confirms Krashen's theory of the acquisition of a foreign language [20] However, this would, of course, need to be verified by conducting focus interviews with the respondents. Similarly, the students who prefer the blended form of instruction prefer the kinaesthetic learning style since this form of instruction might offer more interactive ways of learning.

The same is true also for the Kazakh students because most of them (52%) still welcome the traditional form of instruction and 80% of them prefer the auditory learning style. Moreover, those who prefer the face-to-face classes prefer the auditory learning style, which means that they best learn when they listen to a lecture. On the contrary, those few who fancy the online teaching have the visual learning style which probably best suits to this form of instruction. As for the blended form of instruction, the auditory learning style prevails which might indicate that the online course study materials mostly serve as reference/supporting material for their self-study.

As far as the sex is concerned, there were not any striking differences between the Kazakh males and females in comparison with the Czech males and females whose preferences differed although, of course, the sample of males was small. The Czech male students are rather conservative because they prefer the traditional form of instruction and the auditory learning style like the Kazakh students. On the contrary, the Czech female students seem to be more flexible and non-conformist since they favour the blended learning and mainly kinaesthetic and visual learning styles.

5   Conclusion

In conclusion, the teachers should bear in mind the preferred students' learning styles and attempt to (re)consider the teaching methods and techniques which would match these preferred students' learning styles and forms of instruction. This in fact opens new opportunities for further research in this area where technologies could take a lead.

References

1. CRLT: Strategies for online teaching. The Regents of the University of Michigan (2013)
2. Graham, C.R., et al.: Benefits and challenges of blended learning environments. In: Khosrow-Pour, M. (ed.) Encyclopedia of Information Science and Technology I-V. Idea Group Inc., Hershey (2003)
3. Popelkova, K., Kovarova, K.: Impact of e-learning on stu-dents' study results. In: Proceedings of the 10th International Conference on Efficiency and Responsibility in Education (ERIE 2013), Prague, pp. 510–515 (2013)
4. Bruffee, K.: Collaborative learning. The John Hopkins University Press, Baltimore (1993)
5. Cerna, M., Svobodova, L.: Current social media landscape. In: Proceedings of the 10th International Conference on Efficiency and Responsibility in Education (ERIE 2013), Prague, pp. 80–86 (2013)
6. Coffield, F., et al.: Learning styles and pedagogy in post-16 learning, A systematic and critical review. Newcatle University report on learning styles,
   http://www.Isda.org.uk/files/PDF/1543.pdf
7. Gregorc, A.F.: Learning/teaching styles: potent forces behind them'. Educational Leadership 36, 234–238 (1979)
8. Hubackova, S., Semradova, I.: Comparison of on-line teaching and face-to-face teaching. Procedia – Social and Behavioral Sciences 89, 445–449 (2013)
9. Poulova, P., Simonova, I.: Flexible e-learning: online courses tailored to student's needs. In: Proceedings of the 9th International Scientific Conference on Distance Learning in Applied Informatics (DIVAI 2012), pp. 251–260. UKF, Nitra (2012)
10. Simonova, I.: Information literacy: research reflecting individual learning styles. In: Proceedings of the 10th International Conference on Efficiency and Responsibility in Education (ERIE 2013), Prague, pp. 550–556 (2013)
11. Simonova, I., Bilek, M.K.: Problematice e-learningu adaptujicimu se stylum uceni. Media4u Magazine (1), 4–11 (2010), http://www.media4u.cz/aktualvyd.pdf
12. Frydrychova Klimova, B., Poulova, P.: Reflection on the development of eLearning in the Czech Republic. In: Proceedings of the 16th WSEAS International Conference on Recent Researches in Communications and Computers, pp. 433–437. Corfu, Greece (2012)
13. Kucirkova, L., Kucera, P., Vostra Vydrova, H.: Impact of e-learning on the results of students in the lessons of Business English. In: Proceedings of the 9th International Conference on Efficiency and Responsibility in Education (ERIE 2012), Prague, pp. 294–302 (2012)
14. Simonova, I.: On the process of ICT implementation in the tertiary education reflected in the eLearning conferences and competitions at the FIM UHK'. In: Semradova, I. (ed.) Reflections on the Exploitation of a Virtual Study Environment, pp. 26–62. MILOS VOGNAR Publishing House, Hradec Kralove (2010)

15. Frydrychova Klimova, B.: Blended Learning. In: Vilas, A.M., et al. (eds.) Research, Reflections and Innovations in Integrating ICT in Education, vol. 2, pp. 705–708. FORMATEX, Spain (2009)
16. Frydrychova Klimova, B., Hubackova, S., Semradova, I.: Blended Learning in a foreign language learning. Procedia – Social and Behavioral Sciences 28, 281–285 (2011)
17. Frydrychova Klimova, B., Poulova, P.: ICT in the teaching of academic writing. Lectures Notes in Management Science 11, 33–38 (2013)
18. CEFR, http://en.wikipedia.org/wiki/
19. Dunn, R., Dunn, K.: Teaching secondary students through their individual learning Style. Allyn &Bacon, Needlam Heights (1993)
20. Krashen, S.D.: Second language acquisition or second language learning. Pergamon Press Inc., USA (1981)

Borderless Education: InterUniversity Study – Successful Students' Feedback

Petra Poulova and Ivana Simonova

University of Hradec Kralove, Rokitanskeho 62, Hradec Kralove, Czech Republic
{petra.poulova,ivana.simonova}@uhk.cz

Abstract. The paper introduces the project of interuniversity study running within eight universities (United Kingdom, Ireland, Finland, Latvia, Italy and three institutions from the Czech Republic). The process of instruction ran online in the LMS Blackboard, EDEN and Moodle. The paper is structured in three main parts (1) briefly describing the project and (2) presenting evaluation feedback collected from those students who succeeded in this form of study and (3) providing recommendations resulting from the questionnaire results towards improvements the hybrid learning process for future use.

Keywords: Hybrid learning, borderless education, open access, online, Information Technologies, Financing, Management, higher education.

1   Introduction

Higher education worldwide is in a period of transition, affected by globalization, the requirement for mass access, changing relationships between the university, state and new technologies, among others [1]. Internationalization is one of the major forces impacting and shaping higher education as it evolves to meet the challenges of the 21st century. Overall, the picture of internationalization that is emerging is one of complexity, diversity and differentiation. The internationalization of higher education is a process in rapid evolution, both as actor and as reactor to the new realities of globalization and to the rather eventful times facing higher education [2], [3], [4], [5].

Reflecting demands of the current period, a project of borderless education "Inter-University Study" (IUS) was introduced in the Czech Republic being built on international co-operation of eight universities:

- University of Huddersfield, United Kingdom (UH)
- Galway-Mayo Institute of Technology, Ireland (GMIT)
- Savonia University of Applied Sciences, Finland (SUAS)
- Riga International School of Economics and Business Administration, Latvia (RISEBA)
- University of Genoa, Italy (UG)
- Tomas Bata University, Zlin, Czech Republic (TBUZ)
- University of West Bohemia, Pilsen, Czech Republic (UWB)
- University of Hradec Kralove, Czech Republic (UHK).

S.K.S. Cheung et al. (Eds.): ICHL 2014, LNCS 8595, pp. 232–242, 2014.
© Springer International Publishing Switzerland 2014

The interuniversity study started among three Czech institutions UWB, TB and UHK as the RIUS project (Run-up of interuniversity study) running for one semester as a pilot project and focused on following objectives:

- Create the base of university network in the Czech Republic for the purposes of interuniversity study (IUS), i.e. to prepare and stabilize the infrastructure (organization, processes) for IUS in the network of selected universities.
- Provide financial support to interuniversity educational activities (in the run-up phase) in the hybrid and distance form of study.
- Prepare both pedagogical and administrative workers for IUS realization
- Enhance the quality and attractiveness of study programmess and subjects offered at particular universities by sharing subjects guaranteed by leading experts in the field and thus extending the offer of study subjects.
- Share teaching/learning aids (mainly those for the hybrid process), educational infrastructure and tools.
- Prepare Czech universities for more intensive co-operation with similar organizations in other EU countries
- Prepare conditions (infrastructure, processes, know-how) for the connection of created Czech IUS network to similar networks in other EU countries for the purposes of IUS.

The pilot RIUS project been finished and results analyzed, the objectives were applied for the IUS project without any change. Applying the hybrid learning approach [6] both the RIUS and IUS projects were of identical concept – selected European universities provided distance courses running in a LMS for students of other universities to enroll. Part of each course was held in the distance form except from starting and assessment tutorials. In the starting tutorial students were provided with information about the objectives and structure of the subject, ways of communication in the online course, requirements for successful passing exams etc., and they were provided with student´s access to the online course. The LMSs WebCT/Blackboard, EDEN and Moodle were used for designing the courses. Despite the universities differed in using the LMS, all three learning environments are widely recognized as standardized and user friendly to provide learners with all tools required for simulating the real process of instruction. The assessment tutorial was organized at the end of the semester where students´ knowledge was evaluated by written tests and oral exams. The design of all subjects followed the distance education standards covering both the course design and process of running the instruction (e.g. [7]). In both projects the coordination of teaching/learning related activities was provided by steering committees consisting of participating universities representatives.

Totally, 274 students from eight partner universities participated in the IUS project. As no pre-requisite knowledge was required, each student, enrolled in any year of any partner university study, could attend any subject (except from Industrial Plant Management II and Principles of Management II having pre-requisites in relating subjects I; both subjects could be studied simultaneously).

2   Learning Content

As displayed in table 1, totally 47 subjects were offered to students of partner universities within the IUS project, 5 – 9 subjects per university, having value of 3 – 10 credits and covering fields of Information Technologies, Financing and Management. Finally, students enrolled in 35 online courses, one per subject (non-attended subjects are marked with asterisk). The attendance rate can be considered from two points of view:

- first, amount of accepted students from other universities: the largest amount of students attended courses provided by SUAS (85 students), followed by TBUZ – 70, GMIT – 49, RISEBA – 23, UWB – 19, UHK – 17, UH – 8, UG – 3);
- second, amount of students attending courses at other institutions: most students from UHK (79) studied at other universities, followed by RISEBA – 62, GMIT – 56, TBUZ – 33, SUAS – 26, UWB – 13, UG – 5, UH – 0).

Totally, the most ´active´ institution was SUAS having 111 participants involved in the project, followed by GMIT – 105, TBUZ – 103, UHK – 96, RISEBA – 85, UWB – 32, UH and UG – 8 participants each.

3   Project Evaluation from Successful Students' View

Despite the provided opportunity of studying at foreign universities was challenging and interesting for many students, only the best ones succeeded in the study. The success rate overview is included in table 1. The success rate covered an interval of 0 – 100%. If data were available, the value is presented in the appropriate field and the title of the course/subject is highlighted in light grey. There were two reasons why some data are missing – either data were not provided (UH, RISEBA, UG subjects), or not a single student finished the attendance and successfully passed the exam (i.e. zero success rate, the field is empty). Totally, 114 students from five institutions provided the feedback, which is 41.6 % of the total amount of those who started the study.

4   Evaluation Methodology

Several tools were developed for the complete evaluation of the content and organization of particular subjects during the pilot phase:
- questionnaire for successful students,
- questionnaire for drop-out students,
- questionnaire for teachers,
- evaluation interview with students and teachers.

Below, the selected results from the evaluation questionnaire collected from successful students are presented. The questionnaire was structured in two parts covering 64 items relating to didactic and technical (technology-supported) field of study. The items were provided in the form of statements and evaluated on the five-level scale (1 - fully agree, 5 - fully disagree). The questionnaire focused on areas of project administration (e.g. subject documentation), learning objectives, exam requirements, tutor´s work (motivating and stimulating students, explanation of problems, teaching materials and methods, content and instructions for assignments etc.), quality of methodological instruction on how to study in the distance online course, IT and organizational support and (last but not least) the adequacy of work load during the study. Selected results are presented in table 1 - 3. The blue and dark purple parts of the graphs represent positive feedback to the statements. They cover major part of the graphs (from 51 % in graph dealing with stimulating and motivating the students to 80 % in clearness of instructions for assignments).

Table 1. Successful students' evaluation (selected results) – part 1

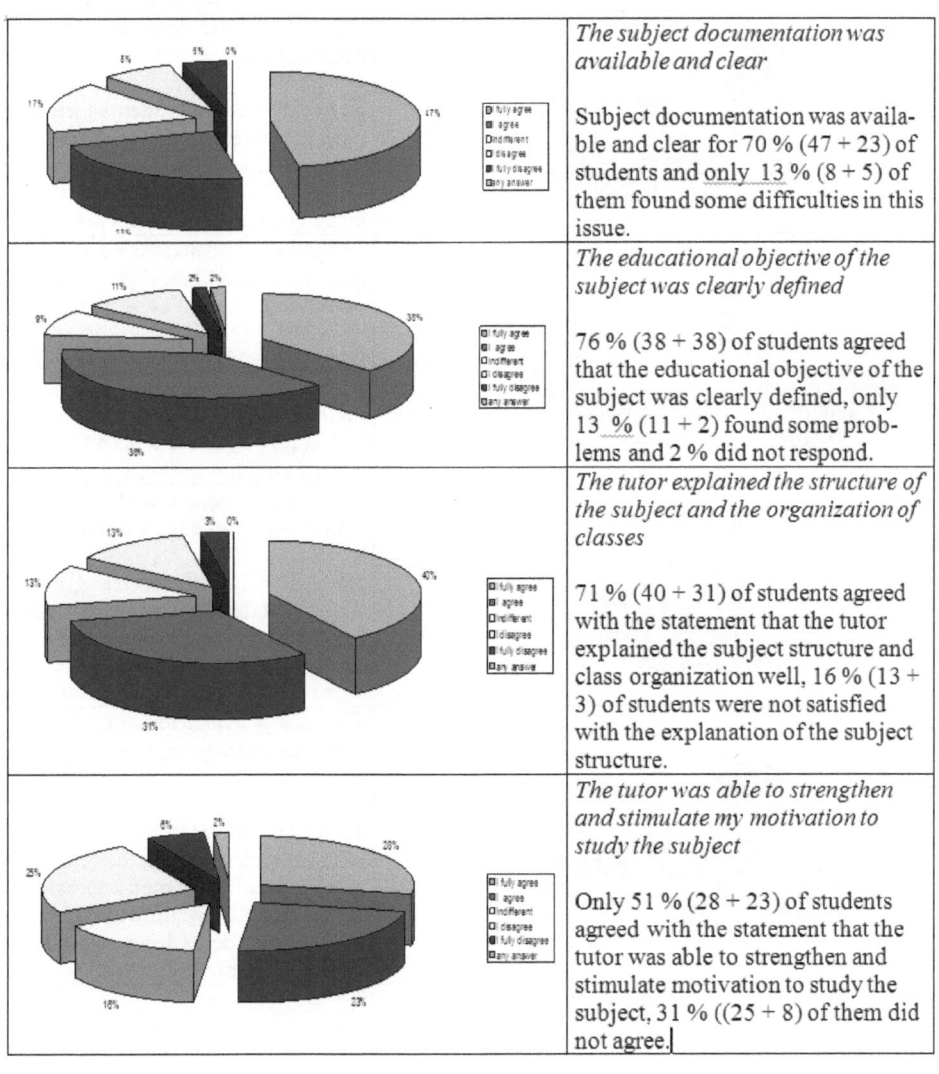

	The subject documentation was available and clear
	Subject documentation was available and clear for 70 % (47 + 23) of students and only 13 % (8 + 5) of them found some difficulties in this issue.
	The educational objective of the subject was clearly defined
	76 % (38 + 38) of students agreed that the educational objective of the subject was clearly defined, only 13 % (11 + 2) found some problems and 2 % did not respond.
	The tutor explained the structure of the subject and the organization of classes
	71 % (40 + 31) of students agreed with the statement that the tutor explained the subject structure and class organization well, 16 % (13 + 3) of students were not satisfied with the explanation of the subject structure.
	The tutor was able to strengthen and stimulate my motivation to study the subject
	Only 51 % (28 + 23) of students agreed with the statement that the tutor was able to strengthen and stimulate motivation to study the subject, 31 % ((25 + 8) of them did not agree.

Table 2. Successful students' evaluation (selected results) – part 2

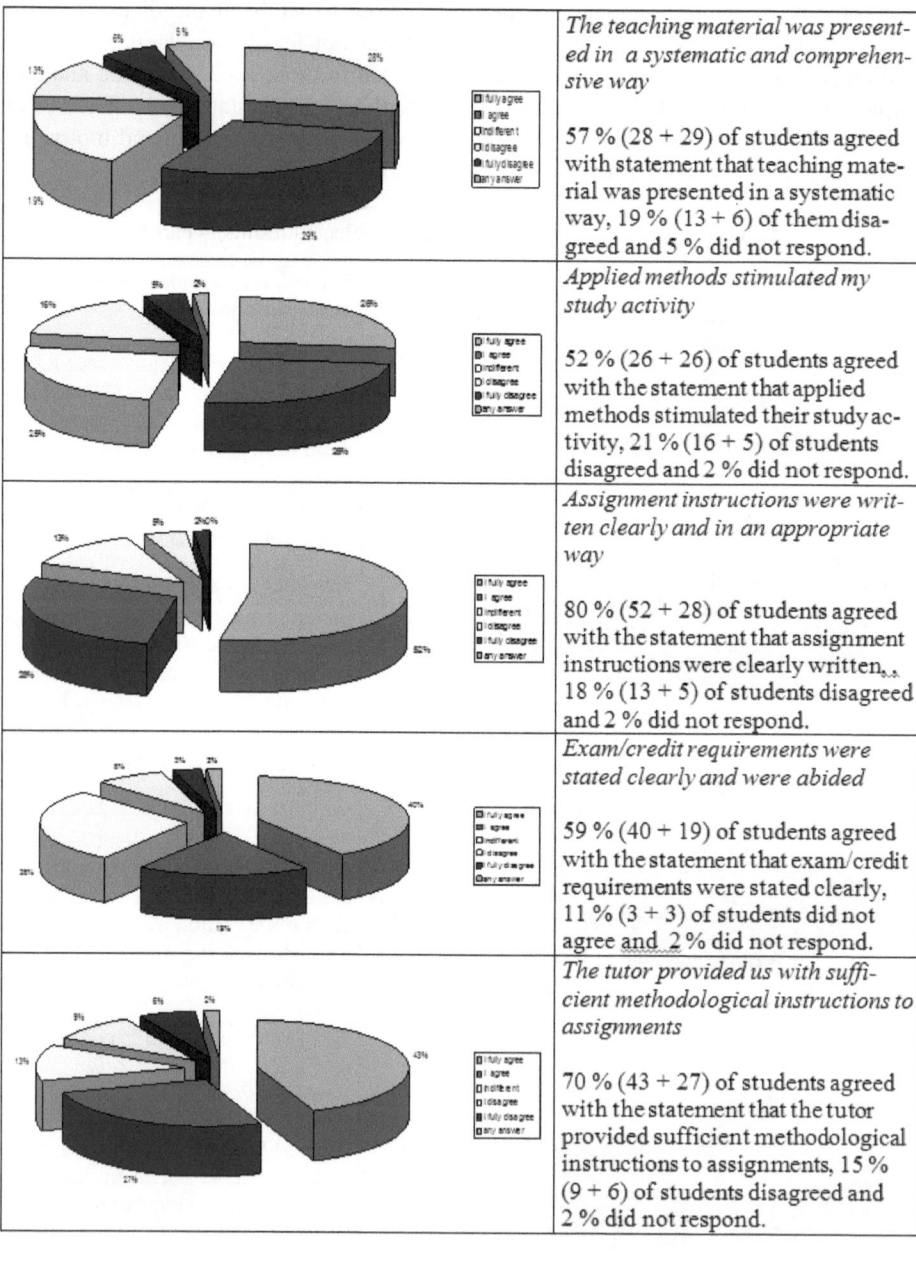

	The teaching material was presented in a systematic and comprehensive way
	57 % (28 + 29) of students agreed with statement that teaching material was presented in a systematic way, 19 % (13 + 6) of them disagreed and 5 % did not respond.
	Applied methods stimulated my study activity
	52 % (26 + 26) of students agreed with the statement that applied methods stimulated their study activity, 21 % (16 + 5) of students disagreed and 2 % did not respond.
	Assignment instructions were written clearly and in an appropriate way
	80 % (52 + 28) of students agreed with the statement that assignment instructions were clearly written, 18 % (13 + 5) of students disagreed and 2 % did not respond.
	Exam/credit requirements were stated clearly and were abided
	59 % (40 + 19) of students agreed with the statement that exam/credit requirements were stated clearly, 11 % (3 + 3) of students did not agree and 2 % did not respond.
	The tutor provided us with sufficient methodological instructions to assignments
	70 % (43 + 27) of students agreed with the statement that the tutor provided sufficient methodological instructions to assignments, 15 % (9 + 6) of students disagreed and 2 % did not respond.

Table 3. Successful students' evaluation (selected results) – part 3

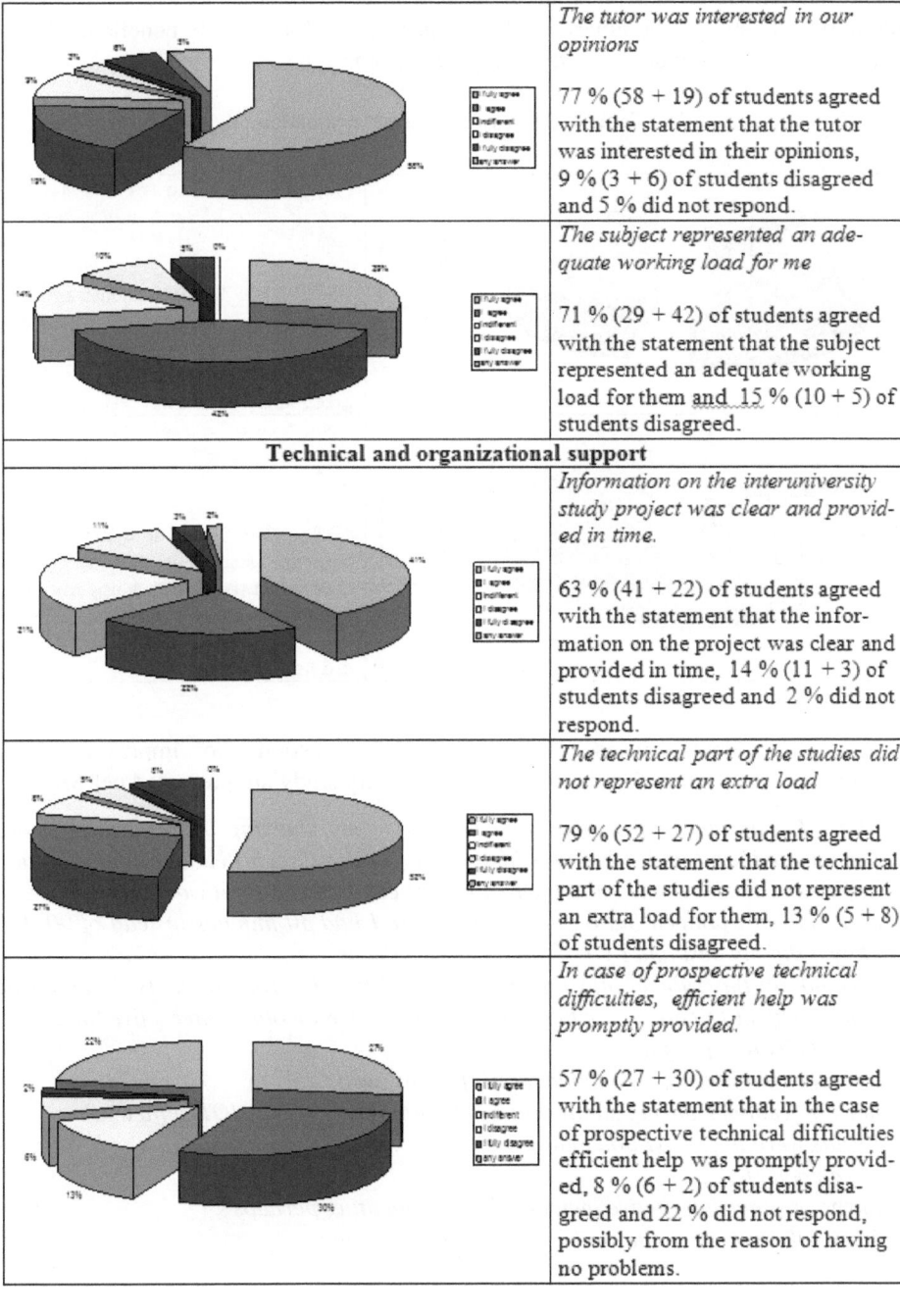

	The tutor was interested in our opinions 77 % (58 + 19) of students agreed with the statement that the tutor was interested in their opinions, 9 % (3 + 6) of students disagreed and 5 % did not respond.
	The subject represented an adequate working load for me 71 % (29 + 42) of students agreed with the statement that the subject represented an adequate working load for them and 15 % (10 + 5) of students disagreed.
Technical and organizational support	
	Information on the interuniversity study project was clear and provided in time. 63 % (41 + 22) of students agreed with the statement that the information on the project was clear and provided in time, 14 % (11 + 3) of students disagreed and 2 % did not respond.
	The technical part of the studies did not represent an extra load 79 % (52 + 27) of students agreed with the statement that the technical part of the studies did not represent an extra load for them, 13 % (5 + 8) of students disagreed.
	In case of prospective technical difficulties, efficient help was promptly provided. 57 % (27 + 30) of students agreed with the statement that in the case of prospective technical difficulties efficient help was promptly provided, 8 % (6 + 2) of students disagreed and 22 % did not respond, possibly from the reason of having no problems.

5   Conclusions and Recommendations

In two final graphs in table 4, highly positive experience of students who succeeded in interuniversity study is summarized. They consider this form highly beneficial (77 %) and are going to continue the study next year (67 %).

Table 4. Successful students' evaluation

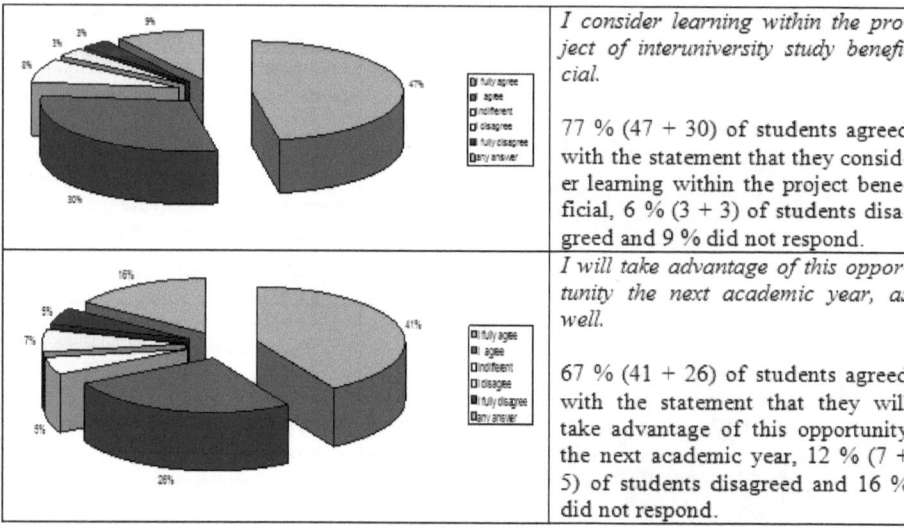

	I consider learning within the project of interuniversity study beneficial. 77 % (47 + 30) of students agreed with the statement that they consider learning within the project beneficial, 6 % (3 + 3) of students disagreed and 9 % did not respond.
	I will take advantage of this opportunity the next academic year, as well. 67 % (41 + 26) of students agreed with the statement that they will take advantage of this opportunity the next academic year, 12 % (7 + 5) of students disagreed and 16 % did not respond.

Selected students´ ideas, comments and suggestions to improvement of learning/teaching within the project of interuniversity study are presented below:

- *'Well, I experienced just one thing that made my studying of this subject more complicated, and it was a time slide, where here in Czech Republic was 9:30 and in Finland 10:30. I was quite interesting, especially because it was "intercultural" and I haven't noticed but on the exam, where I had 30 minutes instead of 90. But okay, I did my best and I got it.*
- *I would put this subject into 1st year of the studies, in order students could decide which subject to choose for the same credits. Skype or other interactive method of communicating perhaps?*
- *use other methods of communication! (forums, web, …)*
- *need of feedback during studies (one mail after half year is NOT sufficient)*
- *results were to pure (I don't know what I did or didn't right, what methods or ideas were good etc…)*
- *Skype or other interactive method of communicating perhaps?*
- *More information to the students during the studying*

- *Start on time, have high quality self-studying materials ready, send emails directly to email addresses of individual students as well as their accounts on a server where they log on to get materials (assurance of getting info), create virtual night video chat meetings of students and teacher – at least few times per semester. I would appreciate of the beginning of study started earlier then in middle of the semester.*
- *Subject should be presented more clearly. I am also not able to get recommended books; there are no books to learn from.*
- *to improve technical staff*
- *I think it necessary to match the various study semesters better. Every school has different dates for the beginning of the semester and different date for getting grades and enclosing the semester. It took us quite long time to start the course – it was a pity because I very enjoyed the course I took.*
- *I think, that is everything good, maybe in English is very important also noise for correct pronunciation.*
- *Learning and teaching within the project of interuniversity study exceeded my expectations so that I have no suggestions on how to improve it.ʹ*

Reflecting the results displayed in table 5 the project of interuniversity study provided positive impact on the involvement of selected Czech universities in the world network of borderless education, despite fewer than 50 % of students met the requirements and successfully passed exams. Emphasis must be paid to the fields which have not proved good performance (i.e. results in the interval of 51 – 63 %). Instead of the above mentioned areas we will mainly focus on:

- keeping the teaching methods maximally stimulating the process of learning and steadily increasing their impact in the affective field of the process;
- improving teaching materials, mainly their comprehensiveness, so that the understanding the topic was as complete as possible;
- providing the exam requirements clear and stable, but reflecting latest pedagogical achievements;
- furnishing interested and enrolled students with more clear and complex information on the IUS project advantages and threats;
- providing fast IT service and methodological support in case of technical difficulties in LMS.

After solving the problem of "passive" partner institutions (possibly by contracting other universities which will be more reliable project partners and more deeply engaged in the project work), the project would be recommended to further implementation in following academic years. The main strengths were detected in the fields of tutorʹs work (explanations provided by hybrid learning tools, setting and leading studentʹs assignments, providing tutorʹs feedback), setting the educational objectives and applying the methodological instruction (interval of 70 – 80 %). Above all, taking the educational contribution of the project into consideration, it definitely provides "added value" to students motivation to further education [8].

Table 5. Students enrolled in subjects in IUS project (n)

	Subject title	CREDITS	UH	GMIT	SUAS	RISEBA	UG	TBUZ	UWB	UHK	TOTAL
U H	Corporate Governance and Business Ethics	7		1	3					4	8
	*Developments in Banking and Finance	10									
	*Digital Innovation and Learning	10									
	*Simulation in Mechanical Engineering	10									
	*Introduction to the Business Dissertation	5									
G M I T	Celtic Studies	5			6			6		5	49
	Computer Business Applications	5			1				1	4	
	Entrepreneurship and Innovation	10			1				2	2	
	Finance	5						1		5	
	Internet Technology	5			2				1	12	
S U A S	Advanced Use of Office Programs	5		5		13		1		11	85
	Budgeting and Budgetary Control	5				4				3	
	Business Research Methods	5				2					
	Human Resource Management	5		1		4	2	8	2	8	
	Intercultural Competence	5		1		7		7	3	3	
R I S E B A	Corporate Finance	5		1	1					1	23
	Corporate Financial Management	5								2	
	Management Accounting	3		3					1		
	Marketing Research and Data Processing in SPSS	6		7				1		1	
	*Microeconomics	3									
	Operational Management	3					3			2	
U G	Industrial Plant	5			1						3
	Industrial Plant Management I	5			1						
	*Industrial Plant Management II	5									
	*Industrial Production Management	5									
	Maintenance Management	5								1	
T B U Z	Advanced Economic Analyses	4		1						1	70
	Business-to-Business Marketing	4		1						1	
	Computerized Data Processing	3		14	5					3	
	DTP and Electronic Publishing	3		4						1	
	E-Marketing	4			3	32				2	
	Enterprise Information System	4		1							
	*Basics of Accounting	5									

	Subject title	CREDITS	UH	GMIT	SUAS	RISEBA	UG	TBUZ	UWB	UHK	TOTAL
UWB	Quantitative Methods for Managerial Decision Making	5							1		
	Basics of Enterprise Management	5		1				6		2	19
	Economics and Financial Management	4								1	
	*Computer Support in Mechanical Engineering	4									
	*Simulation in Mechanical Engineering	3									
	Marketing Study Cases	4						1		3	
	Programming Techniques	5		4						1	
UHK	Basics of Finance	3			1						17
	Managerial Methods	5							1		
	Principles of Management I	3		1					1		
	*Principles of Management II	5									
	System Theory	7									
	Public Finance	4		1							
	Stock Exchange and Financial Markets	4		10				2			
	TOTAL (n)		0	56	26	62	5	33	13	79	274

References

1. Knight, J.: Higher education in turmoil. The changing world of internationalization. Global perspectives on higher education, vol. 13. Center for International Higher Education, Boston (2008)
2. Knight, J.: Internationalization of higher education: New directions, new challenges. International Association of Universities Global Survey Report. International Association of Universities, Paris (2006)
3. Knight, J.: Internationalization: Concepts, complexities and challenges. In: Forest, J., Altbach, P. (eds.) International Handbook of Higher Education, pp. 207–228. Springer Academic Publishers, Dordrecht (2006)
4. Trent, J.: The internationalization of tertiary education in Asia: Language, identity and conflict. Journal of Research in International Education 11, 50–69 (2012)
5. Coryell, J.E., Durodoye, B.A., Wright, R.R., Pateand, P.E., Nguyen, S.: Case Studies of Internationalization in Adult and Higher Education: Inside the Processes of Four Universities in the United States and the United Kingdom. Journal of Studies in International Education, 75–98 (2012)
6. Allen, I.E., et al.: Blending in. Eduventures (2007),
   https://www.uwb.edu/learningtech/elearning/
   hybrid-and-online-learning/hybrid-learning/
   about-hybrid-learning/definition-hybrid-learning

7. NCPSA: Recommended standards for distance education,
   http://www.ncpsa.org/client_data/files/2010/
   13_recommendedstandardsforitdistancelearning.pdf
8. Altbach, P.G., Knight, J.: The internationalization of higher education: Motivations and realities. In: NEA Almanac of Higher Education, pp. 27–36. National Education Association, Washington, DC (2006)

Creating and Delivering Learning Materials for Mobile Phones - Our Findings in Japan

Shudong Wang[1], Jun Iwata[2], and Douglas Jarrell[3]

[1,2] Shimane Unviesity, Japan
[3] Nagoya Women's University, Japan
wangsd@soc.shimane-u.ac.jp, j_iwata@med.shimane-u.ac.jp,
djarrell@nagoya-wu.ac.jp

Abstract. With increasing permeation of mobile devices into people's everyday life, m-learning can be regarded as the next generation of e-learning. Learning via mobile devices, especially mobile phones, is practiced in educational areas all over the world. This paper describes a mobile language learning project which creates English learning materials and delivers the learning materials to Japanese university students. The data collected from this ongoing mobile language learning project allows us to investigate Japanese students' mobile learning styles and learning material preferences as well as their concerns about using mobile learning. The data was collected from various sources: online surveys, server logs, user registered personal information, interviews and actual online quiz results. The findings obtained from this research provide useful information for future mobile learning project/system design, implementation and content delivery.

Keywords: Mobile learning styles, learning preferences, learning expectations, findings, future mobile learning design, Japan.

1   Introduction

Mobile telecommunication networks have witnessed rapid development in bandwidth in recent years. Wi-Fi and 4G wireless networks make data transmission to and from mobile phones as fast as computers in a wired network. On the other hand, swift hardware advances in mobile devices represented by smart phones have begun to erode the difference between handsets and PCs. Much of the work that used to be done only on computers can now be easily completed on mobile phones.

The above changes are leading away from computer based e-learning towards mobile phone based m-learning. Consciously or unconsciously, more and more people use mobile phones to learn. Learning applications are added to the Apple Store or the Google Play Store every day. Mobile phones are no longer tools simply to convey messages.

Even so, compared with PC-based e-learning, mobile learning does not enjoy a similar level of maturity. Neither the technical systems nor learning content of many existing mobile learning projects ideally meet students' needs and expectations [1].

S.K.S. Cheung et al. (Eds.): ICHL 2014, LNCS 8595, pp. 243–253, 2014.

The mobile learning applications currently available for language learning serve as examples of such a misfit. Most mobile language learning applications focus on vocabulary and TOEIC/TOEFL grammar, and the major type of interaction available to users is the vocabulary quiz. Reading, grammar, listening and speaking applications are not yet well developed. Many students start to learn on mobile phones but quit half-way. Furthermore, the majority of mobile learning applications are commercial in nature or linked to advertising. This could have an impact on the number of students willing to use mobile language programs.

In order to have students accept and welcome the concept of mobile learning, teachers or mobile learning system designers should fully understand the mobile hardware readiness of students, their mobile learning styles, the materials they prefer to study, and the format of materials to be delivered.

For the purpose of addressing the above issues as regards Japanese university students, we analyzed the data collected from an ongoing mobile language learning project being carried out at Shimane University, Japan, called the Mobile English Learning Project. Based on this data, the paper tries to answer the following questions:

Is the hardware environment ready for Japanese university students to carry out learning via their mobile phones?

What kind of learning content is suitable for students to study on mobile phones?

During which period of time in a day are students mostly likely to conduct mobile learning?

When students study via mobile phones, what other concerns do they have besides the learning content?

2   A Mobile Language Learning Project

In 2009, a mobile learning project aimed at improving students' English reading and grammar ability, called the Mobile English Learning Project, was initiated at Shimane University, Japan. The project is ongoing, with a total of 341 new students joining the project in 2013. Most of the participants were first-year students at the time they joined. Before the project began, flyers were handed out to every first-year student to encourage them to take part in the project by registering their email addresses.

The project regularly sends out a variety of language materials such as short English essays on different topics, English grammar quizzes, and TOEIC/TOEFL exam strategies. The materials are sent two or three times a week as email texts with attached URLs which students can click in order to leave comments or take quizzes. Students register with the project of their own volition, and they are able to opt out at any time. There are no required tests during the project, its sole purpose being to provide a ubiquitous environment for students to read English and learn or review English grammar without the pressure that they often encounter in the classroom.

In terms of English essays, there is a rich variety of topics: culture differences, entertainment, science and engineering, politics, economics, travel and campus life. English jokes and riddles are also sent out from time to time. In terms of grammar, a different item is explained in an email message sent out once a week. Attached to the email message is a web link to a 5-question quiz designed to reinforce the grammar points (See Fig.1).

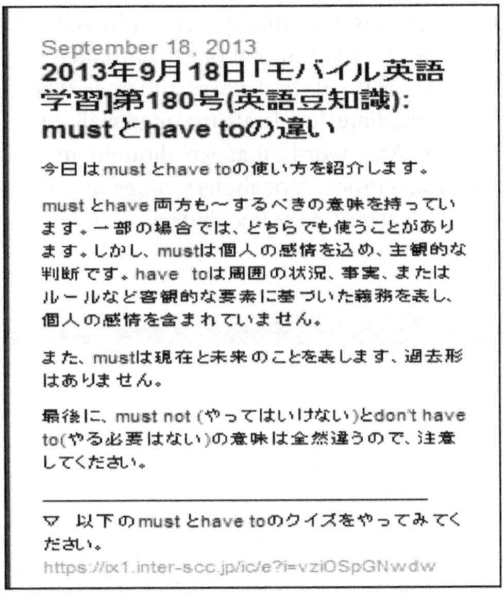

September 18, 2013
2013年9月18日「モバイル英語学習]第180号(英語豆知識): mustとhave toの違い
今日はmustとhave toの使い方を紹介します。
mustとhave両方も～するべきの意味を持っています。一部の場合では、どちらでも使うことがあります。しかし、mustは個人の感情を込め、主観的な判断です。have toは周囲の状況、事実、またはルールなど客観的な要素に基づいた義務を表し、個人の感情を含まれていません。
また、mustは現在と未来のことを表します、過去形はありません。
最後に、must not (やってはいけない)とdon't have to(やる必要はない)の意味は全然違うので、注意してください。
▽ 以下のmustとhave toのクイズをやってみてください。
https://ix1.inter-scc.jp/ic/e?i=vziOSpGNwdw

Fig. 1. Archived grammar material

モバイル英語学習プログラム
Learn English at anytime, anywhere!
March 1, 2014
2014年3月1日「モバイル英語学習」第209号(エッセイ): My Sweet Memory
February 26, 2014
2014年2月26日「モバイル英語学習」第208号(英語豆知識): An Animal Sound Quiz!
February 19, 2014
2014年2月19日「モバイル英語学習」第207号(エッセイ): Movie Goers in Korea and the U.S.
February 16, 2014
2014年2月16日「モバイル英語学習」第206号(エッセイ): The First Day On The Job
next »
発信内容を検索!
SEARCH
テーマ

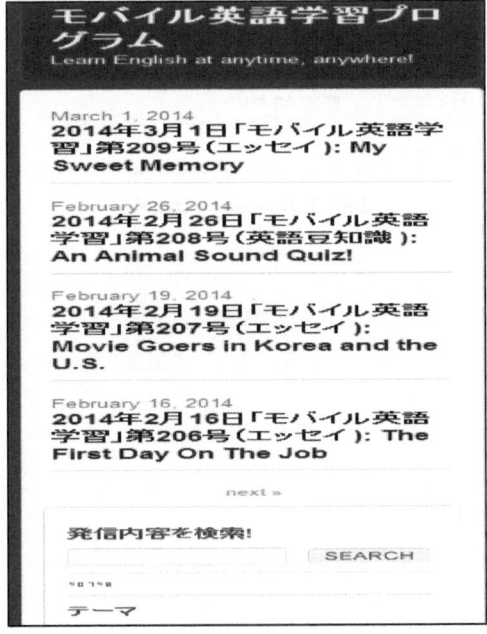

Fig. 2. Archived essays

Students who do not want to register their email addresses but would like to read the content delivered by the project are able to choose to access a blog site designed for both PCs and mobile phones (See Fig.2)

In this project, each composition originally written by teachers is no more than 140 words in length so that it can be read in one or two minutes on a small screen [2][3]. In order to appeal to a majority of first-year students, whose average knowledge of English is at a pre-intermediate level, all the materials are written in simple and easy-to-understand English. Any words that we thought might cause a problem are annotated with Japanese translations. Vocabulary notes are placed at the beginning of the essay to make readers aware of new vocabulary items before they read the essay (See Fig.3).

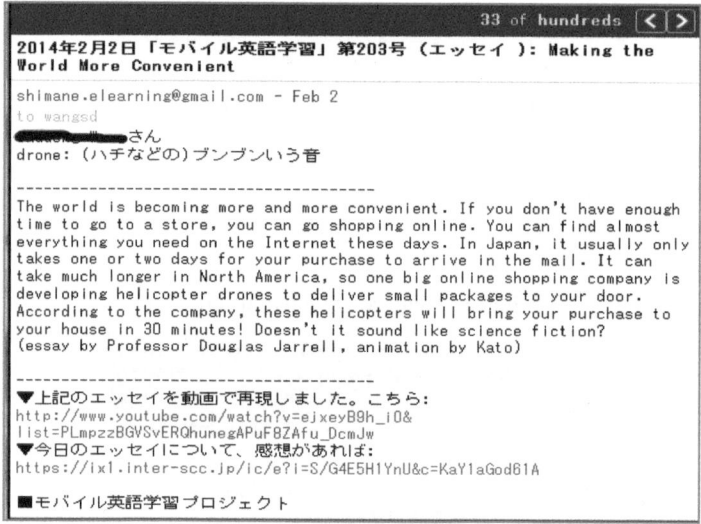

Fig. 3. An essay example

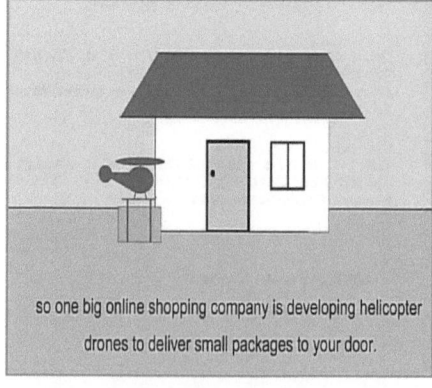

Fig. 4. Student-created animation

There are a number of reasons for using in-house materials. Firstly, creating original reading and grammar materials avoids copyright issues. Japanese copyright law stipulates that a web page and all other related documents are copyright protected. Teachers may reproduce materials from web pages and use them in the classroom only if they do not 'unreasonably prejudice' the copyright owner. In essence, this implies that teachers must be careful to ensure that the only place they use the materials is in the classroom [4]. Secondly, a teacher who is familiar with the students' learning needs is more likely to resonate positively with the students, enhance their classroom learning and, hopefully, increase their motivation towards language learning. Also, from a teaching perspective, creating in-house materials enables teachers to offer material which learners themselves see as relevant and transferable to other situations. In order to appeal to our young cohort, the topics chosen for the mobile learning project are as topical and broad-based as possible. For the purpose of capturing students' interest, the chosen topics are not overly taxing and include jokes and riddles. Although listening skills have never been the main focus of this project, we were aware that reading accompanied by pictures and audio is always more effective than text-only [5]. Therefore, some materials sent by the Mobile English Learning Project include both audio and visual content to support the readings.

In this project, students/readers have also been involved in creating mobile learning content. In the last two decades, there is a trend toward student-led collaborative learning where teachers adopt a supportive role and become learning resources [6] and students are entrusted with new roles as content producers. As mobile learning materials are usually short and independent in terms of content, students are capable of developing such materials both in terms of time and ability if properly instructed. Therefore, the Mobile English Learning Project invited more than 30 students to write essays and create other materials, and up to February 2014, the Mobile English Learning Project had received about 100 student-created materials. Student-created content need not be limited to written learning materials, but can also include multi-media materials. The following is an animation developed by a first-year student (See Fig.4).

3   Findings from the Mobile English Learning Project

3.1   Mobile Learning Devices and Mobile Learning Experiences

On the registration page for the Mobile English Learning Project, students are asked about their reading devices, namely which mobile device they want to use to receive learning materials and whether they have a package payment plan giving them unlimited internet use. In addition, they are asked if they have previously used mobile devices for learning purposes.

The following data was obtained from 137 students registering in May 2013:

Q1 : Which mobile device do you own?

- Smart phone: 86 % ; Japanese style mobile phone: 13 % ; Other (iPad, iPod... etc.)1 %

Q2 : Do you have an unlimited use package payment plan for the internet on your mobile phone?

- Yes: 87%;   No: 13%

Q3 :   Have you ever used mobile devices for learning purposes?

- Yes: 41%;   No: 59%

The above data shows that the majority of these students possess multi-functional smart phones that are internet-connected all the time, indicating that the hardware environment is ready for conducting mobile learning. However, simple ownership of learning-ready devices does not guarantee that students will use mobile phones for learning. About 60% of the students state that they have never engaged in mobile learning before. Many students may still need guidance in order to successfully engage in mobile learning.

3.2   Students' Preferences Regarding Contact Method, Mobile Learning Materials, and Material Delivery Time

Each year, in the Mobile English Learning Project, we ask which communication method students prefer to use when they receive learning materials, PC email or mobile phone email. In 2013, of all the 137 new participants in the project, 79 (58%) preferred to use their mobile phone email address, while 24 (18%) chose to use a PC email address to receive learning materials and 34 participants (24%) thought either method was fine. The majority of young students seem to prefer to use their mobile phone to receive messages from teachers for the sake of convenience. This is because the mobile phone is portable and can be used to deal with any learning task at anytime, anywhere.

As possession of a smart phone has now become the norm for university students, Yahoo email, Gmail and Hotmail - which were formerly regarded as PC email accounts - are now also easily accessible. In spite of this new functionality, however, the majority of students still prefer to be contacted at their mobile phone email address.

A survey is carried out every year to obtain subscribers' feedback about the learning materials sent out from the project. The survey (n=56) conducted on April, 2012 from the Mobile Learning Project suggested that essays (41%) were the most popular, followed by trivia (34%), and grammar quizzes (27%). Further data analysis yielded more information on topic preference in essay writing and triva. In order of preference, topics were ranked as follows: English jokes and riddles (45%), cultural differences (30%), life/living/entertainment (27%), and topics related to society (12.5%). Less popular topics included English learning methodology (5%), science and technology (4%), and politics (4%).

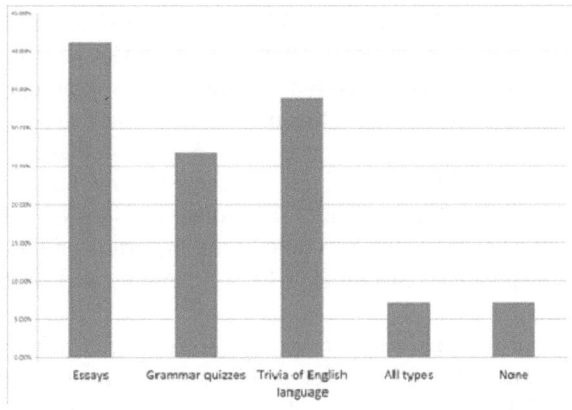

Fig. 5. Students' ranking of favored learning materials

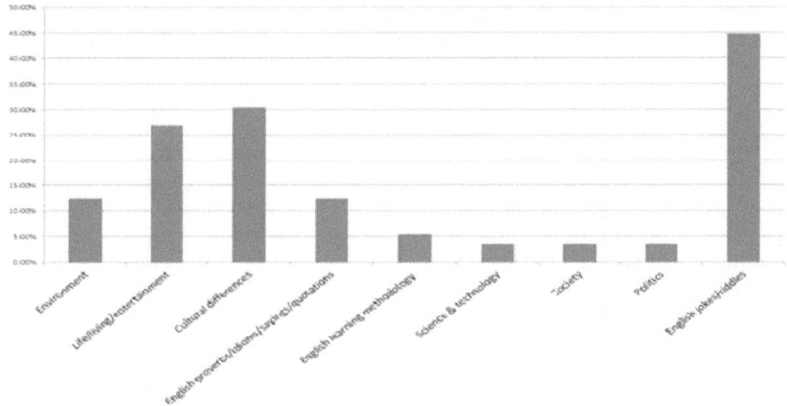

Fig. 6. Students' ranking of favored essay and triva topics

The results imply that students prefer to read essays and trivia rather than study grammar and do quizzes. Amongst all the essay and trivia topics, English jokes/riddles were ranked as the most popular, followed by cultural differences and topics connected to life/entertainment. The fact that essays are preferred to grammar quizzes indicate that materials read or interacted with on mobile phones should not be overly demanding: students may not have the time or the patience to do deep study on small-screen mobile phones. Entertaining materials such as English jokes and riddles, or something light, i.e. cultural differences, or campus life, can better attract students' attention and provide stimulation for this kind of project. Heavier topics such as politics, science and technology are not popular with students, although many of them are either social science majors or engineering majors.

The project has made some students realize that the mobile phone is not only a tool for voice communication, taking photos and gaming, but also a useful tool for learning English. One student interviewed said: "Before this project started, I only used my mobile phone for texting, phone calls and playing games, although I did sometimes use the built-in dictionary. Now I realize that the mobile phone can be used for learning!"

Cognizant of the fact that students can choose to conduct learning via their mobile phones at any time, we wanted to find out whether students had a preferred time of day for conducting mobile learning. The 2013 project registration page asked students what time of day they preferred to receive learning materials on their mobile phones. Students (n=137) responded: Anytime: 61%, Evenings and night: 22%, Lunch time: 14% and Morning: 3%

In order to confirm that the above responses were indeed accurate, we randomly chose the access record data of 7 quizzes and 3 essay comment interfaces which are kept on the server. Table 1 below shows that 72% of quiz and comment submissions occurred in the evenings and at night, followed in frequency by the mornings, then the afternoons, and finally noon.

Table 1. Student mobile learning time

Time of a day	Number of submissions during the time	Percentage
Morning (5:01 ~12:00)	18	12%
Noon (12:01 13:30)	11	8%
Afternoon (13:31~17:00)	13	9%
Evening (17:01 ~20:00)	52	36%
Night (20:01~ 5:00)	52	36%

Although some students acknowledge that they can receive learning materials on their mobile phones at any time, the evenings and night are the time when students have finished their whole day of classes and can start to relax and enjoy their own freedom. This seems to be the proper time to deliver materials for informal learning [1].

4   Challenges of Creating and Delivering Mobile Learning Materials

In this project, the first challenge is how to deliver the content. The project delivers learning content to mobile phones using emails. If the content is an essay, a TOEIC/ TOEFL tip or a joke, then it goes into the body of the email. If it is a quiz, then the quiz

URL is attached to an email explaining the purpose of the quiz. In total, up to March, 2014, 351 email addresses were registered with the Mobile English Learning Project. Unfortunately, not all of the registrants have become permanent participants; 21 subscribers' email addresses were found unreachable. The reasons ascribed to the loss of so many subscribers are fourfold; (a) some students found that the program was not suitable for their learning style and chose to terminate their subscription; (b) Japanese students frequently change their mobile phone email addresses in order to avoid spam, but they forget to pass on this information to the project managers; (c) many students' mobile phones are pre-set by telecommunication companies to prevent receiving emails from PCs; and (d) the emails from the project server are filtered to the spam folder.

Another challenge is the difficulty of determining whether a reader has truly read the content or not. This is impossible unless he or she makes a comment or clicks on the web link attached to the email. The difficulty of tracking students' degree of involvement is the major difficulty that we have faced so far. Of course, we can choose to deliver mobile learning content via the web rather than by email. However, content delivered via web may not have the same readership as emails. After all, students check emails very often, while they do not access web sites as frequently. The choice of mode for delivering mobile learning content depends on students' learning motivation.

To keep readers motivated and responsive to mobile learning content is another great challenge. Although the survey indicated that students like topics in cultural differences and school life, the essays in these areas did not have significantly more responses than other topics did. In the Mobile English Learning Project, each message receives three rankings or comments on average; most of the readers choose to remain silent. Even English jokes that were perceived to be most popular with students received only five responses on average.

Grammar and vocabulary quizzes have been unable to garner much participation among readers. The following figure shows that of 239 subscribers, only 19 students took quizzes. This suggests that no matter how well mobile learning content is designed, it is difficult to maintain a high degree of student involvement if the task is voluntary.

Similarly, student involvement in content creation is hard to sustain. The project invited students/subscribers to contribute content, but the response was limited. Even with the promise to pay authors, the Mobile Learning Project is still not receiving many contributions. For example, in July, 2013, one teacher made a call for content contribution to 156 students in the advanced English classes he taught, sweetened with a promise of payment. Even so, only five responded and joined the content development team.

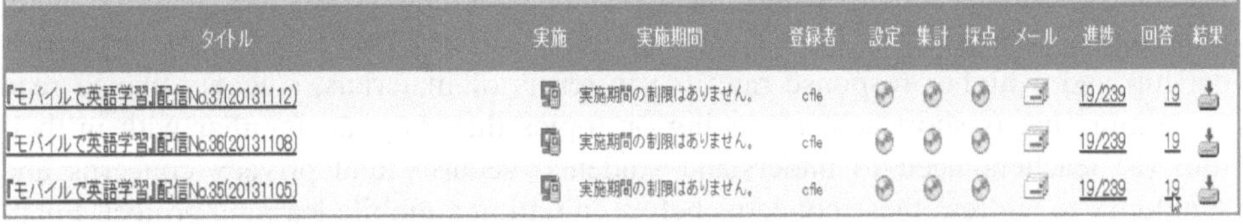

Fig. 7. Low participation of vocabulary/grammar quizzes

5   Students' Concerns over Mobile Learning: Privacy and Security

Although the call for participation in the Mobile English Learning Project goes out to all the first-year students in May every year, only a small portion of students eventually join the project. Of the 1000 first-year students, the number voluntarily registering for the project came to 154 students in 2010, 157 students in 2011 and 106 in 2012. This amounts to a small percentage (about 15%) of the total population. Students' responses show that they may not be interested in any form of study which is not linked to course credits, or they may regard the mobile phone as a private possession and do not want to *study* on it. The project has also had some difficulty in keeping its subscribers. Up to June 2013, the project had lost 179 subscribers out of the original 472 subscribers from 2010-2012, a loss of 38%.

In order to clarify the reasons for dropping out, we interviewed two students. Their comments may represent the concerns of many students towards mobile learning.

"I am already very busy with so many other subjects. I don't want to study anything which is not credit-related. In addition, when taking a quiz or leaving a comment, we need to click a URL. I am afraid of getting spam (by clicking an unfamiliar URL)."

"When taking quizzes, I always feel that I am being monitored by a watchful eye – our teacher. So if I do poorly on quizzes, I will feel embarrassed. As soon as I think that our teacher may see the quiz results, I start to feel pressure. Therefore I choose not to take quizzes on my mobile phone."

These comments indicate that students may not be motivated by a mobile learning project in which they are not rewarded for their work with credits. Furthermore, they may be worried about their online security and privacy.

6   Conclusion

In this research, we observed data from a mobile learning project being conducted in a Japanese university. As regards Japanese university students, the data implies that (1) hardware advancement in mobile devices does provide a lot of potential for students to conduct mobile learning. However, ownership of mobile devices does not necessarily stir enthusiasm for mobile learning; (2) when teachers need to contact students about learning materials, student mobile phone email addresses are preferable to PC email addresses at the present time; (3) students tend to access their learning materials in the evenings or at night, so sending emails after 17:00 may bring a larger readership and a higher response rate; (4) in terms of materials, students like to read something that is short and interesting on topics that they are familiar with in their life; (5) teachers need to understand students' security and privacy concerns and should try to address these concerns before initiating a mobile learning project. Finally, as students are busy and always on move, the content developed for learning on mobile phones should not be only short and topical, but also interesting. If possible, mobile learning should be tied into required coursework and evaluated as a part of students' performance in the course. Otherwise, there will be a great likelihood of a considerable drop-out rate [6].

References

1. Shibatari, D.: Surveys on trends of personal games. In: Ketai White Book 2010, pp. 89–90. Impress R& D, Tokyo (2010)
2. Borau, K., Ullrich, C., Feng, J., Shen, R.: Microblogging for language learning: using Twitter to train communicative and cultural competence. In: Spaniol, M., Li, Q., Klamma, R., Lau, R.W.H. (eds.) ICWL 2009. LNCS, vol. 5686, pp. 78–87. Springer, Heidelberg (2009)
3. Grosseck, G., Holotesch, C.: Can we use Twitter for educational activities? In: Fourth International Scientific Conference eLearning and Software for Education, Bucharest, Romania (2008)
4. Heffernan, N., Wang, S.: Copyright and Multimedia Classroom Material: A Study from Japan. Computer Assisted Language Learning 21(2), 167–180 (2008)
5. Harden, R.M., Crosby, J.R.: The good teacher is more than a lecturer: the twelve roles of the teacher. Medical Teacher 22, 334–347 (2000)
6. Wang, S., Smith, S.: Reading and grammar learning through mobile phones. Language Learning and Technology 17(3), 117–134 (2013), http://llt.msu.edu/issues/october2013/wangsmith.pdf (retrieved)

Instructional Design and Practice of Problem-Based Collaborative Knowledge Building under Network Environment

Haixia Zhao

Network & Educational Technology Institute, Jinan University,
510632 Guangzhou, China
lejb@gsta.com

Abstract. A new hybrid learning model of problem-based collaborative knowledge building (referred to as the CKB) is based on the specific learning CKB under network environment. It can be integrated with knowledge creation to promote advanced cognitive activities and to solve problem together. We expound its connotation, basic elements, characteristics, and explore the main steps and operation process. The model has three main stages including learner community, cognitive conflict-based and integration-based CKB. Taking "structural chemistry" course as an experiment to verify, though action research, questionnaire survey and the interview method, it proves that the model plays active roles in improving student's learning interest, academic performance and high levels abilities, especially social abilities, ability to practice, research and to solve problem in real situations. It is important to take into account whether the teachers have the ability required by the model.

Keywords: Collaborative knowledge building, Hybrid learning model, Basic elements, Instruction Design, Network environment.

1 Introduction

1.1 The Connotation of CKB

The biggest challenge of our education in the era of knowledge, is not to help the students how to obtain the vast factual knowledge and skills, but to help them learn how to produce and apply new ideas to complex situations that are contributed to the process of creating new knowledge. On the rising of social construction theory, situational theory, group dynamics theory, activities theory and interactive teaching theory, the educational idea gradually pays attention to the learning construction and improvement of community knowledge. Gerry Stahl etc. think, sometimes relying on independent learning does not resolve the problem, then you need to construct knowledge meaning through collaboration, so socialization learning process has just begun [1]. A knowledge-based society needs people who can work collaboratively and creatively with critical thinking and adaptive expertise. Therefore, the focus of education should be

S.K.S. Cheung et al. (Eds.): ICHL 2014, LNCS 8595, pp. 254–265, 2014.

transferred from single study out of context to CKB. This concept is proposed the earliest by the Canadian scholars SCardamalia and Bereiter in twentieth Century and early 80's. The CKB refers to the individual in a specific organization where each one is mutual cooperated each other, jointly participate in activities with certain purpose, and ultimately form a certain view, ideas, methods of intellectual products. It is emphasized on the formation of learning public knowledge group approval. Then the learner in the group transfers the public knowledge into individual knowledge. The process of knowledge building is valuable to the community views and thinking and continuous improvement, the purpose is realized the collective contribution through the community than the individual contribution [2]. Koschmann believes that, "learning is a collaborative knowledge construction process of society" [3]. It has been used in many countries and regions, such as American, Canada, Britain and Hong Kong.

Hyo Jeong et al. (2010) found the CKB environment is beneficial for both high-achieving and low-achieving students by quantitative data [4]. This necessitates gaining deep understanding and problem-solving skills. The problem-based CKB is based on the specific learning CKB, has become an important new hybrid learning method in the classroom teaching and internet environment. It can be integrated with knowledge creation to promote the students to carry out a variety of advanced cognitive activities, to promote them to solve problem together. The network technology based on the multimedia and communication technology, due to its characteristics of sharing and collaboration, collaborative knowledge of problem solving can provide a new problem-based CKB environment to successfully achieve knowledge sharing and knowledge innovation. Many scholars research from different perceptions of the CKB theory under the network environment.

1.2   The Construction Perceptions of CKB under the Network Environment

Many scholars research from different perceptions of the CKB theory under the network environment. Scardamalia and Bereiter's research team carries out a large number of experiments mainly through Knowledge Forum and propose a series of the community principles of CKB. The main problem of CKB under the network environment is studied, such as Goodman, stressed the importance of the conversation, Martinez et al. discussed the learners' participation in the construction influence quality of collaborative knowledge, Stahl analyzed social practice of the CKB, think its process has six elements: brainstorming, discourse, reaction, organization, analysis and generalization (Stahl, 1999).

From the students' cognitive development point of view, Nobuko has investigated changes of learner cognition through the construction of qualitative analysis of data in the process of collaborative knowledge [5]. Some researchers study community knowledge assessment in a knowledge building environment. (Huang-Yao Hong and Marlene Scardamalia,2014) [6]. Johannes Moskaliuk et al.(2012) study CKB with wikis [7]. Furthermore, Ralph Barthel et al.(2013) found the shared multi-path video approach of CKB [8]. Other Chinese researchers have studied quantity and quality interactive, dynamic mechanism, community, forum and effect evaluation research, and discusses the group, strategies and models of CKB [9][10][11][12].

1.3   The Stages of CKB under the Network Environment

Many scholars research from different conditions and process of the CKB theory under the network environment. Doherty, Hilberg, Epaloose, Tharp et al. in USA have extended out three conditions for effective knowledge construction: teaching activities and students' previous experiences and knowledge to create meaningful connections; Between the students, teachers and students to cooperate with conversation to each other; Teaching is happened in the zone of proximal development, in which process is full of dialogue. From social orientation of construct knowledge perspective, social theorist Gergen, K.J. has emphasized on the dialogue that make students change from the object to subject in our teaching practice. Harasim (1989) has divided the process of CKB into five stages that includes common viewpoint, evaluation, inspection, negotiation, each questioned that comprehensive [13]. Nonaka Fujiro (1994) has proposed SECI model of knowledge transform, namely socialization, externalization, integration and internalization, and has divided process of knowledge construction into two dimensions: individual CKB and social CKB. From the learner's interaction perception, Gunawardena (1995) has divided it into four stages which include sharing and comparing the information, the discovery and analysis of differences between the views [14]. Hansen et al. (1999) proposed six stages including group formation, the problem setting, planning, research, summary, evaluation, which is not only a good guidance on how to organize the teaching process, research to evaluation, but also embodies the micro process of CKB [15]. Fisher et al. (2002) has proposed four stages, namely: the specific, abstraction of task knowledge, conflict -based and integration –based of the CKB [16]. Gerry Stahl (2003)think it has eleven stages, and described micro process in small steps, which includes problems, language expression, personal public statements, others open statement, discussion, debate and reasoning of choice, meaning clear, shared understanding, negotiation, cooperative knowledge, view of formal and impersonal, artificial products and their representation. By means of the Knowledge Forum platform ,César Coll et al. (2014)   found teacher feedback on learning content, academic task and social participation   supports the process of   online knowledge building [17].

2   A New Model of Problem-Based CKB under the Network Environment

Through the construction of model, process, design and the main problem of network supported CKB, based on analysis and study of problem solving learning, and Hybrid Learning theories, the author constructs a new model of problem-based CKB under the network environment, and puts forward the related concepts, the main stage of the pattern of teaching process and key steps, elements, further forms the teaching design process of the mode.

2.1   Concept of Problem-Based CKB under the Network Environment

Through reference and summary of the existed research, the author think the concept of problem-based CKB under network environment means taking solving problem as the center, through multimedia and network technology providing the resources, tools for students, the learning is set in complex, meaningful problem situation so that students using the knowledge and skills can be involved in collaborative problem solving activities in a particular community collaboration. In the end it ultimately forms a certain view, ideas and methods of intellectual products. Its goal is to improve students' ability of knowledge acquisition, problem solving and autonomous collaboration process, to construct the multi dimension CKB and experience. It has an open and web-based learning environment, takes the concretively coordinate effect and group performance as an incentive, and pays attention to the cultivation of students' personality development and the ability of knowledge innovation.

2.2   The Instructional Design Process of Problem-Based CKB under the Network Environment

Reference and summary of the existing research results, the author thinks that, problem-based CKB under network environment teaching design process can be divided into three main stages that includes learning community, cognitive conflict-based and integration-based collaborative knowledge building, and six key steps (Table 1).The instructional design process (Figure 1) is a process of gradually rising, with no clear boundary, each stage respectively containing the corresponding key steps, each step design, organization, implementation, evaluation and management embodies the characteristics and factors of collaboration construction.

Table 1. The main teaching stages and key steps of Problem-based CKB under network environment

the main stages	key steps
The First stage: the learning community	• Creating a learning community Creating context, setting problem, group planning, division of tasks
The Second stage: cognitive conflict-based on CKB	• Consensus of CKB within group Sharing, negotiation, argument, consensus, reflection and creation • Integrity of CKB between groups achievement exhibition, inter group competition, collaborative agreement, mutual evaluation and reflection • Problem solving Formal and impersonal, intelligence sharing
The Third stage: cognitive Integration -based CKB	• Multiple evaluation, summary and reflection • Multi-dimensional CKB

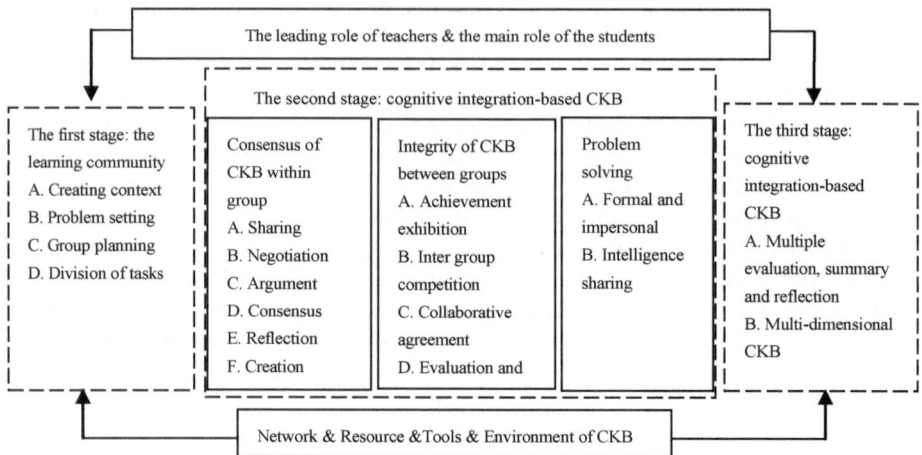

Fig. 1. The instructional design process of problem-based CKB under the network environment

The first stage is the learning community. It is one of the important ways and means to promote students' to construct knowledge collaboration. Its key steps include creating context, setting program, group planning and division of tasks. This process can formulate common learning objectives and operational mechanism of a group.

The second stage is cognitive conflict-based on the CKB. Its key steps includes consensus of CKB within group, integrity of CKB between groups and problem solving. The first key step includes six elements, namely ongoing sharing, negotiation, argument, consensus, reflection and creation. This step is necessary to group formed a positive interdependence, effective face to face and the network environment to study hybrid group collaborative learning, and form six elements' circulation or microcirculation. The second key step in this stage is integrity of CKB between groups which includes achievement exhibition, inter group competition, collaborative agreement, mutual evaluation and reflection. It is necessary to introduce competition mechanism in the group to improve the participation and active performance. The third key step is problem solving which includes formal and impersonal and intelligence sharing. The group show their achievements, generate common knowledge and ideas, make them formal, impersonal and intelligent sharing. The students' thinking mode will be tested, stretched and improved through problem solving key step.

The third stage is cognitive integration-based CKB which key steps include multiple evaluation, summary, reflection and multi-dimensional CKB. Through the view of integration, the formation of public knowledge achieves the ultimate purpose of CKB. At the same time, members of the contribution of ideas and intelligent in the cognitive structure is changed and the construction of individual knowledge, develop continuously, go round and begin again, spiral, eventually completed the collective knowledge construction.

2.3   Essential Factors of Problem-Based CKB under the Network Environment

Combining relevant theories, through structured understanding and comprehensive analysis of CKB system, the author thinks, the essential factors of the new model are:

- Collaborative group. Group is the basic organization form of CKB. Group forms dynamics of the team to remote mutual assistance and encouragement.
- Knowledge construction problems. Problem teaching is a kind of developing teaching which can give the students independence and development of creative ability.
- Knowledge construction task. It is the specific task, not from the teaching practice and the mechanical memorizing some materials. It includes specific content, the task of development process, task division, achievement and group operation mechanism.
- Knowledge construction division. It includes the student's individual responsibilities, specific division of task, process monitoring and evaluation.
- Collaborative strategy. It includes the situation strategy, support strategy, problem strategy and interactive strategy etc.
- Knowledge building environment. Network environment to highlight the knowledge building collaboration, stressed the network as a cognitive and communicative tool.

2.4   Characteristics

According to the related theory, the new model of problem-based CKB under the network environment, in the author's opinion, has the following main characteristics:

- The focus on collaborative knowledge building. Get through collaboration and interaction of knowledge is the core of effective teaching.
- Stressing the construction group of public knowledge. The era of knowledge society idea gradually pay attention to the social, collective community construction and improvement of knowledge.
- Emphasize the subjective role of individual knowledge construction and the leading role of teachers.
- Emphasize problem solving of practice and application of knowledge.
- Emphasizes knowledge construction context and society.
- Emphasize the network as a group, interactive, distributed, powerful tool for CKB.

3   Environmental Design and Construction of the New Model

"Structural chemistry" is the basic course of applied chemistry, chemical, material chemistry. Because it is abstract and difficult, students have lower interest and think it to be of little value. Therefore, there are more problems of teaching and learning, the effect is often not ideal.

This hybrid learning model of problem-based CKB under the network environment, provides a new perspective for the course teaching reform. First, teachers have completed the school-based e-learning project based on Blackboard network teaching platform during 2010-2011. Using this platform we can achieve many learning functions, such as tracking trajectory, group work, wiki, interaction, collaborative forum and learning test, questionnaire survey of students, and can satisfy the need of the problem-based CKB. Then, our research and implementation began as a demonstration of teaching reform project of the higher education in Chinese Guangdong province in 2011,and achieved outstanding award after the project is well finished in 2013.

This research mainly adopted the action research method in the experimental stage, to verify the proposed problem-based CKB in figure 1.According to the characteristics, difficulties and teaching bottleneck problem of the course, the teacher team selected the "molecular symmetry" chapter as the test section. The two rounds of action research lasted two years during 2012 and 2013. Each round lasts 4 weeks in annual autumn semester, every week for three classes (45 minutes each class). The teaching object was 72 undergraduate students whose specialties are including applied chemistry, chemical, material chemistry and other related specialty in the same college. The first round of action has total of 34 students, 15 girls; second rounds of 38 students, 18 girls. Teachers compiled the study guide, and made the learning resources and other supplementary materials resources in Blackboard network teaching platform. The course divided all the students into 8 groups, each group of 4-5 students.

Considering the limits in the attribution of action research method, this research through the questionnaire survey and the interview method, the results are triangulation, in order to improve the reliability of the conclusion. Survey of students to understand the teaching evaluation includes three dimensions (the teaching attitude, method and effect) and ten items. The written interview was aim to understand students' feelings of the course. Anonymous questionnaires and interviews were for all students. Interviews were subsequently measured complete, real name.

4   Teaching Process Design and Implementation of the New Models

4.1   The First Stage: The Learning Community

Creating Context
It includes two parts of teaching situation and network environment. In the classroom teaching, teachers apply situational heuristic teaching to help students effectively understand the structure and principles of symmetry model, strengthen the cognition and application of the depth. The curriculum make full use of the special subject learning website, network teaching platform, network and social media tools, provide "rich" support conditions, promote members opinion divergence and convergence of collective intelligent.

Problem Setting
Based on the question situation, learner centered real situation and problems of collaborative learning situation, carry on scientific research, improve collaboration effectiveness. Problems setting in should be slightly higher than the actual level of students, namely to moderate difficulty, easy to carry out, and divergent and inquiry,

strong feasibility and operation of open. Choose three collaborative themes and uses integrated design ideas for the design. The themes are:

The first theme: symmetry concept and molecular symmetry;

The second theme: the molecular point group and determine the type;

The third theme: physical properties of molecular symmetry and molecular.

In the concrete teaching practice, it is divided into eight groups, each group of 6 people scale. Eight groups of participants are:

A. Methane and 1, 2- Dichloroethene.   B. Phosphoric acid.

C.Benzene and sulfur hexafluoride.   D. Ferrocene.

E. Hydrogen peroxide.   F. Adamantane.

G. White phosphorus.   H. Diborane.

Separate research topic in each group, but in two rounds of action research keep the relative stability of the topic. If the aim of topic in first group is "Methane and 1, 2- two vinyl chloride molecules", then its research content is their symmetry operations of those molecules; problem in second theme is their point; problem in third theme is their dipole moment and rotation.

Group Planning

It follows the "inter group homogeneity, heterogeneity within the group" principle in order to ensure fair competition between each team. The teacher should not only promote the groups to reduce the difference and keep balance, but also promote the group to have some differences and complementarities in learning level, ability etc.

Division of Tasks

Division of tasks includes common goals, group operation schedule, reward and punishment incentives, form the effective feedback mechanism of the clear individual responsibility and team self-processing, ensure collaboration group orbit.

4.2   The Second Stage: Cognitive Conflict-based CKB

Consensus of CKB within Group

Sharing : Students make problem-based independent inquiry learning through network resources and tools combined with face to face and network environment, finish their statement, brainstorming and view sharing.

Negotiation : Response, feedback, interact, cognitive conflict to others' view; discuss, consulate, debate and reason the key cognitive conflict; form the new insights and suggestions.

Argument : Students make a strong argument, revise and improve the personal point of view in the old and new knowledge and experience between the repeated, two-way interaction, expression analysis and discourse organization.

Consensus : Sum up and form the more perfect group views and cooperation agreement.

Reflection : The group and individual reflect to find problems in the whole process, timely adjust and correct, and form benign feedback.

Creation : The form of collaboration knowledge, explicit form intelligent products.

Integrity of CKB between groups
Achievement exhibition: The team will share results, report and presentation.
Inter group competition: Take the group competition mechanism, high level exchanges formed in a wide range of collective concept.
Collaborative agreement: Interactive multi-dimensional construction can take effect.
Evaluation and reflection: The mutual evaluation and shared reflection, positive feedback, to organize and construct.

Problem Solving
Problem solving is not to seek the only answer, but to encourage multi angle thinking, seek the different solution in order to train students' cooperation spirit, critical thinking and compatibility ability.
Formal and impersonal: Characterization of artificial product works, is in the form of design and creative team, can be a report, thesis, design, model etc.
Intelligence sharing: The modified product sharing, mutual correction sustainable use the platform wiki, embodying the learning result generation and visualization.

4.3   The Third Stage: Cognitive Integration-Based CKB

Multiple Evaluation, Summary and Reflection
Though multiple elastic evaluation and cognitive thinking, the students meta-cognitive ability and the transfer of knowledge get relatively developed.

Multi-dimensional CKB
The teams make discussion, mutual assessment, consultation to collaborative knowledge together. Finally the objective of perfect, collective knowledge or ideas can be formed. It eventually shares public knowledge visualization and reaches the final goal cooperative construction.

5   Results and Discussion

In the first round of action research, the surveyed students made specific recommendations for creating more opportunities of communication and providing newer learning resources. Then, teachers enhanced the 3D animation display of resources and updated research theme resources as a stronger scaffold for students. Furthermore, Teachers recorded classroom teaching video and flipped it on the web to add more CKB time and opportunities.

In the second round of action research, in order to mobilize each learning level of students and enlarge their engagement and contribution, teachers conducted a series of initiatives, such as training team leader management and cooperative ability, expanding inter group competition, strengthening the distribution group contribution, and incenting collective and individual awarding mechanism etc. Especially, All initiatives were arranged uninterrupted to ensure continuous and effective function in each CKB stage.

Based on the test, questionnaire and the forum and log, it showed that :

- At the beginning of the experiment and questionnaire survey, students had general interest 52% , had fewer interest 8%. However, in the post experiment questionnaire, 100% of the students thought they improved learning interest, 81% of them effectively improved. In addition, both the interview and questionnaire survey, the data showed students had higher identity on course teaching. According to interviews of students, 32 students surveyed, 84% students liked the problem-based CKB, 80% of students improved their learning enthusiasm; The unit test average score was 91 in centesimal system, compared to the past 86, the overall improvement of academic performance. 83% of them effectively improved the professional knowledge internalization and high levels of thinking ability.
- Practice proved that the model played active roles in improving student's higher level abilities. Through CKB task, students went beyond the static knowledge learning, 92% of students greatly improved research ability and practice ability .Through the inter group confrontation, multiple evaluation, assessment of team contribution,100% of the students improved the independent learning, collaborative learning and information literacy, 78% of them greatly improved the above abilities. On the other hand, 98% of students improved self-education ability, meta-cognitive ability, 60% of them greatly improved the above abilities. This was also confirmed from CKB forum and log.
- Practice proved that continuous the problem-based CKB played active roles in improving student's social abilities and the ability to solve problem in real situations. 100% of students promoted the construction of group public knowledge collaboration.79% of them greatly improve communication, expression, collaboration, compatibility, multiple evaluation and problem solving skills.77% of students greatly improve individual and collective learning responsibility, and it promoted the construction of public knowledge.

In this study, through teaching practice and two rounds of action research test, proved that the problem-based CKB can be applied successfully in the university teaching, also put forward the basic operation process of the mode of teaching in the university. And through all levels of multidimensional CKB so as to enhance the knowledge and professional ability, promote the culture of higher level abilities.

However, the research of process in the network environment is still not perfect. First, there are still a few students who don't be very active. How to fully mobilize the enthusiasm of the students is our further research problem. Then, how to improve the group CKB mechanism also needs more theoretical research and technical support. In addition, students must be rooted in the process and practice so as to take more time and more energy. There are 8% students who think that the process make them spend more spare time so as to add the learning pressure. However, as the proverb goes "Teaching a man to fish is better than giving him fish", all students think that it is worth them spending more time and energy on CKB task. Maybe the last real challenge is whether teachers are qualified as the students' facilitator, timely and effective for students to provide support for the notion, meta-cognitive support, process support and policy support, promote the efficiency and benefit of construction. This is the real key factor restricting the application of new mode in University teaching. Maybe, with the development of MOOC, the future teachers can use the MOOC curriculum resources (including on video) as the basis of their own teaching, attention to act as a guide and exchange activities organizer role.

Acknowledgements. This work was supported by the China Guangdong Province education research project, "Research and practice of learning model of problem-based collaborative knowledge building in college students" (Project number: 2013JK020), China Guangdong Province higher education teaching reform Research project "Research and practice of promoting education information strategy in higher education based on Innovation diffusion theory in the era of MOOC ".

References

1. Stahl, G.A.: Model of Collaborative-Knowledge-Building (EB/OL), http://www.umich.edu/~icls/proceedings/pdf/Stahl.pdf
2. Scardamalia, M., Beretier, C.: Computer support for knowledge-building communities
3. Koschmann, T.D.: CSCL: Theory and Practice of an Emerging Paradigm. Lawrence Erlbaum Associates, Hillsdale (1996)
4. So, H., Seah, L.H., Toh-Heng, H.L.: Designing collaborative knowledge building environments accessible to all learners: Impacts and design challenges. Computers & Education 54(2), 479–490 (2010)
5. Nonaka, I.A.: Dynamic theory of organizational Knowledge Creation. Organization Science 30(2), 15–27 (1994)
6. Hong, H., Scardamalia, M.: Community knowledge assessment in a knowledge building environment. Computers & Education 71, 279–288 (2014)
7. Barthel, R., Ainsworth, S., Sharples, M.: Collaborative knowledge building with shared video representations. International Journal of Human-Computer Studies 71(1), 59–75 (2013)
8. Moskaliuk, J., Kimmerle, J.: Ulrike Cress, Collaborative knowledge building with wikis: The impact of redundancy and polarity. Computers & Education 58(4), 1049–1057 (2012)
9. Zhao, J.: Analysis of CSCL activity process based on Network Forum. China Audio-visual Education 2010(5), 8–15 (2010)
10. Zhao, H.: Collaborative knowledge building in Web environment. The Modern Education Technology 2012(11), 110–116 (2012)
11. Xie, Y., Song, N., Liu, M.: Analysis of collaborative knowledge building and community based on the network. Audio Visual Education Research 2013(4), 38–46 (2013)
12. Chen, J.: Study of interactive teaching of Collaborative knowledge building in Web environment. D. Master's thesis, Fujian Normal University (2011)
13. Harasim, L.M.: Online Education. A new domain. In: Mason, R., Kaye, A.R. (eds.) Mindweave. Communication, Computers, and Distance Education, pp. 50–62. Pergamon Press (1989)
14. Gunawardena, C.N., Lowe, C.A., Anderson, T.: Analysis of a global online Analysis of Interaction in Online Environments debate and development of an interaction analysis model for examining social construction of knowledge in computer conferencing. Journal of Educational Computing Research 17(4), 397–431 (1997)

15. Hansen, T., Dirckinck-Holmfeld, L., Lewis, R., Rugel, J.: Using telematics for collaborative knowledge construction. In: Dillenbourg, P. (ed.) Collaborative Learning: Cognitive and Computational Approaches, pp. 169–196. Pergamon Press (1999)
16. Fisher, F., Bruhn, J., Grase, C., Mand, H.: Fostering collaborative knowledge construction with visualization tools. Learning and Instruction 12, 212–232 (2002)
17. Coll, C., Rochera, M.J.: Supporting online collaborative learning in small groups: Teacher feedback on learning content, academic task and social participation. Computers & Education 75, 53–64 (2014)

Personalized-Adaptive Learning –
A Model for CIT Curricula

Jayshiro Tashiro[1,2,3,4,*], Fred Hurst[3], Alison Brown[3],
Patrick C.K. Hung[1,4], and Miguel Vargas Martin[1,5]

[1] University of Ontario Institute of Technology, Oshawa, Ontario, Canada
[2] MAXIT EDUCATION Systems, Tucson, Arizona, USA
[3] Northern Arizona University, Flagstaff, Arizona, USA
[4] BeaconWall Limited, Hong Kong, SAR, China
[5]PHractal Partnership, Oshawa, Ontario, Canada
jay.tashiro@uoit.ca

Abstract. We studied the complexity of building a personalized and adaptive learning system for computer and information technology (CIT) curricula. Working with an online personalized competency-based CIT curriculum at Northern Arizona University (Flagstaff, Arizona, USA), our research developed a model for layering adaptive capacities into this curriculum to provide enhanced feedback and remediation for students. Additionally the model we developed provided integration of data collection and analysis that could drive evidence-based educational practices for CIT undergraduate and graduate programs. In this paper, we describe the conceptual model for a personalized-adaptive learning CIT educational environment, along with data collected over three years that support the efficacy of the approach we describe. We call the model **SIGNAL CIT Education**—Serial Integration of Guiding Nodes for Adaptive Learning in CIT Education.

Keywords: Personalized learning, adaptive learning, competency-based learning, evidence-based learning, e-learning, learning assessment, misconception development, knowledge systems, CIT curricula, computer and information technology.

1   Introduction

We describe the methodology and research foundation for a personalized and adaptive learning environment called **SIGNAL CIT Education**—Serial Integration of Guiding Nodes for Adaptive Learning in CIT Education The acronym of **SIGNAL** acknowledges emergence of inclusive and adaptive environments during a period of very aggressive implementation of hybrid and totally online courses at all levels of education and training. However, inclusive-adaptive hybrid and totally online environments have been elusive and understudied. Tashiro, Hung, Vargas Martin, and colleagues [1-4] described how the lack of evidence-based frameworks for hybrid and totally online

---

*   Corresponding author.

S.K.S. Cheung et al. (Eds.): ICHL 2014, LNCS 8595, pp. 266–277, 2014.

learning results from complexity in studying and implementing such educational frameworks. Additional complexity results from disagreement about which theoretical frameworks should guide systematic studies of the enormous diversity in hybrid and totally online educational environments [2].

We previously analyzed impacts of healthcare technologies on care planning and delivery and found important analogues between the transformation of healthcare and the transformation of evidence-based practices in education. Through these types of analyses, we identified a variety of problems within education. As we did in previous studies of healthcare, we sorted educational problems into one of three categories—micro, meso, and macro levels. Micro level problems tend to be those appearing at the individual level. For example in education, the individual level would be the student. From our perspective, the critical micro level problems are the gaps in our knowledge related to educational environments and their effectiveness. To date, we feel confident that there are at least 10 gaps in knowledge about how educational environments "really work" to change an individual's learning outcomes and willingness as well as ability to sustain behaviours related to learning [1-3]. Students' formation of misconceptions is a keystone knowledge gap and we developed research models that allow us identify how misconceptions become instantiated. Preliminary studies showed us how understanding misconception development would advance understanding of other knowledge gaps [1-7].

Meso level problems occur at the level of course or learning environment organization, such as educational materials and commercial learning management systems or other educational technology brought into teaching-learning-assessment environments. Meso level problems emerge when educational materials and learning management systems are used to provide singular solutions that seldom meet the idiosyncratic needs of diverse departments and other units within academic institutions. As an example, Tashiro [8] identified unethical issues in ways faculty selected and used educational materials as well as issues with academic publishers' not producing evidence-based instructional materials (books, images, digital learning objects, test banks, content for learning management systems) and educational technologies (course cartridges and websites, learning management systems—some with a capacity for adaptive learning).

We argue one type of macro problem evolves at the level of institutional organizations. Examples include: department structures within a college; collaboration of colleges within a university; and the impact of government mandates typically found within state-funded universities as well as within city or county supported community colleges in the United States. A second type of macro problem evolves when an academic unit or institution decides to create a new model for a teaching-learning-assessment system. Problems become evident when developers must adhere to rigid external requirements (e.g., accreditation, licensing requirements for professional education). This second kind of problem inhibits development of innovative online learning models that are outside the norms of an educational institution's other course structures, even if the proposed model has strong evidence for actually improving students' educational outcomes. Not unrelated to this second macro problem we found a suite of related problems: (1) increased workload required of faculty and administrators to create evidence-based educational environments; (2) lack of resources to create educational environments especially with mandates for integrating emerging educational technology (which may not be sufficiently studied to be called "evidence-based"); and (3) accommodating new types of organizational relationships and change management when new models of education are being implemented within a department, college, or across an entire university.

Certainly, we do not make the claim that micro, meso, and macro problems are independent of each other, which adds to the complexity. However, we have made the argument in earlier papers [1-4] that changes proposed for education should have some kind of empirical support for improving educational outcomes. Sadly, such empirical foundations are the exception rather than the rule.

In order to develop a rigorous framework for evidence-based education, we formed two educational teams to examine the problem areas listed above and explore ways to create and implement evidence-based models for online learning. One team was located at Northern Arizona University (Flagstaff, Arizona, USA). The second team originated at the University of Ontario Institute of Technology (Oshawa, Ontario, Canada), subsequently working as part of a research and development group in the Incubation Programme at the Hong Kong Science and Technology Park and then with a research and development group called Maxit Systems in Tucson, Arizona (USA). A key difference from many online learning development collaborations is that these two teams both focus on competencies rather than credit hours or courses as defined in the traditional sense. Furthermore, before meeting each other these two teams had worked across the micro-meso-macro levels to examine how individuals learn, how misconceptions could be assessed in individual students, and how to build teaching-learning-assessment systems for online learning that were adaptive in the following ways: (1) personalizing an educational experience for students; (2) providing feedback and remediation pathways; and (3) building dynamic knowledge systems integrated into the many facets of any teaching-learning-assessment environment. Finally, these two teams used concepts and technologies from the electronic patient record systems of healthcare to figure out how to create truly personalized-adaptive educational environments. As observed in many healthcare settings, our teams used combinations of commercially available software engines and software developed by academic teams to create the most appropriate educational systems for meeting the idiosyncratic needs of both the institutional operations base and the student populations served by the respective institution.

2   Northern Arizona University Personalized Learning

Northern Arizona University (NAU) has a main campus in Flagstaff, Arizona (USA), as well as an Extended Campus educational system—a network of 34 satellite campuses spread throughout the state of Arizona. The NAU Flagstaff main campus and Extended Campuses have parallel administrative structures. Within the Extended Campus network, NAU faculty and staff built a Personalized Learning online educational environment. Dr. Alison Brown is the head of Personalized Learning. She also serves as Associate Vice President of Extended Campuses. Dr. Brown helped develop the initial structure for Personalized Learning.

Personalized Learning (PL) development was partially funded by a $1 million grant from EDUCAUSE and the Bill & Melissa Gates Foundation. The online interface was designed in partnership with Pearson Learning. PL officially launched on

June 3, 2013 with three Bachelor degree programs: Computer Information Technology, Small Business Administration, and Liberal Arts. These programs are entirely online and self-paced. All content is available to the student at the time of enrollment, so he or she can work as fast, or as slowly, as he or she would like. The student enrolls for 6-month subscriptions, and they are able to complete as many lessons as they would like during the subscription. The subscription is a flat USD$2500 fee, which includes all fees and textbooks.

PL is a traditional degree program that has been deconstructed and reconstructed around specific competencies. Reinforcing key concepts, activities, and assignments can address multiple yet related subjects at once. PL's aim has been to bring back the joy of learning by never treating material as mere information. Instead, everything a student studies will be relevant and interconnected. PL faculty members never want students to: (1) wonder why general education courses are essential; (2) be discouraged because something is too hard; or (3) be bored because something is too easy.

In regards to the topic of competency-based learning, NAU faculty and administrators recognized that except in certain well-defined baccalaureate programs leading to professional licensing (e.g., Engineering, Nursing), there is no universally agreed upon strategy for developing competencies. Review of curricula with defined competencies will reveal that some competencies might come from established program outcomes, others from professional organizations, some could be based on university-wide goals. Currently, Northern Arizona University's Personalized Learning (NAU-PL) has been developed around competencies for baccalaureate programs.

Following best practices of curriculum mapping, a panel of faculty, experts working in the field, subject matter experts, and specialists in teaching and learning developed ten competencies for the Computer Information Technology major. Ten Competency Domains were identified: (1) Information Technology Foundations; (2) Data Management and Administration; (3) IT Business Operations and Leadership; (4) Information Security and Policy; (5) Enterprise Architecture, Network and Telecommunications Technology; (6) Software Engineering and Development; (7) Systems Administration; (8) Business Analysis and Design; (9) Web-based Systems and Technologies; (10) Information Technology. As shown in Figure 1 below, each Competency Domain was expanded into one or more measurable Objectives. In turn, each Objective was analyzed to develop Lessons that would achieve the Objective. Figure 2 shows a schematic representation of how each Lesson environment offers a Lesson Guide, a Pretest, Topics, a Posttest, and Mastery. Each Topic area has direct access to a suite of Learning Activities related to the Topic, and each Activity offers a variety of Learning Objects available to the student.

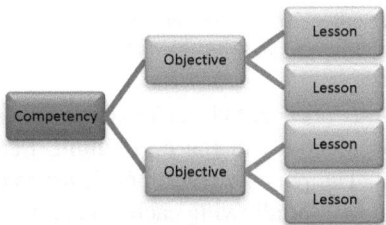

Fig. 1. Competency mapping from Competency Domain to one or more specific Objectives, and then for each Objective mapping to one or more Lesson

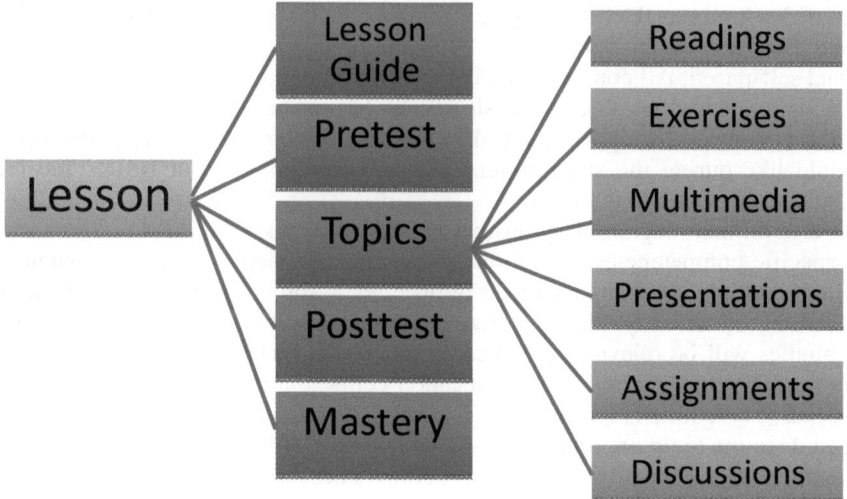

Fig. 2. Lesson components and Learning Activities

To provide more specific detail about the competencies and lessons, the authors of this paper have set up a Website to provide access to the CIT Competency Domains, Objectives, and Lessons, but also to selected interfaces for the Personalized Learning environment developed by the Northern Arizona University Extended Campus.

However, below we show part of Competency Domain 1 — Information Technology Foundations: Objective 1 > Lesson 1 (of 5 Lessons) > Topic 1 (of 7 Topics). Note there are Competency codes in red and Course codes in blue. These codes are used for mapping competencies in the curriculum.

>   **C1:Information Technology Foundations:**   / IT Foundations/ CITmnC1
>   **>Objective 1:**   Demonstrate knowledge of market trends and innovative technology in this fast changing technology industry and its many specialty areas as evidence the graduate has developed a clear understanding of Information Technology / Trends and Innovation /CITmn.C1.O1
>   **>>Lesson 1:**   Examine the history of computers and early computing. / History of Computers /CITmn.C1.O1.L1 (CIT 294 - 0.3)
>   **>>>Topic 1:** History of Computing (Hardware and Software) - Examine key theories on the history of computing and how it has evolved. / History of Computing / CITmn.C1.O1.L1.T1

The CIT major, as well as other NAU Personalized Learning degree programs are tightly structured, with no electives in the curriculum. Each student proceeds on a defined path to graduation. The personalization emerges as a learning plan developed for the student by a faculty mentor allowing each student to enter the lessons where he or she needs to be at any given time. This plan is not set in stone. Rather the plan is a good approximation of a reasonable path for the student, based on the respective student's past work experience and academic accomplishments. Students are freed from working on concepts they know and competencies they have acquired. They take a pre-test for each lesson and if they score an 86% or above, they may move on to the next lesson. If they score below that mark, they enter the exercises and activities as needed. No one spends time on topics and skills they already know so that the effort is placed where that effort affords the best progress through the CIT major.

The current number of students per faculty mentor is set at 150. Mentors meet with students once a week and on an as-needed basis, using the student's preferred environment. Subject-matter mentors meet in tutorials with a student based on the respective student's need related to specific content. Faculty mentors provide life-, academic-, and career- coaching. Lead faculty and faculty mentors are full-time faculty. Subject matter mentors are part-time faculty members.

3   Methodology for Enhancing Adaptive Capacities of PL

3.1   Extant Capacities of the NAU-PL / http://pl.nau.edu/

The Northern Arizona University Personalized Learning (NAU-PL) environment is a well-built teaching-learning-assessment system. In July 2013, the adaptive learning research group from University of Ontario Institute of Technology (UOIT) began a series of Gedanken experiments to study models for improving adaptive learning capacities for systems like the NAU-PL environment. The UOIT team had studied healthcare systems and the transformation of clinical systems for collecting, storing and analyzing electronic patient data in electronic health records (EHR). We realized an analogue to an EHR would be a student's Electronic Learning Record (ELR). Research funded by the Social Sciences and Humanities Research Council of Canada allowed us to build middleware that could be layered into online environments to stream data into an ELR, analogously to the ways and means data stream into EHRs.

The NAU-PL was a good candidate for our studies of middleware that could enhance adaptive learning capacities to create an ELR. Specifically NAU-PL has a fairly extensive web of tools that are used to support learners and to assess other programs. These programs include Pearson's Learning Outcome Manager (LOM) to track some student and course analytics. LOM also is an online repository of students' learning outcomes. Since NAU faculty had developed a sophisticated suite of Competency Domains, the competency maps allowed development of sensible competency-based learning outcomes as well as programmatic and institutional learning outcomes, all of which populate the LOM. Furthermore, the NAU-PL was built to take advantage of the Pearson LOM functionality coupled to a unique NAU user interface built by the IT unit at NAU serving the NAU-PL.

As part of the "in-house" build, NAU staff created their own databases so data from students could be fed into NAU systems and Pearson systems, providing tremendous increases in data collection, management, and analysis without loss of functionality or compromising privacy. Using customized analytics and dashboards, the NAU-PL uses LOM to create reports as data arrays. These reports are available through "Enterprise Reporting." Individual student data, lesson data, or program data can be easily gathered and analyzed. For example, NAU faculty can monitor how long students take to complete a particular assessment, a particular lesson, or the entire program, as well as tracking how many lessons students complete on average within a 6-month subscription. Very specific data analyses are also possible, for example, item analysis on a particular assessment item related to a particular Lesson-Task-Learning Activity.

In other words, the NAU-PL environment is a very good example of a powerful competency-based online degree program that is possible to build within the resource constraints now facing many American state universities. We analyzed how to enhance adaptive learning capacities of such a system with middleware that are layered into the data collection and analysis flows of student outcome data. In addition, we studied how to add a powerful knowledge system that connected databases of learning objects in ways that a student could receive detailed feedback on their progress, as well as recommendations and remediation activities for improving their learning. During the period July 2013-January 2014, we conducted two Gedanken experiments to study ways and means to add adaptive capacity to the NAU-PL environment.

3.2   Gedanken Experiment 1

A research platform we built [1] provided a means to create a Space-Time mapping of each individual's conceptual and performance competencies to their decisions during engagement in educational and knowledge transfer activities [9-12]. Misconceptions identified during assessments of each individual could then be mapped to Space-Time moments in the individual's learning processes. These Space-Time moments could be analyzed in the context of learning outcomes. Misconceptions could be identified then mapped to Learning Activities to help a student improve their learning [13-20].

Gedanken Experiment 1 involved the creation of an abstraction of the NAU-PL environment for the CIT major. By "abstraction" we mean a competency map: for each Competency Domain we delineated the Objectives; for each Objective its Lessons; for each Lesson its Topics; for each Topic its Learning Activities; and for each Learning Activity its Learning Objects. These were modeled abstractly as compartments that were dynamic in the sense of being able to send and receive signals that created database linkages,. Such linkages could assemble components of a teaching-learning-assessment environment related to a particular Learning Activity nested in a particular Topic of a Lesson associated with an Objective.

Our first Gedanken experiment used a research platform called MISSED—Misconception Instantiation as Students Study in Educational Domains, which allowed us to model students moving through the NAU-PL. On our early iterations within the NAU-PL, we realized the critical nature of signals received and sent by any compartment of the teaching-learning-assessment environment. We also realized that the dynamic nature of any given compartment would be critically important to building truly adaptive educational environments that could adapt to a student as he or she worked within a compartment. We use "compartment" herein to represent a Learning Object for a Learning Activity associated with a specific Topic of a specific Lesson within a particular Competency Domain.

Gedanken Experiment 1 led to a refinement of **MISSED**. Basically, analyses of signals and dynamic features necessary for each compartment required layering monitoring middleware across compartments to record each student's navigational and engagement decisions as well as time spent in various activities. Using monitoring data coupled to learning assessment outcomes within the simulations, we could map students' learning and competency outcomes against expectations delineated by expert clinical panels [17-22].

A diagrammatic representation of **MISSED** is provided in Figure 3. Images show preliminary studies with Canadian health sciences students. Refinements resulting from our first Gedanken experiment allowed us to create a set of interconnected software engines that monitor educational activities of CIT students in the following manner: (1) a CIT student is working in the NAU-PL, engaging within a Competency Domain's Lessons, Topics, and their respective Learning Activities and associated Learning Objects—all their work is within a Web-based interface, designed as a personalized Inclusive-Adaptive System that assesses a student's accessibility needs and preferences for a personalized educational environment; (2) the Inclusive-Adaptive Interface collects data on the student's needs and preferences, creating a Student Profile database that becomes part of an Electronic Learning Record; (3) the Student Profile data stream to a MatchMaker system that selects an Instructional Deign Template (IDT) based on a theory of cognition and behavioral change selected by a faculty member and consistent with the course content, but informed by the student's needs and preferences; (4) the MatchMaker engine then reads the metadata from the template; (5) the Assembler Engine reads the IDT and metadata brought to it by MatchMaker, searches Learning Object Repositories to find and collate learning activities, resources, educational scaffolding, learning assessments, and feedback personalized for the learner, and then organizes the assemblage to create a Web-based personalized teaching-learning-assessment-diagnostic Educational Environment; (6) students engage within the Educational Environment (and for some types of hybrid classes also engage in face-to-face settings, such as faculty mentoring, live skills labs, low-fidelity or high-fidelity simulations related to computer information technology); (7) within the Web-based Educational Environments, each student is constantly monitored by middleware called PathFinder that follows choices made within the Educational Environments and also times a student's engagement in learning activities, resources, assessments, and using diagnostic feedback; (8) within the face-to-face environments in some course types (e.g., live skills lab), a student is monitored during learning-demonstration activities, using a video-capture and analysis system called MAXIT EDUCATION [23] that efficiently collects assessment data on students' performance competencies; (9) prior to, simultaneously with, or after learning-demonstration activities, students enter an assessment engine called eXAM^3 [24] which assesses their learning outcomes within a cognitive taxonomy selected by the faculty member (e.g., Bloom's Revised Taxonomy or the a rubric for a CIT Competency Domain); (10) PathFinder, MAXIT EDUCATION, and eXAM^3 stream a student's data to a data analysis and knowledge system called DATUMM; (11) DATUMM, in turn, analyzes the data, creates new information about the student, and sends this information back to the Student Profile. These new information sets are integrated into the Student Profile, with revised data and information facilitating adaptive changes to the flow beginning with the MatchMaker and ending in new configurations of the Educational Environment. Importantly, data from the Student Profile also stream into a subcomponent—the Electronic Learning Record, through time creating a longitudinal record of a student's progress.

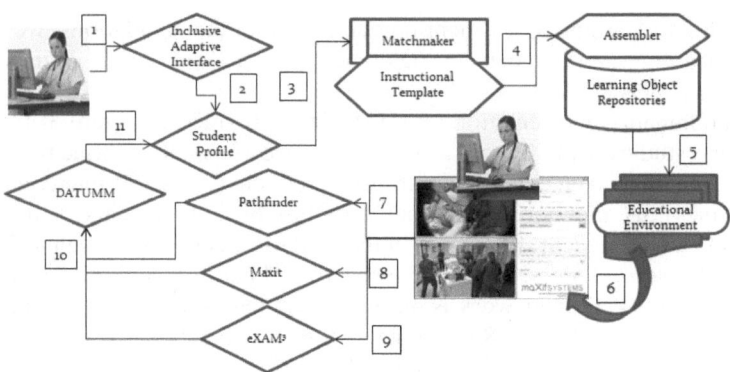

Fig. 3. Diagrammatic Representation of the MISSED Environment piloted in research on Health Sciences education

The **MISSED** research platform collects data on students' conceptual and performance competencies, creating a very detailed Electronic Learning Record. The ELR also can be constructed to receive data and information from multiple courses, and so create a much more detailed and informative multidimensional student transcript. Preliminary studies of this platform provide evidence that it will complement faculty efforts without increasing workload, while providing new tools and types of data for better assessing students' conceptual and performance competencies. The platform also will allow detailed analysis of cognitive processes and behavioral choices to trace development of misconceptions [25-32].

3.3   Gedanken Experiment 2

In the second experiment, we studied the importance of signals received and sent by any compartment within an environment like the NAU-PL and we also explored the dynamic nature of compartments. For our modeling, we focused on the **MISSED's** engines called Matchmaker, Assembler, and the Pathfinder. These engines have the most rigorous requirement for signal integrity and dynamic function.

MatchMaker Engine.—MatchMaker bridges an individual learner to an instructor's educational goals for a course—in the case of the CIT curriculum, these goals are the Competency Domains, their respective Objectives, Lessons, Topics, and Learning Activities. MatchMaker receives Student Profile data, making the first adaptive changes for individual students. NAU-PL has Learning Object Repositories to accommodate many different types of Learning Objects for a particular Learning Activity. To be truly adaptive the Repositories must contain equivalent forms of learning objects that can be selected by MatchMaker, with selection based on Student Profile data. Different students have different needs. NAU-PL must be able to adapt to those needs by choosing different Learning Objects. Furthermore, some curricula may require multiple Learning Object Repositories that could be integrated in ways that allow linked Repositories to have all of the Learning Objects for a particular course. Our modeling in Gedanken Experiment 2 revealed the MatchMaker Engine signal input-output must be able to acquire and interpret metadata for all of the elements comprising any Learning Object in order to identify that object's potential use for: personalized learning, different knowledge or skills domains, diverse courses with specific types of educational goals, and choices of grounded theory for cognition and learning as well as behavioral expression of what has been learned.

Assembler Engine.—MatchMaker provides metadata on the IDT for mapping to the metadata of learning objects within the Learning Object Repositories. The Assembler uses the IDT to select and organize specified learning objects, creating the personalized teaching-learning-assessment-diagnostic Educational Environment. Results of Gedanken Experiment 2 lead us to conclude that the IDT must be built as a multidimensional array that can be filled with metadata related to the diverse types of learning resources, activities, assessments, educational scaffolding and diagnostic feedback likely to optimize a student's learning. The Assembler must be able to interpret the IDT and provide instructions to create the personalized Education Environment—the IDT is an organizing framework. The Assembler then loads into this framework learning activities, resources, educational scaffolding, learning assessments, and feedback for the student's personalized educational environment.

PathFinder.—Gedanken Experiment 2 refined our ideas about how PathFinder creates place-time stamps for every place in which the learner engages within the Educational Environment. Such engagement includes Learning Objects or sub-elements of a Learning Object nested within a Learning Activity, as well as with any resource or scaffolding element made available to a learner. PathFinder also monitors all assessment activities, collects data on each assessment, and retrieves sub-elements of any assessment in which the learner is working. This place-time data set is a record of decisional sequela for the learner (sometimes called Space-Time worm). Basically, the data reveal the sequence of choices made, actions taken within the Educational Environment, and time spent in such places and actions. In our modeling within Gedanken Experiment 2, we studied how Space-Time worms can be articulated with assessment data related to what a student actually learned during their the decisional sequelae of engaging with learning objects.

4   Conclusions

We have studied how and why to add enhanced adaptive capacities to educational environments—our prototype was the Northern Arizona University Personalized Learning environment. We used analogues of electronic health record systems' middleware and customizable graphic user interfaces to create student Electronic Learning Records. In times of limited resources, and without a clear evidence-based framework for education, there are significant advantages to building relatively cheaper solutions than to buying or leasing expensive learning management systems that are difficult to customize. Learning management systems and adaptive learning environments offered by academic publishers still have many weaknesses, often requiring loading of the respective publisher's learning objects. The Northern Arizona University Personalized Learning environment represents an approach of combining commercial systems with in-house built systems that meets the needs of a university and its students. The addition of adaptive capacities to the NAU-PL provides cost-effective customization that could better serve the university, its students, and faculty.

References

1. Tashiro, J., Vargas Martin, M., Hung, P.C.K.: MISSED – Studying Students' Development of Misconception in Hybrid Courses. In: Cheung, S.K.S., Fong, J., Fong, W., Wang, F.L., Kwok, L.F. (eds.) ICHL 2013. LNCS, vol. 8038, pp. 364–376. Springer, Heidelberg (2013)

2. Tashiro, J., Hung, P.C.K., Martin, M.V.: Evidence-Based Educational Practices and a Theoretical Framework for Hybrid Learning. In: Kwan, R., Fong, J., Kwok, L.-f., Lam, J. (eds.) ICHL 2011. LNCS, vol. 6837, pp. 51–72. Springer, Heidelberg (2011)

3. Tashiro, J., Hung, P.C.K., Martin, M.V.: ROAD-MAP for Educational Simulations and Serious Games. In: Tsang, P., Cheung, S.K.S., Lee, V.S.K., Huang, R. (eds.) ICHL 2010. LNCS, vol. 6248, pp. 186–204. Springer, Heidelberg (2010)

4. Garcia-Ruiz, M.A., Tashiro, J., Kapralos, B., Vargas Martin, M.: Crouching Tangents, Hidden Danger: Assessing Development of Dangerous Misconceptions Within Serious Games For Health care Education. In: Hai-Jew, S. (ed.) Virtual Immersive and 3D Learning Spaces: Emerging Technologies and Trends, pp. 269–306. IGI Global, Hershey (2011)

5. National Research Council: How Students Learn: History, Mathematics, and Science in the Classroom. National Academy Press, Washington, DC (2005)

6. American Association for the Advancement of Science: Invention and Impact: Building Excellence in Undergraduate Science, Technology, Engineering and Mathematics (STEM) education. American Association for the Advancement of Science, Washington, DC (2004)

7. Federation of American Scientists: Summit on Educational Games - Harnessing the power of Video Games for Learning. Federation of American Scientists, Washington, DC (2006)

8. Tashiro, J.: Faculty Roles in Building and Using Electronic Educational Products. Journal of Electronic Commerce in Organizations 7(1), 1–17 (2009)

9. Rudak, L., Sidor, D.: Taxonomy of E-courses. In: Islander, M., Kapila, V., Karim, M.A. (eds.) Technological Developments in Education and Automation, pp. 275–280. Springer Science and Business Media, New York (2010)

10. Gasparini, I., Eyharabide, V., Schiaffino, S., Pimenta, M.S., Amandi, A., de Oliveira, J.P.M.: Improving user profiling for a richer personalization: Modeling context in e-Learning. In: Graf, S., Lin, F., McGreal, R. (eds.) Intelligent and Adaptive Learning Systems: Technology Enhanced Support for Learners and Teachers, pp. 182–197. IGI Information Science Reference (2012)

11. Khribi, M.K., Jemni, M., Nasraoui, O.: Automatic Recommendations for e-Learning personalization based on web usage mining techniques and information retrieval. Educational Technology & Society 12(4), 30–42 (2009)

12. Tan, J., Hung, P., Dohan, M., Trojer, T., Farwick, M., Tashiro, J.: Gateway to Quality Living for the Elderly: Charting an Innovative Approach to Evidence-based E-Health Technologies For Serving the Chronically Ill. In: Proceedings of the 13th IEEE International Conference on Computational Science and Engineering, Hong Kong (2010)

13. Kelly, M., Ort, M., Semken, S., Tashiro, J.: Virtual reality excursions - Exploring earth's environment. Prentice-Hall, Upper Saddle River (2000)

14. Fulcher, G.: Virtual Medical Office for Bonwit-West's Clinical Procedures for Medical Assistants, 6th edn. Elsevier-Saunders, Philadelphia (2007)

15. Mathers, D.: Virtual Clinical Excursions - For Black and Hawks Medical-Surgical Nursing: Clinical Management for Positive Outcomes, 7th edn. PAL Elsevier Saunders, Philadelphia (2006)

16. Tashiro, J.T., Sullins, E.S., Long, G.: Virtual Clinical Excursions for Fundamental Concepts and Skills for Nursing. Mosby, St. Louis (2003)
17. Fernandez, A., Regts, M., Tashiro, J., Vargas Martin, M.: Neural network prediction model for a digital media learning environment. In: International Conference on Information and Knowledge Engineering, Las Vegas, USA (2012)
18. Fernandez, A.: Cluster techniques and prediction models for a digital media learning environment. Thesis: Master of Computer Science. University of Ontario Institute of Technology (2012)
19. Regts, M., Fernandez, A., Vargas Martin, M., Tashiro, J.: Methodology for studying health science students' development of misconceptions. In: International Conference on Advances in Databases, Knowledge, and Data Applications, Reunion Island, pp. 112–119 (2012)
20. Regts, M.: A look at simulated online learning environments and undergraduate health science students' development of misconceptions. Thesis: Master of Health Informatics. University of Ontario Institute of Technology (2012)
21. Sorden, S.D.: A Cognitive Approach to Instructional Design for Multimedia Learning. Informing Science Journal 8, 263–279 (2005)
22. Mayer, R.E., Fennell, S., Farmer, L., Campbell, J.: A Personalization Effect in Multimedia Learning: Students Learn Better When Words Are in Conversational Style Rather Than Formal Style. Journal of Educational Psychology 96(2), 389–395 (2004)
23. Tashiro, J., Hung, P.C.K.: Method for Assessing an Individual's Physical and Psychosocial Abilities. No. 61/549,5789. U.S. Patent and Trademark Office, Washington, DC (2011)
24. Tashiro, J., Choate, D.: Method to assess a Person's Knowledge of a Subject Area. US Patent (pending) No. 60/521,329. U.S. Patent and Trademark Office, Washington, DC (2004)
25. Martin, L., Haskard-Zolnierek, K., DiMatteo, M.R.: Health Behavior Change and Treatment Adherence: Evidence-based Guidelines for Improving Healthcare. Oxford University Press, New York (2010)
26. Prochaska, J.O., Redding, C.A., Evers, K.E.: The Transtheoretical Model and stages of change. In: Glanz, K., Rimer, B., Viswanath, K. (eds.) Health Behavior and Health Education, pp. 97–121. Jossey-Bass, San Francisco (2008)
27. DiMatteo, M.R., DiNicola, D.: Achieving Patient Compliance. Pergamon Press, New York (1982)
28. Fishbein, M., Hennessey, M., Kamb, M., Bolan, G., Hoxworth, T., Latesta, M.: Using Intervention Therapy to Model Factors Influencing Behavior Change: Project RESPECT. Evaluation and Health Professions 24(4), 363–384 (2001)
29. Bensley, R., Mercer, N., Brusk, J., Underhile, R., Rivas, J., Anderson, J.: The e-Health Behavior Management Model: A Stage-based Approach to Behavior Change and Management. Preventing Chronic Disease 1(4) (2004)
30. Baranowski, T., Cullen, K., Nicklas, T., Thompson, D., Baranowski, J.: Are Current Health Behavioral Change Models Helpful in Guiding Prevention of Weight Gain Efforts? Obesity Research (suppl.), 23S–43S (2003)
31. Leventhal, H., Halm, E., Horowitz, C., Leventhal, E., Ozakinci, G.: Living with chronic Illness: A Contextualized, Self-Regulation Approach. In: Sutton, S., Baum, A., Johnston, M. (eds.) Handbook of Health Psychology, pp. 159–194. Sage Publications, London (2004)
32. De Feijter, J.M., De Grave, W.S., Muijtjens, A.M., Scherpbier, A.J., Koopmans, R.P.: A comprehensive overview of medical errors in hospitals using incident-reporting systems, patient complaints and chart review of inpatient deaths. PLoS One 7(2) (2012)

A Critical Analysis of the Studies on Fostering Creativity through Game-Based Learning*

Huan Nie, Haiming M. Xiao, and Junjie J. Shang**

Department of Educational Technology, Peking University, Beijing, China
{1301214438,haiming,jjshang}@pku.edu.cn

Abstract. Creativity and game-based learning have long been under heated discussions and studies. In order to clarify whether games-based learning can contribute to fostering creativity, we carried out a literature review of related studies and researches. We concluded that there are generally three approaches adopted to fostering creativity in game-based learning: "Learning in games", "Learning about games" and "Learning both in and about games". In discussing the three approaches and their representative studies, we found that game-based learning is generally an important and effective way of fostering and enhancing creativity, though other influence factors need to be considered. In response, we provide suggestions for further studies.

Keywords: Fostering Creativity; Game-Based Learning; Leaning in Games; Learning about Games; Learning in and about Games; Game Design.

1   Introduction

In order to grasp the current research focuses and achievements on the topic of fostering creativity[1] through game-based learning[2], we carried out a literature review of related studies and researches by searching on SSCI[3] and ERIC[4] with key words: "games" and "creativity". We found 23 essays on SSCI and 161 essays on ERIC (183 in total). After a throughout and intensive reading, we found that 44 essays study "fostering creativity

---

* Funded by: Ministry of Education of China General Project of Humanities and Social Science Research, "The Study on Theories and Practices of Applying Educational Games in Fostering Students' Creativity"(No: 13YJA880061). The corresponding author of the paper is Professor Shang Junjie.

** The corresponding author of the paper is Professor Shang Junjie.

[1] In this paper, we define creativity as an individual's abilities of sensing problems and providing original and effective solutions for the problems.

[2] In this paper, we define game-based learning as a pedagogical approach that applies games in various ways to closely engaging in teaching and learning.

[3] Social Science Citation Index (SSCI), developed from Social Science Index (SCI), is a citation database.

[4] The Education Resources Information Center (ERIC), a well-known online digital library of education research and information.

S.K.S. Cheung et al. (Eds.): ICHL 2014, LNCS 8595, pp. 278–287, 2014.

in games-based learning". Among the 44 studies, we found that there are generally three approaches adopted to foster creativity in game-based learning, according to the different roles games played. We coined three phrases to represent the three approaches: "Learning in games", "Learning about games" and "Learning both in and about games", which are defined and explained as following:

"Learning in games" means learning through playing games. Authors in their studies adopt games to create a playful environment for students to learn. The games adopted in the studies can be either digital or traditional ones. Overall, there are 23 out 44 essays belonging to this category.

"Learning about games" means learning through game design. Authors in their studies adopt game design tools for students to learn by creating their games alone or in cooperation. There are 12 out 44 essays belonging to this category.

"Learning in and about games" is a combination of the previous two approaches, which means learning through playing games first and designing games later by themselves.

In this article, we discuss and compare in detail how the three approaches were adopted by the researchers in their studies and what conclusions they came to. Then some critical responses are made to the studies and some suggestions for further studies are provided. Overall, there are mainly three findings:

First: The results of whether game-based learning is effective in fostering learners' creativity are, in general, positive, although a few of them hold a neutral or even negative opinion on this point. The influence factor is probably the types of games adopted. In consideration of this, more studies on the relationship between types of games and the effectiveness in fostering creativity need to be conducted in the future.

Second: Creativity cannot be fostered through game design alone. Appropriate pedagogical strategies should be applied in "learning about games" in order to foster learners' creativity.

Third: The approach "learning in and about games" is claimed to be helpful in fostering learners' creativity. We suggest that this approach is worth studying in the area of fostering creativity, in terms of in what degree it can improve creativity compared to the other two approaches.

2   Fostering Creativity through Learning in Games

Among all the 44 essays picked out from SSCI and ERIC, there are 23 essays applying the approach of learning in games to fostering creativity, which can be further divided into two secondary sub-approaches: one is "learning in traditional games", and the other is "learning in digital games". And the sub-approach "learning in digital games" can also be further divided into two third-level sub-approaches in terms of the games' original designing goals and ideal users: one is "learning in digital games designed intentionally for instruction", and the other is "learning in digital commercial games adapted to instruction". In total, we have three sub-approaches under the high-level approach "learning in games".

2.1   Learning in Traditional Games

A research conducted by Maciej Karwowski *et al.* is the very case of "learning in traditional games". The study presents a new approach in fostering students' creativity—the Role Play Training in Creativity (RPTC), inspired by RPG games. Forty-seven undergraduate students voluntarily participated in this study, and the effectiveness of RPTC in fostering creativity was tested by two tests –TCT-DP[5] and TCI[6]. The comparison of post-test and pre-test results shows a significant increase in TCT-DP test and two of three TCI scales—fluency and originality. This indicates that students learning through RPTC, a traditional game, can improve their creativity. Besides, there are other cases conducted by embedding features of game in instructional activities rather than using digital games as learning support tools [1], [2]. We concluded from the studies that the process of generating students' motivation, guiding them, enabling them to make connection, etc., instead of games-based activities or technologies themselves, are the major stimulus for fostering creativity.

Traditional games, however, depend so much on physical environment that it limits the possibility of students imagining and exploring. Since the 80s of the last century, digital games have begun to be applied in education and correspondingly scholars have begun to study whether digital games can trigger and enhance creativity. Among all the 23 essays on fostering students' creativity through learning in games, there are 18 essays studying digital games' effectiveness in fostering students' creativity.

2.2   Learning in Digital Games Designed for Instruction

Arabic LOGO, a programming environment developed for children programing instruction in 1966, is considered as the first successful educational game used in instruction and self-directed learning and now remains popular in many areas around the world. A lot of original researches of "learning in games" embedded LOGO as the learning tools [4], [5]. Clements assessed the effects of learning logo computer programing on creativity and specific cognitive skills and metacognitive skills [6], presented us a result that the programing group scored significantly higher a measure of creativity. In 1999, after evaluating a large number of previous studies on the enhancement of creativity through learning in LOGO program environment, Subhi concluded that many of the studies have a positive effect [7].

Later on, online games increasingly attracted more researchers to study their effectiveness of enhancing creativity [8], [9], [10]. Huang *et al.* conducted an experimental research to evaluate the effectiveness of a collaborative and online brainstorming game—Idea Storming Cube (ISC) in fostering problem solving abilities. ISC provides users with a competitive game-based environment and a peer-like intelligent agent. The results showed that the ISC game facilitated diversified ideas in problem solving and were considered beneficial for brainstorming [10]. Hsien-Sheng *et al.*

---

[5]   Test of Creative Thinking—Drawing Production (TCT-DP). [3]

[6]   Test of Creative Imagination (TCI), developed by the Polish educationalist Janusz Kujawski to measure creative potential.

constructed an online game to help students develop the skills for divergent and creative thinking. They proved that playing the proposed game has a positive effect on students' abilities relating to "fluency, flexibility, elaboration", and originality in particular.

Because it is indeed too expensive and inefficient for teachers to develop educational games for instruction, proponents of game-based learning suggest teachers adapt commercial games to courses.

2.3   Learning in Digital Commercial Games Adapted to Instruction

As for commercial games, virtual world games or massive simulation games are adopted by scholars in their studies. One of the most popular massive virtual games is Second Life (SL), an online virtual world developed by Linden Lab. Its unstructured atmosphere and wide-open spaces where student creativity can grow and flourish are two reasons for its popularity. In study, Doyle conducted a study on the effectiveness of the development of a virtual island on the SL in supporting creative practice and creative collaboration [11]. In describing how SL works, Oishi, L. noted that SL benefits students "not only in higher-order thinking required to program object movement and the strategies necessary for successful trading, but also the reinforcement of such 21st-century skills as collaboration and innovation" [12]. Moreover, in order to prove that educational games may offer a viable strategy for developing students' problem-solving skills, Kristian Kiili embedded a business simulation game in the course, and found that the students learning in this game performed better in creative problem-solving skills [13].

Despite the 3-year study on effect of digital games on students' creative skills, Michela Ott *et al.* [14], all studies discussed above are conducted in a short period of time. This brings up a question: Can the creative thinking and problem-solving skills be kept for a long period? Indeed, more studies are suggested to be conducted on this topic. In addition, another issue is worth discussing in the following part: Can playing all kinds of games foster students' creativity?

2.4   Do the Types of Games Influence the Effectiveness of Fostering Creativity?

Among the essays picked out, the games chosen in the studies can generally be categorized into four types: mini-games or mind games, simulation games, games based on subjects, and action games. Ott and Pozzi adopt 45 "mainstream mind games" [14] (also called mini-games) in their study investigating the relationship between digital tools and fostering creativity. As to simulation games, Oishi and Doyle studied on whether Second Life supports creative practice and collaboration in real life [11], [12]. In another study conducted by Squire and Barab [10], students played Civilization III in an interdisciplinary history, humanities, and social studies course. Moreover, Oei and Patterson adopted action games in their study [15].

Although there is no distinct difference in the results of the effectiveness of fostering creativity among the studies discussed above, "such a comparison of multiple genres is important because it is possible that different game types will improve different aspects of cognition and perception" or have different impact on fostering creativity [15]. In order to answer whether types of Games influence the effectiveness of fostering creativity, more studies are suggested.

2.5   Conclusion and Discussion on the Approach "Learning in Games"

Although most researchers reported positive results of fostering creativity through learning in games, there are still some doubts needed to be resolved by more precise studies. Firstly, differences in teachers' background and abilities may be the factors affecting students' learning and thinking skills development. Secondly, there is not enough studies proving students' creativity improved in the short time can be kept for a long time. Thirdly, it is not clear that whether the types of games influence the effectiveness of fostering creativity.

3   Fostering Creativity through Learning about Games

In total, there are 12 essays studying the approach "learning about games", which means learning through game design.

3.1   Fostering Students' Creativity through Game Design

Perhaps as O'Hanlon put it that "game creation as a learning tool is really just a digital-age take on the old learning-by-doing approach to teaching" [16], game design is actually not a novel or fantastic thing. Nevertheless, "a new generation of gamers is not just picking up skills by playing video games—they're learning by designing and creating the games themselves" [16].

Most of the studies on fostering creativity through designing games take a quantitative and qualitative method pre-and-post experiment. In Allsop's study, children "wanted to create games with narratives and reflected their imagination and interests" [17]. The study shows that game authoring activities can provide opportunities for children to develop skills such as critical thinking, problem solving and creativity. Furthermore, Qing Li chooses 21 elementary students (aged between 7 and 11), to participate in the study. In particular, this small-scale study asks students to design games to teach others their concept of Issac Newton's Three Laws of Motion. The analysis of the research data suggests that "creativity, engagement and new identity were the three salient traits displayed by the students when learning by digital game-building" [18]. In 2009, Gary Cheng from The Hong Kong Institute of Education undertook a similar study to test whether *game making pedagogy* (GMP) is helpful for facilitating student learning in a course named Interactive Multimedia. After the whole semester of the course, the study' quantitative and qualitative data indicates that "the GMP model is effective in helping students to enhance their problem solving skills, learning motivation, and creativity" [19].

O'Hanlon introduces a series of game design tools or engines, such as Gamestar Mechanic, Activate!, Level Up! and Globaloria Games [16]. Kiili *et al.* introduced another new game authoring environment MAGOS [38], which was developed to facilitate students learning by developing games. Moreover, Resnick recommends two attractive tools of designing: Crickets and Scratch. Crickets enable learners to create in physical world all types of interactive inventions: musical sculptures, interactive jewelry, dancing creatures, alarm clocks, and so on, which requires a simple knowledge of programming [20]. As to Scratch, children can use it to create games or animations in the online world in a drag-and-drop way, without any need to program.

3.2   Fostering Teachers' Creativity through Game Design

An interesting finding is that 2 out of the 12 researches discuss the fostering of teachers' creativity through designing games. As students need creativity in their learning and life, teachers are suggested to have teaching creativity.

Frossard *et al.* presents in his study "an innovative pedagogical approach where teachers become game designers and engage in creative teaching practices" [21]. In the study, 21 Spanish primary and secondary school teachers are asked to design and implement learning games applied to their specific educational contexts. The study concluded that "the learner-centered game design methodology appeared as a productive and creative approach to teaching and learning, along with difficulties, but worth to explore if we want to promote creative teaching and creative learners and, by extension, creative people" [21].

3.3   Can Game Design Alone Foster Creativity?

Although all the studies discussed above came to have a positive conclusion on whether creativity can be fostered through game design, 4 out of the 12 studies claim that games designing alone cannot foster creativity. Yee explained that digital technology is "not an easy stand-alone option to enhance creativity among students of the 21st century" [22].

Yee *et al.* designed a study which takes different pedagogical strategies in the teaching of computer games development. The study involved 69 Malaysian 13–14 year-old students, who are divided into two groups: the treatment group and the control group. The treatment group adopted appreciative learning approach[7], which consist of discover, dream, design and destiny stages, while control group "adopted self-paced learning, followed by do-it-yourself session" [22]. The pre-to-post-test showed that "treatment group gained a significantly higher score compared to the control group" [22]. This study indicates that applying a pedagogy produces a higher level than applying no pedagogy in the teaching of computer games design.

---

[7] Appreciative learning approach provides many opportunities for students to be heard; explore; dream; taking actions, and share their products and dreams (Yee, 2010).

In addition, there are several studies suggest that different work environments may have different influences on students' development of creativity. In the study by Göttel and Schild, a computer-free meeting place for Computer Science students in game design courses was provided as a learning place [23]. It offered playful and creative elements and had to be rearranged by the students. "Such environments have the potential of countering possible negative attitudes of Computer Science students towards creative processes" [23]. This study shows that Computer Science students "strongly benefit in their creative processes from working in individually arranged playful environments" [23].

3.4   Conclusion and Discussion on the Approach "Learning about Games"

In conclusion, all studies found on "Learning about Games" seem to agree that the way of designing games can foster creativity. Not only students but teachers can benefit from learning through designing games in terms of the ability of thinking or performing creatively. However, this positive conclusion is doubted by some scholars who believe that merely through designing games cannot enhance learners' creativity. They suggest that only combined with appropriate pedagogical strategies, can the approach of learning through designing games have positive influence on fostering creativity. The work environment of designing games is also regarded as a factor that influences the effectiveness of game design in fostering creativity.

As to the question whether the types of game design tools have different influences on fostering creativity, the best response is probably what was put by Yasemin Allsop in her research that "the process of game design itself represented the aspects of creativity where children used their ideas and imagination to make games" [17].

4   Fostering Creativity through Learning in and about Games

"Learning in and about games" means that students learn how to design games through playing games and after that, design games themselves. Among the studies found on SSCI and ERIC, no one adopted this approach in testing its effectiveness in fostering creativity. However, one tool mentioned above can act as an exemplification of this approach, i.e. Gamestar Mechanic. According to its website [24], Gamestar Mechanic is an online game-creation platform targeting at 4th to 9th grade students that is designed to teach kids how to design their own games in a highly engaging and creative environment.

On Gamestar Mechanic, students can play through a game named Quest that is a narrative adventure shown in motion comics and mini-games. As students move through the story in the game, they will encounter some "broken" games they have to edit and fix. By playing and editing/fixing the games, students earn sprites as awards that they can use to design games in their workshop. Then they can make their own games using those sprites in a drag-and-drop way without any need to program. After finishing designing their own games, they can share them in Game Alley, which is Gamestar Mechanic's online community for kids to review or comment each others' games [24].

Editing and fixing the "broken" games and designing their own games are the most critical processes that relate to the fostering of students' creativity. The two processes allow students to learn and think creatively about how systems work and how they can be modified or changed. Through the game design process, students can cultivate their creative problem solving ability. As claimed by Gamestar Mechanic's website, the design of the game is based on researches on discussing how it relates to 21st skills such as systems-thinking and literacy.

With Gamestar Mechanic as an exemplary tool, we suggest the approach "Learning in and about Games" be studied, with regard to in what degree it can improve creativity compared to the other two approaches.

5   Conclusion and Discussion

Based on the discussion and review on the current studies, we found that the results of whether the approach "leaning in games" is effective in fostering learners' creativity are, in general, positive, although a few of them hold a neutral or even negative opinion on this point. It is probably because of the difference in the types of games that the results and conclusions they made are different. In consideration of the possibility, more studies on this topic need to be conducted in future. In addition to game types, teachers and students may also be two factors that influence the results of studies on fostering creativity through "learning in games". For example, teachers' differences in personalities or instructional skills, and students' different pre-experiences in playing games or personalities may be the variables that influence the results.

As to "learning about games", that is learning through designing games, studies applying this the approach seem to arrive at a same conclusion that learning through designing games can contribute to fostering creativity. Nevertheless, some scholars point out that creativity cannot be fostered through game design alone. They suggest that appropriate pedagogical strategies should be applied in "learning about games" in order to foster creativity, and appropriate learning environment is needed.

In discussing the approach "learning in and about games", the famous online game design platform Games Mechanic is discussed for it applies the way of playing games to learning game design. On its website as well as by some scholars, Gamestar Mechanic is claimed to be helpful for improving learners' creative problem solving skills. We suggest that in future the approach "learning in and about games" is worth studying in what degree it can improve creativity compared to the other two approaches.

Creativity is an increasingly important ability in the digital information age. On the whole, it is agreed by scholars that creativity can be trained and fostered through specific training approaches such as playful activities or games. Among the training approaches, game-based learning is considered as an important way and regarded by most scholars as an effective way. We believe that if combined with appropriate pedagogies and conducted in a proper learning environment, game-based learning is a promising approach for fostering and enhancing creativity.

References

1. Doolittle, J.H.: Using Riddles and Interactive Computer Games to Teach Problem-solving Skills. Teaching of Psychology 22(1), 33–36 (1995)
2. Sefer, J.: The Effects of Play Oriented Curriculum on Creativity in Elementary School Children. Gifted Education International 11(1), 4–17 (1995)
3. Urban, K.K.: Assessing Creativity: The Test for Creative Thinking - Drawing Production (TCT-DP) The Concept, Application, Evaluation, and International Studies. Psychology Science 46(3), 387–397 (2004)
4. Clements, D.H., Gullo, D.F.: Effects of Computer Programming on Young Children's Cognition. Journal of Educational Psychology 76(6), 1051 (1984)
5. Papert, S.: The Children's Machine: Rethinking School in the Age of the Computer. Basic Books (1993)
6. Clements, D.H.: Effects of Logo and CAI Environments on Cognition and Creativity. Journal of Educational Psychology 78(4), 309 (1986)
7. Subhi, T.: The Impact of LOGO on Gifted Children's Achievement and Creativity. Journal of Computer Assisted Learning 15, 98–108 (1999)
8. Gee, J.P.: An Introduction to Discourse Analysis: Theory and Method. Routledge, New York (1999)
9. Gee, J.P.: What Videogames Have to Teach us about Learning and Literacy. Palgrave Macmillan, New York (2003)
10. Huang, C., et al.: The Idea Storming Cube: Evaluating the Effects of Using Game and Computer Agent to Support Divergent Thinking. Educational Technology & Society 13(4), 180–191 (2010)
11. Doyle, D.: "Immersed in Learning": Supporting Creative Practice in Virtual Worlds. Learning, Media and Technology 35(2), 99–110 (2010)
12. Oishi, L.: Surfing Second Life: What Does Second Life Have to do with Real-life Learning? Technology & Learning 27(11), 54 (2007)
13. Kiili, K.: Content Creation Challenges and Flow Experience in Educational Games: The IT-Emperor Case. Internet and Higher Education 8(3), 183–198 (2005)
14. Ott, M., Pozzi, F.: Digital Games as Creativity Enablers for Children. Behaviour & Information Technology 31(10), 1011–1019 (2012)
15. Oei, A.C., Patterson, M.D.: Enhancing Cognition with Video Games: A Multiple Game Training Study. PLoS One 8(3) (2013)
16. O'Hanlon, C.: Don't Play It, Make It! The Journal 38(8) (2011)
17. Allsop, Y.: Exploring the Educational Value of Children's Game Authoring Practises: A Primary School Case Study. In: 6th European Conference on Games Based Learning (2012)
18. Li, Q.: Digital Game Building: Learning in a Participatory Culture. Educational Research 52(4), 427–443 (2010)
19. Cheng, G.: Using Game Making Pedagogy to Facilitate Student Learning of Interactive Multimedia. Australasian Journal of Educational Technology 25(2), 204–220 (2009)
20. Resnick, M.: All I Really Need to Know (about Creative Thinking) I Learned (by Studying How Children Learn) in Kindergarten. In: Proceedings of the 6th ACM SIGCHI Conference on Creativity & Cognition, pp. 1–6 (2007)
21. Frossard, F., Barajas, M., Trifonova, A.: A Learner-Centered Game-Design Approach: Impacts on Teachers' Creativity. Digital Education Review 21 (2012)

22. Leng, E.Y., et al.: Computer Games Development Experience and Appreciative Learning Approach for Creative Process Enhancement. Computers & Education 55(3), 1131–1144 (2010)
23. Schild, J., Göttel, T., Grimm, P.: Game Development Inhalte in der Hochschulinformatik. Mensch & Computer, 385 (2011)
24. Gamestar Mechanic, http://gamestarmechanic.com/teachers/about

Exploring Interpersonal Relationship and Growth Need Strength on Knowledge Sharing in Social Media

Sally M. Li[1] and Will W.K. Ma[2]

[1] Department of Accounting, Hong Kong Shue Yan University, Hong Kong SAR, China
mli@hksyu.edu
[2] Online Communication Research Centre, Department of Journalism & Communication,
Hong Kong Shue Yan University, Hong Kong SAR, China
will.wkma@gmail.com

Abstract. Popular social networking sites (SNS) like Facebook and Weibo empower users to connect to people. Active SNS users are leaders of their peer groups. The youths are dedicated to share knowledge and information on SNS in their daily lives. We explore the motivation drivers influencing university applicants' online knowledge sharing behaviour on SNS. Using a survey questionnaire completed by 485 students who enrolled a university degree programme in various majors, the study found that perceived online relationship commitment had a direct, positive and significant effect ($\beta=0.66$, $p<0.001$) and the perceived growth need commitment also had a direct, positive and significant effect ($\beta=0.21$, $p<0.001$) toward online knowledge sharing behaviour, whereas perceived online attachment motivation had a significant but indirect effect on online knowledge sharing behaviour through perceived online relationship commitment. The proposed online knowledge sharing model explained 43% of the observed variance, and its implications are discussed.

Keywords: Perceived online attachment motivation, perceived online relationship commitment, online knowledge sharing behavior, growth need strength, social media.

1 Introduction

The digital youths are keen to connect with others and are immersed in playing online games, chatting and sharing photos and feelings on social media platforms. Popular social networking sites (SNS) like Facebook and Weibo grow exponentially and are indispensable. They are powerful for users to connect to individuals, groups and communities. Active SNS users are leaders of their peer groups. Knowledge and information on SNS are shared and reverted freely, however; effective use relies on users' ability to distinguish good information from bad [1]. Users may enjoy convenient, instant and multi-mediated sharing on SNS simply with their fingertips. After pressing a "share" button, they were being put under the spotlight of a group of people which could never be hidden again no matter they did it yesterday or 10 years ago. Though parents are concerned about any possible addictive behavior of active SNS users, these

S.K.S. Cheung et al. (Eds.): ICHL 2014, LNCS 8595, pp. 288–299, 2014.

tools are around us. Digital divide between teachers and pupils can cause confrontation and behavioral displacement [1]. To help students critically evaluate the quality of massive information that they bring to classes are important [1].

Previous research has also examined knowledge sharing involving the participation and continuous interaction of peer learners through a shared online platform in both academic and workplace contexts to generate and imitate best practices [2, 3, 4]. However, knowledge sharing is a 'complex process [that] differs from interaction and participation and cannot . . . simply [be assessed] through counting [the] frequency of interactions' [5, p. 42]. These studies did not cover particular SNS features like instant gratification and social endorsement. From a social exchange perspective, users may gain wider attention for both intended and unintended outcomes. Thus, we do not have sufficient theoretical model to explain why SNS users are so committed to invest their time and effort in their social groups.

Since knowledge sharing is multifaceted, researchers are interested to understand the youths' motives behind their dedicated sharing behavior on SNS. We explore the factors that influence university applicants' online knowledge sharing behaviour, especially with respect to their innate need to belong to and grow on SNS. The results are expected to provide insights for academics and social leaders into nurturing knowledge sharing and creation.

Our research question was as follows.

RQ: What factors affect students' online knowledge sharing behaviour on social networking sites?

To explore the motivation drivers influencing students' online knowledge sharing behaviour, we examine the literature to find the relevant factors. An online knowledge sharing model is then proposed, and the methodology used to collect data to test the hypotheses is explained. The findings are reported and the implications discussed. We conclude by acknowledging the study's limitations and suggesting areas for further research.

2   Literature Review and Hypotheses Development

Knowledge is ubiquitous and must be recognised and accepted before it can be acquired and applied. Given that knowledge is, by nature, sticky and leaky [6], people who possess knowledge may or may not share with others for self or public interests. In a knowledge society, researchers have shown continued interest in the study of knowledge sharing in different contexts.

2.1   Social Interaction, Learning and Knowledge Sharing

According to Vygotsky [7], learning is social. It involves a process of acquiring knowledge and representing it through social interactions. Sharing with others occur naturally through observations and imitations especially at an infant stage. Over time, people are educated to act and think in similar way. Formal education aims at converging our thinking and behaviour, whereas informal learning ingrains social norm into our mind. Webb and Palincsar [8] explained this of the use the reciprocal teaching process to explain how knowledge sharing in social processes act as a mechanism for learning. Knowledge is contextual and relational [9]. SNS are socialization platforms. Socialization builds on conversation and discussion, which is one of the four stages to convert tacit and explicit knowledge continuously [9]. Ma and Li [10] suggested that learning platform features contributed to learning satisfaction. Brown and Duguid [6] echo that information technology not only supports the transfer of knowledge, but also creates know-how that allows knowledge to be shared. Thus, social interaction is important for an individual to form new bonding with groups and to internalize external rules and build relationship in a community [9].

2.2   Online Knowledge Sharing Behavior

Previous studies suggest that online knowledge sharing behavior (OKSB) occurs when learning takes place in an online learning context when the individual learner understands the details and implications associated with that knowledge so that he or she can apply it through the use of online learning platforms [11, p.213]. OKSB refers to "the online communication of knowledge so that knowledge is learned and applied by an individual" [11, p.212]. The other constructs are defined in the following sections.

2.3   Perceived Online Attachment Motivation

Previous studies have suggested that perceived online attachment motivation (POAM) is a determinant of online knowledge sharing [11, 12]. POAM refers to 'the degree to which an individual believes that he or she can improve his or her social interaction and the sense of communion with others on an online learning platform' [11, p.213]. If an individual expects to have strong social interactions on an online platform, then he or she would be more willing to develop relationships with other members in that community. On social networking sites, all learners share the common goal of connectivity and instant messaging, and thus sharing one's knowledge is a good way to develop relationships. This leads to the following hypothesis.

> *H1: The perceived attachment motivation of an individual learner on a social networking site has a positive effect on his or her knowledge sharing behaviour in that context.*

2.4   Perceived Online Relationship Commitment

Previous studies have suggested that perceived online relationship commitment (PORC) is a determinant of online knowledge sharing [11, 12]. PORC refers to "the degree to which an individual believes that he or she can persist in a relationship with others on an online learning platform" [11, p.213]. The greater an individual's need to persist in an established relationship, the more committed that individual is to the relationship, as manifested by spending more time and effort in consistent and continual interaction with relationship partners. On a social media platform, users establish relationships with fellow members and as sharing is a means of establishing such relationships, it can be viewed as a form of social support and pro-social behaviour. In the process of maintaining established relationships, individual learners become more willing to share with other members of the online community. Knowledge sharing thus comes to be viewed as a positive act that benefits the sharing parties. This leads to the following hypothesis.

H2: The perceived online relationship commitment of an individual learner on a social networking site has a positive effect on his or her knowledge sharing behaviour in that context.

2.5   Growth Need Strength

According to Hackman and Oldham [13], growth need strength (GNS) is a moderating variable in their job characteristics model. They noted that certain people dislike job enrichment such as autonomy or involvement in decision making and, when offered complex tasks, may exhibit lower motivation and performance. A later study by Graen, Scandura and Graen [14] argues that it is the growth increment that motivate employee to perform better. Growth needs are defined as the strong desire for personal challenge and accomplishment in learning and professional development [14, p.484]. They asserted that the subordinates who perceived the challenges are acceptable would perform better with leader support, which they termed it as "vertical collaboration". Thus, growth need is not only a personal trait; it can be cultivated with challenges and leader support that are acceptable by employees. Adler and his colleagues [15] replicated the study of Hackman and Oldham [13] and found that high GNS students are more satisfied and perform better in enriched learning setting.

According to Maslow's [16] hierarchy of needs, esteem and self-actualization are higher order needs which are important for growth. With advanced technology in the material world, people face more challenges to achieve their growth needs. SNS are socialization platforms. Socialization is an iterative process in which a person learns and mutually adjusts with his or her peers in establishing relationship with others [17]. A group socialization model suggested by Moreland and Levine [17] involved a 3-steps process in which a new member evaluate the rewardingness to relate to a group and determine effort to commit to the group before he or she can transit to take the full membership role. Every user goes through the evaluate-commit-transit phases to widen their social context. Sharing occurs between users in reflecting or acknowledging the sharers' or knowledge seekers' understanding of their personal values, ideas and practice [18]. Social interaction is a necessary means to evaluate their likeness and determine further effort to commit and transit to a new community.

GNS is defined in this study as "the degree to which an individual believes that he or she has a strong need for challenge and accomplishment, for learning, and for professional development with others on social networking sites". If an individual possesses high GNS, he or she is expected to engage more in online knowledge sharing as it offers more opportunities to interact with others to foster growth and development. In this study, the Hong Kong Diploma of Secondary Education (HKDSE) graduates selected were pursuing bachelor degree and thus were expected to possess a high GNS. Such students should prefer challenging work, have autonomy to share with others and engage more in online knowledge sharing on SNS because it offers more opportunities to interact with others and foster personal growth and development. This leads to the following hypothesis.

H3: High perceived growth need strength has a positive effect on a user's knowledge sharing behaviour on a social networking site.

3   Methodology

3.1   Background, Subjects and Data Collection

Social media has been very popular. Due to their nature of communication, social media could be divided into a number of different platforms, including social networking, photo sharing, audio sharing, video sharing, publishing, interpersonal, etc. Users could access all these social media through desktop personal computers, tablets, smartphones, etc. Individual users get access and connection throughout seven days a week and twenty-four hours a day. This study was conducted in summer 2013. The subjects in this study were all post-secondary students who had taken the Hong Kong Diploma of Secondary Education (HKDSE). While they were waiting in line to submit their applications to a local university in Hong Kong, they were handed a paper questionnaire, which they were asked to complete and return. Most of them completed the questionnaire in ten minutes. In three days, a total of 485 completed questionnaires were returned for further analysis. The age of the participants were from 17 to 25 with an average age of 18.34 years old.

3.2   Measures

A survey instrument was used to obtain self-reported information from the subjects [11]. The questionnaire was divided into two parts. The first part collected respondents' basic personal information, including gender, age, and most frequently used social networking sites last week. The second part asked respondents for their opinions about their studies, their perceived commitment, and their perceived online knowledge sharing behavior over the use of the social networking sites. All of the questionnaire items were adopted from previous validated scales and were measured on a 7-point Likert-type scale ranging from 1 (strongly disagree) to 7 (strongly agree). Specifically, the respondents were asked to answer items regarding POAM (5 items), PORC (5 items) and the OKSB (5 items) from a validated instrument by Ma and Yuen [11]; and the perceived GNS scale (5 items) [15]. The complete instrument and sources are listed in the Appendix.

4   Findings

4.1   Descriptive Statistics of Respondents

The descriptive statistics of the respondents were presented and self-explained in the below table (see Table 1).

Table 1. Descriptive Statistics of Respondents (*N=485*)

Items / Descriptive	
Gender: Male - 168 (34.6%); Female - 317 (65.4%)	
Average Age: 18.34	
Most frequently used: Facebook (431, 89%); Others (54, 11%)	
In the last week,......	**Mean (1-10)**
how often did you <u>visit</u> there?	7.06
how often did you use the <u>inbox message</u> there?	4.28
how often did you <u>share news</u> there?	3.03
how often did you <u>post message to all friends</u> there?	3.06
how often did you <u>chat</u> there?	3.96
how often did you <u>upload photo(s)</u> there?	3.07
how often did you <u>upload video(s)</u> there?	1.84
how often did you make <u>comment(s)</u> there?	3.93
how often did you <u>edit your profile</u> there?	2.59
how often did you <u>share music</u> there?	2.40

4.2   Descriptive Analysis of Variables

Table 2 presented the mean responses and standard deviations for the constructs on a seven-point Likert-type scale. Factor loadings, AVE and Cronbach's alpha values were included (see Table 2).

Table 2. Descriptive Statistics and Factor Loadings of Constructs

	Min	Max	Mean	Std. Dev.	Cronbach's Alpha	Factor Loadings	AVE
Perceived Online Attachment Motivation (POAM)							
POAM1	1	7	3.47	1.332	0.880	0.71***	0.56
POAM2	1	6	3.21	1.295		0.72***	
POAM3	1	6	3.38	1.291		0.79***	
POAM4	1	7	3.66	1.357		0.74***	
POAM5	1	7	3.64	1.338		0.79***	
Perceived Online Relationship Commitment (PORC)							
PORC1	1	7	3.89	1.329	0.875	0.79***	0.61
PORC2	1	7	3.99	1.459		0.85***	
PORC3	1	7	3.82	1.364		0.85***	
PORC4	1	7	3.52	1.385		0.63***	
PORC5	1	7	3.62	1.278		0.78***	
Online Knowledge Sharing Behaviour (OKSB)							
OKSB1	1	7	4.09	1.295	0.889	0.74***	0.63
OKSB2	1	7	4.24	1.274		0.77***	

Table 2 (*Continued*)

OKSB3	1	7	4.06	1.194		0.82***	
OKSB4	1	7	3.96	1.191		0.87***	
OKSB5	1	7	3.87	1.129		0.76***	
Growth Need Strength (GNS)							
GNS1	1	7	5.06	1.303	0.916	0.78***	0.72
GNS2	2	7	5.40	1.264		0.92***	
GNS3	2	7	5.29	1.232		0.93***	
GNS4	2	7	5.19	1.188		0.85***	
GNS5	1	7	5.18	1.229		0.76***	

4.3   Instrument Validation

Measurement models for each construct were specified with the corresponding items. The measurement models were assessed by confirmatory factor analysis, Structural Equation Modeling (SEM) testing using LISREL. Measurement model validity depends on (1) establishing acceptable levels of goodness-of-fit for the measurement model and (2) finding specific evidence of construct validity [19, p.664]. The measurement models for POAM, PORC, OKSB and GNS all exhibit acceptable levels of goodness-of-fit as suggested by previous literature [19, p.672].

Convergent validity of a construct refers to the items that are indicators of a specific construct should converge or share a high proportion of variance in common. This was assessed by factor loadings, average variance extracted and reliability. Factor loadings assessment: In the case of high convergent validity, high loadings on a factor would indicate that they converge on a common point, the latent construct [19, p.709]. Factor loadings for each item were listed in the Table 2. They were all statistically significant ($p<0.001$) and above the ideal value of 0.70, except PORC4. Average variance extracted assessment: The variance extracted refers to the square of a standardized factor loading that represents how much variation in an item is explained by the latent factor. The average variance extracted was then calculated as the mean variance extracted for the items loading on a construct and is a summary indicator of convergence. As shown in Table 2, all AVE exhibited 0.5 or higher, suggested adequate convergence [19, p.709]. Reliability is an indicator of convergent validity and internal consistency. Coefficient alpha is a commonly applied estimate of reliability [19]. The Cronbach's alpha values were summarized in Table 2, ranged from 0.880 to 0.916, well above the threshold value of 0.7 as suggested by previous studies [20]. Altogether, the constructs exhibited convergent validity.

4.4   Model Testing Using Structural Equation Modeling

The structural model and the hypotheses were tested using structural equation modeling by LISREL. The model fit was analyzed using the various goodness-of-fit indices. It was found that all the goodness-of-fit indices, either above, or very close to the suggested threshold value by previous studies [19].

Table 3. Summary of Goodness-of-fit Indices for Model Testing Results

Chi-sq/df (<3)	GFI (>0.9)	NFI (>0.9)	NNFI (>0.9)	CFI (>0.9)	IFI (>0.9)	RMSEA (<0.1)	SRMR (<0.08)
2.65	0.92	0.95	0.96	0.97	0.97	0.055	0.047

The hypotheses of the model were measured by both the significance and the strength of each of the causal paths. The results were summarized in the Figure 1.

*p<0.05; ***p<0.001; ns: non-significant*

Fig. 1. Extended Online Knowledge Sharing Model

This study found that perceived online relationship commitment has a direct, positive and significant effect (β=0.66, p<0.001) and the perceived personal growth commitment also has a direct, positive and significant effect (β=0.21, p<0.001) toward online knowledge sharing behaviour, whereas POAM had an indirect significant effect on OKSB that was fully mediated by PORC. The proposed online knowledge sharing model explained 43% of the observed variance.

5   Discussion

5.1   Interpersonal Relationship and Growth Needs Strength on Online Knowledge Sharing

H1 posited a direct, positive, and significant relationship between POAM and OKSB. POAM was fully mediated by PORC and showed only an indirect significant effect on online Knowledge Sharing Behaviour. Data analysis revealed that the relationship was not significant, and thus hypothesis 1 was not supported. H2 which posited a significant relationship between PORC and OKSB was supported. These results were just the opposite of previous empirical studies [19, 21]. It is worth noting that the different results as explained by the usage pattern of social media. Previous studies

[19, 21] and many forum usage involved anonymous usage that encouraged a free expression of ideas without any hindrance from one's own physical identities. On the contrary, social media, especially the usage of Facebook, is an extension of the physical relationship where individual users develop their virtual connections based on their physical interpersonal relationships. That is, individual users develop their relationship in social media as a representation of their already known community. Making new friends becomes not a priority. Instead, maintaining relationship becomes the direct and paramount importance. The ability of relationship commitment becomes the key determinant to predict online knowledge sharing in social media. Attachment motivation has only the indirect effect, through relationship commitment to affect online knowledge sharing. That is, the greater the social media satisfies the need to perceived online attachment motivation, the greater the perceived online relationship commitment, and hence, the more online knowledge sharing in the social media environment.

H3 which posited a direct, positive, and significant relationship between GNS and OKSB was supported. In the knowledge era, GNS is not a personal trait. A wider social context can arouse SNS users' personal interests to engage in complex tasks and meet new challenges. We suggest that it is a "perceived growth need commitment" that driving them to seek and repeat the sharing activities on SNS. Growth need commitment may be personal to one's experience which may cause SNS users to commit different effort and time in different communities. However, growth increment like opportunities to take up complex tasks and new challenges are important to stimulate growth need commitment. Previous studies supported that supervisors can exert acceptable challenge with collaborative supports to improve subordinates' performance [14]. Knowledge sharing with their peers can promote lateral support to create new experience. Educators also take a role to provide acceptable challenges to students in order to advance their growth commitment.

SNS communities are unique as their mix and content are user-driven. However, SNS connectivity is fragile. Its cohesiveness and sustainability depend on both users and operators effort. The architecture of SNS is designed to draw users' attention with socially endorsed news and comment. The usages are intensified when users find something interesting. It may reinforce and aggregate people with similar mindset and different ideas may be criticized. Nowadays, teenagers are busy in surfing with all sorts of mobile technology in classes and workplaces. Instead of a need to attach to others, they may perceive a greater need to attach to the mobile gadgets with praises and followers around them.

The fascinating and multi-mediated nature of SNS promotes thought-provoking activities which can be beneficial or detrimental to the society. Wider social issues, like authenticity, indecent usage or cyber-bullying should be studied. Students should be equipped with digital literacy in using SNS, for examples, by evaluating and interpreting the veracity and integrity of the information that one encounters before knowledge sharing [1]. Both learning and connectedness are drivers to foster community interests [22]. A recent study by Li & Ma [23] also urged to include a cultural and social context as a holistic motivational framework to educate accounting undergraduates. In other words, SNS activities can change students experience and understanding with the physical world. Educators have to discover students' metaphors by engaging them in dialogues or group tasks to solve collective problems rather than working alone to become more self-centered. Both academics and social leaders need to nurture the youths with socialization tactics and good etiquette in meeting new friends on SNS.

5.2   Limitations and Further Studies

Despite the usefulness of its findings, this study has several limitations. First, the generalizability of the study is constrained by its specific context of HKDSE graduates in using SNS in Hong Kong. Second, the proposed knowledge sharing model is based on only three constructs. To better understand the complex social interactions process on SNS, future research should consider other variables. For examples, students' learning style, their preferences to be major in which disciplines, academic results, technology efficacy, perceived acceptance of information authenticity and privacy may also influence their knowledge sharing behaviour.

6   Conclusion

In this study, we extended an established online knowledge sharing model that addressed the human need to belong – a desire that was operationalised as perceived online attachment motivation (POAM) and perceived online relationship commitment (PORC) and perceived growth need strength (GNS) into a new context, SNS. These results suggest that designing learning activities need to consider students' prior experience on these social networking sites that facilitate the formation of social bonds and commitment to personal growth is a possible means of promoting knowledge sharing online.

Appendix A. Measurement Items Used in the Study

Construct (Sources) – Measurement Items
Perceived online attachment motivation (POAM) [11]
POAM1   If I feel unhappy or kind of depressed, I usually try to be around other members using the social media to make me feel better.
POAM2   I usually have the greatest need to have other members using the social media around me when I feel upset.
POAM3   I often have a strong need to be around other social media users who are impressed with what I am like and what I do.
POAM4   I mainly like to be around other users who think I am an important, exciting person together.
POAM5   I often have a strong desire to get other users around to notice me and appreciate what I am like together.
Perceived online attachment motivation (PORC) [11]
PORC1   I am committed to maintaining my relationship with other members using social media.

PORC2	I want our relationship with other members using the social media to last for a very long time.
PORC3	I feel very strongly linked to my relationship with other members using the social media.
PORC4	I would feel very upset if my relationship with other members using the social media were to end.
PORC5	I tend toward the long-term future of my relationship with other members using the social media.

Online knowledge sharing behavior (OKSB) [11]

OKSB1	The advice I receive from other members using the social media has increased my understanding.
OKSB2	The advice I receive from other members using the social media has increased my knowledge.
OKSB3	The advice I receive from other members using the social media allows me to complete similar tasks more efficiently.
OKSB4	The advice I receive from other members using the social media allows me to improve the quality of similar work.
OKSB5	The advice I receive from other members using the social media allows me to conduct similar tasks with greater independence.

Growth Need Strength [15]

GNS1	I prefer having opportunities for personal growth and development in my study.
GNS2	I prefer having opportunities to learn new things from my study.
GNS3	I prefer having chances to exercise independent thought and action in my study.
GNS4	I prefer having a sense of worthwhile accomplishment in my study.
GNS5	I prefer having stimulating and challenging study.

References

1. Miller, C., Bartlett, J.: "Digital fluency": towards young people's critical use of the Internet. Journal of Information Literacy 6, 35–55 (2012)
2. Mazzolini, M., Maddison, S.: When to jump in: The role of the instructor in online discussion forums. Computers & Education 49, 193–213 (2007)
3. Kapur, M., Kinzer, C.: Examining the effect of problem type in a synchronous computer-supported collaborative learning (CSCL) environment. Educational Technology Research & Development 55, 439–459 (2007)
4. Fischer, F., Mandl, H.: Knowledge convergence in computer-supported collaborative learning: The role of external representation tools. Journal of the Learning Sciences 14, 405–441 (2005)
5. Ghadirian, H., Ayub, A.F.M., Silong, A.D., Bakar, K.B.A., Zadeh, A.M.H.: Knowledge Sharing Behaviour among Students in Learning Environments: A Review of Literature. Asian Social Science 10, 38–45 (2014)
6. Brown, J.S., Duguid, P.: Organizing Knowledge. California Management Review 40, 90–111 (1998)
7. Vygotsky, L.S.: Mind in society: The development of higher psychological processes. Harvard University Press, Cambridge (1978)
8. Webb, N.M., Palincsar, A.S.: Group processes in the classroom. In: Berliner, D.C., Calfee, R.C. (eds.) Handbook of Educational Psychology, pp. 841–873. Macmillan Library Reference, New York (1996)

 9. Nonaka, I.: A Dynamic Theory of Organizational Knowledge Creation. Organization Science 5, 14–37 (1994)
10. Ma, W.W.K., Li, S.M.: An Exploration of Student Satisfaction in Online Accounting Courses. In: Cheung, S.K.S., Fong, J., Fong, W., Wang, F.L., Kwok, L.F. (eds.) ICHL 2013. LNCS, vol. 8038, pp. 155–166. Springer, Heidelberg (2013)
11. Ma, W.W.K., Yuen, A.H.K.: Understanding Online Knowledge Sharing: An Interpersonal Relationship Perspective. Computers & Education 56, 210–219 (2011)
12. Ma, W.W.K., Yuen, A.H.K.: Understanding online knowledge sharing: An exploratory theoretical framework. In: Tsang, P., Cheung, S.K.S., Lee, V.S.K., Huang, R. (eds.) ICHL 2010. LNCS, vol. 6248, pp. 239–248. Springer, Heidelberg (2010)
13. Hackman, J.R., Oldham, G.R.: Work redesign. Addison-Wesley, Reading (1980)
14. Graen, G.B., Scandura, T.A., Graen, M.R.: A field experimental test of the moderating effects of growth need strength on productivity. Journal of Applied Psychology 71, 484–491 (1986)
15. Adler, R.W., Milne, M.J., Stablein, R.: Situated Motivation: An Empirical Test in an Accounting Course. Canadian Journal of Administrative Sciences 18, 101–115 (2001)
16. Maslow, A.H.: A theory of human motivation. Psychological Review 50, 370 (1943)
17. Moreland, R.L., Levine, J.M.: Socialization in small groups: Temporal changes in individual-group relations. Advances in Experimental Social Psychology 15, 137–192 (1982)
18. Nonaka, I., Takeuchi, H.: The Knowledge-Creating Company: How Japanese Companies Create the Dynamic of Innovation. Oxford University Press, New York (1995)
19. Hair, J.F., Black, B., Babin, B., Anderson, R.E.: Multivariate data analysis: A global perspective, 7th edn. Pearson, Upper Saddle River (2010)
20. Nunnally, J.C., Bernstein, I.H.: Psychometric Theory. McGraw-Hill, New York (1994)
21. Ma, W.W.K., Sun, K., Ma, J.: The Influence of Attachment Styles on Knowledge Sharing in Social Media Environments. In: Cheung, S.K.S., Fong, J., Kwok, L.-F., Li, K., Kwan, R. (eds.) ICHL 2012. LNCS, vol. 7411, pp. 231–242. Springer, Heidelberg (2012)
22. Rovai, A.P.: Development of an instrument to measure classroom community. The Internet and Higher Education 5, 197–211 (2002)
23. Li, S.M., Ma, W.W.K.: Motivational Factors for Accounting Learning - The Development of a Holistic Framework. In: Cheung, S.K.S., Fong, J., Kwok, L.-F., Li, K., Kwan, R. (eds.) ICHL 2012. LNCS, vol. 7411, pp. 243–252. Springer, Heidelberg (2012)

The Analysis of Classroom Teaching Behavior Based on Knowledge Building

Wu Chen[*], Meilin Long, and Qionghua Duan

South China Normal University
No.55 Western Avenue Zhongshan, Tianhe District, Guangzhou, China
scnuchenwu1@163.com

Abstract. As a teaching method, knowledge building has an advantage that it provided a straightforward way to realize knowledge creation and innovation in the present age. The practice of knowledge building in classroom not only helped student to achieve progress, but also promoted the teacher's professional development. Taking the instructional behavior as the object of research, the paper analyzed the process of teaching in classroom with quantitative method, and combining the qualitative analysis of classroom observation, explored the effects of knowledge building on teacher's professional development. The research results were teacher's professional development have been improved in the circumstance of knowledge building theory.

Keywords: knowledge building, teaching behavior, teacher's professional development.

1   Introduction

Nowadays is a time of thirst for knowledge and innovation. Mechanical reciting recite is no longer the requirement of learning, nor the acquisition of knowledge and skills, but pay more attention to promote deep learning and knowledge advancement. Marlene Scardamalia and Carl Bereiter from Ontario Institute for Studies of Education, University of Toronto, proposed the concept of "knowledge building" in 1987, and pointed out that one of the most important advantages of knowledge building is that it resolves the problem of knowledge creation and innovation directly. In the last 20 years, knowledge building had attracted the attention of many scholars and researchers from all over the world, whose researches related to multiple disciplines such as science, mathematics, society, history, etc. What's more, knowledge building theory was applied to the basic education, higher education, vocational education, and other fields, and obtained plenty of study results. However, most scholars launched their researches from the perspective of students, rarely from teachers who adopted knowledge building in teaching. Thus, this paper taking the instruction behavior in knowledge building classroom as studying object to explore the impact of application of knowledge building theory to instruction on teachers' professional development,

---

[*] Corresponding author.

S.K.S. Cheung et al. (Eds.): ICHL 2014, LNCS 8595, pp. 300–311, 2014.

through a quantitative analysis on knowledge construction of classroom teaching, and the qualitative analysis of classroom observation.

Initiated in year 2013, we collaborated with one primary and middle school in Guangdong province (hereinafter referred to as the "S" school) and carried out a project of "knowledge building". The project attracted many teachers involved in. They studied the "knowledge building" theory and applied into their instruction to explore an innovative instruction pattern, cultivate students' innovation ability and the responsibility of a collective cognitive ability and consciousness in the project. In the practice of research, not only students achieved progress, but also teacher's professional development was promoted.

In order to further the understandings on the facilitation of the knowledge building theory to teacher, we discussed the changes of the teachers on education ideas, concepts and teaching skills, through the quantitative analysis of the classroom behavior and qualitative analysis of classroom observation.

2   The Research Methods and Processes

We adopted the Flanders Interaction Analysis System (hereafter referred to as FIAS), created by American scholar Ned Flanders, to analyze teachers' instructional behavior. Flanders Interaction Analysis System is a kind of classroom interaction analysis method, which can divide the instruction process into a series of behavior units based on the classification of behaviors of teachers and students. According to FIAS, the behaviors can be divided into two categories: teacher behavior and student behavior, which will be subdivided into Flanders Interaction Analysis of Coding System, as shown in table 1.In the Coding system, the teachers' behavior can be divided into two kinds, indirect influence and direct influence on students.

Time sampling was used, and corresponding codes was recorded according to FIAS every 3 seconds. In this way, we encoded about 800 ~ 1000 from each class, which can reflect a series of events in chronological order. Each event occupies a small fragment of time, and then connected into a time series which displayed the instructional structure, behavior patterns and style in classroom.

Table 1.   Flanders interaction analysis of coding system

Categories	Codes	Contents
Teacher Talk (Indirect Influence)	1	Accepts Feeling
	2	Praises or Encourages
	3	Accepts or Uses Ideas of pupils
	4	Ask Questions
Teacher Talk (Direct Influence)	5	Lecturing
	6	Giving Directions
	7	Criticizing or Justifying Authority
Pupil Talk	8	Pupil-Talk--Response
	9	Pupil-Talk--Initiation
Silence	10	Silence or Confusion

Following up teacher L who taught Chinese in Grade 8 from S school for 10 months (from 2013.3 to 2013.12), we recorded the classroom instruction for 3 times at June, October and December. Teacher L taught Chinese in Grade 8. The 3 classes we recorded represented different stages of instruction reality since teacher L participated in the project so that we can explore changes of the impact of knowledge building theory on teachers' teaching. The information of the three videos is shown in table 2.

Table 2.   Information summary of video lesson samples

Lessons	Date	Subject	Mins
Lessons one	2013.06	The Thunderstorm	40.21
Lessons two	2013.10	Expository Writing	42.36
Lessons three	2013.12	The Ugly Duckling	41.24

The first video was recorded in June 2013 whose instructional process was the teacher guided students to read the text, to experience the feelings of the lesson and then to reflect their own growing experience. The process of appreciating the lesson was promoted by teacher's questions. The teacher proposed questions, then student answer shortly and the teacher explained them in detail.

The second video was recorded in October 2013 whose instructional process was students studied by grouping (each group assigned different lessons) and then finished a set of exercise based on the lesson. During the class, each group had a representative to give presentation to the whole class. And then the teacher feed backed appropriately and interacted with students.

The third class recorded in December 2013 which discussed based on the previous lesson (in the previous lesson, each student put forward their questions independently according to the lesson and reading material) in group. The students' tasks were choosing question to explore, answering questions, developing question, answering question, developing question again and at last discussing in the whole class. Teacher L provided scaffoldings to students to students to push forward discussions.

In the data analysis phase, we input data from time sampling into the Flanders interaction analysis system supporting software developed by scholars Guo Huilong from Taiwan [6].

3   Result Analysis

3.1   Key Facts

The correlative data is processed by Flanders interaction analysis system supporting software, and 3 interaction matrixes were formulated, as table 3, 4, 5.

Table 3. Interaction matrixes of lesson one

		Teacher				Student						
		(1	(2	(3	(4	(5	(6	(7	(8	(9	(	Total
Teacher	(1	2	0	0	0	3	1	0	0	0	0	6
	(2	0	9	4	3	10	0	0	0	3	4	33
	(3	0	8	28	6	12	3	0	2	1	0	60
	(4	1	0	3	27	4	4	0	17	1	16	73
	(5	1	0	1	22	231	13	0	7	2	4	281
	(6	0	0	2	2	3	14	0	13	5	7	46
	(7	0	0	1	0	0	0	0	0	0	0	1
Student	(8	1	5	16	8	9	3	1	104	2	1	150
	(9	0	7	5	2	1	0	0	0	68	2	85
	(	2	4	0	3	8	8	0	7	3	36	71
	To-	7	33	60	73	281	46	1	150	85	70	806
%		0.8 7%	4.0 9%	7.4 4%	9.0 6%	34. 86%	5.7 1%	0.1 2%	18. 61%	10. 55%	8.6 8%	100.0 0%
		21.46%				40.69%			29.16%		8.6	100.0

Table 4. Interaction matrixes of lesson two

		Teacher				Student						
		(1	(2	(3	(4	(5	(6	(7	(8	(9	(	Total
Teacher	(1	0	0	0	0	0	0	0	1	0	0	1
	(2	0	11	1	1	4	1	0	0	1	0	19
	(3	0	1	8	5	5	1	0	1	8	0	29
	(4	0	0	1	6	5	1	0	10	7	2	32
	(5	0	0	1	14	96	3	0	1	1	4	120
	(6	1	0	0	1	2	1	0	0	0	4	9
	(7	0	0	0	0	0	0	0	0	0	0	0
Student	(8	0	0	6	1	5	0	0	4	0	2	18
	(9	0	3	12	4	0	0	0	1	346	24	390
	(	0	4	0	0	3	2	0	0	27	197	233
	To-	1	19	29	32	120	9	0	18	390	233	851
%		0.1 2%	2.2 3%	3.4 1%	3.7 6%	14. 10%	1.0 6%	0.0 0%	2.1 2%	45. 83%	27. 38%	100.0 0%
		9.52%				15.16%			47.94%		27.	100%

Table 5. Interaction matrixes of lesson three

		Teacher						Student				
		(1)	(2)	(3)	(4)	(5)	(6)	(7)	(8)	(9)	(10)	Total
Teacher	(1)	0	0	0	0	0	0	0	1	0	0	1
	(2)	0	2	1	1	2	0	0	1	3	0	10
	(3)	0	3	58	14	5	0	0	0	6	1	87
	(4)	0	0	4	4	1	4	0	3	11	4	31
	(5)	0	2	2	3	64	2	0	0	1	1	75
	(6)	1	1	0	2	0	9	0	0	7	3	23
	(7)	0	0	0	0	0	0	0	0	0	0	0
Student	(8)	0	0	3	1	1	0	0	0	0	0	5
	(9)	0	2	19	4	0	4	0	0	540	2	571
	(10)	0	0	0	2	3	4	0	0	3	12	24
	Total	1	10	87	31	76	23	0	5	571	23	827
	%	0.12%	1.21%	10.52%	3.75%	9.19%	2.78%	0.00%	0.60%	69.04%	2.78%	100.00%
		15.60%				11.97%			69.65%		2.78%	100%

3.2 The Analysis of Classroom Structure

According to Table 3, 4 and 5, the distribution map of words rate in classroom of the 3 lessons was drawn, as figure 1. From figure 1, the rate of teacher's words of lesson 1 was the highest, which was 62.16%, and the rate of students' words of lesson 3 is the highest, which was 69.65%. In addition, the rate of teacher's words of lesson 1 was higher than students; rate of students' words of lesson 2 was higher than teacher's; rate of students' words of lesson 3 was far higher than teacher's. So we can know that student engagement in lesson 1 was very low, and the lesson 3 was the highest. It is more and more obviously, the students were becoming to be the main body, and the classroom was getting open. The rate of teacher's words in lesson 3 was higher than lesson 2, which is because students spent so much time on simulating teaching and doing exercises in lesson 2, and the percentage of silence or confusion was very high.

3.3 The Analysis of Teacher's Tendency

Comparing the frequency of the code of 1-4 and 5-7, the tendency of teacher's instruction can be analyzed to indirectly or directly influence; and comparing the frequency of the code 1-3 and 6-7, the instruction to students can be judged to positive or negative reinforcement. According to table 3, 4 and 5, the ratio of indirect to direct influence was shown in figure 2 and the ratio of positive to negative influence as figure 3.

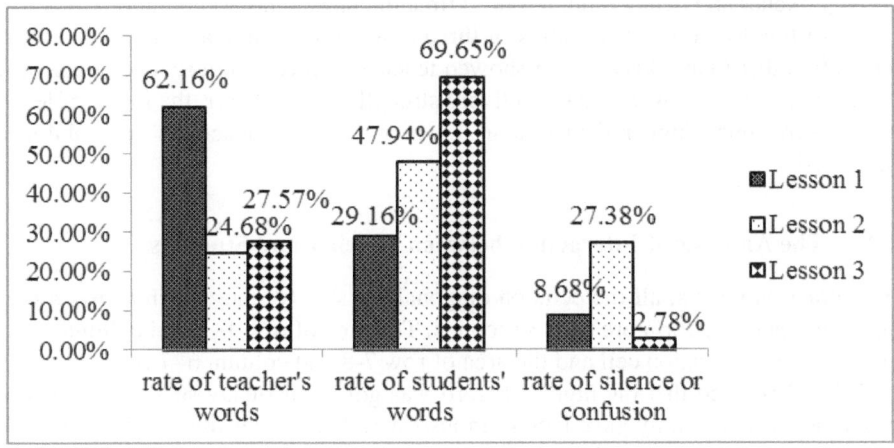

Fig. 1. Distribution map of words rate of 3 lessons

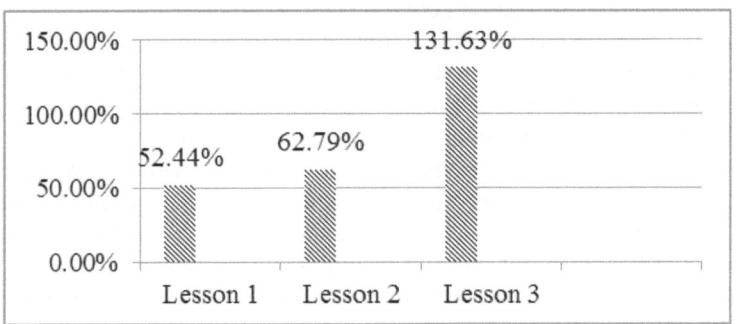

Fig. 2. Ratio of indirect influence to direct influence in three lessons

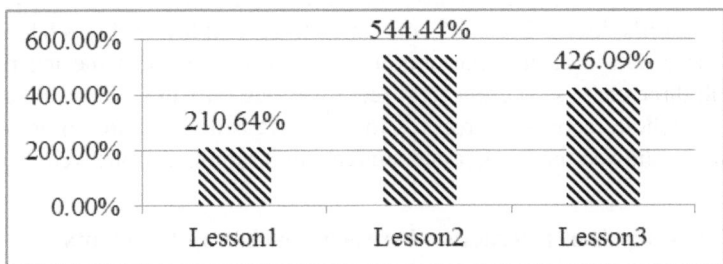

Fig. 3. Ratio of positive influence to negative influence in three lessons

As shown in figure 2, the ratio of teacher's indirect/direct influence was the lowest in lesson 1, was 52.44%, and 62.79% in lesson 2, both less than 100%. It reflected the teacher tended to give direct effect on students, pay attention to own instruction, and rarely give provocative questions. The ratio of lesson 3 was 131.63%, the highest in 3 lessons, much higher than lesson 1 and 2. It was stated that the instruction was becoming opener and democratic, but need time to change and accumulate.

According to the figure 3, ratios of three cases' on positive and negative influence were all higher than 100%, which showed teacher L liked to praise, encourage, affirm or retell students' view, and gave actively strengthen. Moreover, the ratios of lesson 2 and 3 were much higher than lesson 1, which indicated teacher's such skills been improved.

3.4   The Analysis of Interaction between Teacher and Students

In interaction matrix, all the cells on diagonal are steady state which shows a certain behavior appeared for more than 3 seconds. The area of row 1- 3 and column 1 to 3 is constructive integration cell and the area of row 7-8 and column 6 -7 is vicious cell.

Table 3 showed that the highest record was gotten in steady state cell which indicated the teacher mainly gave lecture in lesson 1. And higher frequencies were gotten in steady state cell 8-8 and 9-9 which meant students actively responding to the teacher and interacting with the teacher. During that time, the teacher proposed some open questions inspired the interaction between students and teacher.

From table 4, the highest loading tallies were gotten in steady state cell 9-9, indicating that the students expressed their opinion initiatively. But high records were also found in steady state cell 5-5 cell meant the teacher gave more lecture. In lesson 2, it showed interacting between students and teacher increased.

It was obviously, very high frequencies in steady state cell 9-9 were gained in Table 5. Combining with the observation of lesson 3, teacher's questions were very open and gave more time to group discussions, so the answers from students were creative, multifarious and independent. Several loading tallies in steady state cell 5-5 indicated the teacher mainly gave lecture in that time;   and also several loading tallies in steady state cell 3-3 showed the teacher was good at accepting students' opinion to promote further instruction.

Records in constructive integration cell of lesson 1 were 51, amounted to 6.33% of the whole records; lesson 2 was 21, amounted to 2.47%; lesson 3 was 64, amounted to 7.74%. These data indicated harmonious relationship between the teacher and students in all three classes. There were 4 records of lesson 1 in vicious cell, amounted to 0.5% of the whole records; no records in defective cell was gotten in lesson 2 and 3, which further showed the teacher and students in 3 sample lessons were harmonious.

3.5   The Analysis of Interaction between Teacher and Students

In the interaction matrixes, the records of behavior group (9, 9), (9, 3), (3, 3), (3, 9) and group (4), (4, 8), (8, 8), (8, 4) can show further course instruction model. The former group explored exploring - creating pattern, the latter was instruction - training pattern.

In table 3, the records in behavior groups (4, 4), (4, 8), (8, 8), (8, 4) were more than in (9, 9), (9, 3), (3, 3), (3, 9), which indicated that lesson 1 was question-answer pattern. Among behavior groups (4, 4), (4, 8), (8, 8), (8, 4), the records of behavior groups (4, 8) were 17 and 104 in (8,8), which stated the students responded teacher at the instant and for a long time, but only responded to the questions. High records in behavior group (9, 9) showed students extended teacher's questions with their own views and opinions, and also suggested that the teacher's questions were very open. However, the records of group (8, 4) were only 8 and group (3, 9) only 1, which indicated that the teacher was accustomed to the traditional pattern of asking and answering what were the shortcomings to be the pattern of creative answers.

In table 4, the frequency of behavior group (9, 9) was very high, which showed the students were active to talk during this time. But the records of behavior groups (4, 4), (4, 8), (8, 8), (8, 4), (9, 3), (3, 3) and (3, 9) were lower, indicated the teacher spent little time on guiding students, but gave more time to students' talk. Therefore, the instructional pattern of lesson 2 was not very distinct.

In table 5, the records of the behavior groups (4, 4), (4, 8), (8, 8) were obviously less than the behavior groups (9, 9), (9, 3), (3, 3), (3, 9). The creative enquiry pattern could be concluded in lesson 3. The students taking a long time for group discussion to express their opinion, the frequency of behavior group (9, 9) was very high. And as well groups (9, 3), (3, 3), indicated the teacher accepted the students' answers and then explained and promoted them. At the same time, except the time costing on students' group discussion, most of the class was spent on interaction and communication between teacher and students.

According to the analysis, we could found instructional pattern of teacher L was changing over the time, from the traditional question and answer pattern at the beginning to creative pattern in lesson 3, showed the teacher's ability guiding students been improved.

3.6   Variable Analysis

Flanders analyzed the data gained from the interaction matrix, and put forward 12 indicators (variables) to explain the implied significance behind teaching behavior [1]. According to the "Flanders variables analysis", beside the analysis above, there were several obvious variables reflected the changes of teaching behavior, as shown in table 6.

(1)The teacher question ratio is the time ratio of teacher asking questions to direct instruction (the time of teacher asking questions and the speech), higher the data, more questions used in the instruction. The Norm ("norm" was put forward by the Flanders et al after many studies) was approximately 26. Compared with lesson 1,

Table 6.   Summary of variable analysis results for three lessons

Variable	Abbreviation	Norm	Lesson 1 (2013.06)	Lesson 2 (2013.10)	Lesson 3 (2013.12)
Teacher Question Ratio	TQR	26	20.62%	21.05%	29.25%
Pupil Initiation Ratio	PIR	34	36.17%	95.59%	99.13%
Content Cross Ratio	CCR	55	52.61%	21.50%	17.05%

the teacher question ratio in lesson 2 & 3 were improved, but only lesson 3 was higher than the Norm, which indicated the teacher's ability in guiding was constantly increased however it's slowly.

(2)The pupil initiation ratio means time ratio of active talk amounting to students' talk, higher the data, students more actively expressing their views. The Norm is about 34 in Flanders' research. This ratio in lesson 1 was close to the norm; however, the ratio of lesson 2 and 3 was far higher than the Norm, which indicated students liked to talk in class. With the changing of teacher's instruction style, the classroom was becoming more and more open and democratic, and students did talking initiatively better.

(3) The content cross ratio refers to the time ratio of talk connecting previous discourse and rear to the whole class time. Higher data we got interactions between students and teacher inclines to further around the textbook content. And the Norm is about 55. The content cross ratio in lesson 1 was the highest and lesson 3 was the lowest. It indicated that the instruction content was not limited in text, but paid more attention on extension and integration with extracurricular knowledge, as well as the cultivation of students' abilities.

4   Discussion

According to the interaction analysis of the three lessons, changes of teacher in instruction had been found, and professional development of teacher L was showed.

4.1   The Change in Teaching Philosophy

Lesson 1 taking knowledge teaching as the major task, reflected the teaching idea was teacher-centered. While student-teacher's interactions kept stable friendly in the lesson 1, but it mostly depended on the questions designed by teacher. Students answered one question, and then the next one to reach the objectives, which was still the "question—answer" pattern. And the students could only turn around the teacher, learning passively, student-centered was not been realized.

The second and third Lesson left much time to students, embodying the instruction ideas of "student-centered" and "study first". The second lesson required students to be self-study before courses, and to teach other students as the role of "substitute teacher" in the classroom, giving students opportunity to show themselves. After that, students raised questions to discuss further. Lesson 2 formed a spiraling classroom model of "teacher guiding - students asking - teacher guiding - students asking again", which enabled students' thinking getting constantly development.

Knowledge building theory emphasizes "idea improvement " and "collective cognitive responsibility", and emphasizes on the progress of students' thinking ability and community development. Guiding by knowledge building, teacher L believed developing students' thinking was very important for students' future. The key of students' thinking development lied in guidance of teacher, rather than teacher's instruction. Thus, teacher L gradually gave the class open and democratic, and the idea of student-centered growing significantly. As a consequence, instruction of teacher L changed from "question—answer" pattern to "exploring-creating pattern", student asking questions and developing questions by themselves gradually.

4.2   Changes in the Instruction Model and Strategy

With the change of teacher L's teaching philosophy, instruction pattern and strategy used had also been changed. Instruction pattern of Lesson 1 was "teaching-based", teacher's "talking" accounted for a large proportion, and focused on knowledge imparting and grasping. Therefore, teachers spent a lot of time on the change of the characters' emotion in the lesson. In order to finish knowledge imparting and improve instruction efficiency, teacher L mainly used method of lecture and demonstration, students lightly passively listening.

Teacher L gradually realized the importance of "giving the classroom back to students and making students learn how to learn" after learning knowledge building theory. Therefore, teacher L had students self-studied in the lesson 2, and then solved problems by students. Teacher L changed the teaching methods by using "student-centered" instructional pattern. She integrated self-learning, reading guidance methods and discussion to improve students' enthusiasm and initiative in a certain extent. However, teacher L focused on students' learning on text itself, guiding to students was not enough and discussion among students was not sufficient.

In the third lesson, teacher L focused on the students' discussion using instruction strategies such as "heuristic instruction," "cooperative inquiry", "scaffolding", "discussion ", and "inquiry" and so on to divide students into small groups to inquire and develop questions. Besides asking questions from illuminating perspectives in interaction, teacher L also used "question scaffolding" concerned in knowledge building instruction to promote the in-depth discussions. At the end of lesson 3, students got deeper development in ideas put forward.

From the analysis on teacher L's instruction pattern and instruction strategies, teacher L had a substantial progress in instruction skills. Before that, teacher L studied the ideas of the new curriculum reform, and she also had the ideology of "teacher-directed, student-centered". But the difficulties still existed during the practice, "how to let students learn how to learn", "how to guide students learning better" had been puzzling her for a long time. From teacher L's three lessons, it is obviously she had realized the reason slowly and solved the problems gradually, so gained progress gradually.

4.3   The Development of the Practical Knowledge of Teachers

The practical knowledge of teachers is defined as: "teachers enacted their understanding of teaching based on reflecting and refining on their own teaching experience" [3, 4]. Chen also pointed out that practical knowledge of teachers was the knowledge that teachers doing by them and not only understanding in thoughts, but also work out by them.

As shown in Lesson 1, teacher L learned knowledge building in training at the beginning of March 2013 but had no in-depth understanding about the theory at first. Or she might learn and understand the knowledge building theory, but had difficulties in carrying out in class. Therefore, she still chose the "lecture-based" instruction method and the knowledge building theory brought no change in her general instruction. After a period of accumulation in knowledge and experience, teacher L had some change to make the class more open and democratic. However, teacher L simply returned the class to students and lacked inspirational guidance to students. Thus, students studied as usual and got no change on how to learn. In lesson 3, instruction ideal, pattern, strategy and method showed were enacted with knowledge building theory through learning in past semesters. She did knowledge building and achieved the goal to improve students' thinking capability.

The instruction process, teacher's talk behavior in the three lessons showed the development and improvement of teacher L's practical knowledge of teachers.

5   Conclusion

Teachers and students are the two sides of instruction process and the professional development of teachers can be realized in paying their attention to the development of students' study. The analysis of the teaching behavior and professional development in the three videos showed that teacher L changed and improved her instruction ideal, pattern and strategy as well as made a great progress in practical knowledge of teacher by learning and practicing knowledge building. Guided by knowledge building, the teacher promoted her instructional skill in many aspects.

With further development of global economy today, rapid progress in science and technology and fiercer international competition, education becomes more and more important. Teachers nowadays, are regarded as the foundation of education. Besides necessary professional knowledge and skills, teachers also need to learn advanced educational theory and interdisciplinary comprehensive knowledge. Only in this way, they can keep pace with the time, enhance their quality consistently and cultivate more and more high-quality talents for the development of our country. Although a lot of achievements on the study of teachers' professional development have been gained, it is still relatively lacking of research on combining instruction practice with new theories and new instruction methods teachers learn. How to promote the combination of theory and teaching practice effectively has been a very important question now. To promote teachers' professional development is not only the dimensions we continue to explore and reform further in the future, but also the direction teachers and researchers should be forwarding.

References

1. Flanders, N.A.: Analyzing teaching behavior. Addison-Wesley Publishing Company, MA (1970)
2. Lian, R.: The Teacher Professional Development. Higher Education Press, Beijing (2007)
3. Chen, X.: Setting up the Bridge of Practice and Theory: the Research of Teacher Practical Knowledge. Education Science Press, Beijing (2011)

4. Chen, X.: Qualitative Research Methods and Social Science Research. Education Science Press, Beijing (2000)
5. Xiao, F.: Interactive Analysis of Classroom Speech Act: A Kind of New Classroom Teaching Research Tools. Journal of Liaoning Normal University 2000(6), 40–44 (2000)
6. Guo, H., Lin, J.: The Introduction of Flanders Interaction Analysis System Support Software, http://163.21.34.135/main.htm
7. Zhang, Y., Chen, B., Scardamalia, M., Bereiter, C.: The construction from shallow to deep: the development of the theory of knowledge construction and its application analysis in China. Journal of Electrochemical Education Research 2012(9), 5–12 (2012)
8. Chen, W.: Knowledge Building: the Fusion of Cognition and Technology. Journal of Electrochemical Education Research 2011(6), 15–18 (2011)

Evaluation of Learning Website:
A Social Network Perspective

Nengshan Feng[1] and Xindong Ye[2, *]

[1] Department of Educational Information Technology, East China Normal University,
Zhongshan North Road 3663, 200062,Shanghai,P.R.China
[2] Department of Educational Technology, Wenzhou University
ChaShan Higher Education District , 325035, Wenzhou, P.R.China
shan92316@163.com, yxd@wzu.edu.cn

Abstract. With the rapid development of learning websites, website evaluation attracts more and more attention of the educators. In this paper, we study the current ways of evaluating learning websites and their shortages, and identify the features and advantages of social network in evaluating learning websites. The paper analyzes the possible interaction among learners in learning websites, and tries to find out whether the relevant elements of social network can be used as evaluation indexes in evaluating learning websites. Some initial research is conducted on the correlation between the relevant elements of social network and the evaluation elements of traditional website.

Keywords: Learning website, evaluation, social network, model.

1   Introduction

Different learning websites have different evaluation ways. The current evaluation mainly focuses on the website itself, such as the website's content, technology, effectiveness and development. Technology covers navigation design, information organization, management techniques, searching functions, medium selection etc., namely, the rationality of website interlinking, the balance of the information classification, the standard and entirety of management, the diversity of searching methods, response speed, fault tolerance and so on. Effectiveness covers the effectiveness and interactivity of the website information. Development focuses on click rate, interlinking, resource growth rate, technology progressing rate, information update cycle and the degree of internationalization.

The problem with the current evaluation of learning website is that the evaluation pays too much attention to the research of website as a carrier, ignoring the research of website users' behavior and the evaluation of the websites themselves. However, the current education research shows that learning happens in the interactivity among social organizations; in other words, the interactivity of learners in learning organization is an

---

* Corresponding author.

S.K.S. Cheung et al. (Eds.): ICHL 2014, LNCS 8595, pp. 312–322, 2014.
© Springer International Publishing Switzerland 2014

important reflection of learning happening. Then, can we evaluate website by researching the interactivity in the learning in learning websites? The research of social network provides a new perspective.

Social network is a relation system formed by the interactivity among social individuals. It is a mutual, relatively stable relationship among those individuals or organizations from certain fields. The goal of learning website is to serve learners who are similar to each other in many ways; thus, to evaluate learning websites from a perspective of social network is worthy of our attention and research.

2   Research Sketch

By analyzing the possible interaction of learners in learning websites and using social network's analytical method, the paper tries to find out whether the relevant elements of social network can become the evaluation index of learning websites' evaluation models. By comparing the statistic samples of the behavior features of the learning websites' learners with the data of questionnaire survey, the paper tries to use this objective variable of the social network to replace people's subjective variable and evaluates the learning websites.

2.1   Evaluation of the Relevant Elements of Social Network

The paper evaluates learning websites from five aspects: click rate, network centrality, network density, network intensity and small team, pays close attention to website learners' behavior, and uses the frequency of interactivity between learners and website to inquire into their tendency of development in future.

(a)   Click Rate

Click rate is the percentage of those who visit the website every day or during a certain period in a million people. The rate is the primary evaluation index of a website and also the most direct, convincing quantitative indicators. On the one hand, it is when users click and visit a website that a social network can be formed and we can use the social network's analytical method in analysis. Therefore, click rate is one of the indexes to evaluate learning websites.

(b)   Network Centrality

Network centrality is an index to measure minor activists' dependence to the whole network. In a website, a few learners act as leaders whose posts can attract other learners' attention and thus arouse interactivity among learners. Network centrality includes degree centrality, network central tendency and node mid centrality.

1   Degree centrality: it is an index to measure activists' effectiveness in the whole network, referring to the number of the nodes that have direct relation to a node. In this research, it refers to the sum of the number of a learner's posts, or out-degree, and the one of response posts he or she gets, or in-degree [1].

Out-degree is the number of the linking lines that start from a node when linking lines have direction. It is the sum of lines and ranks that correspond to the node in the linking matrix, namely the sum of posts with which an activist answers other activists [2]. In-degree refers to the number of response posts from other learners that an activist gets.

2   Network central tendency: based on node mid degree, the central tendency of the whole network is analyzed to understand the dependence degree of the whole network on the few activists [1].

3   Node mid centrality: it is an index to measure an activist's control degree on resources. If an activist is located at many network paths, he can be believed to be at an important position, because he can affect the group by controlling or misunderstanding information, and his node gets a higher mid centrality [3].

If the network mid centrality of a learning website is higher, the fixed group in it is more stable. In other words, the centralization of interactivity in a website can explain the order and comprehension of website's information management. Only when the learning resources are classified and managed, can learners rapidly obtain the resources they need and thus take an active part in the learning interactivity. Therefore, network centrality is one of the indexes to evaluate a learning website.

(c) Network Density

Network density is the ratio between the number of actual linking lines and the one of possible linking lines. It is a relevant index that indicates the density of close relationship in the net [2]. There can be a close or distant relation. Generally, a close team has much more cooperation behavior and information circulation is easier and job performance is better. A distant team, however, has some problems such as slow information circulation, less emotional support, low job satisfaction and so on [4].

(d) Network Intensity

Network intensity refers to the times of the interactivity between arbitrary two learners. If a learning website provides learners with many ways of interactivity, such as e-mail address, mailing list and forum, learners will actively participate, which can be indicated by user participation level. Network intensity can be reflected in the times of the interactivity between learners and learning resource, or among learners, and engine's searching information.

When learners are using website to learn, they have interactivity with website content as well as other learners, which forms the website's resources. If a learner faces difficulty in learning and gets help immediately, he or she will have more interest in learning and be more likely to visit the website again. The bigger is the times of interactivity between learners and resources, the bigger the website's network intensity is. If a learning website is linked to many other websites, the possibility of being visited increases, that is, when its click rate increases, its intensity becomes stronger. Therefore, network intensity is one of the indexes in the evaluation system of learning websites.

(e) Subgroup

A subgroup or a clique is a small team whose members are very close and thus form a subgroup. To put it in a popular way, a subgroup can be compared as a party [5]. Gathering degree clearly reflects the interactivity in a subgroup. Gathering degree is the ratio of the actual dual correlation coefficient and the possible dual correlation coefficient, and the index that measures network gathering degree by counting the relevant number of dual correlation [2]. The forming of subgroup greatly benefits the learners' learning in an education website, because a subgroup is usually based on affection and its members have many things in common, or they make up for each other and thus have better interactivity. The number of both its subgroups and members can reflect the participation of learners and also the value of an education website. Therefore, the number and quality of subgroup is an index of website evaluation system.

2.2   Relation between the Relevant Elements of Social Network and the Traditional Elements of Websites

The five aspects above are the relevant elements of social network. We believe that click rate is related with indexes such as the comprehensiveness of learning website's content, the diversity of searching methods, the website's effectiveness and response speed. When learners have high satisfaction and loyalty with the website, they keep joining the society. Meanwhile, network density is related with the service efficiency of website's information, the increase rate of resources, the completeness of interactivity faculty and the effectiveness. When the learners' participation motivation is strong, they are willing to communicate with each other and help each other. The users communicate more times in web site, the density of their social networks is larger. Therefore, we produce a hypothesis as indicated in the following table, and test it.

2.3   Design and Complementation of RESEARCH

1)   Research Methods

  i)   method of literature consultation
  ii) social network analytical methods (social measure, diagram, matrix)
  iii) data statistics
  SPSS 11.5, Ucinet 6.0 and Excel2003 are used to do matrix operation and correlation data analysis and to further research the group feature of website forum.

2)   Data Statistics and Result Analysis

The paper adopts the method of social measure and selects "China English Learning Forum" for testing. The interval times of posting a message and posting a reply are quite different. For example, some host posts get replies just in several minutes (even in one minute); some host posts get replies in several days. In this case, to choose one day as the period time of research cannot reflect the interactivity relation situation [2].

Table 1. The possible relation between social network's elements and learners and evaluation indexes

social network elements	learners' attitude	Website's evaluation indexes from perspective of social network
click rate	satisfaction degree and loyalty degree	the completeness and authority of content; the diversity of searching methods; effectiveness; response speed.
network density	participation motivation and loyalty	the completeness of interactive faculty; the effectiveness of information service; effectiveness degree; the increase rate of resource.
network intensity	participation motivation	user's participation degree; the completeness of interactive faculty; the increase rate of technology; the update period of information.
network centrality	participation motivation	the authority, creative level, individuation of information provider.
subgroup	knowledge management participation motivation	the richness of inner linking; management standard.

Because of this, the research's test time is one week, during which in the forum there are 3210 posts and 203 authors including those who put posts during the week to reply the host posts that are not put in the week. The paper chooses three days of the week for specific analysis. In these three days there are 41 learners whose posts are 672. These authors are this paper's research objects and samples.

i) Diagram Analysis

According to testees' choice and being chosen, the paper uses Ucinet 6.0 to draw a community diagram, which is a social network table formed by learners during their learning in the forum. With the diagram, we can clearly see the whole social network situation in the learning website [4].

According to the three days' community diagrams, we can see that the structure of forum is well-knit. Though there are margin students (referring to those who don't choose nobody else and are not chosen by others), the whole forum forms a complete entirety with a clear gathering center. We can see that learners interact enough during their learning and the structure of learning participation is very stable.

ii) Sample's Matrix Demonstration

The research uses social relation matrix to study the interactivity feature of the learners in the learning website's forum and show the website's quality by analyzing learners'

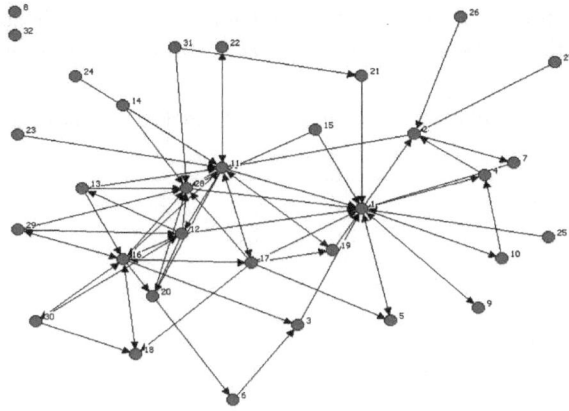

Fig. 1. The community diagram of the forum in the first day

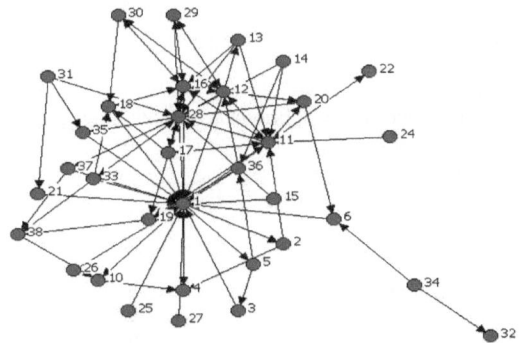

Fig. 2.   The community diagram of forum in the second day

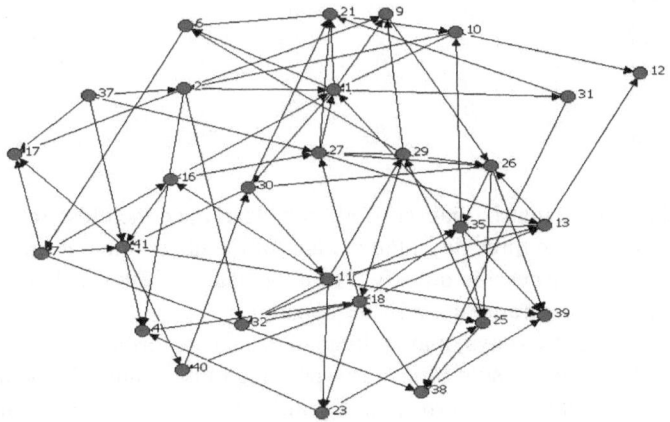

Fig. 3. The community diagram of the forum in the third day

interactivity. Therefore, discussion relation that is embodied by host posts and replying posts should be first marked in relation matrix. Tables are as follows:

Table 2.   Indirect matrix abbreviated simple diagram(the first day)

	1	2	3	4	5	6	7	8
1	0	1	0	1	1	0	0	0
2	0	0	0	0	0	0	1	0
3	1	0	0	0	0	0	0	0
4	0	1	0	0	0	0	0	0
5	1	0	0	0	0	0	0	0
6	0	0	1	0	0	0	0	0
7	1	0	0	0	0	0	0	0
8	0	0	0	0	0	0	0	0
9	1	0	0	0	0	0	0	0
10	0	0	0	1	0	0	0	0
11	1	0	0	0	0	0	0	0
12	1	0	0	0	0	0	0	0
13	0	0	0	0	0	0	0	0
14	0	0	0	0	0	0	0	0
15	1	0	0	0	0	0	0	0
16	0	0	1	0	0	0	0	0
17	1	0	0	0	1	0	0	0

Table 3.   Indirect matrix abbreviated simple diagram(the second day)

	1	2	3	4	5	6	7	8	9
1	0	1	0	1	1	0	0	0	
2	1	0	0	0	0	0	0	0	
3	1	0	0	0	0	0	0	0	
4	1	0	0	0	0	0	0	0	
5	1	0	0	0	0	0	0	0	
6	1	0	0	0	0	0	0	0	
7	1	0	0	0	0	0	0	0	
8	0	0	0	0	0	0	0	0	
9	1	0	0	0	0	0	0	0	
10	1	0	0	0	0	0	0	0	
11	1	0	0	0	0	0	0	0	
12	1	0	0	0	0	0	0	0	
13	0	0	0	0	0	0	0	0	
14	0	0	0	0	0	0	0	0	
15	1	0	0	0	0	0	0	0	
16	1	0	0	0	0	0	0	0	
17	1	0	0	0	0	0	0	0	

According to the matrix diagrams, we can clearly see the close interactivity among learners. During these three days, the number of members remains unchanged and new members can join discussion quickly. From the data, we can see that the network density, intensity and centrality are all very apparent.

Next, we choose two days' matrix diagram to analyze forum's degree. In the diagram, a node's in-degree is the sum of its corresponding ranks' values in the matrix; a node's out-degree is the sum of its corresponding lines' values in the matrix; thus, this node's degree centrality is shown by the sum of all its corresponding lines' and ranks' values.

Based on this, the paper calculates the out-degree and in-degree in the first two days of all members in "China English Learning Forum", which are demonstrated as follows:

Table 4.   Indirect matrix abbreviated simple diagram(the fourth day)

	1	2	4	6	7	9	10	11	12
1	0	0	0	1	0	1	0	0	
2	1	0	1	0	0	1	0	0	
4	0	0	0	0	0	0	0	0	
6	0	0	0	0	1	0	0	0	
7	0	0	0	0	0	0	0	0	
9	0	0	0	0	0	0	0	0	
10	1	1	0	0	0	0	0	0	
11	0	0	0	0	0	0	0	0	
12	0	0	0	0	0	0	0	0	
13	0	0	0	0	0	0	0	0	
16	1	0	0	0	1	0	0	0	
17	0	0	0	0	0	0	0	0	
18	0	0	1	0	0	0	0	0	
21	0	0	0	1	0	0	1	0	
23	0	0	1	0	0	0	0	0	
25	0	0	0	0	0	0	0	0	
26	0	0	0	0	0	0	0	0	

```
                              1               2
                         OutDegree        InDegree
                        -----------     -----------
             16            9.000           7.000
             11            8.000           9.000
             12            7.000           4.000
             17            6.000           2.000
              1            5.000          21.000
             30            3.000           2.000
             13            3.000           1.000
             29            3.000           2.000
              2            2.000           1.000
             18            2.000           3.000
             15            2.000           0.000
             20            2.000           3.000
             19            2.000           0.000
             14            2.000           0.000
             31            2.000           0.000
             24 |         1.000           0.000
              9            1.000           1.000
             10            1.000           1.000
              3            1.000           0.000
              4            1.000           1.000
              5            1.000           1.000
              6            1.000           0.000
              7            1.000           0.000
             28            1.000          10.000
             25            1.000           0.000
             26            1.000           0.000
             27            1.000           0.000
             22            1.000           1.000
             21            1.000           1.000
             23            1.000           0.000
              8            0.000           0.000
             32            0.000           0.000
```

Fig.4. Statistics of the forum in the first day

From the social network analysis of the whole net, we can see that different community members have different in-degree and out-degree and that compared with other members, those whose degree centrality is high have more linking lines and are leaders in the forum [6]. In the above analytical diagram, the degree centrality of 16,11,12,17 is higher and more stable.

3   Relevant Research on Social Network Elements and the Traditional Website's Evaluation Indexes

After analyzing many parameters of "China English Learning Forum", we can't help guessing the relationship between the whole network's relevant elements and website evaluation indexes. Next, we research on the relationship between degree centrality, an element of social network, and community satisfaction degree, community loyalty, community participation motivation, knowledge management and so on. The reason why degree centrality is chosen is that what degree centrality represents is the degree of forum's members' choosing or being chosen. As we know, a person's honor can be reflected by the number of people around him or her; the higher a person's degree centrality is, the higher his or her honor is [7]. Here, we take the relevant data in "China English Learning Forum" as reference data. The relevant data are obtained through questionnaire survey and Likert Scales.

The targets of the survey are members of China English Learning Forum. The questionnaire survey is carried out online and 40 questionnaires are sent out and 32 valid questionnaires are collected. Narrative statistic analysis is done on samples, and the average number and standard deviation of community participation motivation, community satisfaction degree, community loyalty, the satisfaction degree towards information sharing and so on.

Next, we use the software SPSS 11.5 to do a correlation analysis. We get the correlation between social network elements and evaluation indexes after analyzing the data of both network density in China English Learning Forum and questionnaire survey, and adopting the correlation analysis of rank variables in correlation coefficient analytical methods. Through analysis, Table 5's structure is obtained.

According to the data in Table 5, the correlation variable between the degree centrality in China English Learning Forum and community satisfaction degree is 0.053, and the correlation coefficient's confidential level is 0.725 and above 0.01; that's to say, above the notable level of 0.01, the correlation of two groups is normal. The degree centrality and community loyalty of China English Learning Forum is 0.440.The correlation coefficient confidential level is 0.833 and above 0.01, that's to say, above the notable level of 0.01, the correlation of two groups is normal.

The degree centrality and group participation motivation of China English Learning Forum is 0.775, and the correlation coefficient confidential level is 0.702 and above 0.01, that is to say, above the notable level of 0.01, the correlation of the two groups is common. The degree centrality and knowledge sharing activity of China English Learning Forum is 0.230, and correlation coefficient confidential level is 0.934 and above 0.01, that is to say, above the notable level of 0.01, the correlation of the two groups is common.

In order to understand the relationship among them directly, we input the data of point-degree centrality, group satisfaction degree, group loyalty, group participation motivation and knowledge management into Excel 2003, and draw broken lines demonstrated as in Fig.6.

Table 5. The relationship diagram of centrality and satisfaction degree, loyalty, participation motivation and knowledge management

		Centrality	Satisfaction degree	Loyalty	Participation motivation	Knowledge management
Centrality	Person Correlation	1	-.053	.044	.776	.023
	Sig. (2-tailed)	.	.725	.830	.702	.934
	N	32	32	32	32	31
Satisfaction degree	Person Correlation	-.053	1	.665 *	.827 *	.787 *
	Sig. (2-tailed)	.725	.	.000	.000	.000
	N	32	32	32	32	31
Loyalty	Person Correlation	-.044	.665 *	1	.762 *	.811 *
	Sig. (2-tailed)	.830	.000	.	.000	.000
	N	32	32	32	32	31
Participation motivation	Person Correlation	.776	.827 *	.762 *	1	.905 *
	Sig. (2-tailed)	.702	.000	.000	.	.000
	N	32	32	32	32	31
Knowledge management	Person Correlation	.023	.787 *	.811 *	.905 *	1
	Sig. (2-tailed)	.934	.000	.000	.000	.
	N	31	31	31	31	31

**. Correlation is significant at the 0.01 level (2-tailed).

From the figures above, we can see that the higher the degree centrality of learners is, the higher the community satisfaction degree and loyalty are, then the learners are more willing to take part in learning and group activities. Thus, it is feasible to use the relevant elements of social network instead of learners' subjective ways as indexes to evaluate learning websites.

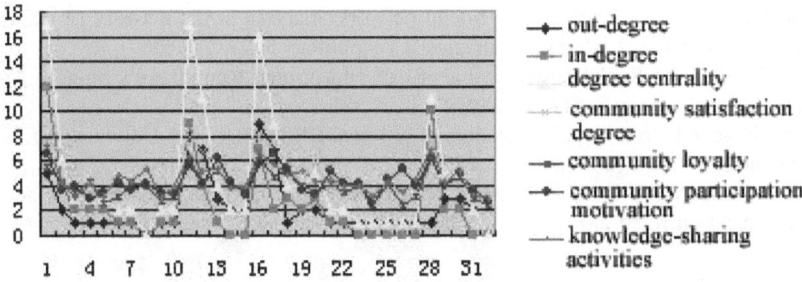

Fig.6. Related diagram of degree centrality and community satisfaction degree, community loyalty, community participation motivation and knowledge-sharing activies

4   Conclusion

No matter where it is, home or abroad, what methods to be taken to evaluate website and how to choose sample website reasonably is a problem researchers must face.

In this research, we try to evaluate learning website through the perspective of social network. By comparing one of the social network's elements and the data of questionnaire survey, the paper can safely make the conclusion that we can use the elements of social network's degree centrality to show learner's satisfaction degree and loyalty towards learning website. In the research, we discover that the higher the degree centrality is, the higher the learners' satisfaction degree and loyalty towards website are. Meanwhile, during the research progress, we also discover that network intensity, subgroup method and click rate can all reflect the participation initiative of learners. The higher the learners' satisfaction degree, loyalty and participation initiative are, the higher the value of an education is. Therefore, we can draw a conclusion that social network can be used as a way of learning websites evaluation, that is to say, with the analysis of the relevant factors of the social network, we can   evaluate the learning website.

Acknowledgments. This work is supported by Zhejiang Provincial Natural Science Foundation of China (LY13F020021) and the Philosophy and Social Sciences Foundation of the Government of Wenzhou(13wsk012). The authors are grateful for the anonymous reviewers who made constructive comments.

References

1.   Shui, H.Y.: Social network analysis on the participation characters of the members of primary school writing virtual communities. Nanjing Normal University, Nanjing (2011)
2.   Bai, S.Y.: Characteristics of internet interaction based on a study of BBS. Journal of HIT (Social Sciences Edition) 3, 91–92 (2002)
3.   Hu, Y., Wang, L.: Social network analysis in CSCL: A case study. J. Open Education Research 5, 57–60 (2006)
4.   Chen, S.J., Ye, X.D., Zhou, W.C.: Social network analyses in the network of curriculum evaluation of research. J. Modern Educational Technology 3, 27–28 (2009)
5.   Ye, X.D., Qiu, F.: Social network analysis of educational technology's blog. J. Modern Educational Technology 5, 51–52 (2008)
6.   Yu, H.: Research on the opinion leaders of political BBS. Huazhong University of Science & Technology, Wuhan (2007)
7.   Li, Y.: Comparative analysis of microblog relationship network and social relationship network based on relationship network analysis perspective. Guangxi University, Nanning (2012)

Chinese Composition Teachers' Commentary Styles and Patterns in a Tablet-Based Marking Environment

K.K. Ying, Kat Leung, Roger Lee, and Daisy Chow

Caritas Institute of Higher Education
Hong Kong SAR, China
{kkying,kleug,rlee,plchow}@cihe.edu.hk

Abstract. This paper is a preliminary study on the general marking process of Chinese writing teachers in a tablet-based marking platform, which focuses on identifying the predominant commentary styles and patterns of the Chinese writing teachers on a newly developed tablet-based marking platform. Two participating teachers were recruited to take part in an on-site experiment in which they were requested to mark four compositions written by their students on a tablet-based marking platform. It is found that one of the participants was over-generic in his overall comments and both of them tended to emphasize evaluation over instruction in their marking. We try to account for these findings in terms of their narrow conception of the role of teachers in composition marking merely as "proofreaders", "evaluators" and "judges", and propose the need to promote a more comprehensive notion of writing teachers.

1 Introduction

Past studies investigated composition marking mainly from the perspective of *scoring* and the research subjects are treated as *raters of examination papers* and only few of them were able to capture the primary concern and complicated cognitive process of the markers as *writing teachers*. These studies are highly inadequate in depicting the intricate relationship among students, teachers and the teaching environment. It is also worth noting that despite a great deal of prior L1 and L2 English writing researches on the topic of teacher responses to student writings, little information has been found that is either relevant to L1 Chinese composition writing or teachers' commentary styles and patterns in an on-screen marking setting. To address these research gaps, the present study in the form of descriptive analysis was guided by the following research questions:

1. What are the predominant commentary styles and patterns of the Chinese writing teachers in a tablet-based marking platform?
2. Are there any commonalities and differences in the characteristics of written feedback provided to their students between the Chinese writing teacher subjects marking on the tablet-based marking platform and those teachers employing traditional paper-based marking method?

This paper is essentially a report on the findings obtained from a relatively small-scale pilot study to a formal and full-scale research in the future, in which two Chinese teachers are recruited for the purpose.

S.K.S. Cheung et al. (Eds.): ICHL 2014, LNCS 8595, pp. 323–334, 2014.
© Springer International Publishing Switzerland 2014

2   Literature Review

Various analytical models and frameworks for composition research regarding teacher responses to student writings have been proposed and adopted by past researchers. Diverse as they are, these models and frameworks can be understood in terms of four basic dimensions of the nature of teacher feedback, namely its focal, functional, scoping and attitudinal dimension.

2.1   Focal Dimension

The focal dimension of teacher feedback refers to the general orientation of the feedback. Teacher feedback is content-oriented if it focuses on substantive issues concerning the content of the composition, whereas it is form-oriented if it focuses on formal issues like mistakes in spelling, vocabulary and other grammatical errors.

The choice between giving students content-oriented or form-oriented feedback has been a source of debate in composition research regarding teacher responses to student writings since the 1970s. Earlier studies reported that English language teachers were more concerned with error correction, focusing on giving students feedback on the surface language errors in spelling, vocabulary and grammar (Beach 1976; Hendrickson 1980; Lalande 1982; Robbs et.al. 1986). Such kind of form-oriented marking approach was criticized by a few writing researchers and they began to question the effectiveness of form-based feedback. Some argued that it was a waste of time and effort for teachers to focus mainly on students' language errors in writing (Knoblauch & Brannon 1982; Robbs et al. 1986). Others even went further to suggest that teachers' emphasis on error correction can produce a negative impact on students' writing ability since it may mislead them to take the task of draft revision merely as a proofreading exercise (Sommers 1982).

2.2   Functional Dimension

The functional dimension of teacher feedback refers to the pragmatic aims of the feedback the teachers attempt to achieve. The distinction between directive and facilitative feedback has been widely discussed. When it comes to the nature of directive feedback, different researchers may have various ways of categorization and classification focuses. Three sub categories of directive feedback have been identified by Ravichandran (1996), namely evaluative comments, instructional comments and questioning comments. Ravichandran's sub-categorization of directive feedback focused on the traditional role of individual writing instructor as a teacher and an evaluator when assessing and marking students' compositions. Instead of the term directive feedback, Straub (1997) grouped "criticism", "commands" and "correction" under the category of "controlling comments". As the terminology suggests, Straub obviously had a low regard for this kind of feedback and tried to highlight the problem with this kind of comments in that they were usually found too directive and appropriative in nature. The concept of directive feedback of Underwood (2008) can be seen as a combination of Ravichandran's and Straub's models. Three types of teacher feedback were classified as "directive feedback": (1) comments that provided students with explicit remarks for revision (including criticism); (2) comments that gave clear and specific direction to student writers (e.g. using grammatical rules to guide students to rewrite their texts); and (3) highlighting or corrections of errors directly on the compositions.

While the researchers mentioned above were divided in their views on the nature of directive feedback, they defined and classified facilitative feedback in more or less the same way. Straub's (1997) distinction between comments of advisory nature and praise bears an uncanny resemblance to Ravichandran's (1996) sub-categorization of facilitative feedback into "teachers own opinion and suggestion" and "positive comments and encouragement". In addition to its advisory nature, Underwood (2008) emphasized that teachers preferred using facilitative feedback to provide students with hints on revising drafts in the forms of questions and reflection.

2.3   Scoping Dimension

The scoping dimension of teacher feedback refers to the specificity of the feedback. Some writing researchers have tried to divide teacher written comments in terms of the scope of feedback, depending on how specific they are. Though findings on the effectiveness of teacher feedback types are still inconclusive to-date, past studies indicated that both researchers and students did not welcome comments that are vague, overly generic and too readily applicable across different student texts (Mc Gee 1999). Remarks such as "explain further", "more details needed" and "develop the idea" have long been considered as a source of frustration to students as they constantly find these comments not very useful (Bardine et al 2000; Ferris 1995). By contrast, results of related studies consistently revealed that students preferred receiving specific feedback from writing teachers, especially those capable of pinpointing the particular writing errors they committed and how to correct them or do better in terms of content and structure on the final drafts (Ferris 1995; Straub 1997; McGee 1999). It was also reported that comments including explicit suggestions on revision have a positive effect on the writing quality of the beginner writers and ESL learners (Bitchener et al. 2005; Suigita 2006).

2.4   Attitudinal Dimension

Finally, the attitudinal dimension of teacher feedback refers to the attitude of marker displayed in his written comments, which can be either positive or negative. Attempts have been made to assess the impacts of negative and positive comments on students' writing performance and revision success respectively. It was evident that students were more likely to accept positive comments, praise in particular, as opposed to negative feedback (Ferris 1995; McGee 1999; Underwood 2008). However, results of a few composition researches reminded us that praise alone does not necessarily enhance students' writing quality, albeit positive changes on students' writing attitude and their amount of writing after receiving positive comment treatment were found in a handful of related studies (Beason 1993). In regard to evaluative feedback, student surveys showed that student writers were generally frustrated by criticism and purely negative comments were found harmful to the motivation and self-image of the students (Ferris 1995; Connors & Lunsford, 1993; Storms & Sheingold 1999). Besides praise and criticism, mitigation language, which refers to comments that include both praise and criticism, is also identified in many composition studies as one of the most prevalent types of evaluative feedback. It can start with a positive comments followed by negative ones, or vice-versa.

3   Methodology

The pilot study was conducted in the form of an on-site experiment, where each of the two participating teachers was asked to mark four pieces of composition written by their students. An interview was then conducted with the participants after they finished marking the first two compositions by students with higher writing ability to understand what they had been going through during the marking process. After the interview, the participants continued with the second stage of the experiment in which they engaged in marking the remaining two compositions by students with lower writing ability. Another interview with the same set of questions was conducted with the participants after they finished marking these two compositions.

3.1   Participants

As a preliminary to a full-scale research, this pilot study recruited two experienced Chinese language teachers, who had been teaching Chinese for over twenty years and possessed rich experience in marking public examination papers in composition writing.

3.2   Instruments

Marking Platform. The general procedure of the pilot study is as follows. Before the commence of the experiment, the four target compositions were scanned and saved as pdf files to the tablets in which our composition marking recording system has been installed. Then, during the experiment, each of the participants was given one of these tablets and requested to mark the compositions on it. They were able to put down any symbols, write down any notes and comments and make any necessary corrections on the screen in exactly the same way as they normally did when they marked on the hardcopies. The system allows the researchers to check up the recordings with the system afterward to review and pinpoint every single symbol, comment and correction marked on the compositions and the verbal description reporting what the participants had in mind during the marking process.

Writing Samples. In this pilot study, a total of eight student compositions were adopted for the on-site marking purpose. Each participating teachers were requested to provide four student writings. Among the four writers of the selected compositions, two of them are outstanding writers, and the remaining two are below average in their writing abilities among their peers.

4   Analysis and Discussion

From the pilot study, the research team discovers two significant points worth discussing, namely the lack of specificity in the overall comments of Teacher A and the general tendency of putting the emphasis on evaluation over instruction of both of the participants.

4.1   Lack of Specificity in the Overall Comments of Teacher A

While there is still no consensus among Chinese and Western scholars on what the most ideal and effective form of feedback is, they do agree that feedback which is vague, overly generic and too easily applicable across different student texts is ineffective as it fails to help students make their corrections and improve their writing (Siegel 1982; Sommers 1982; Straub 1997; Leki 1990;). Do the feedbacks of Teacher A and B suffer from these drawbacks?

Generally speaking, the overall comments written by Teacher A are obviously more generic and formulaic. Most of their wording is used repeatedly, giving the impression that he only treated the marking as some sort of routine work. It can be observed from the following examples:

Table 1. Selected Comments of Teacher A

Selected Comments of Teacher A	
1st text	Smooth and clear expression
	More detailed depiction of the photo should be made
	Able to express feelings with the use of objects
2nd text	Smooth and clear expression
	Thoughtful choice of vocabulary
	Realize one's own happiness from the photo of disaster

Comparatively, the overall comments given by Teacher B are more specific and seem to be tailor-made for each particular student. Examples include:

Table 2. Selected Comments of Teacher B

Selected Comments of Teacher B	
1st text	Only a few parts are relevant to the topic. Hasty writing. Need to redo.
2nd text	Able to write relevantly to the topic. Intentional employment of rhetoric. Brilliant sentences. Beware of typos.
3rd text	The theme never shows up until the last part, which is not appropriate for propositional composition. Better let readers know you have not been off topic in each paragraph. Beautiful wording, yet so many typos that they threaten to distort the meaning.

How much time did the participating teachers spend on their overall comments? Judging from the think-aloud protocol, both of them wrote the overall comments first and scored afterwards. They started writing down their overall comments as soon as they finished marking the last paragraph of each composition. Apart from the length of the comments, the variation in the time they spent on their overall comments was to a large extent due to the different commenting procedures they employed. Teacher B always wrote his overall comment in two separate stages. He wrote the first part of his overall comments right after he finished marking. He then added some further comments after rating the composition. This special practice explains why he spent more time than Teacher A in writing the overall comments. The time consumption of them was shown below:

Table 3. Time Spent on Writing Overall Comment

	Teacher A	Teacher B
1st text (S1/S11)	86 s	43 s
2nd text (S2/S12)	61 s	110 s (82+28)
3rd text (S5/S13)	84 s	193 s (129+64)
4th text (S6/S15)	72 s	102 s (75+27)
Average (single text)	96.8 s	112 s

From the above data, it can be observed that Teacher A is obviously faster than Teacher B in writing the overall comments, with an average difference of 15 seconds. This seems to be the result of the overly generic and formulaic style of Teacher A.

4.2   Emphasis on Evaluation over Instruction

Another noteworthy feature is that the comments of both Teacher A and B are predominantly evaluative and barely instructional. Their comments are predominantly evaluative in that most of their responses are basically value judgments expressing praise or criticism. Moreover, they are barely instructional in that their comments seldom consist in any substantial advice and instructions on how to revise and improve their writing. The distribution of various kinds to responses of Teacher A and B is listed in the following table:

Table 4. Frequency and Percentage of Feedback Offered by Teacher A and Teacher B

	Teacher A		Teacher B		Teacher A + Teacher B	
	Marginal comments	Overall comments	Marginal comments	Overall comments	Marginal comments	Overall comments
Positive Evaluation	0 (0%)	6 (54.5%)	6 (18.8%)	3 (30%)	6 (18.8%)	9 (40.9%)
Negative Evaluation	0 (0%)	2 (18.2%)	13 (40.6%)	2 (20%)	13 (40.6%)	4 (18.2%)
Positive Evaluation followed by Negative Evaluation	0 (0%)	0 (0%)	1 (3.1%)	3 (30%)	1 (3.1%)	3 (13.6%)
Suggestion	0 (0%)	3 (27.3%)	12 (37.5%)	3 (30%)	12 (37.5%)	6 (27.3%)
Total	0 (0%)	11 (100%)	32 (100%)	10 (100%)	32 (100%)	22 (100%)

In the table above, "positive evaluation" refers to praise and positive affirmation given to students' performance, whereas "negative evaluation" is taken as "criticism", usually given against any faults or deficiencies spotted in students' writing. Comparatively speaking, the overall comments of Teacher A are more affirmative, focusing mainly on linguistic expression (e.g. "Smooth and clear expression"), wording (e.g. "Thoughtful vocabulary"), and meaning (e.g. "Able to highlight the gratitude towards mother's care"). Concerning the attitudinal dimension of his feedback, the marginal comments of Teacher B reflect that his feedback is comparatively more negative and critical. The number of different kinds of marginal comments and the time spent on them by Teacher B are listed as follows:

Table 5. The Kinds of Items Commented and the Time Spent on them by Teacher B

Different Kinds of Marginal Comments	Teacher B		
	Frequency	Average Thinking Time for Each Item	Total Commenting Time for Each Item
Wording	2	0.5 s	19 s
Accuracy	2	0.5 s	5 s
Relevancy	14	1.29 s	24.6 s
Incomplete Meaning	10	2.3 s	27.7 s
Structure	4	2.75 s	21.75 s
Total	**32**		

Most of the marginal comments of Teacher B are concerned with the failure of students in writing relevantly to the topic assigned, followed by quite a number of comments on unsubstantial content and incompleteness in meaning. Finally, there are also a few comments on paragraphing, structural, grammatical and wording problems. On the other hand, Teacher B spent the longest period of time, more than 2 seconds on average, on deliberation in face of problems with the structure and content of the compositions. It takes him only about 1.5 seconds regarding relevancy and less than half a second regarding wording and accuracy.

Apart from these, Teacher B liked to comment in a "positive followed by negative evaluation" style. That is, in order to reduce the sense of criticism, he usually talked about the weaknesses of and the problems with compositions only after mentioning their strengths and merits. Examples are:

Table 6. Summary of Comments by Teacher B

		Examples
Positive Evaluation	Marginal Comment	Echoing the topic; relevant to the topic; appropriate to the topic; beginning to touch on the theme.
	Overall comment	Intentional employment of rhetoric; able to express feelings with the use of objects; brilliant sentences.
Negative Evaluation	Marginal Comment	Weird sentence; Still irrelevant to the topic; unsubstantial.
	Overall comment	Illegible handwriting; Only a few parts are relevant to the topic; Hasty writing.
Positive, and then Negative Evaluation	Marginal Comment	Concrete description but the theme is not clear.
	Overall comment	Beautiful wording, yet so many typos that they threaten to distort the meaning.
Suggestion	Marginal Comment	The sentence should be written more smoothly and clearly; proper explanation should be given. A clear account should be provided.
	Overall comment	More detailed depiction of the photo should be made; Feelings should be expressed with the photo.

Such a kind of "positive followed by negative evaluation" response shares a similar ideal with the "sentential" response proposed by Ferris et al. (1997) and the "dialectical" response proposed by the mainland scholar Cai Wei (2004). "Dialectical" response can also be called "Positive-Negative" or "Praise-Criticism" response. Commenting on all the strengths and weaknesses of students' texts, teachers usually praise before they criticize and give more positive comments than negative ones. Although Cai thought that "this type of response is the most effective in composition rating" (page 40), the effectiveness of this responding style is still controversial and demands further investigation to determine due to insufficient empirical researches in the area.

Why the responses of both Teacher A and B are judged as "barely instructional"? From the data collected, we can see that the instructional responses they gave are far outnumbered by the evaluative ones. Since Teacher A mainly marked in the form of direct correction without giving marginal comments, and only 3 items are instructional among the 11 items in his overall comments, we shall focus on the performance of teacher B in the following discussion.

In the past, writing scholars thought that teachers' feedback should provide concrete writing suggestions for students instead of merely pinpointing the merits and problems of the compositions. In other words, evaluative feedback alone is considered inadequate and teachers have to provide instructional advice for revision as well as future writing. Scholars stressed repeatedly that the writing suggestions of teachers should be "constructive" (Ho Man-koon 1997, 2007, meaning that the teachers' feedback should not only tell students what and how but also why to correct. Otherwise, even if the students do the corrections as required, they may not be sufficiently impressed about their problems, let alone really learn from the responses and corrections. Therefore, it is vital to explain to the students the reasons why the revisions and corrections are needed to be done. Can the marginal and overall comments of Teacher B realize this principle? Consider the following excerpts from his rating scripts:

Table 7. Examples of the Marginal and Overall Comments of Teacher B

Marginal Comment		**Better use the words** 「的話」
	1.	Better expand on this paragraph
	2.	Need to explain why it is scaring
	3.	Supplement the point with appropriate explanation
	4.	Appropriate feelings should be added
Overall comment	5.	Better delete the part about Mr Wan and expand on the 2 episodes where someone holding umbrellas passed by and your feelings towards them.

At the first glance, most of the examples above would be generally considered as "concrete" suggestions for revision since they enable the students to know exactly what went wrong with their compositions and how they should revise and correct. However, the feedback of Teacher B usually sounds appropriative in that he never explained to the students the reasons for the changes needed throughout the marking process. He always acted as if he were the writer himself, commanding the students where to expand, where to add more information and which words to be used as better substitutes. Such kind of directive feedback bas been criticized by past researchers (Ravichandran 1996; Staub 1997; Underwood 2008). As early as the

1980's, Brannon and Knoblauch (1982) pointed out a common malady in teachers' feedback, namely that teachers generally focus on the difference between the actual drafts submitted by students and some Ideal Texts supposed to be composed by some ideal students existing only in the mind of the teachers. Brannon and Knoblauch stressed that this practice would, in the long run, produce far worse influence upon the future development of the writing ability of the students than not giving any feedback at all. Sommers (1982) criticized the directive style of feedback on the ground that it tends to divert students' attention from fulfilling their objectives in writing to speculating about the hidden implication behind teachers' feedback. Sometimes, the revisions and corrections are simply done to please and satisfy their teachers instead of improve the quality of their writing. What is said in the literature above deserves all frontline writing teachers to reflect upon the proper purpose and function of their feedback.

From the past researches, we know that English writing teachers prefer to use "hedges" and "rhetoric questions" in their comments in order to avoid the appropriative effect of the comments on the writing process of the students. Unfortunately, empirical researches showed that such feedback strategies were neither effective nor welcomed by students. Firstly, there seems to be no close relationship between the use of hedges by teachers and the active undertaking of correction by ESL students. Moreover, researches also showed that students usually fail to understand, or even misunderstand, the motive and reason why teachers use the hedges (Ferris 1997, 1999; Ferris & Hedgcock 2005)

The "predominantly evaluative and barely instructional" style of both Teacher A and B clearly reflects their views towards composition marking, especially the role played by teachers. They read students' texts basically from the perspective of evaluators, taking the main task of a teacher to be evaluating students' writing performance. They usually forgot about their role of facilitators and neglected making proper use of marginal and overall comments to facilitate students in correcting and revising their compositions by themselves. As mentioned before, a number of local scholars keep urging that the responsibility of correction should be borne by students themselves and should not be transferred to teachers (Ho Man-koon 1997; Tze Shek-kam 1983; Sum Siu-ki 1990). Students should understand that the whole "writing process" includes all the "checking, reviewing, revising and rewriting" phases subsequent to the writing of the first drafts, all of which are indispensable (Ho Man-koon 1997). Accordingly, teachers' comments should be able to guide the students through the steps of "re-reading", "reviewing" and "revising" their own texts and it is not appropriate for teachers to give too concrete suggestions for revision. Only the students themselves are the writing subjects and they should be fully responsible for directing the development of their own compositions.

5   Conclusion

This paper attempts to explore the views of the participants Teacher A and B concerning (1) the role of teachers in composition marking and (2) the allocation of responsibility of revision, based on the findings concerning the types and nature of their feedback to students' compositions collected in the pilot study. We find that, first of all, their marking approaches reveal their restricted understanding of the role of writing teachers in composition marking. In adopting a correction-oriented approach of marking, Teacher A inevitably gives an impression of being only a "proofreader", while the "predominantly evaluative and barely instructional" style of Teacher B renders him as basically an "evaluator" or a "judge". Apart from the role of "proofreader", "evaluator" and "judge", what other roles should a teacher play in marking students' compositions? How can a teacher play a variety of roles in different phases of the marking process regarding the different needs of students and the various learning objectives of the different aspects in writing teaching effectively and purposively? These are the questions worth our contemplation. Second, both Teacher A and B failed to allocate the responsibility of revision effectively. In other words, they were not able to make good use of their marking strategies to cultivate the students' ability to revise and correct on their own. For minor errors like spelling mistakes, wrong punctuations and inappropriate use of dialect, both Teacher A and B still took up the responsibility of revision themselves. Why didn't they let their students handle such simple errors? Past researches suggested that this is usually the result of the marking policy of the schools and the expectation of students and parents toward teachers' feedback. However, these explanations fail to apply to the cases of Teacher A and B.

According to the interviews, their schools do not have any explicit official marking policy and teachers are given great freedom in their marking strategies. Moreover, Teacher B stated that he had practiced the "students write more, teachers revise less" principle for several years, and students enjoyed starting a new piece of composition before they finished revising and correcting the last work. In other words, it was highly unlikely that students' expectation constituted a source of stress to his marking. However, why did they still correct every single mistake and error in great detail in the experiment? This is probably due to their self-imposed demand resulted from their personal endorsement of some kind of traditional idea of teacher. Deep down both of them committed to the idea that it is the responsibility of a teacher to revise and correct the compositions of his students and a responsible teacher should correct all the errors for them as far as possible. Accordingly, the research team observes the need to convince writing teachers to abolish their traditional narrow conception of composition marking and attain a new understanding towards the role, the responsibility, and the different kinds of strategies of marking.

6   Limitations

This paper has attempted a preliminary investigation in the strengths and weaknesses of Chinese writing teachers regarding different kinds and aspects of composition marking. While the scale of this investigation is very limited, the data and information collected by the experiment are valuable in furthering our understanding of the marking behaviors of secondary school Chinese teachers and facilitating future studies in the related areas, as there have been very few relevant researches on this topic. Certainly, the results of the current study, like the classification of "teacher comments", are only based on preliminary observations and descriptive analysis and have to be further verified.

Limited by our manpower and resources, the result is inadequate in its representativeness as only two teachers as recruited for the experiment. For example, in analyzing their performance in marking grammatical items, the discussion focused only on Teacher A as Teacher B did very little marking in this aspect, undermining the statistical significance of the findings. Therefore, when relevant research is to be done in the future, teachers coming from different schools with different teaching experiences should be recruited as subjects such that the diversity of the sample can be increased, strengthening the representativeness and significance of the research conclusions.

Finally, the tablet-based "think aloud" method, which has overcome the inadequacy of the traditional paper-based feedback analysis and interviews, has succeeded in facilitating the research team to collect a lot of valuable raw data. Participants were positive about this research method in general. They thought that the method had some influence on their marking speed but did not affect the procedure of the marking process. This matches the findings of Crisp (2008). In one of his experiments, Crisp recorded the marking process of six markers of writing examination scripts with the method of "think aloud" conducted in the traditional paper-based writing assessment environment. The result showed that their marking speed was a little bit lower and they were more stringent and demanding in their marking. In the interviews afterwards, Teacher A and B said that the time they usually spent on marking a composition is about 5 to 10 minutes and around 10 minutes respectively, more or less the same as the measurement in our experiment with the tablet-based marking platform. With the growing use of the tablet-based marking platform, it is highly likely that the potential effect of this new type of marking mode on teachers' marking behavior will turn out to be a vital issue of concern among composition researchers and writing teachers. In view of this consideration, the research questions stated in this study needs further exploration and investigation with larger samples and modified research designs and methodologies.

Reference

1. Bardine, B.A., Bardine, M.S., Deegan, E.F.: Beyond the red pen: clarifying our role in the responses proves. English Journal 9(10), 94–101 (2000)
2. Beach, R.: Self-evaluation strategies of extensive revisers and nonrevisers. College Composition and Communication 27(2), 160–164 (1976)
3. Beason, L.: Feedback and revision in writing across the curriculum classes. Research in the Teaching of English 72(4), 395–422 (1993)
4. Branon, L., Knoblauch, C.H.: On students' rights to their own texts: a model of teacher response. College Composition and Communication 33(2), 157–166 (1982)
5. Cai, W.: Analysis of teacher feedback type. Chinese Language Pedagogy 12, 39–41 (2004) (in Chinese)
6. Connors, R., Lunsford, A.: Teachers' rhetorical comments on student papers. College Composition and Communication 44, 200–223 (1993)
7. Ferris, D.R.: One size does not fit all; response and revision issues for immigrant student writers. In: Harklau, L., Losey, K., Siegal, M. (eds.) Generation 1.5 Meets College Composition, pp. 143–158. Lawrence Erlbaum, Mahwah (1999)
8. Ferris, D.R., Hedgcock, J.: Teaching ESL Composition: Purpose, Process, and practice, 2nd edn. Lawrence Erlbaum, Mahwah (2005)

9. Ferris, D.R.: Student reactions to teacher response in multiple-draft composition class-rooms. TESOL Quarterly 29(1), 33–53 (1995)
10. Ferris, D.R.: Teacher commentary that communicates: practicing what we preach in the writing class. Journal of Teaching Writing 6, 307–317 (1997)
11. Hendrickson, J.M.: Error correction in foreign language teaching: recent theory, research and practice. In: Croft, K., et al. (eds.) Readings on English as a Second Language, pp. 153–173. Winthrop, Cambridge (1980)
12. Ho, M.K.: Correcting Chinese composition with the use of cassette tapes. Education Journal 25(2), 1–16 (1997) (in Chinese)
13. Ho, M.K.: Language teachers' abilities of evaluating essay marking qualities. Education Journal 35(1), 113–139 (2007) (in Chinese)
14. Knoblauch, C.H., Brannon, L.: Teacher commentary on student writing: the state of the art. Freshman English News 10(2), 1–4 (1981)
15. Lalande, J.F.: Reducing composition errors: An experiment. Modern Language Journal 66, 140–149 (1982)
16. McGee, S.J.: A qualitative study of student response to teacher-written comments. Diss. Purdue U. (1999)
17. Ravichandran, V.: Responding to student writing; motivate, not criticize. GEMA Online Journal of Language Studies 2(1) (2002)
18. Robb, T., Ross, S., Shortreed, I.: Salience of feedback on error and its effect on EFL writing quality. TESOL Quarterly 20, 83–93 (1986)
19. Shum, S.K.: A study on the effects of methods of evaluation on senior secondary school Chinese students. Unpublished M. Phil Thesis, the Chinese University of Hong Kong (1990)
20. Siegel, M.E.A.: Response to student writing form new composition faculty. College Composition and Communication 33, 302–309 (1982)
21. Sommers, N.: Responding to student writing. College Composition and Communication 33(2), 148–156 (1982)
22. Straub, R.: Students' reactions to teacher comments: an exploratory study. Research in the Teaching of English 31(1), 91–119 (1997)
23. Truscott, J.: The case against grammar correction in L2 writing classes. Language Learning 46(2), 327–369 (1996)
24. Tze, S.K.: Analysis on high school teachers' cognitive process of Chinese writing. Unpublished M. Phil thesis, the Chinese University of Hong Kong (1983)
25. Underwood, J.S.: Effective feedback: guidelines for improving performance. Retrieved from Google Scholar (2008)

An Empirical Research on Teachers' Self-Efficacy in Distance Learning

Jiangsheng Zhang, Juan Li, and Fengshan Liu

Liaocheng University, No. 1, Hunan Road, Liaocheng, Shandong, China
{zhangjingsheng,lijuan,liufengshan}@lcu.edu.cn

Abstract. Distance education in now a new platform for the continuing education of teachers. This education form, characterized by its autonomy in organization, pertinence in content, flexibility in form, has become one of the most important methods for teachers' professional development in network age. The efficiency of distance education depends on greatly on teachers' active participation, so a study of teachers' self-efficacy is very important. This study, based on relevant theories on self-efficacy, provides a clear definition about teachers' self-efficacy in distance learning, and focuses on an empirical research on the self-efficacy of the teachers participating distance education with the help of a scientific questionnaire.

Keywords: Distance learning, self-efficacy, empirical research.

1   Introduction

Li points out that it has become the goal of Chinese educational reform to enhance teachers' professional development in order to improve the quality of education to meet the demands of the age for various professionals [1]. As a major method for teachers' professional development, on-the-job training for teachers is gaining more and more attention from various educational institutions. In order to improve the comprehensive quality of the primary and high school teachers, a series of explorations have been made into teachers' training mode in Shandong Province. In the recent years, based on modern information technology, distance education becomes the major form to fulfill the training of primary and high school teachers in Shandong Province.

With development of educational information technology, with the help of internet and communication technology, distance learning plays a more and more important role in the continuation education and professional development of teachers. Distance education in Shandong Province developed very well. And this kind of distance education facing all primary and high school teachers proves to be very useful to improve teachers' professional level and ability. Ding states that teachers' distance learning is a kind of teacher performance combining learning, work and research into one, abiding by three principles of "practice and reflection", "communication and cooperation", "leading and innovation", and has formed a dialog system between teachers and their selves, teachers and their colleagues, practice and theory, so as to promote teachers'

S.K.S. Cheung et al. (Eds.): ICHL 2014, LNCS 8595, pp. 335–343, 2014.
© Springer International Publishing Switzerland 2014

professional development [2]. Distance education has been carried out in Shandong Province for several years and has played an important role in improving teachers' teaching ability, their professional level and in constructing new courses of information technology. Teachers' self-efficacy becomes the life source of distance education. So how to improve teachers' self-efficacy in distance learning becomes something critical in distance education program.

2   Literature Review

The concept of self-efficacy was put forward by Albert Bandura in his 1977 article "Self-efficacy: Toward a Unifying Theory of Behavioral Change" Bandura argues that when one accepts any form of enforcement, he or she may recognize the co-relationships between activities and enforcement, so as to expect the next phase of enforcement, and this kind of expectation depends the appearance of activities. Bandura and others also point out that self-efficacy has such functions as: depending one's choice of an activity and his or her persistence in this activity; influencing one's attitude in the face of difficulties; influencing one's acquirement of new activities and learning performance; influencing one's mood in an activity. It can be seen that the level of self-efficacy will directly influence one's way of thinking, feeling and acting.

Zhang provides a comprehensive review of the studies on self-efficacy in China since the 1980s, and discusses the background of self-efficacy, its theoretical framework, its studies and its future [3]. There are some studies on learners' self-efficacy in distance learning, mainly including analyses of the factors influencing self-efficacy, strategies to cultivate self-efficacy, the relationships between self-efficacy and academic achievements. Chen provides a study on the relativity between the achievements of internet self-learning and self-efficacy, finding that there is a positive relativity between these two [4]. Song finds in his study about learners' self-efficacy in distance learning that the score for distance learners' self-efficacy is over 1.5, but self-efficacy in computer handling, mood management, time management is lower [5]. Former studies also cover teachers' self-efficacy. Pang provides a study on the role of self-efficacy in teachers' professional development [6]. But as a whole, studies on teachers' self-efficacy in distance learning are not enough, especially lacking empirical studies.

3   Methods

3.1   Instrument

Likert Scale is the common tool to study self-efficacy. Generally speaking, the object of the investigation voluntarily reports their choice and reaction in specific environment.

According to Feng, efficacy in distance learning includes "general efficacy in distance learning" and "specific efficacy in distance learning" [7]. General efficacy refers to the value of distance learning, its efficiency and usefulness or whether one can learn something in this process, like believing distance learning and classroom learning can produce the same effect. Specific efficacy refers to learners' subjective cognition, conviction or feeling about whether they can complete various specific learning tasks, like whether they can understand the online lecture. Specific efficacy includes two dimensions of "skill" and "course learning". Self-efficacy in skill refers to distance learners' judgment on their abilities to use computers and internet, to fulfill learning tasks, like whether they can login the learning platform, open the online course, or whether they can communicate with the teacher or other learners through internet communication tool BBS. Self-efficacy in course learning refers to distance learners' judgment on their abilities to fulfill various learning phases, to understand textbooks or learn any skill.

So this study defines teachers' self-efficacy in distance learning as including three dimensions: general self-efficacy, self-efficacy about skill and self-efficacy about course learning.

3.2   The Design of Question Items

This study begins with the above-mentioned three dimensions of self-efficacy, and employs the research tool of Likert Scale, 5 scales from "strongly disagree" to "strongly agree" calculated as from 1 point to 5 points. A scale about teachers' self-efficacy in distance learning is made, including 30 items. Then 50 primary and high school teachers are chosen as the object of the investigation. Factor analysis is employed to analyze the scale's popularity, differentiation, structure and reliability. Based on this analysis, some corrections are made to the scale and finally a scale with 25 items is adopted.

Each item is done in the above-mentioned three dimensions. General self-efficacy includes teachers' opinion about the educational value of distance learning, its efficiency, its usefulness, whether something can be learned, altogether 7 questions. Self-efficacy about skill including items like whether they can login the learning platform, open the online course, and whether they use communication tool to communicate with the teacher and other learners, altogether 9 questions. Self-efficacy about course learning include their judgments on whether they fulfill every phase in the learning process, whether they can understand the textbook, whether they grasp specific skill, altogether 9 questions.

Table 1. Distribution of the question items in the questionnaire

General Self-Efficacy	Skill Self-Efficacy	Course Self-Efficacy
7	9	9

3.3   The Subjects of the Investigation

This empirical study, based on the convenience principle in choosing samples, take as the research object the primary and high school teachers in Liaocheng City of

Shandong Province where the authors works, including No. 1, No. 2, No. 3 and No. 6 Middle School of Liaocheng, Shuicheng Middle School, Experiment Middle School of Liaocheng, Subsidiary Primary School of Liaocheng University, with 200 teachers involved. The questionnaire in paper form is distributed. The questionnaire is done and collected in the presence of the authors of this paper. 200 copies of the questionnaire are distributed, and 200 retrieved, among which 196 copies are effective. The rate of questionnaire retrieved is 100%, and those effective is 98%. The basic information of the investigated teachers is shown in Table 2.

Table 2. Teachers' basic information

Item	Group	Percentage
Sex	male	35
	female	65
Age	20-30	40
	30-40	45
	40-50	15
Teaching Age	1-5 years	35
	5-10 years	35
	10-15 years	10
	Over 15years	20

It can be seen from Table 2 that 35% of the chosen objects are male, 65% is female; female teachers are more than male teachers, which truly reflects the real composition of primary and high school teachers in Shandong Province.

In terms of the age of the investigated, those between 20 and 30 years occupy 40%, those between 30 and 40 years 45%, and those between 40 and 50 years 15%. It is clear that the main body of teachers in primary and high schools are young teachers, which is in accord with the real situation in Shandong Province.

In terms of their teaching age, those who have been teaching for 1 to 5 years occupy 35%, those for 5 to 10 years 35%, those for 10 to 15 years 10% and those for over 15 years 20%. It can be seen that most of the teachers have been teaching for 1 to 10 years, and those over 10 years are the major teaching force.

4   Results

Enter the data collected from the retrieved questionnaire into the computer and processed them with SPSS19 for descriptive and relative analysis, to find factors that may influence teachers' self-efficacy in distance learning, which will finally be used to improve teachers' self-efficacy in distance learning.

4.1   Scores for Teachers' Self-efficacy in Distance Learning in Three Dimensions

A descriptive analysis of the three dimensions of teachers' self-efficacy in distance learning is done, and the average number of the scores for every item in three dimensions is calculated, as is shown in Table 3. Because every single scale had different numbers of items, the average numbers for every dimension are not comparable. According to statistical theories, analysis of this kind of problem is done by dividing the average number for each single scale by the number of items in each single scale, to get the average number of every item.

Table 3. S Scores for teachers' self-efficacy in distance learning in three dimensions

Measure Variant	Average	Item Number	Item Average
Skill Self-Efficacy	37.15	9	4.13
Course Efficacy	36.25	9	4.03
General Self-Efficacy	27.15	7	3.88

It can be seen from Table 3 that the average value of the investigated teachers' skill self-efficacy and course self-efficacy is higher, all above 4.00, which means they have higher approbation degree about the two dimensions of skill and course self-efficacy. Yet their general self-efficacy gets only 3.88, which suggests that the investigated have lower approbation degree about the dimension of general self-efficacy. All these suggest that during the process of their distance learning, the investigated teachers are not so active in distance learning through internet. So it is necessary to make further investigation into the factors influencing teachers' self-efficacy in distance learning and the degree to which each factor influence their general self-efficacy.

4.2   Individual Difference Analysis

Compare the individual differences in how statistic variable sex influences general self-efficacy, skill self-efficacy and course self-efficacy, using mainly the common average differentiation. Individual sample t test: when independent variables are two discrete random variables and dependent variables are continuous variables, t test statistic method is used for individual difference test; when independent variables are three or over three, and dependent variables are continuous variables, one-actor difference analysis is used.

It can be seen from Table 4 that of the t value of dependent variables about relationship between the sex of the investigated teachers and their self-efficacy, only that of course self-efficacy is obvious, whose p value is less than 0.05, which means different sexes correlates with different course self-efficacy. Male teachers' course self-efficacy (M=36.5000) is higher female teachers (M=36.1429); in terms of average analysis, male teachers' skill self-efficacy (M=36.3333) is lower than female teachers (M=37.5000). This suggests that male teachers' skill efficacy needs to be improved.

Table 4. Self-efficacy difference test of teachers of different sexes

Test Variable	Group	Average	Standard Deviation	T Value
General Self-Efficacy	male	27.0000	2.44949	-0.112
	female	27.2143	4.33552	
Skill Self-Efficacy	male	36.3333	3.77712	-0.549
	female	37.5000	4.55311	
Course Self-Efficacy	male	36.5000	1.64317	0.195*
	female	36.1429	6.35921	

Note: **p<0.01 *p<0.05

4.3   Self-efficacy Difference Test of Teachers of Different Ages

The self-efficacy difference test of teachers from different age groups in distance learning is shown in Table 5.

Table 5. Self-efficacy difference test of teachers of different ages

Dependent Variable	Age (I)	Age (J)	Mean Difference (I-J)	Standard Error	Significance
Skill Self-Efficacy	20-30	30-40	1.41667	1.88623	.758
		40-50	6.33333	2.58789	.077
	30-40	20-30	-1.41667	1.88623	.758
		40-50	4.91667	2.62801	.204
	40-50	20-30	-6.33333	2.58789	.077
		30-40	-4.91667	2.62801	.204
Course Self-Efficacy	20-30	30-40	2.18056	2.66345	.720
		40-50	2.88889	3.65422	.736
	30-40	20-30	-2.18056	2.66345	.720
		40-50	.70833	3.71088	.982
	40-50	20-30	-2.88889	3.65422	.736
		30-40	-.70833	3.71088	.982
General Self-Efficacy	20-30	30-40	1.45833	1.81637	.729
		40-50	4.00000	2.49204	.301
	30-40	20-30	-1.45833	1.81637	.729
		40-50	2.54167	2.53067	.613
	40-50	20-30	-4.00000	2.49204	.301
		30-40	-2.54167	2.53067	.613

Note: **p<0.01 *p<0.05

It can be seen from Table 5 that there is no significant difference between teachers of different ages in their general self-efficacy, skill self-efficacy, and course self-efficacy.

This suggests that teachers in the informational age are improving greatly their level of information technology, capable of accepting all the technology and conception needed in distance learning, including interpersonal communication. It means that teachers' self-efficacy in distance learning doesn't change significantly among different ages.

Besides, a further analysis about the average value of teachers' self-efficacy in distance learning across different ages is made, and the result is shown in Figure 1:

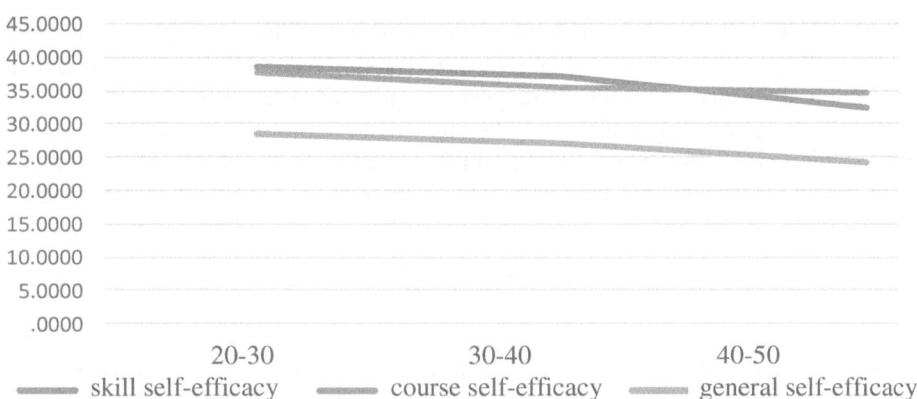

Fig. 1. Average value of teachers' self-efficacy in distance learning across different ages

It can be concluded from Figure 1 that the average value in the three dimensions of general self-efficacy, skill self-efficacy, course self-efficacy decreases with the growing of one's age. That means that with their aging, teachers' self-efficacy is decreasing.

4.4   Correlation Analysis of the Teaching Age and Self-efficacy

A Pearson correlation analysis is done to test the difference of self-efficacy among teachers of different teaching ages. The result is shown in Table 8.

Table 6. Correlation analysis of the teaching age and self-efficacy

		Teaching Age
Skill Self-Efficacy	Pearson correlation	-.558[*]
	Significance (bilateral)	.011
Course Self-Efficacy	Pearson correlation	-.241
	Significance (bilateral)	.306
General Self-Efficacy	Pearson correlation	-.383
	Significance (bilateral)	.095

Note: **. means significantly correlated at .01 level; *. means significantly correlated at 0.05 level (lateral).

It can be seen from Table 8 that the significant approbation value (p<0.05) suggests that skill self-efficacy and teaching ages are significantly and negatively correlated at 0.05 level, and course self-efficacy and general self-efficacy are not significantly different across different ages.

5   Discussion

In an age when information technology has penetrated into education and school teaching, distance education as a new form of training has a bright prospect. But the application of all kinds of mode presupposes proper environment and conditions, so in the training programs for teachers relying on distance learning, it is quite important to improve teachers' self-efficacy. Based on the discussion in the above, some strategies are provided for teachers participating distance-learning to improve their self-efficacy.

5.1   Design of Training Content Should be Based on the Trainees' Demands

Distance education serves teachers on the job. They accept training with a very definite purpose, so if the training deviates from their teaching practice, and their demands can't be met, they will lose interests in the program. Therefore, the design and implement of the training should be based on the trainees' demands to improve their course self-efficacy.

Investigation into the teachers about their demands participating the training

Investigation about teachers' demands for the training is the basis to design a training program. Those who hold the training program should organize a special workshop to investigate into the trainees' demands, taking into consideration the demands of teachers from different areas. Typical schools should be chosen, followed by interviews, class observations and questionnaires to know fully what their teachers want from the training.

Meeting teachers' internal demands for the training

Teachers from different areas, different grades and different academic statuses have different demands about the training. In order to meet teachers' demands about the training and at the same time to make the training easy to handle, the courses should be arranged into different modules, so different teachers can chose whatever desired training contents according to their own situation and conditions.

5.2   Construction of Powerful Distance Education Platform

To guarantee the effect of distance education, a comprehensive and powerful system can improve teachers' interests and enthusiasm in participating the training so as to produce a good result, to improve teachers' skill self-efficacy and general self-efficacy.

Improvement of internet platform

When the assignments submitted through internet have too many problems, a medium system is needed to deal with, to sort out these problems, then the experts and instructor may give response as to typical problems. This can guarantee the solution of the trainees' questions and give instant feedbacks, so as to get an ideal result.

Extension of the range of distance education

When distance education ends, the training platform should be still available for the trainees to make full use of the information on the platform, to communicate with experts, instructors and other trainees to get help or direction.

6   Conclusions

Distance education is on its way to perfection. In order to improve teachers' self-efficacy in distance learning, not only are proper and scientific guidance and training for the teachers needed, but also betel school environment is necessary. With continuous exploration and reforms, this new form of teacher training project will be more and more promising.

This study provides a detailed study of teachers' self-efficacy in distance learning, but it is not free of some limitations, like limited data, limited object schools and teachers, etc. More research objects will be included in the following studies to produce more comprehensive data.

References

1. Li, X.: An Investigation into Distance Education for Primary and High School Teachers in Shandong Province. D. Shandong Normal University (2012)
2. Ding, J.: A Study of Teacher Community for Distance Education. D. Nanjing Normal University (2008)
3. Zhang, D.: Self-Efficacy Theory and its Studies. Psychology Research Trends 1, 39–43 (1999)
4. Chen, Y.: A Correlation Study of the Internet Self-Learning Achievements and Self-Efficacy. Computer-assisted Foreign Language 8, 32–36 (2007)
5. Song, J.: An Investigation into Distance Learners' Self-Efficacy. Modern Education Technology 3, 67–70 (2008)
6. Pang, L.: Teachers' self-efficacy: An important intrinsic motivation mechanism of teachers' autonomous development. Teacher Education Research 7, 43–46 (2005)
7. Feng, F.: Influence of support characteristics on distance learners' self-efficacy. Distance Education in China 3, 30–34 (2008)

Author Index

Bai, Jing 129
Brown, Alison 266
Byrne, Julia 16

Chan, Kelvin K.L. 196
Chan, Wai-lap 208
Chen, Wu 300
Chen, Xiangdong 140
Cheung, Simon K.S. 196
Chow, Daisy 323
Chu, David W.K. 93
Chu, River 164
Chung, Vincent 184

Duan, Qionghua 300

Feng, Nengshan 312
Fong, Joseph 184
Frydrychova Klimova, Blanka 220

Guo, Haijun 1

Hsu, Jenq-Muh 152
Huang, Wen-Feng 152
Hung, Patrick C.K. 266
Hurst, Fred 266

Ip, Horace H.S. 16
Iwata, Jun 243

Jarrell, Douglas 243

Kwok, Lam-for 208

Lai, Donny C.F. 173
Lai, Ivan K.W. 164, 173
Lam, Jeanne 80
Lee, Kelvin K.W. 196
Lee, Roger 323
Leung, Kat 323
Li, Guanjie 129
Li, Juan 335
Li, Kam Cheong 105
Li, Sally M. 288
Li, Yan 164
Liu, Fengshan 335
Liu, Huan 1
Long, Meilin 300
Lu, Beirong 1

Lu, Chun 24
Luk, Louise 56

Ma, Will W.K. 288
Martin, Miguel Vargas 266

Ng, Kwan Keung 56
Nie, Huan 278

Poulova, Petra 220, 232

Qiao, Chen 140
Qiu, Feng 36
Quan, Jianqiang 1

Ren, Youqun 1

Shang, Junjie J. 278
Shi, Yinghui 24, 116
Simonova, Ivana 232

Tashiro, Jayshiro 266
Tsai, Cheng-Yu 152
Tsai, Hung-Hsu 152

Wang, Fu Lee 56
Wang, Sen 68
Wang, Shudong 243
White, Bebo 11
Wong, Kenneth 93, 184
Wu, Di 24, 116
Wu, Minyu 1

Xiao, Haiming M. 278
Xie, Youru 129

Yang, Harrison Hao 24, 116
Yang, Zongkai 116
Ye, Xindong 312
Yin, Rui 129
Ying, K.K. 323
Yu, Pao-Ta 152
Yu, Xiaorong 24

Zhang, Jiangsheng 335
Zhang, Jiping 49
Zhao, Haixia 254
Zhu, Zhiwei 164